Survey of Contents

THIS CONTRIBUTION HAS BEEN FINANCIALLY SPONSORED
BY THE STIFTUNG VOLKSWAGENWERK IN HANNOVER (GERMANY)

Chapter 16

REMEDIES FOR BREACH OF CONTRACT (COURSES OF ACTION OPEN TO A PARTY AGGRIEVED)

Guenter H. Treitel

I. GENERAL INTRODUCTION*

1. *Classification of remedies: Specific and substitutionary relief; termination.* – The courses of action open to a party who is aggrieved by the other party's failure to perform a contract[1] may be divided roughly into three kinds.

First, the aggrieved party may be able to claim *specific* relief, that is, actual performance of the defaulting party's untertaking. Such specific relief will hardly ever in fact give the aggrieved party exactly the performance to which he was entitled, if for no other reason than that the enforced performance resulting from this form of relief will generally take place at a time other than that stipulated in the contract.

Secondly, the aggrieved party may be able to claim *substitutionary* relief, that is, compensation for not having received the promised performance. Almost always the substitute is a sum of money, although this is not invariably the case.[2] Where the substitute is not a sum of money, the distinction between substitutionary and specific relief becomes, in fact, somewhat blurred and is drawn in different places in different legal systems.

The third course of action open to the aggrieved party is less easy to describe compendiously. It consists of a combination of two elements: a refusal on the part of the party aggrieved to accept further performance from the other contracting party, coupled with a claim by the aggrieved party to recover back any performance which he may have rendered. This is the *Rücktritt* at GERMAN law, and the *résolution* of FRENCH law. The process is often referred to as "rescission" in COMMON LAW countries, though the use of the term has been criticised[3] and is open to the objection that it has many, insufficiently differentiated, shades of meaning. The process will be referred to in this chapter as "putting an end to" or "terminating" the contract.

This third course of action is closely related to the *exceptio non adimpleti contractus* which is discussed in ch. 15 above. The difference between the *exceptio* and the remedy discussed in the present chapter is that the *exceptio* is purely defensive, involving simply the withholding by a party of his own performance, while the process of putting an end to the contract is usually a more drastic measure in that it may involve the actual reversal of acts done in pursuance of the contract. For this reason, legal systems may impose stricter limitation on the remedy of putting an end to the contract than on the availability of the *exceptio non adimpleti contractus.*

The broad threefold division of courses of action available to an aggrieved party exists in all WESTERN systems, though the exact conditions in which each remedy is available, and the precise effects of the remedy when granted, differ considerably in legal theory, and often in actual practice.

The three remedies discussed above are by no means always mutually exclusive; in particular a claim for money compensation may often be available together with a claim for specific enforcement or for one for putting an end to the contract (*infra* s. 183, 184).

2. *Judicial remedies and self-help.* – The remedies considered in this chapter are primarily *judicial* remedies. Self-help plays a relatively small part: as a general rule a contractual creditor is not entitled simply to seize the object owed. The policy against self-help is strongest in FRENCH law, where the maxim "*nul ne peut se faire justice à soi-même*" (no-one is allowed to mete out justice personally) has been exceedingly influential. In that system even the process of putting a contract to an end requires, at least in theory and as a general rule, a judgment of a court. At the other extreme, in the UNITED STATES OF AMERICA, the Uniform Commercial Code (UCC) expressly recognises "self-help" as a "remedy" available to an aggrieved party.[4] But the reference is to steps which can be taken without the exercise of physical force against the person or property of the debtor: *e.g.* to reselling goods against a buyer in

* The discussion is, with minor exceptions, confined to systems expressed in languages in which the author was able personally to check the original sources.

SOCIALIST systems of law are discussed in subch. V by Prof. *Eörsi* of Budapest, and a general comparison of remedies in SOCIALIST and WESTERN systems will be found at the end of that subchapter.

[1] For the purpose of this chapter, it is assumed that there is an effective contract, that one party has failed to perform his undertaking, and that there is no lawful excuse for this failure.

[2] *E.g.* in times of scarcity it has been held in GERMANY that delivery of a substitute even for a non-fungible thing may be ordered: *Zweigert and Kötz* 166.

[3] *Corbin* § 1105.

[4] Comment to s. 1-201 (34).

default or to making a cover purchase.[5] Purely defensive self-help is allowed by all the systems: this is simply a withholding of performance which may be subsequently justified by pleading a defence in the nature of the civil law *exceptio non adimpleti contractus.*

3. *Criminal and civil remedies.* – The remedies available to an aggrieved party are generally by way of civil action. Criminal remedies for breach of contract are rare, since the failure to perform a private obligation is not usually a matter of sufficient public concern to justify the punishment of the defaulting party. There are, however, cases in which conduct amounting to a breach of contract also violates laws for the protection of consumers against the sale of dangerous goods or against dishonest statements; or laws for the protection of tenants against undue harrassment by landlords.[6] Breach of a contract may also involve dishonest misappropriation of property in the nature of theft and be punishable as such.[7]

In these cases an offence is not committed merely because a contract is broken, nor is a breach of contract essential to criminal liability. The overlap between contractual and criminal liability is largely coincidental, but there are some cases in which a breach of contract is essential or sufficient to constitute an offence. Such cases are obviously based on the public policy of individual states.

ENGLAND, for obvious reasons, has traditionally imposed criminal sanctions on seamen neglecting their duty; and although the severity of the law has recently been mitigated in this respect, under an Act of 1970 it was still an offence for a seaman wilfully to disobey certain lawful commands.[8] In NORTH DAKOTA a law is still in force by which a person who refuses without lawful excuse to accept a shipment of potatoes or other produce for which he has contracted thereby commits an offence.[9] In general, the aggrieved party will not benefit from such criminal proceedings which will result either in imprisonment of the offender or in the imposition on him of a fine, payable to the state.

Provisions do exist in many legal systems for ordering a defendant in criminal proceedings to pay a sum of money, or to restore property, to the person injured by his crime;[10] and such provisions may apply where the offence also amounts to a breach of contract.[11]

4. *Penalties in civil actions.* – Remedies in the nature of criminal penalties may be available for the enforcement, not of contractual obligations as such, but of certain types of judgments based on such obligations. Sometimes judgments may be enforced by levying a fine on a recalcitrant defendant and in such cases the fine, if it becomes exigeable, will normally be paid to the state and not to the plaintiff. This is the position in GERMAN law when a fine may be used to enforce a judgment to do an act which cannot be performed vicariously (*unvertretbare Handlung*);[12/13] and in ANGLO-AMERICAN law when an order for specific performance or an injunction may be enforced by a fine levied in contempt proceedings.[14] In FRENCH law, the result of an *astreinte* (*infra* s. 24) may similarly be to impose a penalty on the recalcitrant party, with the significant difference[15] that in this case the penalty (if in fact it is exacted) goes not to the state but to the injured party. The institution has been criticised on this ground among others.[16]

The COMMON LAW occasionally awards a sum of money to an injured party with the object not so much of compensating him as of punishing the defendant. Such awards of "punitive" or "exemplary" damages are rare in contractual actions (see *infra* s. 45). They must be distinguished from damages for injured feelings, which are also uncommon in contract cases (*infra* s. 110 ss.). Such damages have been described as a sort of private penalty[17] on the ground that they are awarded even though the plaintiff suffers no pecuniary or patrimonial loss. But where they are available it

[5] UCC s. 2-706, 2-712; comment 1 to s. 2-704 describes resale as the seller's "primary remedy"; and comment 1 to s. 2-712 describes the buyer's right to "cover" as "the buyer's equivalent of the seller's right to resell".

[6] See, for example, *Kessler and Gilmore,* Contracts. Cases and Materials (ed. 2 Boston 1970) 472-478; *Dekkers* no. 833; UNITED KINGDOM: Trade Descriptions Act 1968 (c. 29); GREAT BRITAIN: Rent Act 1965 (c. 75) s. 30.

[7] *E.g.* under the ENGLISH Theft Act 1968 (c. 60) s. 15, 16.

[8] UNITED KINGDOM: Merchant Shipping Act 1970 (c. 36) s. 29.

[9] NORTH DAKOTA Century Code (1959) § 4-10-16.

[10] See, for example, the GERMAN *Strafgesetzbuch* (PC) § 188, 231; FRENCH *Code pénale* (PC) art. 53; ENGLISH Criminal Justice Act 1972 (c. 71) s. 1. See this Encyclopedia vol. XI ch. 8 s. 49-59.

[11] *E.g.* where there is a violation of the GERMAN PC § 223 b or of the ENGLISH Theft Act 1968 (*supra* n. 7) s. 15, 16, or of the UNITED KINGDOM Trade Descriptions Act 1968 (*supra* n. 6) s. 1, 14.

[12/13] GERMAN CCProc. § 888; *cf.* CCProc. § 890.

[14] ENGLAND: Rules of the Supreme Court (Supreme Court Practice, 1972) – RSC – Order 52 rule 9.

[15] *Zweigert and Kötz* 174.

[16] *Idem* 186; *Carbonnier* IV 531.

[17] *Carbonnier* IV 306.

seems preferable to regard them as compensatory rather than punitive, even though the injury for which they are awarded cannot be precisely valued in money.

5. *Declarations.* – The judicial remedies so far mentioned all have some coercive effect, in that they result in the making of orders against a defendant which can be enforced against him by some process of execution. A party may, in some countries, simply sue for a declaration of his rights under a contract without claiming any consequential relief; or he may couple the claim for a declaration with one for consequential relief.[18] Such a remedy may be available even though neither of the parties is strictly speaking "aggrieved". Both parties may wish simply to obtain the court's decision on a disputed point as to the construction of the contract, or as to its legality. Where a breach has occurred, there is normally no reason why the injured party should wish to confine his claim to such a declaration. But exceptional circumstances may justify such a course, for example where an executable judgment cannot be given against a defendant on the ground of sovereign immunity.[19] And where there is a *bona fide* dispute between businessmen as to their respective rights and duties under a contract a judicial declaration of the legal position may, for practical purposes, be as effective as an executable judgment.

6. *Administrative remedies.* – A final group of remedies available to a party aggrieved by a breach of contract are administrative or "police" measures. These are aimed principally at preventing breaches of penal laws passed, for example, for the protection of consumers, or other sections of the community.[20] Sometimes disputes are referred to an administrative body for attempted solution in the first instance, and it is only when these attempts have failed that resort may be had to judicial proceedings.[21] Sometimes the function of the administrative body is not merely to settle disputes but to supervise a legislative scheme for the protection of a class such as borrowers to ensure that its provisions are in fact observed.[22]

[18] ENGLAND: RSC Order 15 rule 16; UNITED STATES: Uniform Declaratory Judgments Act, Uniform Laws Annotated – ULA – 9B; SCOTLAND: *Walker* II 1179; SOUTH AFRICA: Supreme Court Act 1959 (no. 59) s. 19 (1) (c).

[19] *E.g.* GREAT BRITAIN: Crown Proceedings Act, 1947 (10, 11 & 12 Geo. 6, c. 44) s. 21 (1) (a).

[20] *E.g.* UNITED STATES: Consumer Credit Protection Act 1968 (15 U.S.C.A. § 1601 ss.); *cf.* GREAT BRITAIN: Equal Pay Act 1970 (c. 41) s. 2 (2).

[21] *E.g.* GREAT BRITAIN: under Race Relations Act 1968 (c. 71) which may apply to breach of a contract to provide hotel accommodation; UNITED KINGDOM: under Fair Trading Act 1973 (c. 41) part III: s. 34 (3) refers expressly to breaches of contract; *cf.* Industrial Relations Act 1971 (c. 72) s. 146 (*unfair* dismissal – not necessarily in breach of contract).

[22] *E.g.* UNITED STATES: under Uniform Consumer Credit Code, ULA 7, art. 6 part 4; UNITED KINGDOM: Fair Trading Act 1973 (*supra* n. 21) part II.

II. ENFORCED PERFORMANCE

A. CONCEPT OF ENFORCED PERFORMANCE[23]

7. *Meaning.* - By enforced performance is meant, in its broadest sense, a process whereby the creditor obtains as nearly as possible the actual subject-matter of his bargain, as opposed to compensation in money for failing to obtain it. Such compensation is also, in a sense, "enforcement" of the contract[24] and may from this point of view be contrasted with the remedy by way of putting an end to the contract. But it is not "enforced performance" in the sense here under discussion in that its object is not to give the creditor the very thing for which he bargained.

In considering the availablity of enforced performance, it is first of all necessary to determine exactly what it was that the defendant undertook.[25] If he undertook to bring about a certain physical or legal state of affairs, enforced performance will mean bringing about that state of affairs; if he undertook to forbear from doing something, it will mean destroying a state of affairs brought into existence in breach of the undertaking, or preventing a breach of the undertaking in the future.

The debtor may, however, promise *either* to bring about a certain state of affairs (or to forbear from doing so) *or* to pay or repay or allow a sum of money should he fail to bring about the state of affairs (or to forbear) in accordance with his promise. It is obvious that the distinction between enforced performance and compensation in money tends to disappear when the debtor's only undertaking is of the second kind. The point may be illustrated by taking the case of defective goods delivered under a contract of sale. In such a case the seller may have undertaken that the goods shall not be defective; in which event "enforced performance" would require him either to put right the defect or to make a delivery of conforming goods (if the sale was of generic goods). Alternatively, the seller may have merely undertaken a guarantee-type of liability referred to in GERMAN law as *Gewährleistung*. The word "guarantee" in this context is not used in the sense of a promise by one person to make a payment to the creditor if the principal debtor fails to perform. It refers rather to the liability of the seller to certain financial consequences: either in the form of a price reduction or of having the contract set aside on account of the defect.

This is the position on the sale of specific goods in many CIVIL LAW systems;[26] and where the rule applies there is no question of "enforced performance" being available against the seller in the sense of condemning him to cure the defect, unless the contract expressly so provides.[27] The guarantee liability which rests on the seller under such systems is not even equivalent to liability in damages, from which in turn it will have to be distinguished. The liability of a seller of generic goods who makes a defective delivery stands in these systems on a different footing. It is not a mere guarantee liability but an undertaking to deliver goods of a certain quality; and accordingly the seller can in principle be compelled to "cure" his defective delivery by making a fresh, conforming one.[28] The position is similar in GERMAN law in the case of a *Werkvertrag*, such as a contract for the execution of building work. The customer can in principle sue for enforced performance, that is he can claim to have the defect put right.[29]

In COMMON LAW systems a seller *is* held to undertake that the thing sold is free from certain defects, so that some kind of "enforcement" of this obligation is available against him, but this invariably takes the form of damages. He may have the privilege of avoiding liability in damages by curing the defect (*infra* s. 174), but he cannot be compelled actually to effect the cure. Similarly a building contractor is liable for defects, but generally his liability is in damages. These are sometimes measured by the cost of curing the defect (*infra* s. 66). A judgment ordering the contractor actually to effect cure is not generally available (*infra* s. 35).

Under the Uniform Law on International Sales[30] (hereafter referred to as ULIS) a seller

[23] *Dawson*, Specific Performance in France and Germany: 57 Mich.L.Rev. 495 (1959); *Szladits*, The Concept of Specific Performance in Civil Law: 4 Am. J.Comp.L. 208 (1955).

[24] *De Page* III no. 98C; the position is the same under COMMON LAW.

[25] *Enneccerus and Lehmann* § 108 I.

[26] See this Encyclopedia vol. VIII ch. 3 *sub* II D.

[27] *Enneccerus and Lehmann* 452.

[28] GERMAN CC § 480 par. 1; SWISS CO art. 206.

[29] GERMAN CC § 633 par. 2. See this Encyclopedia vol. VIII ch. 8.

[30] For texts of the Law, see Diplomatic Conference on the Unification of the Law Governing International Sale of Goods (The Hague 1966) I 336.

of goods, whether specific or not, is in breach if he delivers defective goods (art. 33(1)). Generally, the buyer will claim damages or a price reduction in respect of such defects, but in two cases ULIS allows him to claim actual cure. If the sale relates to goods to be produced or manufactured by the seller, the buyer may require him to remedy the defects, provided that the seller is in a position to do so (art. 41(1)(a)). And if the sale relates to unascertained goods, the buyer may require the seller to deliver other conforming goods, except where the purchase of goods in replacement is in conformity with usage and reasonably possible (art. 42(1)(c)).

8. *Claims for an agreed sum.* – Enforced performance of a party's obligation also takes place where that obligation is simply one to pay an agreed sum of money and an action is brought for that sum. This is the position where a buyer of goods is sued for the price and an employer for the agreed remuneration. Claims of this kind are not, however, normally subject to the restrictions which most systems of law place on the availability of enforced performance. These restrictions are based on the difficulty or undesirability of compelling a person actually to do something against his will (*infra* s. 10). Such considerations are inapplicable to a judgment simply for the payment of a sum of money as such a judgment can be executed without any physical constraint on the debtor's person.

In COMMON LAW countries actions for an agreed sum are not referred to as suits for specific performance.[31] Nor are they actions for damages,[32] the measure of recovery being generally neither more nor less than the agreed sum plus in appropriate cases interest (*infra* s. 114-117). There may sometimes be a question whether the plaintiff is entitled to the agreed sum or only to damages; but this question is determined in accordance rather with the rules relating to mitigation of loss (*infra* s. 103) than with those which limit the availability of enforced performance.

9. *Differences in terminology.* – The process of enforced performance is described in different legal systems by words which are superficially similar, and which do indeed have a considerable common core of meaning. But such expressions as the FRENCH *exécution en nature*, the GERMAN *Naturalherstellung* and the ANGLO-AMERICAN specific performance are by no means identical in significance.

The ANGLO-AMERICAN notion is, in fact, much narrower than the corresponding CIVIL LAW concepts. It is restricted to a decree directed against the defendant personally, ordering him to perform the contract and entailing the possibility of punishment for contempt of court in case of disobedience.[33] It means, moreover, an order which could only have been made in a court of equity and not in one of common law in the days when these systems were administered in separate courts. This point still retains some significance in that the remedy may be refused on "equitable" grounds, such as unfairness or hardship which would not be a defence to an action for damages. And in the UNITED STATES a claim for specific performance is not subject to the right to trial by jury, as it is not an action "at common law" within the relevant provision of the Constitution.[34]

In CIVIL LAW countries the terms used to describe enforced performance are not used in this narrow sense but may include any process by which the creditor receives the substance of what he bargains for. They include, for example, the process whereby the creditor can have the contract executed or a defect cured at the expense of the debtor, and the process whereby a substitute may be bought at the expense of the debtor.[35] In these cases no order to perform is directed to the debtor, but the result from the creditor's point of view is similar. He does not of course get precisely what he bargained for, but that may be true as well where a decree of specific performance is issued. In COMMON LAW jurisdictions the obtaining of a substitute for the performance promised is also a common process, but it leads to a claim for *damages* for the difference between the cost of the substitute and the contract price and is not considered as a process of enforced performance.[36]

The doing of an act at the expense of the defendant is a process available in ENGLISH law, but only as a method of *executing* a decree of specific performance when such a decree has first been made.[37] In theory this differs from damages in that the whole expense is placed on the shoulders

[31] *Corbin* § 1145; unlike Chancery decrees, judgments for the agreed remuneration are not enforceable by contempt proceedings.

[32] *Corbin* § 995; *Treitel* 832.

[33] *Jackson*, Specific Performance in Louisiana, Past and Future: *Dainow* (ed.), Essays on the Civil Law of Obligations (Baton Rouge 1969) 195.

[34] Amendment VII.

[35] FRENCH CC art. 1143, 1144; as to GERMAN law, see *infra* s. 15.

[36] See, for example, the "cover" provisions of the AMERICAN UCC s. 2-712.

[37] ENGLAND: RSC Order 48 rule 5; the GERMAN rules stated *infra* s. 15 seem to be of a similar character.

of the defendant directly; it is not incurred by the plaintiff and then recoverable. But in practice the distinction is unlikely to make any difference save in exceptional cases.

B. AVAILABILITY OF ENFORCED PERFORMANCE

i. *General Considerations*

10. *Reasons for restricting its availability.* – In theory enforced performance is the most appropriate remedy from the point of view of the creditor who in that way gets what he may be supposed to want, namely the performance for which he bargained. But this ideal is counterbalanced by a number of factors.

First, the enforced performance may be regarded as an undue interference with the personal freedom of the debtor. This is particularly true where performance can only be rendered by the debtor personally; but even where this is not the case enforced performance is often felt to be too strong a measure when the creditor could for most practical purposes be put into almost as good a position by the award of a sum of money. Enforced performance might, moreover, cause hardship to the debtor which would not be occasioned by an award of money, particularly where such an award would be subject to reduction under the mitigation rules.[38] Secondly, enforced performance may be thought to impose strains on the machinery of law enforcement which are too severe when balanced against the benefit derived by the creditor from enforced performance.

For these reasons the availability of enforced performance is in fact limited in all the legal systems under discussion. Three main approaches to the problem may be distinguished. Under the first, the general principle of enforced performance is accepted, subject to certain exceptions; under the second enforced performance is available in respect of obligations of a certain content but not in principle in respect of others; and under the third enforced performance is regarded as an exceptional, discretionary remedy. These may be called respectively the GERMAN, FRENCH and COMMON LAW approaches; it should be said at the outset that the difference between them is probably more marked in theoretical approach than in practical effect. A fourth or mixed approach, combining elements of some of the others, will finally be considered.

11. *The option to claim enforced performance.* – Before discussing these various approaches, two preliminary questions must be raised.

First, assuming that specific enforcement is, in principle, available, is the creditor bound to pursue this remedy, or can he (if he prefers it) claim substitutionary relief? In COMMON LAW countries there has never been any question about this: the creditor always has the option of claiming damages even though specific enforcement is available. This is also true of those CIVIL LAW systems which, by political association with COMMON LAW countries, have adopted some of their habits of thought: for example of SCOTLAND,[39] QUEBEC (CC art. 1065), LOUISIANA (CC art. 1926), and SOUTH AFRICA.[40] It is also the position under ULIS.[41] If, in any of these systems, a seller of "unique" goods wrongfully refused to deliver, it would be perfectly open to the buyer to choose to claim damages even though specific enforcement was an available remedy.

The same option is given to the creditor by some CIVIL LAW writers, particularly in FRANCE;[42] while others maintain that the creditor has no such right of choice.[43] According to the latter view, the creditor must *prima facie* sue for performance where this remedy is available: he has no right to damages for non-performance *merely* because the debtor has failed to perform.[44]

This is the starting principle in GERMAN law,[45] though obviously it does not apply where performance is impossible.[46] In cases of delayed performance, the creditor as a general rule cannot claim damages until the expiry of a *Nachfrist* (*infra* s. 149). This is a notice calling on the debtor to perform within an additional period of time and stating that the creditor will after the end of the period refuse to accept performance. Under this institution, the creditor has indeed an option as to the form of relief, but one that can only be exercised by taking certain formal steps. In addition he can claim damages for delay or for breach of subsidiary duties where enforced per-

[38] *Treitel* 835.
[39] *Walker* I 579.
[40] *Willie and Millin (-Coaker and Schutz)* 88.
[41] *Supra* s. 7. See, *e.g.*, art. 24, 41.
[42] *Mazeaud and Tunc*, Traité III (ed. 5) no. 2306.
[43] *De Page* II no. 1026 p. 1069; *idem* III no. 94 (1); *Dekkers* no. 341; *von Mehren* 793-794.
[44] *De Page* III no. 94 n. 1; it does not follow that the creditor can only claim damages after *claiming* termination (*résolution*) (*idem* no. 98) but if the contract is not terminated, the debtor's option to perform remains open.
[45] Under CC § 326, 283; see also CC § 250, 251.
[46] CC § 280, 325.

formance will not fully compensate him: *e.g.* where he has suffered lost gain as well as deprivation of the actual subject-matter of the contract.[47]

In SWISS law, the creditor is said to have the option of claiming performance or *Schadenersatz* (*i.e.* reparation by way of substitutionary relief);[48] but the creditor's option is subject to the judge's discretion as to the form of relief.[49]

The second question is whether, assuming specific enforcement to be at some stage available, the creditor may lose his option to claim it. Both COMMON LAW and CIVIL LAW systems recognise the possibility that the defaulting party may be prejudiced if, long after breach, he is faced with a claim for enforced performance.

The problem is of comparatively small importance in COMMON LAW systems since in them specific enforcement is a discretionary and somewhat exceptional remedy. Where (as in contracts for the disposition of an interest in land) specific enforcement is the normal remedy, the danger of prejudice to the defaulting party is met by the so-called doctrine of "laches", under which specific enforcement will be refused if it is sought after undue delay.[50]

More elaborate rules exist to protect the debtor in systems, such as the GERMAN, which accept the availability of enforced performance as a general principle. In cases of delay in performance, the general rule is that the claim for performance is excluded on expiry of the *Nachfrist*.[51]

In such cases, SWISS law also entitles the creditor to set a *Nachfrist* (CO art. 107); but it differs from GERMAN law in several respects. First, the notice need not state that the creditor will refuse performance at the end of the term. Secondly, the creditor can still sue for performance after the expiry of the *Nachfrist;* indeed this remains his principal remedy unless he makes a further immediate declaration of intention to refuse further performance and to claim compensation. This provision has been criticised;[52] the party in default might well be taken by surprise by being ordered to perform unless he has received two notices, one requiring him to perform and the other stating that performance will no longer be accepted. Cases of hardship could, however, be dealt with under the judge's discretion as to the form of relief.

In both GERMAN and SWISS law, special rules apply to so-called *Fixgeschäfte* (*infra* s. 150) in which the time of performance is of the essence of the contract. If such a transaction is a commercial sale, GERMAN Comm.C § 376 par. 1 provides that the aggrieved party can only claim performance if he notifies the defaulting party at once on expiry of the stipulated time that he will insist on performance. The SWISS CO art. 190 par. 2 is to the same effect. If the transaction is not a commercial sale, the aggrieved party's right to claim performance is governed by the rules already stated, though he may terminate at once on expiry of the stipulated time.[53]

In dealing with failure to perform at the date fixed, ULIS distinguishes between cases in which the failure is a "fundamental breach" and those in which it is not. The breach may be "fundamental" (*infra* s. 162) if the delay is so long as to frustrate the purpose of the aggrieved party in entering into the contract (whether or not the contract specifies the time for performance). In either case, the contract is "*ipso facto* avoided" if the aggrieved party does not within a reasonable time (of the occurrence of the breach, or of its becoming fundamental) notify the other that he requires performance. Unless he gives such a notice, the aggrieved party cannot claim performance. This rule applies whether the default is that of the seller[54] or that of the buyer (art. 62(1)).

If the breach is not fundamental, the aggrieved party's right to claim performance is unaffected unless he sets an additional period for performance. This resembles the *Nachfrist;* but unlike the German version of the institution the notice does not have to state that he will refuse to accept performance after the end of the period. Moreover, if the notice is given by the buyer, he does not lose the right to claim performance immediately on expiry of the period. The sole effect of such expiry is to turn the breach into a fundamental one,[55] so that the buyer has a further reasonable time within which to give notice of his intention to claim performance.[56] If the notice is given by the seller, its expiry in no way affects his right to

[47] For this distinction see *infra* s. 51. CC § 251; *cf.* the express provisions as to performance and damages for delay in AUSTRIAN CC § 918.

[48] *Guhl* 50. *Schadenersatz* should not in all contexts be translated as "damages": see *infra* s. 12.

[49] *Infra* s. 16. SWISS CO art. 43 (*infra* s. 99) applied to contracts by CO art. 99 par. 3.

[50] *Chitty (-Morris)* I § 1651.

[51] CC § 326, 283; see also CC § 250. *Infra* s. 149.

[52] *Guhl* 193.

[53] GERMAN CC § 361.

[54] Art. 26 (1); the seller can abridge the period under art. 26 (2).

[55] Art. 27 (2), 30 (1).

[56] *I.e.* under art. 26 (1).

claim performance (*i.e.* the price): this right is only lost if he declares the contract avoided (art. 62(2)), in which case the remedy becomes an action for damages. Since in either event the buyer will have to pay a sum of money, the risk of prejudice to him as a result of enforced performance is reduced. It only exists where the seller should have mitigated by resale, but in such a case the remedy of claiming performance is not, under ULIS, available to the seller at all (*infra* s. 104).

In cases of non-conforming delivery there is no "*ipso facto* avoidance" under ULIS so that the buyer's right to claim performance, where it exists (*supra* s. 7), is not affected unless he declares the contract avoided.[57]

ii. *Four Typical Solutions*

a. Enforced Performance Subject to Exceptions

12. *German law – general rule.*[58] – GERMAN law starts with the principle that the creditor is entitled to a judgment for performance. This is nowhere stated in so many words, but it underlies a number of provisions in the Civil Code. For example CC § 241 provides that the creditor is entitled "to claim performance from the debtor" (*eine Leistung von dem Schuldner zu fordern*). The Civil Code is concerned rather to state the right of the creditor than to say anything about the remedy by which it is enforced; but there is no doubt that the creditor's right to performance is considered to give him simultaneously a claim to a judgment for performance or *Leistungsklage*.[59]

It is tempting, for a common lawyer, to contrast the *Leistungsklage* with a judgment for *Schadenersatz*[60] and to translate the latter term as "damages". Such a translation would, however, be misleading for it is clear from the first sentence of CC § 249 that the primary duty of a debtor who is bound to make *Schadenersatz* is to bring about the state of affairs which would have existed had the circumstances giving rise to the duty to make reparation not occurred.[61] This duty is generally referred to as one to make *Naturalherstellung*. It is contrasted with a duty to make compensation in money, a duty described by the phrase *Ersatz in Geld* in CC § 250 and by similar phrases elsewhere.[62]

However, the terminology is not absolutely consistent, for there are places in which such expressions as *Schadenersatz* or *Schaden zu ersetzen* seem to refer primarily to compensation in money, that is to "damages" in the COMMON LAW sense. This is the position, for example, under CC § 280 par. 1 which provides for the case where performance has become impossible through circumstances for which the debtor is responsible. In such a case the debtor is obliged to make reparation for the damage resulting from non-performance ("*den durch die Nichterfüllung entstehenden Schaden zu ersetzen*"). Obviously the reference must be to compensation in money. The same is true under CC § 286 par. 2 which deals with the case of delayed performance by the debtor. If such performance is of no interest to the creditor, he can refuse it and claim *Schadenersatz* which must again clearly be compensation in money. The provisions of CC § 325 and 326, giving the creditor in a reciprocal contract the option of claiming *Schadenersatz* or putting an end to the contract in cases of impossibility or delay for which the debtor is responsible also clearly refer to compensation in money.

While *Schadenersatz* is, therefore, not an exact equivalent of the COMMON LAW concept of damages, the *Herstellung* or restoration referred to in CC § 249 and 250 should not strictly speaking be translated as *specific* restoration or bringing about of the exact situation which would have existed, had there been no breach of duty. It may refer to this but is wider, including substitute performance otherwise than in money: *e.g.*, by delivery of other goods equivalent to those which were the subject matter of the contract, where those goods have been irrevocably disposed of.[63] In such a case it would seem that the creditor's claim is for *Schadenersatz* and not for *Leistung* (that having become impossible); but insofar as the judgment may condemn the seller to deliver actual goods and not just to pay a sum of money it in fact bears a closer analogy to the ANGLO-AMERICAN judgment for specific performance than to that for damages.

13. *German law – the exceptions.* – The first exception to the general principle of GERMAN law, that the remedy is by way of enforced performance, is of small importance in the law of contract. It is contained in CC § 249: reparation

[57] Art. 43, 44 (2).

[58] For a similar view in AUSTRIAN law, see *Klang and Gschnitzer (-Gschnitzer)* IV 1 § 859 no. B II 2.

[59] *Enneccerus and Lehmann* 10; *Zweigert and Kötz* 165. *Cf.* CC § 283.

[60] *Supra* s. 11 at n. 47.

[61] *Enneccerus and Lehmann* § 18; *cf.* AUSTRIAN CC § 1323.

[62] CC § 249 sent. 2; 251 par. 1.

[63] *Enneccerus and Lehmann* 92; *Zweigert and Kötz* 165–166; for a similar view under AUSTRIAN CC § 1323 see *Klang (-Wolff)* VI § 1323 no. I 3.

for injury to the person or damage to property can be claimed in money at the option of the creditor.

The second exception arises out of a number of provisions to the effect that the creditor can set a *Nachfrist* (*supra* s. 11, *infra* s. 149). If the debtor fails to comply with a valid notice of this kind, the creditor can claim compensation in money[64] but the claim for performance is excluded (*supra* s. 11).

The third exception arises in cases in which actual reparation or performance is impossible (but in which impossibility does not operate as an excuse): here the only possible enforcement claim is for *Schadenersatz*, usually in money,[65] but conceivably in substitute goods (*supra* s. 12).

The fourth exception arises when reparation in kind is inadequate to compensate the creditor.[66] This might be the case, for example, where a profit-earning thing was damaged: here repair of the damage would not adequately compensate the injured party for his loss of profits while the thing was undergoing repair.

The fifth exception arises where the cost of putting the plaintiff into the position in which he would have been but for the default involves unreasonable efforts or expense (CC § 251 par. 2); or where the result of so doing would leave him with a more valuable thing than he had before. In the latter case, the plaintiff can only demand specific restoration on making allowance for the amount by which he is better off, *e.g.* as a result of the repairs undertaken by the defendant.[67]

The sixth exception arises in cases of so-called *positive Vertragsverletzung* (see *infra* s. 75) which gives rise to a claim for *Schadenersatz*. Having regard to the nature of the injury, this will generally (though not invariably) be a claim for compensation in money.[68]

14. *Their practical importance.* – In practice these exceptions are far more important than the general rule.[69] The creditor will usually find it more convenient, even when performance is still possible, to set a term on the expiry of which he can claim *Schadenersatz;* in fact he can do so even after he has obtained a judgment for performance (CC § 283). Since it is expressly provided that after the expiry of the term the creditor can no longer claim performance,[70] the debtor is also protected in the sense that he is assured that his sole liability will be one to make reparation: thus he need no longer hold himself ready to perform (*supra* s. 11, *infra* s. 149). In most cases *Schadenersatz* is as effective a remedy for the creditor as enforced performance; and even where this is not the case the difficulties and delays encountered in executing a judgment for enforced performance will as a practical matter reduce the utility of such a remedy. For these reasons it is more common to claim compensation in money.

15. *Methods of enforcement.* – The method of enforcing a judgment for performance in GERMAN law depends on the nature of the obligation upon which the judgment is based. Generally execution is against property; but personal constraint is not excluded.

If the obligation is to transfer moveable property, the judgment may be enforced by taking the property from the debtor and giving it to the creditor;[71] in the case of immoveables and ships the debtor can be compelled to vacate the property and the creditor can then be put into possession (CCProc. § 885). In either case the acts necessary to execute the judgment are done by an officer of the court.

If the obligation is to do an act which can be performed vicariously, the creditor can ask the court to authorise him to have the act done at the expense of the debtor; and he may ask the court to condemn the debtor to pay the cost of such performance in advance, without prejudice to his right to claim additional expenses should they exceed the amount of the advance payment (CCProc. § 887). This method of execution is available, for example, for the enforcement of judgments directing performance of a contract to build, or to heat or light premises, or to operate a lift. It is available even in respect of services if they require no special bodily or mental skills.[72]

Where the judgment is for an act which cannot be vicariously performed, execution is by means of fines and imprisonment, but this method of execution is not available for the enforcement of a judgment to render services under a contract of

[64] CC § 250, 326 par. 1; cf. CC § 283 which entitles the creditor to set a term for performance after judgment. For the principle of setting a term under AUSTRIAN law, see CC § 918 and in SWISS law CO art. 107.

[65] GERMAN CC § 251, 280, 325; AUSTRIAN CC § 920; SWISS CO art. 97 par. 1.

[66] CC § 251 par. 1; *Enneccerus and Lehmann* 91.

[67] *Enneccerus and Lehmann* 91; contrast the ENGLISH case of *Harbutt's "Plasticine", Ltd. v. Wayne Tank & Pump Co., Ltd.*, [1970] 1 Q.B. 447 (C.A.) (*infra* s. 44).

[68] *Enneccerus and Lehmann* 237.

[69] *Zweigert and Kötz* 167.

[70] CC § 250, 326.

[71] CCProc. § 883, 884, 897.

[72] For these and other illustrations, see *Baumbach and Lauterbach*, Zivilprozessordnung (ed. 30 Munich 1970) § 287 no. 6; *Zweigert and Kötz* 168.

service and in a large number of other cases.[73]

Where the judgment orders the debtor to forbear or suffer something, it can be enforced by fines and imprisonment if the debtor acts contrary to the terms of the judgment (CCProc. § 890).

Where the judgment requires the debtor to make a declaration of will (for example an entry in a land register) the judgment is self-executing in the sense that the declaration is regarded as made as soon as the judgment has become final and conclusive (CCProc. § 894).

The first noteworthy feature of this scheme of enforcement is the great variety of means of execution provided by the law. The exercise of physical force against the person of the debtor (which is usually considered to be an argument against enforced performance) is a comparative rarity. Generally, the method of enforcement is specifically tailored to the needs of the judgment to be enforced; the exception is the use of penal sanctions to enforce a judgment that the debtor should suffer, or forbear from doing something. There appears to be no provision corresponding to the FRENCH CC art. 1143 (*infra* s. 21) by which the creditor can be authorised at the expense of the debtor to destroy things done, in violation of a contractual undertaking to forbear.[74] It may be that a creditor who acts in this way can recover the expense of so doing on the principle of *negotiorum gestio*.[75]

The second remarkable feature of the scheme is its treatment of judgments for services due under a contract of service. Such judgments are excepted from the general rule that judgments for acts which cannot be vicariously performed are enforceable by fines and imprisonment. The result is that these judgments for services cannot be enforced at all;[76] the only effective remedy is a claim for damages. AUSTRIAN law at least in theory avoids this inelegance by allowing direct execution, even by imprisonment, where a judgment can be given to enforce the performance of obligations of personal service, but, if execution is not allowed, by refusing to render the judgment.[77] In SWISS law a judgment for the enforced performance of obligations to do an act (including personal service) can be rendered; and in some cantons it can apparently be enforced by the imposition of criminal penalties in case of malicious nonperformance.[78]

16. *Swiss variations.* – The SWISS position with regard to the availability of judgments for enforced performance is analogous to that prevailing in GERMANY, though there are some significant differences. In principle the creditor may sue for performance; or for *Schadenersatz* in certain cases, namely if performance is not possible, or if the creditor has set a term calling for performance, or if the case is one in which the normal requirement of the setting of a term is dispensed with.[79] The *Schadenersatz* may take the form either of compensation in money or of *Naturalersatz*, the former being in practice the more common.[80] The rules are very flexible in actual operation because of the discretion given by SWISS law to the judge in determining the mode and extent of reparation.[81] In the exercise of this discretion, the judge may combine the two forms of relief where this is appropriate.[82] In practice the general rule is to award money compensation, this being relatively easier to assess and to execute.[83]

b. Enforced Performance Based on Content of Obligation

17. *French law – preliminary distinctions.* – FRENCH law and systems based upon it distinguish, like GERMAN law, between various forms of *réparation* or *exécution:* it may take the form of actually restoring (or bringing about) the state of affairs which would have existed if the wrong had not occurred (*réparation ou exécution en nature*) or of compensating the creditor by a substitute (*réparation par équivalent, exécution en équivalent*) which generally takes the form of money.

Where performance has become impossible, FRENCH law differs from GERMAN law in that it does not generally admit liability to delivery of a substitute object: *e.g.* where a borrower has lost the object borrowed he is only liable to a pecuniary condemnation and not to a judgment for delivery of a thing in substitution for the one he has lost.[84] A quasi-exception to this rule, of no

73 CCProc. § 888; *Zweigert and Kötz* 168.

74 For a similar provision see SWISS CO art. 98 par. 3.

75 For this suggestion in AUSTRIAN law, see *Klang* (-*Wolff*) VI § 1323 no. I 3.

76 RG 24 Jan. 1910, RGZ 72, 393, 394.

77 *Klang and Gschnitzer (-Gschnitzer)* IV 1 § 859 no. B II 1; *idem (-Adler and Höller)* V § 1162a no. II.

78 *Guhl* 51; *Oser and Schönenberger* V 1 art. 97 no. 22.

79 *Guhl* 50; CO art. 97, 98, 107, 108.

80 *Guhl* 76.

81 CO art. 43, applied to contracts by CO art. 99 par. 3.

82 *Guhl* 76.

83 *Ibidem.*

84 *Carbonnier* IV 254; but in times of scarcity or of fluctuating currency values this view has not always been followed: see *Marty and Raynaud* II no. 511 p. 557; Cass.civ. 20 Jan. 1953, D. 1953, 222.

importance in the law of contract, is the possibility of condemning a defendant to publication of an apology where he has been found guilty of an attack on the plaintiff's honour.[85] This is sometimes regarded as a form of *réparation par équivalent* by other means than the payment of money.

The FRENCH and related systems do recognise in principle the availability of *exécution en nature* or what is called "direct" execution.[86] But the general principle is subject to an important exception which is in turn subject to qualification, so that the actual position is complex. It should be said at the outset that the complexities about to be discussed are of more theoretical interest than practical importance; for in practice the most important remedies of the injured party are the claim for damages and his right to put an end to the contract.

18. *Obligations to do and not to do, and to convey.* – The FRENCH Civil Code, more perhaps than any other, was concerned to safeguard the debtor against undue personal constraint resulting from an obligation.[87] It was considered less onerous to owe money than to be liable to compulsion actually to perform an act or forbearance. Hence the Code declares in art. 1142 that every obligation to do or not to do ("*de faire ou de ne pas faire*") resolves itself into damages in case of non-performance by the debtor. The obligation to do or not to do is constrasted (CC art. 1101) with the *obligation de donner* or to transfer property.

An *obligation de donner* often does not require "enforcement"; it is self-executing in the sense that ownership in specific things may be transferred by the mere agreement of the parties.[88] It is true that in such a case the debtor, if still in possession of the subject-matter of the contract, may remain under an obligation to deliver the thing. At first sight, this might appear to be an obligation to do an act (*de faire*); and indeed an obligation to deliver, when it does not arise from an obligation to transfer ownership, appears to be so regarded. But where the obligation to deliver arises out of an obligation *de donner* it is not regarded as falling within art. 1142, whether because in such a case it is regarded as simply an aspect of the obligation *de donner* or because enforcement of the obligation is thought to be based on the creditor's right of ownership rather than on contract.[89] In any event, the creditor has the right in the case of a sale of specific property to be put into possession of the subject matter: in the case of goods this is accomplished by the remedy of *saisie-revendication;* in the case of immoveables, expulsion of the vendor may be effected by act of an officer of the court who can then put the purchaser into possession.[90]

Where the nature of the property is such that its transfer is not effected by the mere agreement of the parties, but requires the execution of a formal instrument, direct enforcement is available in the sense that the judgment may itself operate as the required transfer if the debtor fails to execute it.[91]

Where a sale is of generic goods, the seller's duty to appropriate and deliver appears to be an *obligation de faire* which cannot therefore be directly enforced; but in this case the buyer is entitled to a judgment authorising him to buy against the seller at the latter's expense.[92] This appears to be regarded as indirect *exécution en nature* though in practical effect it appears to differ little from damages. Certainly the recovery of the resulting sum would be so regarded in ANGLO-AMERICAN law. The FRENCH view of the matter seems to be based on the result of the process from the point of view of the creditor, in that he gets (at least very nearly) the thing he bargained for. The ANGLO-AMERICAN view is based on the process as it affects the debtor, who is not actually obliged to do anything, where the creditor obtains a substitute at his expense, except to pay money.

The view that performance at the expense of the debtor is a kind of indirect *exécution en nature* is, perhaps, open to the objection that the expense will be incurred in the first instance by the creditor, who will run the risk that he may not actually be able to recover it from the debtor. FRENCH law does not appear to have any provision analogous to the GERMAN one (see *supra* s. 15) by which the creditor can recover the cost of substitute performance from the debtor *in advance.* The FRENCH also differs from the GERMAN rule in that in FRENCH law the creditor actually

[85] *De Page* III no. 98 p. 129.

[86] See CC art. 1184 par. 2 ("*forcer l'autre à l'exécution*"), art. 1610 ("*demander ... sa mise en possession*").

[87] *Carbonnier* IV 258, 523.

[88] CC art. 1583 and *cf.* CC art. 1138.

[89] *Mazeaud,* Leçons II no. 946; *De Page* III no. 97.

[90] CCProc. art. 826 (*saisie-revendication*); *Mazeaud,* Leçons II no. 946; *Carbonnier* IV 526.

[91] *Carbonnier, ibidem.*

[92] CC art. 1144; *Mazeaud,* Leçons II no. 946; *De Page* III no. 97; there is no corresponding Code provision entitling the seller to *resell* in case of the buyer's failure to take delivery, but such a right appears in fact to be recognised: *Houin,* Sale of Goods in French Law: Some Comparative Aspects of the Law Relating to Sale of Goods (I.C.L.Q. Suppl.Publ. no. 9) (London 1964) 16 ss., 26.

gets a *judgment* for *substitute* performance; while the GERMAN provisions under which substitute performance can be obtained are a method of *executing* a judgment for *performance*. The FRENCH *faculté de remplacement* also suffers (in common with the analogous GERMAN institution) from the disadvantage that it cannot be exercised except with the authorisation of the court,[93] save in cases of extreme urgency;[94] and the court in its discretion may refuse to authorise it and award damages instead. In the case of "commercial" contracts the right may be exercised without prior judicial authorisation.[95]

19. *Scope of CC art. 1142.* – The principle upon which CC art. 1142 is based is that "*nemo potest praecise cogi ad factum*". The article does not expressly draw any such distinction as exists in GERMAN law between acts which can and acts which cannot be vicariously performed. But the distinction does exist; and CC art. 1142 only in fact prevents the direct enforcement of obligations of the latter class. Thus it prevents the direct enforcement of a contract by an artist to complete and deliver a picture; of a contract by a workman to render services; and even of a contract by an actor not to appear in a rival play:[96] it is interesting to note that such a negative promise *can* be directly enforced in ANGLO-AMERICAN law,[97] even though in theory these systems give a narrower scope than FRENCH law to direct enforcement.

The terms of CC art. 1142 are not applied to *all* obligations to do or not to do and the broad language in which the article is drafted has often been criticised.[98] Two particular qualifications of the apparently wide scope of CC art. 1142 occur in the two following articles 1143 and 1144.

20. *Substitute performance.* – CC art. 1144 has already been considered in one particular context, the right of a buyer of generic goods to buy goods of the contract description elsewhere at the expense of the seller (*supra* s. 18). The same principle of obtaining substitute performance applies to other obligations: *e.g.* to an obligation to repair leased premises. But the principle is excluded where the performance promised was either such that there can be no replacement, *e.g.* where it related to a specific object which has been destroyed; or where the promised performance was such that it could not be rendered without the personal co-operation of the debtor, *e.g.* where the promise was one by an actor to act in a play.[99] In the first of these cases, it seems that FRENCH law does not generally recognise the possibility (present in GERMAN law) of enforcing the contract by ordering the delivery of a substitute object instead of money compensation (*supra* s. 12). In the second case (of an obligation requiring personal co-operation) CC art. 1144 is excluded on the ground that it provides for a kind of *exécution en nature*, and that obligations of this kind are not susceptible to this mode of *exécution*. The argument is scarcely adequate to show why an actor who breaks his contract to appear in a particular play should not be held liable under CC art. 1144 for the expense of hiring a substitute actor. But the law is nevertheless settled in the sense stated above. Of course the actor would be liable in damages.

21. *Obligations to forbear.* – CC art. 1143 deals with violations of obligations to forbear and provides that the creditor has the right to demand the destruction of what has been done contrary to the agreement, or alternatively he can be authorised to destroy it at the expense of the debtor. This provision could, for example, be applied to order a lessor to destroy structures, erected in violation of the terms of a lease, which interfere with the lessee's enjoyment of the premises.[100] As under CC art. 1144, a judgment is necessary and the judge may at his discretion award damages instead.

In practice this discretion is not often exercised when *exécution en nature* of the obligation remains physically possible. (It would not be possible, for example, where the obligation to forbear was for a limited time which had passed.) CC art. 1143 refers to the destruction of something done in contravention of an obligation. This includes both physical destruction and also what has been called the destruction of legal acts such as alienations in breach of an obligation not to alienate.[101] It does not seem to include mere prevention of human activity which cannot be "destroyed". For this reason CC art. 1143 cannot be applied to the case

[93] Cass.civ. 5 June 1953, D. 1953, 601.

[94] *Vasseur*, Urgence et droit civil: Rev.trim.dr.civ. 1954, 403, 421, 424; *Deprez*, Distinction des obligations de donner, de faire et de ne pas faire: J.-Cl.Civ. art. 1136-1145 fasc. I no. 15.

[95] *Deprez*, *supra* n. 94; *Hémard*, Les contrats commerciaux (Paris 1953) no. 254-256.

[96] Cass.civ. 14 March 1900, D. 1900.1.497; Cour d'appel Paris 21 April 1896, S. 1897.2.9; *Carbonnier* IV 524.

[97] Under the rule in *Lumley v. Wagner* (1852), 1 De G.M. & G. 604, 42 E.R. 687; *infra* s. 33.

[98] *E.g.*, *Zweigert and Kötz* 170.

[99] *Mazeaud and Tunc*, Traité III (ed. 5) no. 2309-2313; *cf.* the BELGIAN decision Cass. 12 Sept. 1958, Pas. 1959.I.45.

[100] *Carbonnier* IV 524.

[101] *Deprez* (*supra* n. 94) no. 17-18.

in which an actor has broken a contract not to appear in a rival play.

22. *Possession of property.* – A further possible exception to the principle of CC art. 1142 arises in the situation, already noted, where a person fails to surrender possession of premises which he has sold, or of which his tenancy has expired. The obligation which he has thus failed to perform may, perhaps, be described as an *obligation de faire* but the remedy of expulsion may nevertheless be granted by the court.[102] It does not follow that the public officers whose business it is to enforce the judgment will be prepared to exercise the amount of physical force necessary to ensure actual compliance with the court's decree, and their occasional reluctance to do so has been one factor leading to the development in FRENCH law of other methods of bringing pressure to bear on a recalcitrant debtor.[103]

23. *Criticism of CC art. 1142.* – The underlying policy of CC art. 1142, that it is undesirable to enforce private obligations by remedies which unduly restrict the personal liberty (as opposed to diminishing the patrimony) of the debtor, is sensible enough. But the very wide terms of the article, with its reference to *all* obligations to do and not to do, has been a source of unnecessary trouble, and a frequent target for criticism.[104] It may be noted that the article has not been adopted in two NORTH AMERICAN Civil Codes which are based on FRENCH law, those of LOUISIANA and QUEBEC. Its scope in FRENCH law is restricted by the various qualifications discussed above, and also by a device developed by the FRENCH courts, the *astreinte*.

24. *Astreintes.* – An *astreinte* is a judgment for performance, coupled with a condemnation by which the debtor has to pay a fixed sum for each day (or other named period) that he remains in default. There are two kinds of *astreintes:* provisional and definitive *astreintes.* The institution has in the past aroused much controversy[105] but it is now fully established in FRENCH law (*infra* s. 28).

25. *Provisional astreinte.* – The provisional *astreinte* simply fixes a sum which is to be paid for each specified period of non-performance. The sum so fixed is not based on the actual or prospective loss to the creditor; its object is not to compensate the creditor but to coerce the debtor into complying with the judgment to perform the principal obligation. It may therefore be assessed with reference to such factors as the means of the debtor, the degree of his fault, and the extent of his obstinacy which the order seeks to overcome.[106] This form of *astreinte* is called provisional because (whether or not the debtor eventually performs) the creditor has no automatic right to recover the amount specified. He must make a fresh application to the court for this purpose; and at this stage the *astreinte* is subject to revision or "liquidation". When this process takes place, the court may have regard to the creditor's actual loss, so that the *astreinte* may become compensatory by being reduced to the amount of the actual loss suffered. Conversely, if the debtor continues to be recalcitrant, the *astreinte* may be increased in amount with a view to overcoming his obstinacy.[107]

In theory, the process of reduction of the *astreinte* to the actual loss suffered would appear to deprive it of its coercive effect; but in practice the assessment of damages on the liquidation of a provisional *astreinte* tends to be somewhat severe on the debtor. It may also take account of his fault, not only in relation to the non-performance of the original contractual obligation, but also in relation to his disobedience to the court's decree.[108] Certainly, an *astreinte* may be upheld even though it exceeds the creditor's actual loss; it has been held in a leading case that the court is not bound to "liquidate" the *astreinte* at the loss actually suffered. In the case in question an electric company was condemned in the sum of frs. 900000 (in 1956 about US $ 2550) for refusing after repeated and increasing *astreintes* to modify works done in violation of a landowner's rights. It was held on appeal that the lower court had acted correctly in awarding this sum, even though it bore no direct relation to the loss suffered by the landowner.[109]

The original judgment will normally fix a period during which the *astreinte* operates; if at the end of the period the debtor has still not performed, the creditor may apply for a liquidation of the *astreinte* and for the issue of a further *astreinte.*[110]

[102] *Carbonnier* IV 526.

[103] *I.e. astreintes,* discussed *infra* s. 24 ss. In the context of leases, statutory restrictions were however imposed on the availability of this remedy: see *Mazeaud,* Leçons III no. 1150 (Law of 21 July 1949).

[104] *E.g., De Page* III no. 94; *Zweigert and Kötz* 170.

[105] *Carbonnier* IV 530.

[106] *Idem* IV 526-527; *Marty and Raynaud* II no. 668, 674; Cass.civ. 20 Oct. 1959, D. 1959, 537.

[107] *Carbonnier* IV 526-527.

[108] *Idem* IV 530-531.

[109] Cour Riom 10 Dec. 1956, S. 1957, 112, confirmed by Cass.civ. 20 Oct. 1959, D.1959, 537; *cf.* Cass. civ. 20 Jan. 1960, J.C.P. 1960.II.11483.

[110] Cour Riom, *supra* n. 109.

26. *Definitive astreinte.* – The definitive *astreinte*, as its name suggests, is not subject to revision unless the defendant's failure to perform is due to certain events outside his control. Except in such a case the creditor is entitled simply to the fixed sum multiplied (where appropriate) by the number of periods of delay specified in the judgment.[111] This form of *astreinte* may, like the provisional *astreinte*, be fixed at an amount greater than the prejudice actually suffered (or likely to be suffered) by the creditor;[112] and in view of its definite nature it would at first sight appear to have a considerably greater coercive force than the provisional *astreinte*. In practice the distinction between the two kinds of *astreinte* has not been of great significance.[113] The definitive *astreinte* must be distinguished from a judgment which simply assesses the actual damages at so much for each specified period of non-performance. Such a judgment is purely compensatory and not primarily intended to be coercive; it would not seem strictly speaking to be an *astreinte* at all.[114]

27. *Use of astreintes.* – The chief use of *astreintes* in the law of contract is to secure the performance of obligations to do or not to do which, by reason of CC art. 1142, cannot be directly enforced: for example, to compel an agent to render accounts, or an employer to give a testimonial, or to restrain an actor from breach of an undertaking not to act for a rival theatre, or to compel a buyer of goods to take delivery in accordance with his contract.[115]

But its use is by no means limited to such situations.[116] Thus *astreintes* have been used to secure delivery of the subject matter of a sale even though a judgment for delivery was also available. *Astreintes* were also used where a judgment for performance could be given but not enforced because of the reluctance of public authorities to use force where this might lead to public disorder. This was the position in relation to judgments for possession of premises at the end of a lease, until a Law of 1949 provided that in these cases the amount at which the *astreintes* was liquidated could not exceed the actual loss, thus removing the coercive effect of the *astreinte*.[117]

An *astreinte* can also be used in cases to which CC art. 1143 and 1144 apply. Where a buyer of generic goods could "*se remplacer*" by buying against the seller, its use would be rare; but it could be used in times of shortage to compel delivery, for in such cases the buyer's power to obtain a substitute would be more theoretical than real.[118] It is interesting to note that this is the sort of situation in which the more extensive GERMAN right to specific enforcement has been described as particularly useful;[119] and there is some (though rather scant and dubious) support for the view that shortage of supply is a ground for specific performance in ANGLO-AMERICAN law.[120] *Astreintes* may be used even to enforce a judgment for a sum of money, *e.g.* if the defendant is a public authority against which the judgment cannot be enforced in the normal way.[121]

28. *Criticism.* – The *astreinte* has been a highly controversial institution. Arguments against it were that it was not justified by any provision of the Civil Code, which only provides for compensatory damages; that it was a kind of *fraude à la loi* to achieve indirectly that which CC art. 1142 prevents the court from doing directly;[122] and that it amounted to a penalty for disobedience to the court's order, which should, if exacted at all, go to the state and not serve to enrich the injured party (*cf. supra* s. 25). For such reasons, the institution has been rejected in BELGIUM;[123] and it has not been adopted by such FRENCH-based systems as those of LOUISIANA and QUEBEC; though it should be added that those systems are not troubled by the provisions of CC art. 1142 and have other effective means of direct enforcement, in particular enforcement by means of personal constraint against the debtor.[124]

FRENCH law has, however, taken the view that the *astreinte*, with all its faults, is preferable to the gap in methods of enforcement which CC art. 1142, even narrowly construed, would otherwise

[111] *Marty and Raynaud* II no. 668. Doubts as to the validity of this form of *astreinte* appear to be ill-founded; *Mazeaud*, Leçons II no. 953. *Cf. infra* n. 128.

[112] The amount at which it is fixed is not open to review: Cass.civ. 30 June 1964, Gaz.Pal. 1964.2.354.

[113] *Zweigert and Kötz* 176.

[114] *Capitant*, Les grands arrêts de la jurisprudence civile (ed. 5 Paris 1970) 303; *Marty and Raynaud* II no. 668.

[115] *Carbonnier* IV 527; *Mazeaud*, Leçons III no. 1025.

[116] *Zweigert and Kötz* 172–173.

[117] Law of 21 July 1949 (*cf. supra* n. 103).

[118] *Zweigert and Kötz* 173.

[119] *Riegert*, The West German Civil Code, Its Origin and Its Contract Provisions: 45 Tul.L.Rev. 48, 81 (1970/71).

[120] *Corbin* § 1146.

[121] *Zweigert and Kötz* 173.

[122] *Carbonnier* IV 530–531.

[123] Cass. 24 Jan. 1924, Pas.1924.I.151.

[124] *Baudouin* 570; *Jackson* (*supra* n. 33) 202; LOUISIANA CCProc. (West's Louisiana Statutes Annotated – L.S.A. – Civil Procedure 4) art. 2502.

leave in existence.[125] At any rate, the *astreinte* is now well established as a method of indirect specific enforcement of contractual obligations by the practice of the FRENCH courts.[126] The existence and legality of the institution are assumed in a number of legislative provisions,[127] and it has been expressly confirmed by a recent enactment.[128]

The *astreinte* seems to have no parallel in systems not based on FRENCH law, though the concept of giving a remedy so as to bring pressure to bear on the debtor to perform an obligation which cannot be directly enforced is not unknown in COMMON LAW jurisdictions.[129]

29. *Methods of enforcement.* – Execution of judgments in FRENCH law is by seizure of the defendant's property which may then be handed over to the plaintiff where it is the subject-matter of an *obligation de donner.*[130] Similarly, an owner of premises who has obtained a judgment for possession may have the defendant physically expelled and himself put into possession of the premises.[131] Where a contract itself operates (as it often does in FRENCH law: see *supra* s. 18) as a transfer of title, the creditor may be entitled to have the subject-matter seized by virtue of his ownership. Where enforcement is required of an obligation to transfer title, the judgment itself operates as the transfer.[132] In other cases, satisfaction of the creditor is monetary resulting from proceeds of sale of the property seized. Personal constraint of the debtor of a private, civil obligation has not existed since 1867.[133]

c. Specific Performance as a Discretionary Remedy

30. *The basic approach of Anglo-American law* is that the primary remedy for breach of contract is an action for money compensation called damages, and specific enforcement is only exceptionally available. Where the obligation which it is sought to enforce is a positive obligation to do or convey something the remedy is called an order or decree of specific performance; where the obligation is a negative obligation to forbear, it is called injunction. The distinction is not invariably used, so-called "mandatory injunctions" being sometimes issued to enforce positive obligations.

Specific performance and injunction are still called "equitable" remedies, as they were developed in the Court of Chancery; they are commonly contrasted with the "common law" remedy of damages which at one time was available only in courts of common law. The separate administration of "common law" and "equity" no longer exists, but the old distinction between equitable and common law remedies still has some significance (*supra* s. 9).

Disobedience of a court's order of specific performance or of an injunction amounts to contempt of court and is punishable by fines (which go to the state) and imprisonment. The fact that this was originally the standard way of securing compliance with these remedies still affects their scope at the present day, even though other methods of securing obedience to the court's decrees are now available. An award of damages, on the other hand, could always be enforced, without personal constraint, by levying execution on the debtor's property. The old alternative method of enforcing such a judgment by personal constraint on the debtor is almost completely obsolete.[134]

31. *The "adequacy" of damages.* – ANGLO-AMERICAN law starts with the principle that specific performance of a contract will only be ordered where damages (or other common law remedies) afford inadequate protection to the creditor. This principle was originally adopted to minimise the conflict between courts of common law and courts of equity, the latter only claiming the right to intervene where the former could not give satisfactory relief. In this connection it should be stressed again that the process whereby the aggrieved party obtains a substitute and claims the expense of so doing from the party in default is, in ANGLO-AMERICAN law, regarded merely as a step on the road to damages and not as enforced performance. If the creditor could obtain satisfaction in this way equity would not (and generally speaking does not) intervene. Thus contracts for the sale of shares in companies, or of generic

[125] *Tunc*, Le renouveau de l'astreinte en droit français: Festschrift Riese (Karlsruhe 1964) 397, 404.

[126] See *supra* n. 106, 109.

[127] *E.g.* FRENCH Labour Code (*Code du travail*) Book I art. 29 p.

[128] Law of 5 July 1972 (JO 9 July p. 7181, D.S. 1972 Lég. 361) art. 5–8.

[129] See *Lumley v. Wagner*, *supra* n. 97; *infra* s. 33.

[130] *Carbonnier* IV 519–520.

[131] *Idem* IV 526.

[132] *Ibidem.*

[133] *Herzog*, Civil Procedure in France (The Hague 1967) 558; Cass. crim. 16 Feb. 1960, D. 1960, 243.

[134] The limited power of imprisonment which existed in ENGLAND under the Debtors Act, 1869 (32 & 33 Vict., c.62) s. 5 has been further restricted by the Administration of Justice Act 1970 (c. 31) s. 11.

goods, which are available in the market at an ascertainable price, are not as a general rule specifically enforced.[135]

But equity did intervene in two types of cases: those in which the loss was of such a kind that the damages were particularly hard to quantify;[136] and those in which the plaintiff had a recognised interest in having the very thing contracted for as opposed to a substitute which money, awarded as damages, would enable him to buy. The typical situation in which specific performance would be ordered was that in which *no* satisfactory substitute was obtainable: *e.g.* if the subject-matter was land or a house, or goods of a "unique" kind such as heirlooms or great works of art, or perhaps goods which were "commercially unique" such as ships or machinery that could not readily be obtained elsewhere.[137]

ENGLISH law has been reluctant to recognise the specific enforceability of contracts for the sale of goods other than specific goods, and even contracts for the sale of such goods are not as a general rule enforced specifically.[138] But in the UNITED STATES OF AMERICA the courts have extended the remedy of specific performance even to buyers of generic goods whose need for the actual supply was particularly urgent, or who would in fact be unable to get a substitute.[139] This tendency has been confirmed by UCC s. 2-716(1), under which "Specific performance may be decreed where the goods are unique *or in other proper circumstances.*" This section is an indication of the growing tendency of AMERICAN courts to order specific performance without first asking whether damages are an "adequate" remedy; the stress is rather on the appropriateness of specific performance than on the "adequacy" of damages.[140]

The same tendency is illustrated by the fate of certain statutory provisions in some of the UNITED STATES which were based on the draft Civil Code prepared for the state of NEW YORK in 1865 by *David Dudley Field.* The Code was not adopted in NEW YORK but was adopted in a number of other states. That Code originally provided that specific performance might be compelled where pecuniary compensation did not provide "adequate" relief.[141] This form of words is still in force in MONTANA,[142] and it was also adopted by the INDIAN Specific Relief Act, some of the provisions of which are based on *Field's* Code.[143] But it has been repealed in other jurisdictions which have adopted *Field's* Code, such as CALIFORNIA, NORTH DAKOTA and SOUTH DAKOTA. In MARYLAND there is an express statutory provision to the effect that specific performance is *not* to be refused merely because the plaintiff has an "adequate" remedy at law.[144] The tendency of case law in other states is in the same direction.[145]

In ENGLAND the requirement that damages must be inadequate before specific performance will be ordered continues to be stated; but there are signs that the ENGLISH courts may be in the process of accepting the view recently stated in AUSTRALIA that specific performance should be ordered when it is the most appropriate remedy, even though damages may be an "adequate" remedy in the sense of the older authorities.[146] If this trend continues, ENGLISH and AMERICAN law on this point will tend to move more closely together and the requirement that damages must be an "inadequate" remedy will be restored in ENGLISH law to its proper function. There is obvious good sense in restricting the plaintiff's claim to monetary relief if he can thereby be put in as good a position as by actual performance, for a judgment for money is quicker and easier to execute than

[135] *Corbin* § 1146; *Treitel* 836.

[136] *Corbin* § 1142; *Treitel* 837; *cf.* Specific Relief Act, 1877 (Act I of 1877) s. 12 (d), which remains in force in PAKISTAN though there is no corresponding provision in the new INDIAN Specific Relief Act 1963 (Act XLVII of 1963) s. 10.

[137] *Corbin* § 1142, 1143, 1146; *Treitel* 836-837. Statutory provisions sometimes create a presumption that damages are an inadequate remedy for breach of a contract to sell land: *e.g.* CALIFORNIAN CC (West's Annotated California Codes 12) § 3387; others create an additional presumption that damages are an adequate remedy where the subject-matter is personal property, *e.g.* ALABAMA Code (Code of Alabama Recompiled (1958) vol. 4) § 9-52; Revised Codes of MONTANA (1947) Annotated (Replacement vol. 2 Pt. 2) § 17-804.

[138] *Treitel* 837-838.

[139] *Corbin* § 1142.

[140] In fact there have been few cases under UCC s. 2-716, presumably because the remedy of "cover" provided by UCC s. 2-712 is generally more convenient.

[141] *Field* Civil Code (Albany 1865) § 1887.

[142] MONTANA Revised Codes (*supra* n. 137) § 17-801 (2); for a similar provision, see GEORGIA Code (Code of Georgia Annotated Book 12A) § 37-801.

[143] INDIAN Specific Relief Act 1963 (*supra* n. 136) s. 14 (1) (a) (replacing s. 21 (a) of the INDIAN Specific Relief Act, 1877 (*ibidem*) which remains in force in PAKISTAN).

[144] MARYLAND Code (Annotated Code of Maryland (1957) Replacement vol. 2A) art. 16 § 169.

[145] *Corbin* § 1136.

[146] See *Beswick v. Beswick*, [1968] A.C. 58, 88, 102 (H.L.) and the citation *ibidem* of *Coulls v. Bagot's Executor and Trustee Co., Ltd.* (1967), 40 A.L.J.R. 471 (H.C. of A.).

one for actual performance, and its execution is likely to cause less hardship to the debtor. It is in this sense that the "inadequacy of damages" requirement is likely to be applied in ANGLO-AMERICAN law now that its original justification (the rivalry between courts of common law and equity) has disappeared.

32. *Discretionary grounds for refusing specific performance.* – Even granted that damages will be an inadequate remedy, specific performance will not be ordered as a matter of course. It is a "discretionary" remedy. This does not mean that it may be refused arbitrarily; the discretion is governed by fairly definite rules which in fact lay down a number of grounds in which specific performance may be refused.[147] Some of these are invalidating causes such as misrepresentation and mistake. But others do not fall into this category, and it is these which lend force to the view that specific performance is a "discretionary" remedy.

Thus specific enforcement may be refused if this form of remedy causes severe hardship to the defendant, for example where the cost of performance to the defendant would be out of all proportion to the benefit thereof to the plaintiff;[148] if the transaction was of a grossly unfair nature;[149] if the court disapproves of the plaintiff's conduct, for example because he has refused to perform a promise which undoubtedly formed part of the bargain but which could not be enforced against him for want of written evidence,[150] or if he has in times of economic depression without cause dismissed a servant who has served him well for many years.[151] The court may also refuse specific performance if to grant it would be contrary to the interests of the public.[152]

These limits on specific enforceability are of particular interest when viewed against the general absence of any doctrine of lesion, or good faith in the enforcement of contracts in ENGLISH law. In the UNITED STATES it is arguable that such doctrines are infiltrating into the general law by virtue of certain provisions in the Uniform Commercial Code,[153] under which good faith is required in the enforcement of contracts, and contracts may be struck down or modified on the ground of "unconscionableness". The courts tend to apply these provisions even to contracts which do not strictly speaking fall within the provisions of the Code. In some AMERICAN states the mere "inadequacy" of consideration is, by statute, a sufficient ground for refusing specific performance.[154] But the general view of the AMERICAN and of the ENGLISH courts is that *mere* inadequacy of consideration is not sufficient to induce the court to refuse specific performance; it must be accompanied by some form of inequitable or unconscionable conduct on the part of the plaintiff.[155] This is also the position under the INDIAN Specific Relief Act.[156]

It should be stressed that these discretionary bars to specific performance do not in principle affect the validity of the contract or the possibility of awarding damages for breach of it; they only affect its *specific* enforceability.

33. *Undesirability and impracticality of specific performance.* – The availability of specific performance is restricted finally by a group of factors which relate to the desirability of granting this form of relief and to the practicality of enforcing the court's decree.

Thus it has always been considered undesirable in ANGLO-AMERICAN law specifically to enforce a contract which requires one party to render services of a personal nature, such as a contract of employment. To force the employee to work is thought to interfere unduly with his personal liberty; and to compel the employer to reinstate an employee wrongfully dismissed is thought to involve undesirable coercion in enforcing the continuance of a personal relationship.[157] The principle that an employee cannot be compelled by court order to work is maintained in the most recent ENGLISH legislation; and although provision is made in this legislation by which a tribunal may recommend the re-engagement of an unfairly dismissed employee, such a recommendation cannot be specifically enforced. The sole sanction for failure to comply with the recommendation

[147] *Corbin* § 1136; *Treitel* 839.

[148] *Corbin* § 1162; *Treitel* 839. For a statutory statement see Revised Codes of MONTANA (*supra* n. 137) § 17-810. *Cf.* GERMAN CC § 251 par. 2.

[149] *Corbin* § 1164; *Treitel* 839-840.

[150] *Corbin* § 1167; *Treitel* 840-841.

[151] *Economic Grocery Stores Corp. v. McMenany*, 290 Mass. 549, 195 N.E. 747 (1935).

[152] *Corbin* § 1169.

[153] UCC s. 2-203, 2-302.

[154] ALABAMA Code (*supra* n. 137) § 9-56; CALIFORNIAN CC (*ibidem*) § 3391; GEORGIA Code (*supra* n. 142) § 37-805; Revised Codes of MONTANA (*supra* n. 137) § 17-808; NORTH DAKOTA Century Code Annotated (1960) vol. 6 § 32-04-08; SOUTH DAKOTA Compiled Laws Annotated (1967) vol. 7 § 21-9-3.

[155] *Corbin* § 1165; *Treitel* 840.

[156] INDIAN Specific Relief Act, 1877 (*supra* n. 136) s. 22 (I), 28 (a); INDIAN Specific Relief Act 1963 (*ibidem*) s. 20 (2) (a) (see *supra* n. 143).

[157] *Corbin* § 1204; *Treitel* 840.

is an award of compensation.[158] Actual reinstatement is only available as a legal remedy in certain cases of public employment.[159] Subject to this, the rule applies whether the remedy sought is specific performance or injunction; an employee cannot be restrained from breaking his obligation to serve, nor can an employer in general be restrained from wrongfully dismissing his employee.[160]

However, obligations to forbear contained in contracts for personal service may be enforceable by injunction: for example an undertaking by a singer not, during the period of her employment, to sing for a rival impresario.[161] Such enforcement does not actually compel the singer to perform the affirmative obligation to sing. But it may put considerable economic pressure on her to do so; and for this reason the rule, though generally followed in the UNITED STATES, has been criticised there[162] and restricted in particular in two directions. First, it is said to apply only to cases where the services in question are of a "unique" kind; and secondly, the injunction will be granted only if it leaves open to the defendant some reasonable alternative way of earning a living.[163] There is some evidence that ENGLISH law may be moving towards acceptance of the second restriction.[164]

In CALIFORNIA an additional restriction was introduced in 1919, that the contract must be for an annual remuneration in excess of US $ 6000 (CC § 3423(5)), but inflation has deprived this rule of almost all of its practical importance. In some states legislation in general terms prohibits the grant of an injunction "to prevent the breach of a contract which will not be specifically enforced"[165] but this form of words probably does not prevent the enforcement of obligations to forbear of the kind just mentioned. This qualification is made clear in the INDIAN Specific Relief Act,[166] which uses an otherwise identical language to restrict the availability of injunctions.

34. *Mutuality.* – The so-called doctrine of mutuality of remedy, in its simplest form, lays down that specific performance will not be enforced at the suit of one party unless it could, at the time when the contract was made, have been enforced at the suit of the other.[167] The basic idea was that the court should not order one party to perform if it could not ensure that the counter-performance for which he had bargained would in fact be received by him. Obviously this reasoning did not apply if the counter-performance had already been rendered; and there were so many other exceptions to the rule in the simple form stated above that its existence was widely questioned and later denied in many jurisdictions in the UNITED STATES.[168]

The better view is that specific performance may be granted against a party, although it could not have been obtained by him, so, long as the performance of the other party's obligation is satisfactorily assured.[169] But some of the UNITED STATES retain, by statute, a provision that neither party to a contract can claim specific performance unless the other party has performed or is compellable[170] (or in one state *compelled*)[171] specifically to perform.

35. *Difficulty of supervision.* – Specific performance is sometimes refused in cases in which a partyis bound by continuous duties. In such cases it is thought that specific enforcement would require "that constant superintendence by the court, which the court . . . has always refused to give."[172]

[158] GREAT BRITAIN: Industrial Relations Act 1971 (*supra* n. 21) s. 128 (1), 106 (4) and (5).

[159] See *Ridge v. Baldwin*, [1964] A.C. 40 (H.L.).

[160] This is the orthodox position, based on *Whitwood Chemical Co. v. Hardman*, [1891] 2 Ch. 416 (C.A.). For a recent departure in exceptional circumstances, see *Hill v. C.A. Parsons & Co., Ltd.*, [1972] Ch. 305 (C.A.).

[161] *Lumley v. Wagner*, *supra* n. 97; for the same principle in the Roman-Dutch law of SOUTH AFRICA, see *Roberts Construction Co., Ltd. v. Verhoeff*, 1952 (2) S.A. 302 (W.L.D.).

[162] *Corbin* § 1209.

[163] *Ibidem.*

[164] *Treitel* 851-852.

[165] Revised Codes of MONTANA (*supra* n. 137) § 93-4203; NORTH DAKOTA Century Code (*supra* n. 154) § 32-05-05; SOUTH DAKOTA Compiled Laws (*ibidem*) § 21-8-2 (5).

[166] INDIAN Specific Relief Act, 1877 (*supra* n. 136) s. 56 (f), 57; illustration (d) to the latter section is inconsistent with the later ENGLISH case of *Whitwood Chemical Co., Ltd. v. Hardman*, *supra* n. 160. The corresponding provisions in the INDIAN Specific Relief Act 1963 (*supra* n. 136) are s. 41 (e) and 42 (see *supra* n. 143).

[167] *Fry*, Specific Performance (ed. 6 London 1921) 219.

[168] *Corbin* § 1180, and see p. iv of the preface to vol. 5 A.

[169] *Idem* § 1181, 1186; CALIFORNIAN CC § 3386 (b).

[170] Revised Codes of MONTANA (*supra* n. 137) § 17-803; NORTH DAKOTA Century Code (*supra* n. 154) § 32-04-08; SOUTH DAKOTA Compiled Laws (*ibidem*) § 21-9-4.

[171] ALABAMA Code (*supra* n. 137) § 9-51.

[172] *Ryan v. Mutual Tontine Association*, [1893] 1 Ch. 116, 123 (C.A.).

This is one reason why, as a general rule, contracts to build are not specifically enforced in ENGLAND and in the UNITED STATES.[173]

The rule has been criticised both in ENGLAND and in the UNITED STATES on the ground that the alleged "difficulty" of supervision is much exaggerated.[174] In practice the difficulty has not been acute in cases of building contracts when, exceptionally, these have been specifically enforced; and there are various devices short of actual supervision by the court for enforcing the decree against a recalcitrant defendant. The court could appoint an expert to supervise the performance, or authorize the plaintiff to appoint a person to do the required act as agent for the defendant,[175] or use a device common in CIVIL LAW countries by authorising the plaintiff to have the obligation performed at the expense of the defendant.

In the UNITED STATES, courts are increasingly making use of such measures and are now tending to make orders of specific performance in cases of this kind if they feel that the plaintiff has a strong interest in actual performance.[176] There are signs that ENGLISH law is moving in the same direction.[177] An interesting compromise solution may be found in the INDIAN Specific Relief Act which excludes the specific enforcement of any contract "the performance of which involved the performance of a continuous duty *extending over a longer period than three years* from its date."[178]

36. *Flexibility.* – The remedy of specific performance is an extraordinarily flexible one. It may be granted on terms: *e.g.* as to the currency of payment;[179] or be made conditional on the plaintiff's performing his part or giving adequate security for his performance, or even on his assenting to a modification of the contract.[180] When the subject-matter supplied under the contract is greater or smaller in quantity than that contracted for, the court can in certain circumstances order specific performance with "compensation", that is with an appropriate price adjustment.[181] In some cases the party in default may be given the option of specifically performing the contract or of restoring what he has obtained under the contract, together with damages for any loss sustained.[182] The court may, on a claim for specific performance, refuse the decree and instead award damages.[183]

37. *Criticism.* – The development of the law relating to specific performance has been much influenced by its history. For example, the rule that specific performance would not be granted where damages were an adequate remedy was originally justified by two factors: the rivalry between the courts of common law and equity and the reluctance to use the process of contempt of court (which was the traditional method of enforcing Chancery decrees) to redress private wrongs where less drastic methods of enforcement could do adequate (if not perfect) justice to the plaintiff. This reluctance became stronger in the nineteenth century, as imprisonment for civil debt was curtailed. The notion that contempt proceedings were the prime method of enforcement was also responsible for the unavailability of specific performance where the contract called for the performance of continuous duties. The courts were slow to exploit the possibilities offered by other, less drastic but more satisfactory, methods of execution in such cases.

COMMON LAW countries have, however, come to recognise many methods of execution apart from committal for contempt, such as orders for the delivery of goods or for giving possession of land, sequestration and authorising the act to be done at the expense of the defendant.[184] In ENGLAND such authorisation is a method of executing a judgment for specific performance, rather than a separate form of judgment (*supra* s. 9). It is true that where a contract provides, for example, that a buyer shall be entitled to remove the things bought from the seller's land, an injunction to restrain the seller from interfering with this process may be granted.[185] But such an injunction

[173] *Corbin* § 1172; *Treitel* 844.

[174] *Corbin* § 1171; *Treitel* 843.

[175] See, for example, *Gibbs v. David* (1870), L.R. 20 Eq. 373 (receiver appointed in a rescission action).

[176] *Corbin* § 1171.

[177] See *Lugunda v. Service Hotels*, [1969] 2 Ch. 209 (C.A.).

[178] INDIAN Specific Relief Act, 1877 (*supra* n. 136) s. 21 (g). This interesting provision has been dropped from s. 14 (1) (d) of the INDIAN Specific Relief Act 1963 (*ibidem*), which refers to "a continuous duty *which the court cannot supervise*" (see *supra* n. 143).

[179] *Willard v. Tayloe*, 75 U.S. 557 (1869).

[180] *Corbin* § 1137.

[181] *Idem* § 1160; *Chitty (-Treitel)* I § 1555, 1556.

[182] *Tarry v. Johnston*, 114 Neb. 496, 208 N.W. 615 (1926); *Greenwood v. Turner*, [1891] 2 Ch. 144; *Maskell v. Ivory*, [1970] 1 Ch. 502.

[183] *Corbin* § 1161; *Chitty (-Treitel)* I § 1565, 1556.

[184] See for example ENGLAND: RSC Orders 45, 46 rule 5; *cf.* INDIAN Specific Relief Act, 1877 (*supra* n. 136) s. 5 (this section is not reprocuded in INDIAN Specific Relief Act, 1963 (*supra* n. 136, 143); CALIFORNIAN CC § 3367; NEW MEXICO Statutes Annotated (1953) vol. 5 § 22-1-1 (70); *Corbin* § 1171.

[185] *James Jones & Sons, Ltd. v. Tankerville*, [1909] 2 Ch. 440.

does not enable the buyer to act at the expense of the seller; it merely restrains the seller from interfering with the exercise of the buyer of his rights under the contract. In some of the UNITED STATES, however, a judgment entitling the buyer to undertake such acts on the seller's property may be obtained even though the contract envisaged that the acts should be done by the seller.[186] In many COMMON LAW jurisdictions, a judgment for the transfer of title is either self-executing (in that it transfers title) or it can be enforced by appointing an officer of the court to execute the transfer.[187] In view of the availability of these various methods of enforcement, some of the limitations on specific performance are beginning to have an out-of-date appearance; and in the UNITED STATES at any rate they are being progressively discarded.

d. Mixed Approaches

38. *Comparison and fourth or mixed approach.* – The leading distinction between the systems so far discussed is between CIVIL LAW systems which in principle recognise specific enforcement, and COMMON LAW systems which regard specific enforcement as exceptional and discretionary. In practice the gap between the two approaches is not as great as might appear. On the one hand specific enforceability in CIVIL LAW countries is subject to important exceptions; in particular, most of them observe the principle that obligations to render personal services cannot, in the last resort, be specifically enforced;[188] orders for enforced performance of other obligations are sometimes more difficult to enforce than in COMMON LAW countries; and, perhaps most important of all, an aggrieved contracting party will often prefer to claim compensation in money, as that is generally a quicker and to that extent a better remedy. On the other hand, some of the restrictions on specific performance are beginning to disappear in COMMON LAW countries, particularly in the UNITED STATES, as their historical foundations are eroded. That is not to say that there are no differences at all between CIVIL and COMMON LAW systems, but they are less considerable than the starting theories of the two approaches might suggest.

The narrowing of the gap between the two approaches can best be seen by looking at CIVIL LAW countries such as SCOTLAND, LOUISIANA, QUEBEC, SOUTH AFRICA and SRI LANKA which have been exposed as a result of political association to COMMON LAW influence. Of course the influence has not all been one way; for example the provision in the UNITED KINGDOM Sale of Goods Act, 1893 which gives the court power to order specific performance no doubt owes its origin to SCOTS law.[189] But in the matter of specific relief the preponderant flow of influence in these countries has been the other way; the picture is one of acceptance of the general CIVIL LAW principle of specific relief, followed by qualification of that principle very much along COMMON LAW lines.

Thus in SCOTLAND there is said to be a "general right" to the remedy of "specific implement"; but at the same time the remedy is said to be a discretionary one, and the circumstances in which it will be refused are such that in practice there is no wide divergence between ENGLISH and SCOTS law on this point.[190]

In SOUTH AFRICA the election between specific performance and damages is with the injured party who is said in principle to have a right to specific performance; but that right is subject to limitations which closely resemble those which exist in ENGLISH law, even to the extent that specific performance is said to be excluded where damages are an adequate remedy.[191] Indeed it has been said that in this context the SOUTH AFRICAN courts will "be guided by the general principles which underlie the English decisions."[192] The position is the same in SRI LANKA.[193]

Under the LOUISIANA CC art. 1926 the plaintiff may "at his option" claim damages or "in cases which permit it" specific performance; but CC art. 1927 then sets out the COMMON LAW principle that the action for damages is the normal remedy and that specific performance is only available when this remedy is inadequate. Other

[186] *E.g., Rector of St. David's Church v. Wood*, 24 Or. 396, 34 P. 18 (1893).

[187] *E.g.*, MAINE Revised Statutes Annotated – M.R.S.A. – vol. 15 § 33-4; NEW MEXICO Statutes (*supra* n. 184) § 22-18-4, 21-1-11; OHIO Revised Code (Page's Ohio Revised Code Annotated) s. 2323.08; OKLAHOMA Statutes Annotated § 12-687; WEST VIRGINIA Code (West Virginia Code Annotated (1966) vol. 15) § 55-12-7.

[188] *Carbonnier* IV 528 points out this analogy between CIVIL and COMMON LAW.

[189] See *Treitel*, Specific Performance in the Sale of Goods: 1966 J.B.L. 211, 216-217.

[190] *Walker* I 585-586, II 1897; *Smith* 855.

[191] *Willie and Millin (-Coaker and Schutz)* 88-90; *Kerr*, Principles of the Law of Contract (Durban 1967) 213.

[192] *Wessels* II § 3117.

[193] *Weeramantry* II 957 ss.

COMMON LAW principles have been imported by judicial decisions, so that specific performance has been denied in LOUISIANA on the same grounds as in COMMON LAW jurisdictions.[194]

In QUEBEC, CC art. 1165 begins by asserting the general right to damages for breach of an obligation and then provides for specific enforcement "in cases which admit of it" ("*dans les cas qui le permettent*"). From this wording it is not clear which remedy is intended to be the primary one; but from the case law it appears that specific performance is regarded as exceptional and limited in the same way as in COMMON LAW countries.[195] The remedy, it has been said, was introduced "in imitation of the law prevailing in England."[196]

Enforcement of the court's order by contempt proceeding is possible in all these CIVIL LAW countries which have been subjected to COMMON LAW influence.[197] The smooth acceptance of the COMMON LAW restrictions in these CIVIL LAW systems lends considerable support to the view that the clash between COMMON and CIVIL LAW principles in this area is of comparatively small practical importance.

39. *Uniform Law on International Sales.* – The provisions of this Law show an interesting combination of CIVIL and COMMON LAW influences.

ULIS resembles CIVIL LAW systems in recognising that the buyer is in principle entitled to the remedy of "requiring performance".[198] This means that the seller may be ordered to deliver the goods, or to make a fresh conforming delivery, or even in certain cases (*supra* s. 7) to cure defects in the goods.

The scope of the remedy is, however, limited by the rule that it is not available if "it is in conformity with usage and reasonably possible for the buyer to purchase goods to replace those to which the contract relates".[199] This rule is based on considerations similar to those which, in COMMON LAW systems, lead to a refusal of specific performance where damages are an adequate remedy. A similar limitation on the availability of the action for the price is discussed in s. 104 below.

The scope of the remedy in any particular country is further limited by the rule that a court is not *bound* (though it might be entitled) to order the seller to perform in a case governed by ULIS if this remedy would not be available under its own domestic law.[200]

[194] *Jackson* (*supra* n. 33) 207-208.

[195] *E.g., Guaranteed Pure Milk Co. v. Patry,* [1957] Q.B. (Que.) 54; *Shaw Schools, Ltd. v. Fells,* 1932 S.C. 483; *Baudouin* 568.

[196] *Wills v. Central Rly. of Canada* (1914), 24 Que. K.B. 102, 107.

[197] QUEBEC: *Baudouin* 570; LOUISIANA: *Jackson* (*supra* n. 33) 220; SOUTH AFRICA: *Willie and Millin* (*-Coaker and Schutz*) 90; SCOTLAND: *Gloag and Henderson* 123.

[198] Art. 24 (1) (a), 30, 41 (1) (a), 42.

[199] Art. 25, 42 (1) (c).

[200] This is the effect of art. 16.

III. SUBSTITUTIONARY RELIEF IN MONEY

A. GENERAL INTRODUCTION

40. *Availability of "damages"*. – The availability of this form of relief has been inferentially discussed in s. 11 of this chapter. In COMMON LAW jurisdictions, relief of this kind is always available, "damages" being the primary remedy for breach of contract. In CIVIL LAW countries the availability of damages for non-performance[201] as opposed to specific enforcement is sometimes said to be circumscribed (*supra* s. 11); but the limits to its scope are of more theoretical than practical importance. ULIS (*supra* s. 7) here follows the COMMON LAW approach, making damages available as of right in all cases.[202]

A judgment for a sum of money may be available either by way of enforced performance (that is to say, in cases in which an action is brought for the agreed price or remuneration) or by way of substitutionary relief in money. The distinction can be illustrated by the case of an employee who is wrongfully dismissed before the end of his agreed period of service. In COMMON LAW countries the employee in such a case is not entitled to recover his agreed remuneration but only damages which will consist of the agreed remuneration less the amount (if any) that he earned in other employment or that he could have earned in any other employment which it would have been reasonable to seek and accept.[203] This may be contrasted with GERMAN and AUSTRIAN law which recognise a right to the agreed remuneration, subject to deduction of what the employee earned or maliciously or deliberately (*infra* s. 102) omitted to earn during the period in question; in AUSTRIA the employee has an immediate right to full earnings to the extent that the period does not exceed three months.[204] The practical result of the two approaches will often be the same; but the theories are quite different, being founded in the COMMON LAW systems on substitutionary relief and in GERMAN and AUSTRIAN law on enforced performance.

The question exactly when each type of claim is available will be further discussed in s. 103 of this chapter. Here we are only concerned to draw the distinction before discussing the principles which govern *substitutionary* relief in money. For ease of reference such relief will here be called by its COMMON LAW name of damages.

41. *Summary of general principles*. – Many of the basic principles relating to the assessment of damages are in fact common to the principal WESTERN systems of law. The most important of these principles are as follows. First, damages are compensatory and are awarded to protect certain recognised interests of the plaintiff. Secondly, the interest most generally protected is that which the plaintiff has in the performance of the contract. That is, he is entitled to be placed, so far as money can do it, into a position as good as that in which he would have been if the contract had been performed. This, however, is not the only recognised interest. Sometimes compensation is awarded for loss which the plaintiff suffered by acting in reliance on the contract; or the defendant is made liable to the extent to which he has benefited from the plaintiff's performance. The third main principle is that all the systems under discussion stop short of fully protecting these interests. The object of fully compensating the plaintiff must often give way to the generally felt need to lay down certain limits beyond which the defendant will not be held liable.

B. THE COMPENSATORY PRINCIPLE

42. *Damages are compensatory*. – The definition of the interests protected by the law of contract (*infra* s. 49–52) contains in itself some limitation of liability. It is based on the assumption that there must be some injury to these interests before damages will be awarded. In other words, it reflects the principle that damages are compensatory. This principle limits the extent of recoverable damages in various ways.

43. *Loss to plaintiff the criterion*. – In the first place, damages are based on loss to the plaintiff and not generally speaking on gain to the defendant. If, for example, an employee in breach of contract leaves his job and takes up one that is better paid, he is not liable to account to the employer for the extra remuneration thus earned. Similarly, a person who agrees to put capital into a business but instead invests it in another, more

[201] As distinguished from damages for delay which are in principle available provided that the necessary requirements with respect to putting the debtor in default are complied with.

[202] Art. 24, 41, 55, 63, 68, 70.

[203] *Corbin* § 1095; *Treitel* 731.

[204] GERMAN CC § 615; AUSTRIAN CC § 1162 b.

profitable, enterprise is liable to the aggrieved party for the loss suffered by the business, but not for the extra profit made in the other enterprise.[205] Again, suppose that A sells goods to B for £ 100 and before delivery is due he resells them to C for £ 150. If at the date fixed for delivery to B the goods have a market value of £ 100 or less, B will not recover any substantial damages. The fact that A has made a profit of £ 50 is irrelevant since B has suffered no loss.[206]

Gains which have accrued to the party in breach may be recoverable on the principle of unjust enrichment, for example where he has wrongfully, in breach of contract, made use of the aggrieved party's property and thus saved expense;[207] or where he has committed a breach of "fiduciary" duty.[208] But profits to the party in breach are not recoverable *merely* because they have accrued as a result of the breach of contract.

44. *Damages not to exceed loss.* – The second consequence of the principle that damages are compensatory is that an award of damages should not enrich the plaintiff: he cannot recover more than his loss. In some of the UNITED STATES there are express statutory provisions to the effect that damages shall not as a general rule exceed full compensation; and even in the absence of such enactments the principle applies in other states. One application of the principle can be seen in the situation discussed in s. 43 above; but the principle is of general application and is not restricted to cases in which the defendant has made a profit out of the breach of contract.

The compensatory principle is, in particular, the basis of certain aspects of the law relating to mitigation or *Vorteilsausgleichung*, as it is known in the laws of GERMANY, AUSTRIA and SWITZERLAND. This subject is discussed in detail in s. 104 to 105 below. Here it is only necessary to give a few illustrations of situations in which the plaintiff will not be allowed to recover more than his loss. If a seller of goods defaults, the buyer may as a result save storage charges; any such savings must be brought into account on the buyer's claim for damages. If an employee is wrongfully dismissed, and in consequence is able to take other employment, any sums earned in that employment must be brought into account on a claim for damages against the original, defaulting, employer. Equally, he must bring into account sums saved as a result of being relieved from his obligation to perform the original contract.

One aspect of the rule that the plaintiff should not be enriched by the award of damages gives rise to some difficulty. The plaintiff may be put by the defendant's breach into the position of having to procure a substitute and that substitute may actually represent an improvement on his position as it was before the contract (see *supra* s. 13). In general allowance should be made for such improvements. But in an ENGLISH case[209] the plaintiff's factory was as a result of the defendant's breach of contract burnt down; and the plaintiff reconstructed the factory. The result was an improved, more modern, building. It was held that the plaintiff could recover the whole cost of rebuilding, without giving credit for the "betterment". The explanation for this decision seems to be that the plaintiff had no reasonable alternative but to rebuild and that he was indeed bound to do so in performance of his "duty" to mitigate the loss (*infra* s. 100–102).

45. *No punitive damages.* – The third consequence of the principle that damages for breach of contract are compensatory is that generally speaking "punitive" (also called "exemplary") damages will not be awarded for breach of contract. Such damages may be awarded in tort cases, not to compensate the plaintiff but to indicate the tribunal's disapproval for the conduct of the defendant.[210] They should strictly speaking be distinguished from damages for injured feelings or mental suffering which are regarded as compensatory in the sense that they are based on the hurt to the plaintiff and not on a desire to punish the defendant, though in practice courts or juries seem sometimes to lose sight of the distinction.[211]

The concept of punitive damages is largely confined to COMMON LAW jurisdictions, though it has penetrated into some CIVIL LAW countries which are or have been in political association with COMMON LAW ones.[212] It is true that the FRENCH *astreinte* (*supra* s. 24 ss.) to some extent punishes the

[205] *E.g., Teacher v. Calder* (1899), 1 F. (H.L.) 39, [1899] A.C. 451 (H.L.).

[206] *Acme Mills v. Johnson*, 133 S.W. 784 (Ky.C.A. 1911).

[207] *E.g., Penarth Dock Engineering Co., Ltd. v. Pounds*, [1963] 1 Lloyd's Rep. 359 (Q.B.). See this Encyclopedia vol. X ch. 9.

[208] *E.g., Reading v. Att.-Gen.*, [1951] A.C. 507 (H.L.); *Timco v. Useful Homes Corp.*, 168 A. 824 (Ch. N.J. 1933). See this Encyclopedia vol. X ch. 10.

[209] *Harbutt's "Plasticine", Ltd. v. Wayne Tank & Pump Co., Ltd., supra* n. 67.

[210] See this Encyclopedia vol. XI ch. 8 s. 107–114.

[211] *E.g., Chelini v. Nieri*, 32 Cal.2d 480, 196 P.2d 915 (1948) (*infra* s. 110).

[212] See, for example, *Weeramantry* II § 932 with reference to the Roman-Dutch law of SRI LANKA. In SCOTLAND, punitive damages are not awarded.

defendant, but it does so for his contumacy in the face of the court's decree rather than for his failure to perform the primary obligation of the contract

The general rule that punitive damages will not be awarded for breach of contract is well established.[213] In a number of the UNITED STATES there are express statutory provisions to this effect and the same general principle is stated in the Uniform Commercial Code.[214] There are, however, exceptions to the general rule. The most general of these is that exemplary damages can be awarded for breach of promise of marriage in those jurisdictions which still impose contractual liability for such conduct.[215] In the UNITED STATES, punitive damages have also been awarded in a miscellaneous collection of other cases of which the following constitutes a representative selection: against a person who induced another to buy a gelding by fraudulently representing that it was a colt;[216] against a carrier who recklessly carried a passenger beyond his destination;[217] against an employer who wrongfully dismissed an employee and at the same time publicly called him a liar;[218] and in some cases against public service corporations.[219] In all these cases it could be said that the basis of liability was not purely contractual but contained tortious elements.

46. *Multiple damages.* – In some COMMON LAW countries there are also statutory provisions for multiple damages in respect of conduct which could be described as breach of contract. For example, a tenant failing to vacate premises after the termination of a lease or after he has given notice that he will quit may be liable for twice or three times the rental value or agreed rent.[220] The purpose of these rules appears to be to coerce the defendant, rather than (as in the case of punitive damages) to express disapproval of his conduct.

47. *Plaintiff must suffer loss.* – The fourth consequence of the rule that damages are compensatory is that no damages are recoverable if the plaintiff has suffered no loss. An apparent exception is the availability in some countries of "nominal damages" consisting of a trivial sum awarded to indicate that the contract has been broken, even though the breach has caused no loss.[221] This was a device by which COMMON LAW courts evaded the rule (long since abrogated) that they could not make purely declaratory judgments (*supra* s. 5). In effect an award of nominal damages is a declaration of rights rather than an award of compensation in money for the breach of contract, and the power to make such an award is not in substance inconsistent with the principle that damages are compensatory.

For the present purpose, loss may be broadly defined to include any harm to the person, personality or property of the plaintiff. Harm to the person requires no explanation. Harm to the personality includes such things as injury to feelings, honour and reputation. Compensation for such harm is known in FRENCH law as *dommage moral* and in GERMAN law as *Schmerzensgeld.* The question whether such harm gives rise to a claim for compensation in a contractual action is discussed later in this chapter (*infra* s. 110–113). Harm to property includes physical harm to particular things as well as patrimonial loss. The latter concept will require elaboration, but it may provisionally be defined as the difference between the patrimony of the plaintiff as it is and as it would have been, had the defendant duly performed his contract. It is this kind of loss which gives rise to most difficulty in the present context; for the question whether the plaintiff's patrimony was in fact diminished by the breach is often a very complex one.

In a celebrated GERMAN case a bread dealer delivered a quantity of dough to a baker on the terms that the baker was to bake rolls and deliver these to the dealer, who required them for the

[213] *Corbin* § 1077; in ENGLISH law this is usually thought to follow from *Addis v. Gramophone Co., Ltd.*, [1909] A.C. 488 (H.L.); it was applied in *Perera v. Vandiyar*, [1953] 1 W.L.R. 672 (C.A.).

[214] ALABAMA Code (*supra* n. 137) § 9-3294; CALIFORNIAN CC § 3294; GEORGIA Code (*supra* n. 142) § 20-1045; Revised Codes of MONTANA (*supra* n. 137) § 17-208; NORTH DAKOTA Century Code (*supra* n. 154) § 32-03-07; OKLAHOMA Statutes (*supra* n. 187) § 23-9; SOUTH DAKOTA Compiled Laws (*supra* n. 154) § 21-1-4; UCC s. 1-106.

[215] *Corbin* § 1077; *Weeramantry* II § 932; in many of the UNITED STATES and in ENGLAND the cause of action for breach of promise of marriage has been abolished.

[216] *Grandi v. Le Sage*, 74 N.M. 799, 399 P.2d 285 (1965).

[217] *St. Louis and S.F.R. Co. v. Lilly*, 52 Okl. 727, 153 P. 810 (1916).

[218] *Scheps v. Giles*, 222 S.W. 348 (Ct.Civ.App.Tex. 1920).

[219] *Corbin* § 1077.

[220] ENGLAND: Landlord and Tenant Act, 1730 (4 Geo. 2, c. 28) s. 1; Revised Codes of MONTANA (*supra* n. 137) § 17-501, 502; NORTH DAKOTA Century Code (*supra* n. 154) § 32-03-28; OKLAHOMA Statutes (*supra* n. 187) § 12-69; SOUTH DAKOTA Compiled Laws (*supra* n. 154) § 21-3-7.

[221] The power to make such awards is largely confined to COMMON LAW countries (see for example *Corbin* § 1001), but it also exists in some CIVIL LAW systems, *e.g.* in ROMAN-DUTCH law: *Weeramantry* II § 925.

purpose of resale. The baker abstracted some of the dough but baked the agreed number of rolls, though of a reduced size, and the dealer nevertheless in good faith sold the rolls to customers for the same price as full-sized ones. The baker was held liable in contract or alternatively for unjust enrichment.[222] Some commentators prefer the latter basis of liability taking the view that, although the baker may have been enriched, the dealer suffered no loss. In a sense he did suffer loss: as he received rolls of a smaller size than he had bargained for his patrimony was diminished.

The case illustrates a recurring problem: whether regard should be had to the use to which the aggrieved party intends to put certain items of property in order to determine whether his patrimony was diminished. An ENGLISH statute suggests an affirmative answer to this question by providing that a landlord cannot recover damages for breach of his tenant's obligation to repair if the tenant can prove that the landlord was going to demolish the premises.[223] It is also true that the amount of damages recoverable by a buyer of goods for non-delivery may be affected by a subsale if it was of the very same goods which formed the subject of the original sale.[224] And it is possible that damages for delayed delivery may be reduced or wholly eliminated if it can be proved that the subject-matter would not have been used at all during the period of delay.[225]

What these cases show is that affirmative evidence may be given to show that no loss was suffered or that the loss was reduced by reason of the intended use of the subject-matter (*infra* s. 72). In the absence of such evidence, the possibility remains that the mere fact that the plaintiff did not get the subject-matter is regarded as a loss. He does not have to show that he would have put it to profitable use. Thus in a SCOTTISH case contractors were guilty of delay in delivering warships to a foreign government. They argued without success that the government had suffered no loss as warships were not put to profitable use, and as the ships, if delivered on time, would probably have been sunk in a naval battle in which the fleet which they were to have joined suffered defeat. The House of Lords considered that the government suffered loss in not having the ships, irrespective of the use to which they might have been put.[226]

48. *Loss due to factors other than breach.* – Damages will be awarded only where the plaintiff can show that a diminution in his patrimony resulted from the fact that the contract has not been performed. It may be that he has suffered no loss at all. Suppose a person has bought property after being negligently advised by his lawyer or architect. If he has nevertheless paid no more than the true market value or the amount he would have paid even if he had been properly advised, he is not entitled to damages.[227] Alternatively, the plaintiff may have suffered loss, but not because of the fact that the contract was broken. This is the position where a buyer of goods has made a bad bargain and then receives delivery of non-conforming goods which are worth no less than those contracted for. In such a case no damages (or only nominal damages) are available for the non-conformity of the goods; though if the buyer is able to reject the goods or to revoke his acceptance he will in effect avoid the loss resulting from the fact that he made a bad bargain either by withholding payment or by recovering payment already made on the ground that he has put an end to the contract.[228]

These cases should be distinguished from those in which the plaintiff's damages are limited by the principles of "causation" (*infra* s. 91 ss.). These principles determine whether the event of which the plaintiff complains was brought about by the breach. Our present concern is with cases in which it is undisputed that the event (*e.g.* the delivery of non-conforming goods) was so brought about, but in which it is alleged that the event is not disadvantageous to the plaintiff.

C. THE INTERESTS PROTECTED[229]

49. *Expectation interest.* – The starting principle is that the object of awarding damages is to put the aggrieved party into as good a financial position as that in which he would have been if the contract had been duly performed. This pro-

[222] OLG Braunschweig 26 Jan. 1891, SeuffA. 46 no. 173; *Enneccerus and Lehmann* 59.

[223] Landlord and Tenant Act, 1927 (17 & 18 Geo. 5, c. 36) s. 18.

[224] *Re R. & H. Hall, Ltd. and W.H. Pim, Jr., & Co's Arbitration* (1928), 139 L.T. 50 (H.L.).

[225] *Kolker v. U.S.*, 40 F.Supp. 972 (D.C.Md. 1941).

[226] *Clydebank Engineering Co. v. Don Jose Ramos Yzquierdo y Castaneda*, [1905] A.C. 6 (H.L.) (where the actual decision turned on the validity of a "penalty" clause: *infra* s. 134).

[227] *Ford v. White*, [1964] 1 W.L.R. 885 (Ch.); *Sykes v. Midland Bank Executor and Trustee Co., Ltd.*, [1971] 1 Q.B. 113 (C.A.).

[228] *Treitel* 792.

[229] *Fuller and Perdue*, The Reliance Interest in Contract Damages: 46 Yale L.J. 52, 373 (1936).

cess has been called compensating the aggrieved party for loss of his expectation interest. This interest is referred to in GERMAN law as *Erfüllungsinteresse* or positive interest. Of course in order to determine exactly what expectations merit protection it is again necessary to ask just what it is that the debtor has undertaken; and the distinction drawn in s. 7 above between liability for defective performance and "guarantee" liability is again relevant at this point. A person who is under such a "guarantee" liability may be condemned to pay a sum of money in an action for price reduction or redhibition, involving mutual restoration of benefits (*infra* s. 57); but such liability is not regarded in the systems which recognize it as liability in damages. Not only is the basis of liability different; its extent is also quite different from the liability of a person who has undertaken that the performance shall not be defective.

It is the protection of the expectation interest which is a characteristic feature of an action based on contractual default. Indeed, in ENGLISH law it is *the* distinguishing feature of such an action, damages for loss of expectation being available *only* in a contractual action.[230] The same is true of many COMMONWEALTH or EX-COMMONWEALTH countries,[231] though in many of the UNITED STATES expectation loss is also recoverable in an action in tort for fraudulent misrepresentation irrespective of contract;[232] and in GERMANY a seller who fraudulently conceals a defect is liable for expectation loss in a case in which, but for the fraud, he would not be liable *in damages* at all (but only to a price reduction or to a setting aside of the contract) (CC § 463). The seller's liability in such a case is, however, regarded as contractual.

The statement that protection of the expectation interest is the characteristic feature of a contractual action is liable to give rise to some misunderstanding. It is of course true that compensation for the loss of certain expectations is regularly awarded in actions based on tort or delict. In COMMON LAW countries it is, for example, common to talk of an award of damages in tort for "loss of expectation of life". Similarly, damages for loss of earnings suffered as a result of personal injuries or of damage to a profit-earning thing are in a sense damages for loss of an expectation. But the expectations for the loss of which compensation is thus given exist quite independently of the acts of the party who is liable for the loss. In a contractual action the defendant is liable for loss of an expectation which exists solely by virtue of, and is created by, the contract for the breach of which the action is brought.

50. *Alternative principles: reliance and restitution.*– An alternative principle, also of general application, is to put the aggrieved party into the situation in which he would have been if the contract had never been made. This may be done by compensating him for expenses or other losses incurred in reliance on the contract. Here it is common to talk of protection of the reliance interest (known in GERMAN law as *Vertrauensinteresse* or negative interest).

Sometimes the award is based on a third principle which has been called protection of the restitution interest: this terminology is used to describe the situation in which the aggrieved party seeks to recover from the defaulting party a benefit which the former has conferred on the latter by performing his obligations under the contract. A buyer's claim for repayment of the price on account of non-delivery would be the most obvious illustration of a claim for restitution.

Protection of the restitution interest of course overlaps to a considerable extent with protection of the reliance interest, since performance by the aggrieved party constitutes a form of reliance, and the notion of "benefit received" is an elastic one, capable of referring at the one extreme to any reliance that is bargained for, and at the other only to actual "enrichment" of the opposite party by additions to his patrimony. But many forms of reliance falling short of those which "benefit" the other party may be recoverable on a claim for reliance loss, and in spite of the difficulty of distinguishing between restitution and reliance in borderline cases, the two concepts remain basically distinct. The phrase "restitutionary damages" has indeed been used in SOUTH AFRICA to cover both concepts in order to emphasize the distinction between them and damages for loss of expectation.[233] But this usage is confusing, leading to the imposition of conditions, *e.g.* as to the restoration of benefits received by the plaintiff on a claim for reliance loss which are only appropriate where restitution is claimed.

The relationship between claims for expectation, reliance and restitution will be more fully discussed in s. 54 to 65 below. Here it is only neces-

[230] Not, for example, in an action based on fraudulent misrepresentation inducing a contract: *Treitel* 302-303.

[231] *E.g., Snarski v. Snarski*, [1969] W.A.R. 39; *Caxton Printing Works (Pty.), Ltd. v. Transvaal Advertising Contractors, Ltd.*, 1936 T.P.D. 209.

[232] *Prosser*, Law of Torts (ed. 4 St. Paul 1971) 733-736.

[233] *Willie and Millin (-Coaker and Schutz)* 103.

sary to stress the general point that protection of the reliance and restitution interests is not regarded as adequate.[234] A contracting party cannot limit his liability by simply restoring what he has received, or by compensating the other party for his reliance loss. He is in principle bound to perform or to compensate the other party for loss of his bargain. The plaintiff in a contractual action may have the option of claiming damages on one or the other of these bases; but the defendant has no corresponding option.

51. *Two kinds of expectation.* – A contract may give rise to two quite separate expectations: that of receiving the promised performance and that of putting it to some particular use. For example, a person who buys raw materials for manufacturing purposes will expect both to get the goods bargained for and to use them in the process of manufacture. The distinction between these two kinds of expectations is drawn by many CIVIL LAW systems. It is one sense in which actual loss (*damnum emergens*) is contrasted with lost gains (*lucrum cessans*) in the FRENCH Civil Code and in Codes derived from it, in GERMAN, AUSTRIAN and SWISS law, and in ROMAN-DUTCH law.[235] Sometimes the same distinction is said to be between positive and negative damage.

This last usage must not be confused with the distinction between positive (expectation) and negative (reliance) *interest*. Negative damage (*i.e.* loss of profit) is often an element in positive (*i.e.* expectation) interest; though of course negative damage may be an element of negative interest: *e.g.* if the aggrieved party forbears in reliance on the defaulting party's promise from making some profitable use of the subject-matter of the contract. Thus if a contract for the lease of premises is broken by the tenant, the landlord's expectation interest is in the receipt of rent, but he may also suffer a reliance loss in foregoing the opportunity of letting the premises to another person.[236]

Unfortunately, the distinction between *damnum emergens* and *lucrum cessans* is also used in a second sense to refer to the difference between reliance and expectation loss. Thus an example discussed in the FRENCH literature is the case of an actor who breaks his contract to appear in a play.[237] In such a case it is said that the impresario can recover his expenses (*i.e.* reliance loss) as "*la perte qu'il a faite*" (*damnum emergens*) and his loss of profits as "*le gain dont il a été privé*" (*lucrum cessans*).[238] Of course in this case the first of the two kinds of expectation mentioned at the beginning of this section (*i.e.* that of receiving the actor's services) would be almost impossible to value independently. The use of the distinction in two quite different senses is perhaps due to the fact that the FRENCH Civil Code, after drawing the distinction, makes no actual use of it; though, as in GERMAN law (CC § 252), it is in practice relevant for the purpose of limiting the extent of recoverable damages. AUSTRIAN and SWISS law do make express use of the distinction for this purpose, linking it to the degree of fault of which the defendant was guilty.[239]

In COMMON LAW countries there is no doubt that the expectation interest also covers the two elements above. It is sometimes said that a contracting party is entitled to recover for losses caused and gains prevented;[240] but there is little analysis of the distinction and the terms *damnum emergens* and *lucrum cessans*, or any possible ENGLISH equivalents, are not in practice much used. Some statutes, such as the INDIAN Contract Act, 1872, do use the expressions "loss or damage";[241] but these words seem to refer rather to the distinction between financial loss and physical harm than to that between *damnum emergens* and *lucrum cessans* or to that between expectation and reliance loss.

52. *Expenditure.* – Expenditure by the injured party may be recoverable as expectation loss or as reliance loss or on some other basis. For the purpose of this discussion "expenditure" will be used in a broad sense, to include not only disbursements of money, but also the transfer, use or consumption of property, and the performance of work.[242]

The aggrieved party may have a claim for the cost of curing a defective performance (*infra* s. 66). Recovery of this amount is best regarded as compensation for loss of the expectation interest in having performance in accordance with the contract. Such a claim can be combined with one for loss of the different expectation interest in deriving a profit from the subject-matter, so long as this does not result in a duplication in the elements of recovery.

So far as reliance loss is concerned, a distinction

[234] *Corbin* § 996.

[235] FRENCH CC art. 1149; QUEBEC CC art. 1073; LOUISIANA CC art. 1934; GERMAN CC § 252; *Guhl* 72 citing SWISS CO art. 195 and 208 par. 2 and 3; AUSTRIAN CC § 1293; SRI LANKA: *Weeramantry* II § 928.

[236] *Enneccerus and Lehmann* 62.

[237] *Planiol and Ripert* VII no. 855.

[238] *De Page* III no. 105 p. 138.

[239] *Infra* s. 78, 79. SWISS CO art. 195, 208 par. 2 and 3; AUSTRIAN CC § 1324.

[240] *Corbin* § 992, citing Restatement of Contracts (1932) § 329.

[241] INDIAN Contract Act, 1872 (Act IX of 1872) s. 73.

[242] *Corbin* § 1032.

must be drawn between expenditure incurred before and after the contract. Expenditure incurred before the contract obviously cannot be incurred in reliance on it; and an AMERICAN case accordingly holds that such expenditures are not recoverable.[243] But other AMERICAN decisions take the opposite view,[244] which is also supported in ENGLAND.[245] This view may be justified where the precontract expenditure is lost by reason of reliance on the contract, in the sense that the contract induces the aggrieved party to forbear from taking steps to utilize the expenditure. This would be the position, for example, where a leading actor broke his contract to take part in a play or film, so that expenses incurred in relation to the production (whether before or after the actor's engagement) were rendered useless.[246] On the other hand, expenditure incurred after wrongful repudiation of the contract may be irrecoverable on the ground that the aggrieved party ought to have refrained from incurring it in the exercise of his duty to mitigate loss (*infra* s. 103). The most common case, therefore, in which expenditure incurred in reliance on the contract is recoverable is that in which it is incurred after the contract was made but before it was repudiated.

There are, however, many cases in which expenses incurred after breach will be recoverable: for example, expenses incurred in taking care of non-conforming goods, or in taking steps (such as making a cover sale or purchase) to avoid the loss which would otherwise result from the breach. In the UNITED STATES, the Uniform Commercial Code refers to such expenses as "incidental damages" (s. 2-715(1)). They should be distinguished from expenses incurred in "incidental reliance"[247] on the contract, for they are not properly speaking incurred in reliance on the contract, but rather in consequence of its breach. Nor does it seem that expenses of this kind can properly be regarded as forming part of the plaintiff's expectation; indeed they are in principle recoverable in addition to the normal damages for loss of expectation. Thus a buyer who on a seller's failure to deliver makes a "cover" purchase of other goods of the contract description is entitled not only to the difference between the cost of that purchase and the contract price (his expectation interest) but also to the expenses involved in making the second contract.[248] If there is no difference between the contract price and the cost of cover, the incidental damages are still recoverable. The right to recover "incidental damages" does not appear to be based on the principles of expectation, reliance or restitution; it shows that a contracting party's right to damages is by no means exhausted or fully described by these categories.

53. *Consequential damages.* – The same observation is to some extent true with regard to a contracting party's right to recover what in COMMON LAW countries is called "consequential damages". This term is not used at all precisely.

In the legislation of one of the UNITED STATES, it is simply used to refer to loss which is too remote to be recoverable;[249] but more generally it refers to items of loss which in principle are recoverable, though of course they may in an individual case in fact be too remote. Sometimes the term refers simply to the loss of gain which a party suffers in consequence of not receiving the thing contracted for: here its equivalent is the *lucrum cessans*, or "negative damage" of CIVIL LAW systems.[250] In this sense, it forms part of the expectation interest of the aggrieved party.

But the expression is also used in another (which is probably its principal) sense to refer to such things as personal injury or damage to property suffered as a result of the breach. It is used in this sense, for example, when a seller of infected cattle is held liable for loss suffered by the buyer when the infection spreads to other cattle owned by him.[251] In such a case it would strain language to say that the buyer expected not to lose the other cattle; and to say that he did not expect to lose them is of course quite a different matter. Consequential damages of this kind are not confined to physical harm; they may for example include amounts which a buyer of goods has to pay to a sub-buyer by reason of the seller's failure to deliver in accordance with the contract. The view that such "consequential" damages are not properly characterised as compensation for expectation losses has been expressed in GERMANY,

243 *Gruber v. S.-M.News Co., Inc.*, 126 F.Supp. 442 (S.D.N.Y. 1954).

244 *E.g., Security Stove and Mfg. Co. v. American Ry. Express Co.*, 227 Mo.App. 175, 51 S.W.2d 572 (1932).

245 *Lloyd v. Stanbury*, [1971] 1 W.L.R. 535 (Ch.); *Anglia Television, Ltd. v. Reed*, [1972] 1 Q.B. 60 (C.A.).

246 As in *Anglia Television, Ltd. v. Reed, supra* n. 245.

247 *Fuller and Perdue* (*supra* n. 229) 78.

248 See *Robert Stewart & Sons, Ltd. v. Carapanayoti & Co., Ltd.*, [1962] 1 W.L.R. 34 (Q.B.); INDIAN Contract Act (*supra* n. 241) s. 73 Illustration (b); UCC s. 2-714 (3); see *infra* s. 57 and 58 for rights to expenses in FRENCH and GERMAN law.

249 GEORGIA Code (*supra* n. 142) § 20-1406.

250 It seems to bear this meaning in UCC s. 2-715 (2) (a).

251 *Smith v. Green* (1876), 1 C.P.D. 92; *cf.* UCC s. 2-715 (2) (b).

where it has been said that damages of this kind in cases of so-called *positive Vertragsverletzung* (*infra* s. 75) go beyond the aggrieved party's *Erfüllungsinteresse*.[252] The fact that the point has been made in GERMANY shows that the present argument does not depend on the connotations attached to the ENGLISH word "expectation".

Nor can it be said without straining language that consequential damages (in the principal sense) necessarily represent reliance loss. Reliance is most commonly based on a positive belief that performance will take place. The defects in performance which give rise to consequential loss are usually not the subject of such a belief. The point may be illustrated by referring again to the liability of a seller of infected cattle for the spread of the infection to other animals. The loss of those animals is consequential loss, but it seems strange to say that the buyer put the infected cattle with his other stock in reliance on their not being diseased. It is more realistic to admit that the possibility of disease was not present in the buyer's mind at all.

D. RELATIONSHIP BETWEEN EXPECTATION, RELIANCE AND RESTITUTION

54. *Availability and overlap*. – Under the rules stated in s. 49-52 above, the aggrieved party may be entitled to damages for loss of his bargain and for reliance loss and to restitution.

A number of questions remain as to the relationship between these various claims. How is it determined in an individual case which of the possible interests is to be protected? And what is the relationship between them when, as sometimes happens, they overlap? In trying to answer these questions, the temptation to proceed from certain *a priori* assumptions must be strongly resisted.

One possible view might be that, as the object of damages is to put the aggrieved party into as good a position as that in which he would have been in if the contract had been performed, damages should be assessed on the basis of the expectation interest in all cases. In fact no system of law accepts such an argument, both reliance and restitution being recognised as alternative and sometimes as cumulative bases of recovery.

Another possible approach might be to say that protection of the positive interest was meant to put the aggrieved party into the situation in which he would have been, had the contract been performed; while protection of the negative interest was meant to put him into the situation in which he would have been, had the contract never been made. It would be tempting to go on to say that the positive interest is protected when the aggrieved party seeks damages for the other party's failure to render due performance and that the negative interest is protected when the aggrieved party seeks damages consequent on his putting an end to the contract. But this would again be misleading. For we shall see that in both COMMON and CIVIL LAW systems claims for negative or reliance interest are sometimes allowed where damages are claimed by way of a substitute for the enforcement of the obligation, while claims for positive or expectation interest are not ruled out by the aggrieved party's termination of the contract. All that is generally ruled out by such termination is the claim for actual performance (including the right to claim an agreed sum).[253]

The danger of *a priori* arguments in this area is perhaps best illustrated by a problem which does not strictly fall within the scope of the present chapter, as it is not necessarily concerned with default in the performance of a contract. The problem is: on what basis is a creditor to be compensated when performance is antecedently impossible and the debtor is aware of this fact? It is generally agreed that there is some liability, but there is considerable divergence as to which of the creditor's interests (expectation, reliance or restitution) is protected. FRENCH law holds the debtor liable in delict, but apparently for positive interest.[254] GERMAN law holds him liable in contract, but only for negative interest; however, it limits the damages so that positive interest is not exceeded (CC § 307 par. 1). SWISS law similarly makes a party who is unable to perform on account of a self-induced mistake liable for the loss suffered as a result of the failure of the contract (which appears to mean negative interest), though the judge has a discretion to award further damages.[255] Most AMERICAN states would follow the FRENCH view if the circumstance gave rise to a cause of action in deceit (*supra* n. 232). In that event ENGLISH law would allow recovery but would base it on negative interest only (*supra* n. 230). If there were no deceit, ENGLISH law would in principle allow restitution only;[256] but it might in some circumstances hold the debtor liable on the footing that he had "warranted" that perfor-

[252] *Enneccerus and Lehmann* 238.

[253] See *Treitel* 732; confusingly such claims are sometimes called claims for "damages" in COMMON LAW countries.

[254] *Zweigert and Kötz* 203.

[255] CO art. 26; *Guhl* 73-74.

[256] On the ground that the money had been paid under a "void" contract: *Treitel* 863-864.

mance was possible. This reasoning was applied in an AUSTRALIAN case, and it could in principle have led to recovery based on expectation loss. But as the value of the aggrieved party's expectation was not satisfactorily proved, he in fact recovered his reliance loss.[257]

It is, as the foregoing account shows, impossible to find any general principles which determine when an aggrieved party can claim reliance loss or restitution in lieu of, or together with, damages for loss of expectation. Different systems of law have different approaches to the relationship between these various interests. In some systems, the relationship is determined by the provisions of a Code; in others it is left to the discretion of the court; and in yet others it is left to the choice of the aggrieved party. One principle of general application, however, is that the injured party cannot combine the various types of claim so as to obtain compensation in excess of his actual loss.

55. *The relationship in German, Swiss and Austrian law.* – Regulation by the provisions of a Code is attempted in GERMANY, where the Civil Code uses three expressions. The first is *Schadenersatz wegen Nichterfüllung*, or compensation for non-performance.[258] This is measured on the basis of the expectation interest; and the effect of the relevant Code provisions is to establish a general right to damages for loss of expectation in case of the debtor's default. A second expression is used in CC § 307 which deals with the case of antecedent impossibility, discussed in s. 54 above. Here the reference is to loss suffered by the claimant in reliance on the validity of the contract (*cf.* CC § 122): that is, to negative or reliance interest. Finally, the restitution interest is referred to in CC § 346 which obliges each party to restore to the other any performance received (or where this is not possible its value) in case of termination of the contract (*infra* s. 181). Where the party obliged to make restitution is not responsible for the circumstances giving rise to the right to terminate the contract, his liability is limited by CC § 327 to the extent of his actual unjustified enrichment (*infra* s. 157).

The principles which emerge from these provisions are that, generally, the expectation interest is protected; but that, in cases in which the aggrieved party puts an end to the contract, the restitution interest is protected; and that in cases of invalidity of the transaction the reliance interest may be protected. Assuming the existence of a valid contract and default giving rise to a right to terminate, the aggrieved party thus has a choice: he can uphold the contract and claim his expectation interest; or he can terminate the contract and claim his restitution interest. He will pursue the former course if he has made a good bargain or if the market has risen, and the latter course if he has made a bad bargain or if the market has fallen.[259] The GERMAN Civil Code does not entitle the aggrieved party to recover in respect of reliance interest if he puts an end to the contract (*infra* s. 184) though the SWISS Code of Obligations does expressly allow this.[260]

AUSTRIAN law starts with the same principle as GERMAN law, that the aggrieved party can claim compensation based on expectation interest (*Schadenersatz wegen Nichterfüllung*), or put an end to the contract (CC § 920). But it goes on to say that termination of the contract does not affect the claim for compensation in respect of damage caused through non-performance where such non-performance was due to the debtor's fault. This form of compensation is described as "*Ersatz des durch verschuldete Nichterfüllung verursachten Schadens*" (CC § 921) and is not the same as *Schadenersatz wegen Nichterfüllung*. The claim is regarded not as one for *Erfüllungsinteresse* but as a *Differenzenanspruch:* in other words, as a claim based on the difference (and not on the exchange) theory (*infra* s. 73) by which the aggrieved party can, even though he puts an end to the contract, claim the difference in value between his performance (which he will keep) and the performance promised to him and not rendered.[261] This is in reality a sort of protection of expectations: it certainly cannot be explained simply on the basis of reliance or restitution. It would seem that the AUSTRIAN provision is also broad enough to cover reliance loss.

56. *The relationship in French law.* – The distinctions between the expectation, reliance and restitution interests are relatively undeveloped in FRENCH law. One reason for this is that the FRENCH Civil Code does not, with some possible exceptions to be discussed below, make use of the distinctions. Another is that the *Cour de Cassation* (whose reviewing power only extends to ques-

[257] *McRae v. Commonwealth Disposals Commission* (1950), 84 C.L.R. 377 (H.C. of A.), esp. at 411; *infra* s. 60.

[258] See CC § 280, 283, 286 par. 2, 325, 326, 463.

[259] *Enneccerus and Lehmann* 210.

[260] CO art. 109 par. 2 (the debtor can avoid such liability by disproving "fault").

[261] *Klang and Gschnitzer (-Gschnitzer)* IV 1 § 921 no. 1.

tions of law) will only review an assessment of damages by a lower court if that court has applied wrong principles of law,[262] and this rule has tended to inhibit analysis of the various elements constituting damages for breach of contract.

One provision in the part of the FRENCH Civil Code dealing with obligations in general which is capable of referring to the distinction between expectation and reliance loss is art. 1149. This provides that the damages due to the creditor consist of two elements: the loss which he has suffered ("*la perte qu'il a faite*") and the gain which he has failed to make ("*le gain dont il a été privé*"). These phrases refer to the well-known distinction between *damnum emergens* and *lucrum cessans*, which is sometimes used to differentiate between reliance and expection loss (*cf. supra* s. 51). It is so used in the case of an actor who breaks his contract to appear in a play.[263] The result is said to be that the impresario can recover disbursements already made at the time of the actor's repudiation (reliance loss or *damnum emergens*), and also the net profit which he would have made had the play been performed (expectation loss or *lucrum cessans*). There is no reference in the FRENCH sources to the distinction, sometimes drawn in ANGLO-AMERICAN law (*supra* s. 52), between pre- and post-contract expenditure.

However, the distinction drawn in CC art. 1149 between *damnum emergens* and *lucrum cessans* may also be used in quite a different sense, to refer to two kinds of expectation loss (*supra* s. 51). It is used in this sense in an illustration of goods lost in the course of carriage by sea to an agreed destination for the purpose of resale. Here the *damnum emergens* has been said to be the value of the goods and the *lucrum cessans* the profit which might have been made on resale.[264] Both types of loss form elements of the consignee's expectation; neither can be described as reliance loss. Similarly, where a seller of goods wrongfully fails to deliver, the buyer can *prima facie* recover in respect of both types of loss of expectation: his *damnum emergens* in not having the goods and his *lucrum cessans* in losing resale profits. But in the case of a commercial sale of goods for which the buyer has not yet paid the latter had been held the sole recoverable loss since the buyer was free to make other profitable use of his capital.[265]

FRENCH law differs from GERMAN law in that it does not normally restrict the aggrieved party to recovery based on restitution where he is allowed to put an end to the contract. CC art. 1184 (which provides for termination (*résolution*) in the case of synallagmatic contracts) expressly entitles the aggrieved party to seek this remedy together with damages; and the damages will, it appears, be assessed in accordance with the general principles based on CC art. 1149 to 1151.[266] Of course if, as a result of termination the aggrieved party gets back his own performance, he will have to give credit for its value, so that the first element of his damages will be the difference between the value of that performance and the performance promised to him. But recovery of expectation loss is not precluded by termination; nor, it seems, is recovery of reliance loss such as expenses incurred in reliance on the contract.

FRENCH law further differs from GERMAN law in that it does not (at least in principle) give the aggrieved party the option to choose between termination and damages. Termination is, in principle, a remedy which requires the intervention of the court, and it may be refused if in the opinion of the court the aggrieved party would be adequately compensated by damages (*infra* s. 147). Thus the option of the aggrieved party to claim protection of his restitution interest where he has made a bad bargain is restricted by judicial discretion. Of course, the statement that damages are available in addition to termination presupposes that the other requirements for an award of damages have been complied with: for instance that the defendant is guilty of "fault" and that a *mise en demeure* has, where necessary, been issued.

57. *Special application of the distinction to latent defects in the thing sold*[267] – *French law.* – The general principles stated above apply in FRENCH law in cases of sale where the buyer is aggrieved by non-delivery within the agreed time (CC art. 1610, 1611): that is the buyer can at his option claim performance or termination together with damages. Once again, termination is at the discretion of the judge and damages are assessed in accordance with general principles, so that they may comprise expectation and reliance losses.

Liability for latent defects in the subject-matter

[262] *Planiol and Ripert* VII no. 855; J.-Cl.Civ. art. 1146 to 1155 fasc. VIII (2e cahier) no. 125.

[263] See *supra* n. 238. For similar AMERICAN and ENGLISH cases see *Chicago Coliseum Club v. Dempsey*, 265 Ill.App. 542 (1932) (*infra* s. 60) and *Anglia Television v. Reed*, *supra* n. 245 (*supra* s. 52).

[264] *Carbonnier* IV 232-233; *cf.* Cass.civ. 3 Jan. 1893, D. 1893.1.223.

[265] Trib.civ.Seine 23 Oct. 1942, D.C. 1943 J.83 and note *Tunc*.

[266] *Infra* s. 82, 95. *De Page* III no. 104.

[267] For details see this Encyclopedia vol. VIII ch. 3 *sub* II D.

of a sale is, however, governed by certain special rules in CIVIL LAW systems. The basic principle is that the buyer's restitution interest is protected; but he has quite extensive rights to reliance loss. Occasionally he can recover for loss of expectation.

The mere presence of a latent defect in the subject matter of a sale does not constitute default; but it does give the buyer a choice of remedies. He can either claim a price reduction, or "redhibition". The first of these remedies differs, in CIVIL LAW systems, from damages: it is, as we shall see, generally based on a restitutionary principle (*infra* s. 67). Our present concern is with redhibition, which involves restoration of the subject-matter of the sale on the one hand and of the price on the other. In other words, it protects the buyer's restitution interest. It cannot, in principle, be combined with damages since the seller is not considered to undertake that the defects do not exist but only to assume certain guarantee liabilities in case they do exist (*supra* s. 7). The enforcement of these liabilities does not in principle protect the buyer's expectations that the subject-matter is free from defects. However, the aggrieved buyer is not always limited to recovery of his own performance in the redhibitory action.

If the seller knew of the defect he must not only restore the price but is in addition liable (under CC art. 1645) for "all damages" suffered by the buyer. The phrase "all damages" appears to be broad enough to include both of the two elements mentioned in CC art. 1149 (*supra* s. 56), and thus to include expectation and reliance loss. The corresponding provision of the LOUISIANA Civil Code expressly provides that the seller is liable to restitution, repayment of the expenses and damages (art. 2545). The scope of the FRENCH CC art. 1645 has been extended by judicial interpretation which has laid down certain presumptions of knowledge of defects against professional sellers.[268]

If the seller did not know of the defect he is liable (in addition to restoring the price) to reimburse the buyer for "*les frais occasionnés par la vente*" (the expenses occasioned by the sale) (CC art. 1646). This phrase seems to refer, most naturally, to a particular kind of reliance loss, namely to expenses incurred in connection with or in reliance on the sale. In fact the courts at one time interpreted the phrase very much in favour of the buyer, particularly so as to include consequential loss caused by the defect in the thing,[269] such as personal injury, or the cost of resowing a crop where defective seed had been supplied.[270] The justification for this broad view was what the Code referred to "*les frais occasionnés par la vente*" (the expenses occasioned by the sale) – not "*les frais de la vente*" (the expenses of the sale) which might be taken to refer only to the administrative expenses of the sale. But more recently the courts have to some extent resiled from this very broad view, on the ground that it virtually obliterated the distinction drawn in the Civil Code between bad faith and good faith vendors. It is of course arguable that even the broad interpretation of "*les frais occasionnés par la vente*" did not protect the buyer's expectations, *e.g.*, of profiting from the subject-matter of the sale;[271] but if this is the sole distinction between the liability of a good faith and a bad faith seller, it is hard to deduce it from the language of the relevant articles of the Civil Code.[272]

The LOUISIANA Civil Code adopts a middle way by allowing the buyer "expenses occasioned by the sale and those incurred in preserving the thing" (CC art. 2531). This is similar to the GERMAN solution discussed below though it provides somewhat less extensive remedies for the buyer.

58. *Special application of the distinction to latent defects in the thing sold – German law.* – In GERMAN law the rules relating to latent defects in the subject-matter of a sale refer to defects in specific things in existence at the time of the passing of risk (CC § 459). If the sale is of generic goods, and in certain other cases to be discussed below, the buyer has the remedies available under the general law of contract;[273] though if defective goods are appropriated to a contract for the sale of generic goods the buyer may, instead of claiming a substitute conforming delivery, assert the remedies available in the case of specific goods which suffer from a latent defect at the time of the passing of risk.[274]

In such a case, GERMAN law starts with the same

[268] *Mazeaud*, Leçons III 816; for a similar rule in SOUTH AFRICA, see *Willie and Millin (-Coaker and Schutz)* 185.

[269] *Mazeaud*, Leçons III 815-816; *cf. Radouant*, Les dommages-intérêts dus par le vendeur dans la garantie des vices cachés de la chose en droit français: Mélanges Roger Secrétan (Montreux 1964) 241; *Baudry-Lacantinière and Saignant*, Droit civil (ed. 3 Paris 1908) XIX 456.

[270] *Baudry-Lacantinière and Saignant* (*supra* n. 269) XIX 456.

[271] *Planiol and Ripert* X no. 134.

[272] *Radouant* (*supra* n. 269) 243.

[273] *Enneccerus and Lehmann* 452, 457; CC § 480.

[274] *Enneccerus and Lehmann* 458.

principle as FRENCH law, namely that the aggrieved buyer is entitled at his option to a price reduction (*Minderung*) or to *Wandelung*, that is, to recovery of his performance against return of the performance which he has received. As in FRENCH law, it is basically the buyer's restitution interest that is protected, and the seller is not in principle liable to compensate the buyer for loss of his expectation that the subject-matter is free from defect.

Such liability does, however, exist under the GERMAN CC § 463, which makes the seller liable for *Schadenersatz wegen Nichterfüllung* (reparation for non-performance)[275] in two cases: if the goods lack a quality which they are expressly warranted to have, and if the seller fraudulently conceals a defect. A fraudulent representation to the effect that the subject-matter has certain qualities which in fact it lacks appears to have the same effect although this situation is not expressly mentioned in CC § 463.[276] This provision (unlike FRENCH CC art. 1645) makes the claim for damages *alternative* to the claims for *Wandelung* and *Minderung*, in accordance with the general GERMAN policy of making the termination of a contract and damages for non-performance alternatives (*infra* s. 184). There is no doubt that the claim under CC § 463 extends to one for loss of expectation. In this respect it is to be contrasted with other claims for fraudulent misrepresentation which give rise to a claim for negative interest only, that is for reliance loss.[277]

The theoretical justification for the different treatment of a seller who is guilty of fraudulent concealment of defects or of fraudulent misrepresentation as to quality is that a buyer of goods which turn out to be defective really *is* disappointed in his expectation; that the general principle by which the seller is only liable on a guarantee basis and not for the full expectation interest is adopted out of leniency to sellers who cannot be expected to know of hidden defects; but that this leniency ought not to be extended to fraudulent sellers.[278] As against this, a possible rationale of the general rule limiting the seller's liability to *Wandelung* or *Minderung* is that the buyer has *no* right to a thing free from defects: if he had known of the defect he would either not have bought at all or only for a lesser price. In other words, his prejudice is that he parted with his money, or with too much money, and not that he has got defective goods.[279] On this view, the special provisions relating to a fraudulent seller are only explicable (if at all) by the need to provide some effective deterrent for fraud; but this explanation is not wholly satisfactory since a fraudulent representation which does not relate to the quality of the goods only entails liability for reliance loss.

Even in the absence of express warranty or fraud, the buyer may in GERMAN law have two further claims, which are additional (and not alternative) to *Wandelung* or *Minderung;* but these do not protect his expectation interest. The first is a claim for *Vertragskosten* (contract expenses) given by CC § 467: these have been held to include not only the administrative expenses of making the contract, such as stamp duties, postal expenses and agency fees, but also the expenses of obtaining expert advice.[280] The second is a claim for expenses (*Verwendungen*) incurred in relation to the thing.[281] Under this head insurance, freight and even installation costs incurred in relation to the subject-matter have been recovered.[282] This head of recovery seems to go beyond expenses incurred in reliance on the sale and to include items more properly described as consequential loss. The rights of the buyer are therefore more extensive than those which he has in FRENCH law under his entitlement to "*les frais occasionnés par la vente*"; but in both systems pure expectation losses and consequential losses other than *Verwendungen* appear to be excluded.

59. *Special application of the distinction to latent defects in the thing sold – Austrian and Swiss law.* – In AUSTRIAN law, where the seller acted in good faith, the buyer is only entitled to *Wandelung* and *Minderung*. He is not even entitled to *Vertragskosten* if the seller was not at "fault".[283] Thus it is only his restitution interest that is protected. If the seller is at "fault" he is liable in damages, the exact extent of which depends on the degree of fault (*infra* s. 78).

SWISS law goes further than any of the systems so far discussed in protecting the buyer's interests. The seller is again liable to *Minderung* and *Wandelung*. Where the latter remedy is sought, CO art. 208 provides that the seller has to restore the price and in addition to recompense the buyer for the cost of litigation with third parties, expenses

[275] *I.e.* for loss of expectation interest: *idem* 436.

[276] BGB-RGRK § 463 no. 6.

[277] *I.e.* under CC § 249: *Enneccerus and Lehmann* 438.

[278] BGB-RGRK § 463 no. 5.

[279] *Enneccerus and Lehmann* 431.

[280] *Palandt* § 467 no. 3b.

[281] CC § 347 sent. 2, made applicable by CC § 467.

[282] *Palandt, supra* n. 280.

[283] *Klang and Gschnitzer* (-*Gschnitzer*) IV 1 § 932 no. AIII1a; he is however liable for *Verwendungen*: *ibidem.*

incurred in relation to the thing and "direct" damages; and also for all other damages unless he can prove that he was in no way at fault. If he cannot prove this, he is fully liable for loss of expectations.[284] For this purpose a seller may be at "fault" even though he is not guilty of fraud. The effect of fraud is simply to remove the need to give immediate notice of the defect to the seller (CO art. 203). It is not a necessary condition of his liability for loss of expectation.

The "direct" damage for which the seller is liable under CO art. 208, even though he is not at "fault", refers primarily to reliance loss. An award of "direct" damage is meant to put the buyer into the position in which he would have been if the contract had never been made.[285] It follows from this principle that certain types of consequential loss (such as damage caused to the subject-matter by an explosion resulting from the defect) are also recoverable. But pure expectation loss (such as loss of resale profits) is "indirect" and cannot be recovered from a seller who is innocent of "fault".[286]

CO art. 208 only allows the buyer to recover "direct" loss on a claim for *Wandelung*. There is no such claim if the buyer wishes to keep the thing and to claim a price reduction against a seller who is innocent of fault.[287] Here the buyer's only claim is for *Minderung*, based on restitutionary principles (*infra* s. 67): his reliance and expectation interests are not protected at all.

60. *Relation between expectation and reliance interests in Anglo-American law.* – In COMMON LAW countries, recovery by the aggrieved party may be based on the expectation, reliance and restitution interests; and as there is no statutory provision specifying the circumstances in which these various bases are available their relationship is far from clear.

ENGLISH law starts with the principle that the plaintiff is entitled to choose between claiming on an expectation and a reliance basis: thus it has been held that the buyer of a machine which is less efficient than it would have been, had it been in accordance with the contract, can recover *either* its cost and the expenses of installing it *or* the profit he would have made by use of the machine; but he cannot recover both as this would give him his profit and also the cost of earning it.[288] Similarly, in the UNITED STATES it has been held that a buyer of oil could recover, as damages for non-delivery, the market value of the oil, but not in addition the expense wasted in attempting to collect it.[289]

However, claims for loss of profits and expenses are not in all cases mutually exclusive. Thus in the case of the defective machinery it is possible for the plaintiff to recover both his actual outlay (less the present value of the machinery) plus the excess over this sum of the estimated net profits which he would have made had the machinery been in accordance with the contract.[290] There is no theoretical objection to combining items of recovery in this way so long as the plaintiff is not allowed double recovery: if he has to incur expense to earn a profit he cannot recover his full "profit" *and* his capital expenditure since his profit only amounts to excess of receipts over expenditure.

Sometimes the court may award reliance loss even though the plaintiff claims for loss of expectation. This may be done where the value of the plaintiff's expectation is too uncertain to enable the court to base an award upon it.[291] In such a case one possible solution is to award damages for a *different* expectation from that which the plaintiff in fact had: for example it may award him rental value of property which he hoped to put to a particular profitable use,[292] or it may award him a reasonable profit falling short of that which he expected in fact to make.[293] But another possibility is to award reliance loss. This was done in an AMERICAN case where a boxer broke his contract to take part in a fight (*supra* n. 263). The promoter recovered his expenses but not the lost-box-office receipts as these were regarded as too speculative. Similarly, in an AUSTRALIAN case a company bought the wreck of a tanker and fitted out an expedition to salvage the wreck which, as it turned out, did not exist. The company recovered the amount of its payment and the cost of the expedition, but *not* the alleged value of the wreck if it had existed – apparently because there was insufficient evidence of such value. If there had been evidence of such value it could, in principle, have been recovered as damages for breach of contract, for it was held that the vendors

284 *Guhl* 287.

285 BG 14 Dec. 1937, BGE 63 II 401, 403.

286 BG 17 Nov. 1953, BGE 79 II 376.

287 BG 14 Dec. 1937, BGE 63 II 401.

288 *Treitel* 797.

289 *Globe Refining Co. v. Landa Cotton Oil Co.*, 190 U.S. 540 (1903); *Corbin* § 1035, 1036.

290 *Corbin* § 1031; *Treitel* 797.

291 *Corbin* § 996; *Treitel* 796.

292 *E.g., Evergreen Amusement Corp. v. Milstead*, 206 Md. 610, 112 A.2d 901 (1955); *Corbin* § 1029.

293 *Cf., Cory v. Thames Ironworks Co.* (1868), L.R. 3 Q.B. 181 (where the actual profit was not too speculative but too remote); *Treitel* 805.

had contractually undertaken that the wreck did exist.[294]

61. *Reliance limited by expectation.* – In the UNITED STATES it is generally recognized that an aggrieved party claiming damages on a reliance basis should not be put into a position better than that in which he would have been if the contract had been performed.[295] The problem has not been discussed in ENGLAND, but no doubt similar results would be reached. One may take the case of a manufacturer who agrees to make something for a buyer for a fixed price. If the buyer repudiates, the manufacturer may recover expenses incurred in the process of manufacture on a reliance basis; but he should not recover expenses in excess of the agreed price for the goods.[296] Similarly, in the case of the non-existent wreck mentioned in s. 60 above the buyer should not recover the entire cost of the salvage expedition if such cost exceeds the highest possible value of the wreck, had it existed. In these cases the loss suffered by the aggrieved party in excess of his expectation is suffered, not because the contract was broken, but because the contract was for him a bad bargain; or, to put the point in another way, the reliance loss in excess of expectation was not caused by the breach.

The principle appears to be that the court will not, by an award of reliance loss, put the aggrieved party into a position demonstrably better than that in which he would have been if the contract had been performed. It does not follow that a plaintiff will never be better off by basing his claim on reliance rather than expectation. If his expectation is highly speculative, a claim based on it may well yield nothing, or less than his proved expenditure. It is only where the lower value of the expectation is clearly established that it operates as a limit on recovery.

Reference should further be made to the distinction drawn in s. 52 above between expenses incurred in reliance on the contract and those incurred in consequence of its breach. For example, a buyer of an animal which turns out to be diseased and then dies can recover its value, plus veterinary expenses reasonably incurred even though the total sum exceeds the value of a sound animal.[297] In such a case the extra loss *is* caused by the breach and the result of awarding it is not to put the plaintiff in a situation better than that in which he would have been, had the contract not been broken.

62. *Relation between restitution and expectation in Anglo-American law.* – Recovery on the basis of the restitution interest is, in principle, available to the aggrieved party in a number of cases. A party who has paid money and received no counter-performance, or one that is so defective that he justifiably rejects it, is entitled to recover back his money; the conditions in which this action lies are further discussed in s. 181 below. Conversely, a party who has rendered some other performance for which he was to be paid may sometimes be entitled to get the reasonable value of his performance by way of restitution.

A good deal of conceptual difficulty has arisen with regard to these remedies, partly because of the terminology used in connection with them and partly because of the theory on which they are thought to be based. Actions for the recovery of money paid by the aggrieved party are commonly contrasted with actions for "damages" and in the UNITED STATES it used to be said that the two types of action were inconsistent, the purpose of the action for "damages" being to "enforce" the contract, and that for the recovery of money or for restitution to "rescind" it.[298] From this it was sometimes thought to follow "logically" that an aggrieved party cannot have both damages and restitution.[299] This type of reasoning is not an AMERICAN peculiarity. It has its counterpart in the GERMAN rule[300] that the aggrieved party can *either* claim damages for non-performance *or* put an end to the contract.

The view that "damages" and "restitution" are mutually exclusive remedies has been cogently criticized in the UNITED STATES[301] where the Uniform Commercial Code (s. 2-711 (1)) now expressly provides that an aggrieved buyer may, in appropriate circumstances, both recover any part of the price that he has paid and also obtain damages. To avoid the theoretical difficulties noted above, the Code carefully avoids the use of such words as "rescind" or "rescission" in this

[294] *McRae* v. *Commonwealth Disposals Commission*, *supra* n. 257.

[295] *L. Albert & Son v. Armstrong Rubber Co.*, 178 F. 2d 182 (2 Cir. 1949).

[296] *Stolper Steel Products Co. v. Behrens Mfg. Co.*, 10 Wis.2d 478, 103 N.W.2d 683 (1960); *Corbin* § 1033.

[297] *Harling v. Eddy*, [1951] 2 K.B. 739 (C.A.).

[298] See, for example, *Balon v. Hotel and Restaurant Supplies Inc.*, 6 Ariz.App. 481, 433 P.2d 661 (1967); and *infra* s. 183.

[299] *Corbin* § 1219, 1223.

[300] *Supra* s. 57, *infra* s. 119.

[301] *Corbin* § 1121.

context,[302] but the judges nevertheless continue to use them.[303]

The statement that "restitution" and "damages" can only be claimed in the alternative now remains true, even in the UNITED STATES, only in the limited sense that "*full* damages and *complete* restitution ... will not both be given for the same breach of contract."[304] Obviously a buyer of defective goods cannot both keep them and claim restitution of the price: if he wants to keep the goods his only claim is for damages. Similarly a buyer who has paid in advance for goods which are not delivered cannot recover both his payment and the value of the goods. Such conclusions are obvious enough; they are based not on any "logical" inconsistency between restitution and damages but on the policy against double recovery. There is no reason in principle why an aggrieved buyer should not, on restoring the thing sold to the seller, recover back his payment, expenses incurred in reliance on the contract, and the excess cost of a substitute.[305]

In the UNITED STATES the possibility of claiming restitution and damages is now widely recognized, under the influence of the Uniform Commercial Code, even in the case of contracts to which its provisions do not directly apply. It is certainly common to allow restitution claims to be combined with claims for reliance and consequential loss;[306] though there is still, under the influence of the reasoning of the pre-Code decisions, some reluctance to allow a restitution claim to be combined with one for loss of expectation.[307] Perhaps the reason for this is that such claims are sometimes pleaded as claims for *full* expectation which cannot be combined with *complete* restitution.

The theoretical difficulties which have troubled the AMERICAN courts have scarcely been noticed in ENGLAND, where the different elements of recovery have been readily combined subject only to the overriding policy that there must be no double recovery in respect of the same loss.[308]

63. *Advantages of restitution: claim for the recovery of money paid.* – We saw in s. 61 above that an aggrieved party will not be allowed to recover more by way of reliance than he could have obtained on the principle of expectation. The same is not true of a claim for restitution of a sum of money, in which the measure of recovery is what the defendant has received and not what the plaintiff has lost, whether by way of reliance or by way of disappointed expectation. Moreover, once it is established that the breach is sufficiently serious to give rise to a claim for restitution (*infra* s. 181), a COMMON LAW court has no discretion (as a FRENCH court has when it is asked to grant termination (*résolution*)) to award damages instead of restitution. The discretion of COMMON LAW courts comes rather in determining whether the aggrieved party has any right at all to claim restitution. In reaching this decision the court may well be influenced by the fact that recovery based on restitution will give the plaintiff more than his loss assessed on the basis of expectation. In one AMERICAN case an appellate court took the view that a claim for restitution ought not to have been allowed by the trial court, specifically on the ground that "by choosing the alternative remedy of rescission the plaintiff has obtained more than the damages which she suffered and more than she is entitled to receive."[309]

Yet there are no doubt many cases in which an aggrieved party can put himself into a better position by "choosing the alternative remedy of rescission" than that in which he would have been, had the contract been performed.[310] The stock situation in which this is the case is that in which the plaintiff has bought goods, which turn out to be defective, at a price which exceeds their value at the time of delivery. In such a case the plaintiff can terminate the contract even though the amount by which the defect affects the value of the goods or the cost of curing it is less than the amount by which the price of the goods exceeds their present value. Thus the plaintiff is better off financially if he rejects the goods and claims restitution than he would be if he had accepted them and claimed damages for loss of expectation. The same is obviously true where the buyer has paid in advance for goods which are not delivered at all, and the market then falls. If the buyer claims

[302] Except that it refers in s. 2-720 to the use of such words *by the parties*.

[303] *E.g.*, *Dailey v. Holiday Distributing Corp.*, 151 N.W.2d 477 (Iowa 1967).

[304] *Corbin* § 1221.

[305] *Blumrosen v. Silver Flame Industries*, 334 Mich. 441, 54 N.W.2d 712 (1952).

[306] *E.g.*, *Clark v. Ohio Prefab. Homes*, 54 Ohio L. Abs. 120, 84 N.E.2d 251 (Ohio C.A. 1949); *Sheridan Drive-In Inc. v. State*, 16 A.D.2d 400, 228 N.Y.S.2d 576 (1962); *Marks v. Lehigh Brickface, Inc.*, 19 Pa.D. &C.2d 666 (1959).

[307] *E.g.*, *Balch v. Newberry*, 208 Okl. 46, 253 P.2d 153 (1953).

[308] *Millar's Machinery Co., Ltd. v. David Way & Son* (1934), 40 Com.Cas. 204 (K.B. and C.A.).

[309] *Donovan v. Aeolian Co.*, 270 N.Y. 267, 200 N.E. 815, 817 (1936).

[310] *Palmer*, The Contract Price as a Limit on Restitution for the Defendant's Breach: 20 Ohio State L.J. 264 (1948).

restitution he will get back the whole price; while if he had claimed damages he would only get the lower market value.

In many cases of this kind the buyer will not have paid the price;[311] he will simply reject the goods and refuse to pay. This is a situation which would in CIVIL LAW countries be dealt with under the principles relating to the *exceptio non adimpleti contractus* (which is discussed in ch. 15 above); while the case of the plaintiff who had paid and sought to recover his money would depend on the principles relating to termination of the contract, which are discussed in s. 143 ss. below. But in COMMON LAW countries there is no difference in principle between the two situations: the right to refuse payment and the right to reject goods (and so to recover back a payment already made) depend at least in theory on the same rules. It is true that an aggrieved party who has both paid for and received the defective performance is more likely to have lost the right to reject than one who has not done either of these things; but it will by no means always be true that exchange of performances will deprive him of the right to reject and claim restitution.

In ENGLAND under the Sale of Goods Act, 1893 a buyer can reject defective goods if the defect amounts to a breach of "condition" so long as he has not "accepted" them;[312] and on such rejection he is entitled to recover back the price.[313] "Acceptance" is a technical concept, and it certainly does not take place merely because the goods have passed into the possession of the buyer and he has paid the price.[314] If a breach of "condition" is established and no "acceptance" has taken place, the buyer's rights to refuse to pay and to reject and recover back any payment that he has made are simultaneously established. There is no rule that the defect must be more serious for the latter purpose than for the former; and the fact that the buyer is not seriously prejudiced by the defect is quite irrelevant.

Under the AMERICAN Uniform Commercial Code the buyer may even after he has "accepted" (s. 2-606) the goods be entitled to revoke his acceptance, "cancel" the contract and recover back the price or any part of it that he has paid (s. 2-608, 2-711(1)). Here a sharper distinction is, indeed, drawn between the case of a buyer who has never accepted at all and one who seeks to revoke an acceptance: the right to reject may be asserted on account of *any* nonconformity of the goods to the contract (s. 2-601) while the right to revoke acceptance depends on the nonconformity being a serious one.[315] But the distinction between a simple rejection and a revocation of acceptance does not depend on the buyer's having paid the price. The right to restitution may therefore arise on a simple rejection for a non-conformity which is not serious.

In ENGLAND there is another situation in which the aggrieved party may, by claiming "rescission" put himself into a position better than that in which he would have been, had there been no breach. As a general rule, the party seeking restitution must restore the performance which he has received and any benefits derived from it. But this requirement is not insisted upon when such restoration is prevented by the very defect of which the aggrieved party complains: for example, if the seller lacks title and the subject-matter of the sale is taken away from the buyer by the true owner;[316] or if the subject-matter is defective and perishes on account of the defect (*infra* s. 182). In a case where the seller had no title it was held that the buyer could recover back the *whole* of the price which he had paid, without any allowance for benefits derived by him from the use of the thing. The rule has been criticised[317] but for the time being it remains law.

In theory, the same principle would seem to apply if physically defective subject-matter remained available for restoration: *i.e.* the aggrieved party could recover the full price without any deduction for intermediate use. But this problem is unlikely to arise, since any but an inconsiderable amount of use would in practice tend to deprive the buyer of his right to reject[318] and consequently of his right to claim restitution of the full purchase price. His only right therefore would

[311] *E.g., Arcos, Ltd.* v. *Ronaasen,* [1933] A.C. 470 (H.L.).

[312] UNITED KINGDOM Sale of Goods Act, 1893 (56 & 57 Vict., c. 71) s. 11 (1) (c), 34 and 35 as amended by Misrepresentation Act 1967 (c.7) s. 4.

[313] *E.g., Baldry v. Marshall,* [1925] 1 K.B. 260 (C.A.).

[314] UNITED KINGDOM Sale of Goods Act, 1893 (*supra* n. 312) s. 34, 35 as amended by Misrepresentation Act 1967 (*supra* n. 312) s. 4.

[315] UCC s. 2-608 (1). *Infra* s. 169.

[316] *Rowland v. Divall,* [1923] 2 K.B. 500 (C.A.); *infra* s. 181.

[317] *Law Reform Committee,* Twelfth Report (Transfer of Title to Chattels) (Cmnd. 2958) (London 1966) par. 36; *The Law Commission and The Scottish Law Commission,* Exemption Clauses in Contracts. First Report. Amendments to the Sale of Goods Act 1893 (Law Com.Paper no. 24) (Scot.Law Com. Paper no. 12) par. 16.

[318] On the ground that it amounted to "acceptance": *infra* s. 186.

be one to claim "damages". In one case of this kind these have been held to consist of the price paid (which seems to have been regarded simply as evidence of value) plus expenses of the kind known in GERMAN law as *Verwendungen*;[319] but it is also clear that allowance could, on a claim for "damages", be made for any benefit obtained by the aggrieved party from the use of the thing.[320] If the thing without the defect had been worth more than the contract price a claim based on loss of expectation would no doubt have been available to the aggrieved party.

64. *Advantages of restitution: claims in respect of benefits other than money.* – Suppose that a buyer pays in advance and the seller fails to deliver. If the buyer has paid more than the goods are worth, he will obviously want to claim restitution (and not damages for loss of expectation); for in that way he will escape from his bad bargain. Subject to the limitations discussed in s. 62 above and s. 181 below, the buyer is entitled to use the restitutionary claim for this purpose. But the same possibility is not, in ANGLO-AMERICAN law, open to a seller who has delivered goods on credit and has not been paid. His only claim is for the price; and if he has sold the goods for less than they are worth, he cannot escape from his bad bargain by reclaiming his goods from the buyer or by claiming their reasonable or market value. The general principle of ANGLO-AMERICAN law is that a person to whom a fixed sum has become due under a contract cannot recover more than that sum on the theory of restitution.[321]

The same distinction operates in relation to contracts other than those for the sale of goods. Thus a person who pays in advance for services which are not rendered can claim his money back, and will do so if he has made a bad bargain; while a person who had rendered services on credit and is not paid can claim the agreed remuneration[322] but not the reasonable value of his services.

However, a contracting party may be prevented from earning the agreed sum by the other's breach. A contract for services may provide for payment on completion of performance; and if the person to whom the services are to be rendered wrongfully refuses to receive them, the other party will be unable to claim the agreed sum, as it will not have been earned. No doubt the aggrieved party can claim *either* damages for loss of his expectations *or* the reasonable value of his services by way of restitution. If he has made a good bargain, he will obviously take the first course so as to get compensation for the loss of his expected profit. The difficult question is how far he can improve his position by taking the second course where he has made a bad bargain.

Suppose that A agrees to build 10 miles of road for B at a price of £ 1m. per mile, the whole price of £ 10m. being payable on completion of the work. The bargain is a bad one for A, the reasonable value of the work being £ 4m. per mile and the cost of the whole work to A would be £ 30m. After A has built 5 miles of the road, B wrongfully repudiates. There are at least three possible solutions.

First, A should recover the reasonable value of his work, *i.e.* £ 20m. This result is accepted by some AMERICAN cases;[323] but it seems paradoxical that A should get more for doing half the work than he would have got for doing it all. Secondly, A should recover nothing. The argument in favour of this solution admits that A would thus lose £ 20m. worth of work, but relies on the fact that he would have lost exactly this amount (*i.e.*, the cost to him less the agreed price) if he had been allowed to complete the work in accordance with the contract. This view, too, seems unacceptable as it results in B's getting half the work for nothing in consequence of his own breach of contract. It has been rejected by the Privy Council in a NEW ZEALAND case.[324] Probably the best solution is the third: that A should recover *pro rata* at the contract rate, at least where such a method of assessment is a sensible one. This solution, too, finds some support in AMERICAN cases.[325] It enables the aggrieved party to improve his position by claiming restitution to the extent of partially avoiding a loss; but not to the extent of actually making a profit out of the breach.

319 *Harling v. Eddy, supra* n. 297 (veterinary fees); *cf., Mason v. Burningham*, [1949] 2 K.B. 545 (C.A.) (a case of defect of title).

320 *Treitel* 861. Where the breach consists in delivering defective goods the "benefit" may be very little (as in *Charterhouse Credit Co., Ltd. v. Tolly*, [1963] 2 Q.B. 683 (C.A.)) or nothing (as in *Farnworth Finance Facilities, Ltd. v. Attryde*, [1970] 1 W.L.R. 1053 (C.A.)).

321 *Corbin* § 1100. *Cf.* in cases of sale GERMAN CC § 454. Contrast FRENCH CC art. 1654 and ULIS (*supra* s. 7) art. 62 and 78 (2), under which the unpaid seller may be able to terminate. The question whether the effect of such termination is personal or proprietary is discussed in vol. VIII ch. 3 *sub* II D.

322 *Corbin* § 1100.

323 *Palmer* (*supra* n. 310) 268 ss.; for a particularly striking illustration, see *Boomer v. Muir*, 24 P.2d 570 (Cal.App. 1933).

324 *Lodder v. Slowey* (1901), 20 N.Z.L.R. 321, [1904] A.C. 442 (P.C.).

325 *E.g., Kehoe v. Borough of Rutherford*, 56 N.J.L. 221, 27 A. 912 (1893).

65. *Ordinary remedies apply to sales in Anglo-American law.* – It will be obvious from the examples discussed in s. 60 to 64 above that in COMMON LAW countries the remedies ordinarily available for breach of contract apply to the case of defects in the subject-matter of a sale. An aggrieved buyer indeed has certain special remedies, such as the right to "cover" under the Uniform Commercial Code (s. 2-712), but these do not exclude the normal remedies for breach of contract. A defect in the subject-matter of a sale is regarded as an ordinary breach of contract; in accordance with the usual COMMON LAW rule fault is not necessary. There is nothing in ANGLO-AMERICAN law that corresponds to the CIVIL LAW principle that redhibition and price reduction are the only remedies normally available for such a defect. ULIS in this respect follows ANGLO-AMERICAN rather than the CIVIL LAW doctrine, in that non-conformity of the goods gives the buyer the right to all the remedies (including damages) provided by that Code (art. 41).

E. BASES OF ASSESSMENT

i. *Difference in Value or Cost of Cure*

66. *Valuing the loss.* – Once it is determined for what loss the plaintiff is to be compensated, that loss must next be translated into money terms, since damages normally consist of a sum of money.

Where the plaintiff claims for reliance loss, there is relatively little difficulty as to the basis of assessment, which is in principle the expense incurred by the aggrieved party, though some of this may be too remote (*infra* s. 82 ss.). Similarly, in claims for restitution the general principle is clear. Recovery is based on the benefit received by the defaulting party though many problems can arise in this connection: for example, whether the benefit must be received at the expense of the aggrieved party, and whether the defaulting party's liability to restore is limited to benefits retained by him at the time of the proceedings.

Where, however, the claim is for expectation loss or for consequential loss (in the third of the senses distinguished in s. 53 above) there are two wholly different bases of assessment: cost of cure or difference in value. Sometimes it makes no difference which of these methods is adopted. If a seller wrongfully fails to deliver, the buyer is entitled to damages based on the cost of substitute goods; and this can either be described as the difference in value between what he got (nothing) and what he should have got (the goods), or as the cost of "curing" the seller's breach. But in other cases it may be crucial which basis is adopted. The most striking illustration is to be found in an AMERICAN case[326] in which a coal company took a mining lease of farmland, covenanting to restore the land to its original state at the end of the lease. The cost of doing this would have been $ 29000 and the company in breach of contract refused to do the work. The result was to reduce the value of the land by $ 300 and the damages were assessed at the latter sum.

Many legal systems recognise both these methods of assessment and will apply one or the other according to which is the more appropriate. This is, for example, the position reached in SWISS law by virtue of the judge's discretion as to the assessment of damages.[327] The same option is given to AMERICAN courts by a provision in the Uniform Commercial Code under which damages for breach by the seller are to be "determined in any manner which is reasonable" (s. 2-714(1)).

A slightly different approach, which in the end reaches much the same results as that just outlined, is to start with *prima facie* rules in certain specific contracts, leaving it open to the courts to depart from them in appropriate cases. For example, in ENGLISH law the measure of damages where a seller delivers goods which are defective in quality is "prima facie the difference between the value of the goods . . . and the value which they would have had if they answered to the warranty."[328] The AMERICAN Uniform Commercial Code lays down a similar *prima facie* rule (s. 2-714(2)). The assumption is that the defect cannot be cured, but if it can be cured at a reasonable cost there is little doubt that damages based on the cost of such cure could be awarded.[329] Indeed if a reasonable but unsuccessful attempt is made to cure the defect, the cost of it may be recovered in addition to difference in value.[330]

In the case of a building contract, on the other hand, the *prima facie* rule in many systems is that damages are based on the cost of putting the defect right or of completing performance.[331] This mea-

[326] *Peevyhouse v. Garland Coal & Mining Co.*, 382 P.2d 109 (Okla.S.Ct. 1962); *cf.* in ENGLAND Landlord and Tenant Act, 1927 (17 & 18 Geo.5, c.36) s. 18 (1).

[327] Under CO art. 43; see *Guhl* 76.

[328] Sale of Goods Act, 1893 (*supra* n. 312) s. 53 (3).

[329] *Wagner Tractor Co. Inc. v. Shields*, 381 F.2d 441 (9 Cir. 1967); *Charterhouse Credit Co., Ltd. v. Tolly*, *supra* n. 320 (hire-purchase).

[330] *Harling v. Eddy*, *supra* n. 297.

[331] *Corbin* § 1089; *Treitel* 786; INDIAN Contract Act, 1872 (*supra* n. 241) s. 73 ill. (f); *Gloag and Henderson* 126.

sure is particularly appropriate where the difference in value which might have resulted from the work is entirely speculative: *e.g.* where the contract was one to sink an exploratory shaft or well.[332] On the other hand, where the process of curing the defect would involve expense *out of all proportion* to the benefit which would accrue from it, the courts tend to adopt the alternative basis of difference in value,[333] at least if certain conditions are satisfied: *e.g.* that the breach was not deliberate and did not destroy the utility of the work to the aggrieved party.[334] This does not mean that cost of cure will be refused merely because it is *greater* than difference in value. Cost of cure may be allowed even though performance would not have increased the value of the property at all: *e.g.* if the contract was one to build an ornamental fountain which was so ugly that it would actually reduce the value of the customer's house.[335]

ii. *Price Reduction*

67. *Price reduction for defects of quality.* – Where goods are defective, the *prima facie* rule in ENGLISH and AMERICAN law is that the buyer can recover the difference between the value of the goods actually delivered and the value which the goods would have had if they had been in accordance with the contract. Alternatively, he may, in appropriate cases, be entitled to the cost of putting the defect right (*supra* s. 66).

This position should be contrasted with the liability for defects in specific goods which exists in CIVIL LAW countries and is derived from the ROMAN *actiones redhibitoria* and *quanti minoris*. The first action has already been considered (*supra* s. 57). At this point we are only concerned with the latter action, in which the buyer is entitled to a price reduction. Of course in COMMON LAW systems damages may in such a case be deducted from the price,[336] indeed, this possibility is not confined to sales of goods. The right to such a deduction exists as well under contracts for work and labour[337] and in AMERICA (though not in ENGLAND) under contracts for the carriage of goods by sea.[338] But such a deduction is calculated on a different basis from that adopted for the "price reductions" of CIVIL LAW systems, or at any rate of GERMAN law and related systems.

The FRENCH Civil Code simply refers to a price-reduction determined by experts (art. 1644); and the process of making the reduction has been described as one of setting off damages against the price.[339] Generally, however, liability to price reduction in CIVIL LAW systems is not conceived of as liability for contractual default: the liability does not depend on "fault" and is not assessed on the basis of protection of the expectation interest.[340] The buyer is not (in the absence of express warranty, deliberate concealment or fraud) entitled to the cost of having the defect cured, nor is he entitled (as in COMMON LAW countries) to the difference between the value of the thing as it is and as it would have been if it had been in accordance with the contract. Nor even is he entitled to the difference between the price paid by him and the actual value of the thing, though there is some support for this view in the law of SOUTH AFRICA.[341] The buyer's claim in principle is merely one to have the price reduced in the proportion which the actual value of the thing bears to the value which it would have had if it had not been defective;[342] in SOUTH AFRICA he is only entitled even to this amount if the goods are in fact worth less than the price.[343]

The amount of the price-reduction may be more or less than the damages which would be available in COMMON LAW systems, according to whether the buyer made a bad or a good bargain,

[332] *Corbin* § 1089; *Sunshine Exploration, Ltd.* v. *Dolly Varden Mines, Ltd.* (1969), 8 D.L.R.(3d) 441 (Canada S.C.).

[333] The leading AMERICAN case is *Jacob and Youngs v. Kent*, 230 N.Y. 239, 129 N.E. 889 (1921) discussed *supra* ch. 15; *Corbin* § 1090; *Treitel* 786; *Gloag and Henderson* 126. *Cf.*, *Peevyhouse v. Garland Coal & Mining Co.*, *supra* n. 326.

[334] See *Jacob and Youngs v. Kent*, *supra* n. 333; *Bellizzi v. Huntley Estates*, 3 N.Y.2d 112, 164 N.Y.S.2d 395, 143 N.E.2d 802 (1957).

[335] *Corbin* § 1091.

[336] UNITED KINGDOM Sale of Goods Act, 1893 (*supra* n. 312) s. 53 (1)(a); UCC s. 2-717.

[337] *Gilbert-Ash (Northern), Ltd. v. Modern Engineering (Bristol), Ltd.*, [1974] A.C. 689 (H.L.); GERMAN CC § 634.

[338] *Compania Naviera Puerto Madrin S.A. Panama v. Esso Standard Oil Co.*, 1962 A.M.C. 147 (S.D.N.Y. 1961); *Dakin v. Oxley* (1864), 15 C.B.N.S. 646, 143 E.R. 938; *Henriksens Rederi A/S v. T.H.Z. Rolimpex (The Brede)*, [1973] 3 W.L.R. 556 (C.A.).

[339] *Mazeaud*, Leçons III no. 947.

[340] *Cf. supra* s. 49. *Zweigert and Kötz* 183-184.

[341] *Willie and Millin (-Coaker and Schutz)* 190; *Lee and Honoré*, The South African Law of Obligations (Durban 1950) 342.

[342] GERMAN CC § 472; AUSTRIA: *Klang and Gschnitzer (-Gschnitzer)* IV 1 § 932 no. A III 2; SWITZERLAND: *Guhl* 287; SCANDINAVIA: *Rodhe*, The Quantum of Damages Under the Scandinavian Sale of Goods Act: Scand.Stud.L. 10 (1966) 149, 162; ULIS (*supra* s. 7) art. 46.

[343] *Willie and Millin (-Coaker and Schutz)* 196.

or according to whether the market has risen or fallen since the contract was made. The principle on which price-reduction is assessed seems rather to be that the seller was unjustifiably enriched, than that the buyer is to be compensated for not having received what he bargained for. The buyer is entitled to damages on the latter basis in certain exceptional cases, *e.g.* if the seller has given an express warranty or is guilty of fraudulent concealment[344] or (in SOUTH AFRICA) if he was an expert or commercial seller;[345] though it seems that the buyer can still opt for a price-reduction in such cases if that course of action is more favourable to him.[346]

COMMON LAW systems do not recognise the principle of price-reduction for defects in goods (as opposed to damages which can be set off against the price). But an analogous principle may apply where the courts order specific performance of contracts for the sale of land with "compensation" (*supra* s. 36). This jurisdiction primarily concerns deficiencies in area and defects of title, with which we are not here concerned; but it seems that it can also apply to physical defects. However, in an ENGLISH case of this kind the "compensation" was in fact assessed on the principle of COMMON LAW damages rather than on the principle of CIVIL LAW price-reduction.[347] But where the diminished value of the subject-matter of a sale of goods is set up by way of price-reduction the right to further damages is not in principle excluded.[348] Under the Uniform Commercial Code there is also a right in certain circumstances to accept goods which have been damaged with an "allowance";[349] but it is not clear whether the allowance is assessed on the principle of COMMON LAW damages, or of CIVIL LAW price-reduction, or on some other principle.

Where the sale is of generic goods the buyer's right to a price reduction is as stated above if he accepts a tender of defective goods in performance of the contract. Alternatively, he can reject the goods, in which case under CIVIL LAW his claim in principle is one for performance, *i.e.* for a conforming delivery; but in practice this will generally be turned into a claim for damages for loss of his expectation interest and for consequential loss if any has been suffered. The basic claim for damages would appear to be the cost to the buyer of obtaining substitute goods, less the price which he agreed to pay for the rejected goods if that has not already been paid. This is also the mode of assessing the buyer's damages in cases of non-delivery where he makes a cover purchase.

The detailed rules relating to damages for failure to perform contracts of sale are not our primary concern in this volume.[350] The only general point to be stressed is that defects of quality are, to some extent, given special treatment in that CIVIL LAW systems do not generally protect the aggrieved party's expectation interest.

68. *Price reduction for defects of quantity.* – The principle of price reduction may also apply where performance is quantitatively defective. Here some systems, such as GERMAN and AUSTRIAN law,[351] ISRAELI law[352] and ULIS[353], seem to apply the same principles as in cases of qualitative defects. Other systems, such as FRENCH and ENGLISH law (and to a lesser extent the laws of the UNITED STATES) apply a different principle: namely that the price is reduced simply in proportion to the amount which the shortage bears to the full quantity contracted for. This price reduction is not based (as in the case of qualitative defects) on *reduced value* as such, though where the sale is at so much a unit this will often be the practical effect of the principle. The detailed rules on this matter are discussed in this Encyclopedia vol. VIII ch. 3. Our only concern here is to illustrate the special principle of price reduction for defects of quantity and to determine its limits.

In sales of land FRENCH law draws a sharp distinction[354] between sales of land by measure ("*à raison de tant la mesure*", CC art. 1617), to which the principle of *proportional* price reduction applies with full force, and sales which are not by measure, though they may make mention of it. In the latter type of sale a quantitative deficiency is (in the absence of a contrary stipulation) disregarded if it does not exceed 1/20, having regard to the value of the total subject-matter of the sale ("*eu égard à la valeur de la totalité des objets vendus*", CC art. 1619). The last phrase suggests that in this type of sale price reduction for shortage

[344] FRENCH CC art. 1645; GERMAN CC § 463.

[345] *Willie and Millin* (*-Coaker and Schutz*) 185.

[346] GERMAN CC § 463.

[347] *Shepherd v. Croft*, [1911] 1 Ch. 521.

[348] UNITED KINGDOM: Sale of Goods Act, 1893 (*supra* n. 312) s.53(4).

[349] UCC s. 2-613 (b); *cf.* SCANDINAVIAN Sale of Goods Act (see *Zweigert and Kropholler* (ed.), Sources of International Uniform Law I (Leyden 1971) E 158) s. 42.

[350] See this Encyclopedia vol. VIII ch. 3 *sub* II.

[351] *Enneccerus and Lehmann* 441 (it is assumed that the deficiency is not so great as to justify termination under GERMAN CC § 468); *Klang and Gschnitzer* (*-Gschnitzer*) IV1 § 859 no. B II 1.

[352] ISRAELI Sales Law, 5728-1968 (22 LSI 107) s. 28.

[353] *Supra* s. 7; art. 46.

[354] *Mazeaud*, Leçons III no. 938.

exceeding 1/20 is in fact based on diminution in value and not on shortage in quantity as such. This is obviously the sensible solution where a house is sold together with land of a specified area but less land is conveyed.

COMMON LAW jurisdictions reach much the same results under the rules relating to specific performance with "compensation" (*supra* s. 36) which would be based on shortage in the case of a sale by measure but on diminution in value where a house was sold together with adjoining land.[355] The power to order specific performance with compensation only exists before conveyance, but compensation can usually be awarded after conveyance by virtue of express contractual provisions to that effect.[356] Where the deficiency is "substantial", specific performance with compensation will not be ordered against the party prejudiced by the deficiency;[357] but he may elect to claim performance *without* compensation.[358]

Two of the articles of the FRENCH Civil Code which deal with quantitative defects refer expressly to land;[359] and the third has been held to be similarly restricted.[360] A buyer of goods to whom short delivery is made appears to have the ordinary rights of claiming performance, damages or *résolution*. In ENGLAND the Sale of Goods Act, 1893 applies a principle very much like that of price reduction to the case of short delivery of goods: it provides that the buyer may accept delivery of goods less than the quantity contracted for, and pay for them at the contract rate (s. 30 (1)). The position remains substantially the same in the UNITED STATES, though the sharp ENGLISH distinction between qualitative and quantitative defects has been abandoned by the Uniform Commercial Code.[361]

Our present concern is with the buyer's right to a price-reduction. In ANGLO-AMERICAN law there is no reason in principle why a buyer of land or goods should not claim damages for loss of expectation (if otherwise available[362]) in cases of shortage of quantity. The only possible exception to this rule, for which there is some ENGLISH authority, arises where the shortage is substantial and the prejudiced party nevertheless elects to seek performance without compensation.[363] In such a case he has no right to further performance, compensation or damages.[364] The right to claim damages for defects of quantity would appear to exist equally in FRENCH law, the case being one of partial non-performance. There is a similar right in GERMAN law.[365]

The aggrieved buyer may also be entitled to terminate the contract for defects of quantity. This topic is discussed generally in s. 143 ss. below and with special reference to sales in vol. VIII ch. 3.

In practice it is common for sales of land to deal in express terms with quantitative defects.[366] Such provisions are *prima facie* valid, though they may not be effective to deprive a purchaser of his right to terminate the contract on account of a substantial shortage.[367]

iii. "*Concrete*" *and* "*Abstract*" *Assessment*

69. *Statement of the distinction.* – Where the assessment of damages is based on the cost (or proceeds) of a substitute contract, a distinction is drawn in many systems between the so-called "concrete" and "abstract" method of quantifying that cost. The distinction is most easily illustrated by reference to contracts for the sale of goods, though it also applies to, for example, contracts of carriage where a substitute contract may be made to acquire cargo space or (as the case may be) to dispose of it; or where the goods are lost and the consignee acquires substitute goods at the destination.

In the case of a seller's failure to deliver goods, the "concrete" method of quantifying the loss to the buyer looks to the actual cost incurred by him in procuring a substitute, while the "abstract" method is based on the market price at which a substitute could be obtained. In the case of a buyer's failure to accept and pay the "concrete" method is based on the amount for which the seller has actually resold the goods and the "abstract" method is based, once again, on the market price. Of course neither method necessarily forms the limit of recovery, which may include

355 *Aspinalls to Powell and Scholefield* (1889), 60 L.T. 595 (Ch.); *Chitty (-Treitel)* I § 1556.

356 *Chitty (-Treitel)* I § 1556.

357 *Idem* I § 1555.

358 *Durham v. Legard* (1865), 34 Beav. 611, 55 E.R. 771.

359 CC art. 1617, 1618.

360 CC art. 1619; Cass.civ. 17 Dec. 1923, D.P. 1924. 1.14.

361 UCC s. 2-601 (c), 2-607 (1).

362 They may not be available because of the rule in *Bain v. Forthergill* (1874), L.R. 7 H.L. 158; *infra* s. 118.

363 See text *supra* at n. 358.

364 INDIAN Specific Relief Act, 1877 (*supra* n. 136) s. 15; INDIAN Specific Relief Act 1963 (*ibidem*) s. 12 (3) (b) (iii) (see *supra* n. 143); semble expressing a general COMMON LAW principle.

365 *Enneccerus and Lehmann* 441.

366 *Chitty (-Treitel)* I § 1555.

367 *Idem* I § 1556; *Mazeaud*, Leçons III no. 938.

incidental and consequential loss (*supra* s. 52, 53). In connection with the latter, we shall see that the distinction between "concrete" and "abstract" quantification is used in senses other than that now under discussion (*infra* s. 72), but its primary meaning is that which distinguishes between assessment by reference to the actual cost of a substitute (or proceeds of a substitute transaction) and assessment by reference to market prices.

The concrete method of assessment forms the starting point in many systems, though in some systems it is not regarded as "damages" in the sense of a pecuniary *substitute* for performance, but rather as indirect *specific* enforcement (*supra* s. 9). Thus in FRENCH law recovery of an amount based on the actual cost of obtaining a substitute is available on the principle of CC art. 1144, under which the creditor may be authorized to perform himself at the expense of the debtor (*supra* s. 20). In the case of a contract for the sale of generic goods the buyer may under this provision buy at the seller's expense: this is the so-called *faculté de remplacement*.[368]

This principle is also recognised in GERMANY.[369] It is only expressly made available by the Commercial Code in the case of a commercial sale with fixed delivery dates[370] but judicial practice has extended it beyond this area.[371] It is however disputed whether it extends to non-commercial sales.[372] "Concrete" assessment is also available in SWITZERLAND, where the Code of Obligations provides for abstract assessment only in commercial sales.[373] This restriction, while it may operate justly in the majority of cases, is hard to defend as a matter of principle; and it has not been adopted anywhere in the COMMON LAW world.

In the UNITED STATES, the principle of "concrete" assessment is likewise available under the provisions of the Uniform Commercial Code entitling a buyer of goods to "cover" and a seller to resell in the event of the opposite party's breach.[374] In either case the aggrieved party is entitled to recover the difference between the cost of cover or (as the case may be) the proceeds of resale and the contract price.[375] It is clear from the comments to the Code that this difference is regarded as "damages".[376] Resale is regarded as the seller's primary remedy and cover purchase as "the buyer's equivalent of the seller's right to resell."[377] If the aggrieved party does not resell or cover, damages are assessed abstractly, by reference to market prices;[378] where the aggrieved party does resell or cover, market prices are relevant only in determining whether the actual cover transaction satisfied the requirement of reasonableness.[379] The choice between the two remedies of resale and cover on the one hand, and damages based on the market on the other, is that of the aggrieved party; and it is open whether or not the transaction was a commercial one.[380]

ULIS (*supra* s. 7) distinguishes between cases in which the contract is not avoided and those in which it is avoided (*infra* s. 154, 177).

In the first type of case, the general rule is that the injured party recovers his loss, subject to the foreseeability test.[381] The assumption is that performance has been received, but it is late, at the wrong place, or defective. No rule as to the method of assessment is laid down, but the method is presumably "concrete". Where the contract is avoided and there is a market, the general rule is one of abstract assessment, by reference to the market (ULIS art. 84). But (as under the Uniform Commercial Code) if a substitute sale or purchase has in fact been made, the damages will be assessed concretely by reference to the substitute contract (ULIS art. 85), at any rate if the injured party acted reasonably in making it. If there is no market, the damages are assessed concretely.

Where the abstract method is used, the damages are recoverable even though no actual substitute contract has been made. This rule is most clearly stated in the SWISS Code of Obligations;[382] but it is implicit in the other systems discussed above.

ENGLISH law, while recognising a general principle of "concrete" assessment (in that the actual cost of substitute performance is in principle recoverable as damages for breach of contract as one way of fulfilling the expectation interest) curiously states no such principle in its Sale of Goods Act, 1893, under which "abstract"

368 *Mazeaud*, Leçons III no. 946.

369 *Enneccerus and Lehmann* 227.

370 GERMAN Comm.C § 376 par. 3. In AUSTRIAN law, CC § 1332 gives rise to some difficulty in connection with the principle of concrete assessment.

371 *Rabel* I 169.

372 *Idem* I 170.

373 CO art. 191 par. 2, 215 par. 1.

374 UCC s. 2-712 (1); 2-706 (1).

375 UCC s. 2-712 (2); 2-706 (1).

376 UCC s. 2-706 comment 1.

377 UCC s. 2-704 comment 1; s. 2-712 comment 1.

378 UCC s. 2-713 (1), 2-708 (1).

379 UCC s. 2-706 comment 3.

380 UCC s. 2-712 comment 4; the same is true under UCC s. 2-706, which is not restricted to "merchants" as defined by UCC s. 2-104.

381 *Infra s.* 82 ss. ULIS art. 82.

382 CO art. 191 par. 3, 215 par. 2. *Cf.* GERMAN Comm.C § 376 par. 2.

assessment based on market price constitutes the *prima facie* rule in case of buyer's or seller's breach.[383]

There is in ENGLISH law no express provision for assessing damages "concretely", by reference to actual cover purchases or resales. Where there is a market, the "concrete" method of assessment does not seem to be a possible one: in other words, if the aggrieved party in fact covers or resells at a price different from the market price, that fact is irrelevant. "Concrete" assessment is only adopted in cases in which there is no market, in which case the Sale of Goods Act, 1893 simply provides that the measure of damages is to be "the estimated loss directly and naturally resulting in the ordinary course of events from the . . . breach of contract."[384] There is no doubt that damages under this provision could in appropriate cases be based on the cost of a substitute.[385] ENGLISH (like AMERICAN) law draws no distinction (for the present purpose) between commercial and non-commercial sales.

In practice the difference between ENGLISH law, which tends to favour "abstract" assessment, and most other systems which in principle allow "concrete" assessment, is not likely to be considerable. The distinction is of course only significant if there *is* a market for the goods. In such a situation, a buyer who covers or a seller who resells at a cost considerably above or below the market is in fact unlikely to recover more than the market price.

Under the AMERICAN provisions, the aggrieved party might be held not to have covered or resold in accordance with the statutorily required standard of reasonableness.[386] It is true that this does not follow *merely* because he has "covered" or resold at a price above or below the market. Indeed in the case of a resale the Comment to the Uniform Commercial Code says that the market price is "relevant only on the question of whether the seller acted in a commercially reasonable manner in making the resale."[387] But if the resale was at a price considerably below that which could have been obtained in an available market the seller would only in exceptional circumstances be able to show that he had acted reasonably. Alternatively, he might be held to have partly caused, or to have failed to mitigate, his loss (*infra* s. 106). This reasoning is also applicable in GERMAN law.[388]

In FRENCH law, the claimant theoretically requires the authority of the court before proceeding to cover or resell[389] and the court may in its discretion refuse to authorise him to do this and restrict him to the remedy of damages. Even where the requirement of prior judicial authorisation is not insisted upon, the court has, when it is asked to award the difference between the proceeds of resale and the contract price, a considerable discretion as to the amount actually awarded. If there was a market price for the goods at the relevant time, the court may (though it is not obliged to do so) base its award on that price; and in commercial cases it is common practice to do so.[390]

70. *Different kinds of resale.* – A seller's right to recover damages on a "concrete" basis arises when he has made an actual resale. This right should be distinguished from other rights which a seller has under various rules of law which entitle him to resell but which serve different purposes than that of quantifying damages. GERMAN and SWISS terminology conveniently distinguishes between *Deckungsverkauf*[391] which serves to quantify damages, and *Selbsthilfeverkauf*[392] which does not serve this purpose but rather the purpose of enabling a seller to get the goods off his hands if the buyer fails to take delivery of them. A sale of the latter kind is, in principle, simply a method by which a debtor gets rid of his obligation in cases of so-called *Gläubigerverzug*, – or unjustified refusal by the creditor to accept performance.[393] When this has occurred, the debtor can discharge his obligation either by depositing the subject-matter, or by selling it for the account of the creditor and depositing the proceeds.[394] Such a *Selbsthilfeverkauf* is available even though there was no breach of duty by the creditor, who may have been under no duty to accept performance. Of course in the ordinary

[383] UNITED KINGDOM Sale of Goods Act, 1893 (*supra* n. 312) s. 50 (3), 51 (3).

[384] S. 50 (2), 51 (2).

[385] *E.g., C.Sharpe & Co., Ltd. v. Nosawa & Co.*, [1917] 2 K.B. 814.

[386] UCC s. 2-706 (1); s. 2-712 (1) requires the buyer to act "in good faith and without unreasonable delay": this probably comes to much the same thing in practice as the requirement to act reasonably under UCC s. 2-706 (1).

[387] UCC s. 2-706 comment 3.

[388] CC § 254; *infra* s. 102, 106.

[389] Since a judgment is required under FRENCH CC art. 1184 for termination (*infra* s. 147).

[390] *Rabel* I 229.

[391] A term not in common use but appropriately employed by *Larenz* I 352.

[392] *Enneccerus and Lehmann* 274; *Guhl* 204.

[393] *Enneccerus and Lehmann* 241-248.

[394] GERMAN CC § 383-386; GERMAN Comm.C § 373; SWISS CO art. 93; *cf.* ULIS (*supra* s. 7) art. 94, 95.

case of failure to accept goods, the buyer will be in breach of his duty to accept; and the seller's right to damages for non-acceptance is in no way affected by a *Selbsthilfeverkauf*.

The buyer is obviously interested in the proceeds of a *Selbsthilfeverkauf* and many systems contain rules designed to protect his interests:[395] *e.g.* in requiring the sale to be public or to be authorised by the court, unless the subject-matter has a market price.[396] The buyer may also (though less directly) be interested in a *cover sale* as it may form the basis of "concrete" assessment of damages. The AMERICAN Uniform Commercial Code accordingly contains provisions designed to ensure that a fair price is realized on a resale of this kind.[397]

71. *Time for "abstract" assessment.* – The time with regard to which damages are assessed gives rise to no difficulty where the method of assessment is "concrete"; for in that case assessment is in principle the difference between the cover sale or purchase and the contract price. It is true that the cost (or proceeds) of cover may be disregarded if the cover transaction is undertaken at an unreasonably late time, but in that event "concrete" assessment is not available at all: the problem is not one of the time of such assessment.

The problem as to the time of assessment does, however, arise where damages are quantified "abstractly", with reference to the market price, for in such a case there need be no actual cover sale or purchase. The legal systems to be considered present a great variety of solutions to the problem, ranging from assessment at the time of default (or in some cases even earlier) to assessment at the time of judgment; almost every conceivable intermediate stage is adopted by one legal system or another. The systems will be discussed, so far as possible, in the chronological order at which they place the time of assessment. At the outset the point should perhaps be made that postponement of the date at which the damages are assessed will usually tend to favour the aggrieved party, who may be prejudiced by being required to act promptly in relation to what may well be a disputed default.

In ENGLISH law, the starting principle is, or is generally assumed to be, that damages are assessed by reference to the time of breach. So far as contracts for the sale of goods are concerned, the principle is stated in the Sale of Goods Act, 1893 (*supra* n. 312). Where a buyer wrongfully refuses to accept and pay (or a seller to deliver) the damages are *prima facie* based on the market price of the goods at the time or times when the goods ought to have been accepted (or delivered), or, if no time was fixed for acceptance (or delivery) at the time of the refusal to accept (or deliver).[398] The principle is of general application: for example, it applies also where a vendor of land wrongfully refuses to convey.[399]

The courts do not, however, regard the principle as an inflexible one. It is based on two assumptions: that the injured party knows of the breach as soon as it has occurred, and that he is at that point of time in a position to take steps to mitigate the loss that is likely to flow from the breach. Even where these assumptions are true, the aggrieved party may be allowed some latitude. Thus in one case a seller's breach was known to the buyer but an exact substitute could not be obtained. It was said that the buyer had "a reasonable time to consider the position"[400] – amounting to about ten days – and the damages were assessed by reference to market prices at the end of the ten days.

If the breach is not known to the aggrieved party until some time after its commission, the general principle does not apply. For example, a seller may commit a breach of contract by *appropriating* defective goods, but the time by reference to which damages are assessed is that of *delivery*.[401] This time is relevant because it is then possible for the buyer to find out about the defect. If the defect is in fact not discoverable till some later time – for example when the goods are unpacked – the damages may be assessed by reference to that time, provided that the buyer was not guilty of any unreasonable delay.[402] Similarly, in building contracts damages for defective work will normally be assessed by reference to the time when the customer, acting with reasonable diligence, discovered the defect.[403]

Even if the aggrieved party does know of the breach, he may in fact be unable to take steps to avoid its harmful consequences. For example, a buyer may wrongfully refuse to pay for goods while they are on the high seas; and if there is no

395 GERMAN CC § 383-385; GERMAN Comm.C § 373 par. 2, 3, 5; SWISS CO art. 93 par. 1.

396 GERMAN CC § 385; GERMAN Comm.C § 373 par. 2; SWISS CO art. 93 par. 2.

397 S. 2-706 (2) to (4).

398 S. 50 (3), 51 (3).

399 *Diamond v. Campbell-Jones*, [1961] Ch. 22, 36.

400 *C.Sharpe & Co., Ltd. v. Nosawa & Co.* (*supra* n. 385) 814, 821.

401 Sale of Goods Act, 1893 (*supra* n. 312) s. 53 (3).

402 *Van den Hurck v. Martens*, [1920] 1 K.B. 856.

403 *East Ham Corp. v. Bernard Sunley, Ltd.*, [1966] A.C. 406 (H.L.); *Applegate v. Moss*, [1971] 1 Q.B. 406 (C.A.).

market for such goods afloat the seller will be unable to effect a cover sale until they reach the destination. The damages will then be assessed by reference to that time, at the earliest. Or a buyer may be financially unable to buy a substitute on a rising market[404] and in such cases the damages may (subject to the rules of remoteness) be assessed by reference to a later time - possibly as late as the time of judgment.[405]

If a general principle can be deduced from all these cases, it is that damages are assessed by reference to the time at which the aggrieved party could reasonably have taken steps to avoid the harmful consequences of the breach. Even this principle, however, does not apply in cases of so-called anticipatory breach, in which one party declares before performance is due that he will not perform.[406] In these cases of anticipatory breach, ENGLISH law in general adheres to the principle that damages are assessed by reference to the time (if any) fixed for performance.[407] The time of refusal to perform is however relevant for the purpose of assessing damages where there is no time fixed for performance.[408] And if the aggrieved party "accepts" the repudiation he comes under a duty to mitigate his loss. Performance of that duty may, and if there is a market probably will, require him to make a cover sale or purchase; and *prima facie* he will be required to do this at the time at which the repudiation is accepted.[409] If he makes no such sale or purchase, damages will nevertheless be based on the market price at the time when he should have done so. But since the duty to mitigate only requires the aggrieved party to act reasonably the rule as to the time of assessment may not be as rigid as most statements of it tend to suggest.

Under ULIS (*supra* s. 7) damages are assessed abstractly only when the contract has been avoided (*supra* s. 69), and the rule is that they are assessed by reference to the market at the time of avoidance (art. 84). This will sometimes be after the time of breach. In some cases the contract is *ipso facto* avoided on the occurrence of a fundamental breach unless the aggrieved party within a reasonable time declares it subsisting.[410] Presumably, if the aggrieved party simply does nothing the contract is avoided when the breach occurs or becomes fundamental. In other cases, the contract is not avoided unless the aggrieved party after breach makes a prompt declaration of avoidance.[411] In such cases avoidance presumably takes place at the date of the declaration. The same is true of cases of anticipatory breach: the contract is avoided at the time of the injured party's declaration, and abstract assessment takes place by reference to that time.[412]

In the UNITED STATES the time at which the market is relevant for the purpose of abstract assessment differs, under the Uniform Commercial Code, according to whether the party in default is the buyer or the seller. In the former case the seller's damages are quantified by reference to the market price at the time for tender,[413] while in the latter case they are quantified by reference to the market price at the time when the buyer learned of the breach (s. 2-713(1)). The latter rule is obviously based on the consideration that the buyer cannot in practice take steps to procure a substitute until he knows of the seller's default. In the case of a buyer's default, it seems to be assumed that the seller will have the corresponding state of knowledge at the time when his tender is refused, but this is not necessarily the case. The seller may tender the goods and not know at once that the buyer will wrongfully refuse to accept them; indeed the buyer may initially accept the goods and then wrongfully revoke his acceptance, in which case the remedy of damages for non-acceptance is open to the seller.[414] Of course the seller can resell and so quantify his damages concretely (s. 2-708(2)); but so far as abstract quantification is concerned the Code refers only to the time for tender.

The rules in the Uniform Commercial Code with regard to the time at which the market price is relevant apply not only to cases of non-acceptance and non-delivery, but also to cases of

[404] *Trans Trust S.P.R.L. v. Danubian Trading Co., Ltd.*, [1952] 2 Q.B. 297 (C.A.).

[405] *Wroth v. Tyler*, [1973] 2 W.L.R 405 (Ch.).

[406] UNITED KINGDOM Sale of Goods Act, 1893 (*supra* n. 312) s. 50 (3), 51 (3); *C.Sharpe & Co., Ltd. v. Nosawa & Co., supra* n. 385.

[407] *Roper v. Johnson* (1873), L.R. 8 C.P. 167; in relation to sale of goods the principle is more clearly stated in the GHANA Sale of Goods Act (no. 137 of 1962) s. 48(2)(a), 54(2)(a) than in the UNITED KINGDOM Sale of Goods Act, 1893 (*supra* n. 312).

[408] Under UNITED KINGDOM Sale of Goods Act, 1893 (*supra* n. 312) s. 50 (3) and 51 (3); *cf.* INDIAN Contract Act, 1872 (*supra* n. 241) s. 73 ill. (c). The INDIAN Sale of Goods Act, 1930 (Act III of 1930) s. 56, 57 lay down no rules as to time of assessment.

[409] *Tredegar Iron & Coal Co., Ltd. v. Hawthorn Bros.* (1902), 18 T.L.R. 716 (C.A.); *Melachrino v. Nicholl and Knight*, [1920] 1 K.B. 693.

[410] *E.g.* art. 26 (1), 62 (1).

[411] *E.g.* art. 26 (3), 43, 44 (2), 62 (2).

[412] Art. 76, 77.

[413] UCC s. 2-708 (1); as to tender see UCC s. 2-503.

[414] S. 2-703, 2-711 (1) and (2).

"repudiation".[415] But in cases of anticipatory repudiation, special provisions apply; these entitle the aggrieved party (amongst other courses of action) to claim damages or to await performance by the repudiating party "for a commercially reasonable time" (s. 2–610(a)). These words appear to restrict the unfettered right which ENGLISH law gives to the aggrieved party to refuse to accept the repudiation; and, together with the principle that good faith must be observed in the enforcement of a contract (s. 1–203), they seem to support the conclusion that an aggrieved party who refuses to accept a repudiation is not necessarily entitled to quantify damages by reference to the market at the time for tender or at the time when he learned of the breach.

If an action based on anticipatory repudiation comes to trial before the time for performance, the Uniform Commercial Code provides that damages based on market price shall be determined by reference to the market when the aggrieved party learned of the repudiation (s. 2–723(1)). This provision does not mean that the aggrieved party must always safeguard himself by buying in the market as soon as he learns of the repudiation; it is merely intended to provide a measure where the court would otherwise have to speculate as to future market movements. Where this difficulty does not exist, the aggrieved party has a commercially reasonable time before he must go into the market or suffer any adverse consequences of his failure to do so.

In ANGLO-AMERICAN law all the rules which lay down the market principle for abstract quantification are only *prima facie* rules and they do not lay down the limits of recovery where the aggrieved party suffers additional, legally recoverable, loss.

In FRENCH law the Civil Code lays down no time for abstract assessment and the case law on the point has fluctuated considerably. According to the most recent authorities, the general principle is that damages are to be evaluated *at the time of judgment*.[416] Thus if a carrier loses the thing to be carried, he is liable for its value at the time of judgment;[417] so, if a seller fails to deliver and the thing has risen in value above the contract price by the time of default and has risen further by the time of judgment, it is the latter value which is in principle recoverable.[418] Only in this way, it is said, will the creditor get full reparation. To the objection that he might have made a substitute contract and so have avoided the prejudice caused by rising prices, the reply is made that the debtor could equally have avoided it by performing or by making good the loss earlier, as the case may be.[419] But the reply is hardly conclusive and the FRENCH rule seems to be oddly inconsistent with the solicitude generally shown by FRENCH law for the protection of the debtor. The rule seems to be justifiable only where the creditor cannot in fact make a substitute contract before the time of judgment, or where it would be quite unreasonable to expect him to do so. It is sometimes said that the rule is subject to the broad discretion given to the trial judge in the matter of evaluation of damages;[420] but his discretion will not protect his decision from reversal if he adopts a wrong principle in assessing damages.

The principle that damages are to be assessed at the time of judgment is also sometimes stated in other systems, for example in GERMANY.[421] But there it refers to "concrete" assessment (with which we are not at this point concerned). It is expressly made subject (as it is not in FRANCE) to the duty to make cover sales or purchases;[422] and is not intended to displace the rule as to the time for abstract assessment of damages which is the date of default or expiration of the *Nachfrist* (*infra* s. 149) at the option of the aggrieved party.

In FRENCH law, a date earlier than that of judgment is taken if the creditor has in fact entered into a cover transaction before judgment, but not merely because he might have done so.[423] The danger that this might enable the creditor to speculate at the debtor's expense is partly met by the rule that if the debtor makes an offer of reasonable compensation which is refused by the creditor with a view to profiting from a rise in the market, then any further rise in market values taking place after the offer will be disregarded.[424] The main defect in FRENCH law is that it does not appear to recognize any obligation to mitigate damages by entering into a cover transaction;

[415] S. 2–708 (1), 2–713 (1).

[416] *Carbonnier* IV 255, 258–259; *Mazeaud and Tunc*, Traité III (ed. 5) no. 2420, esp. 2420–4 and 2420–12; *Mazeaud*, Leçons II 596–601; *De Page* III no. 108; Cass. soc. 19 Nov. 1953, J.C.P. 1954.II.8039 (depreciation of currency).

[417] Cass.civ. 16 Feb. 1954, D. 1954, 534.

[418] *Mazeaud and Tunc*, Traité III (ed. 5) no. 2420–4.

[419] *Idem* III no. 2420–12.

[420] *Anon.*, Sanctions de l'obligation de délivrance: J.-Cl.Civ. art. 1610–1613 no. 78; but *cf. supra* s. 56, *infra* s. 86 as to control of discretion exercised on wrong principle.

[421] *Enneccerus and Lehmann* 89.

[422] *Ibidem*.

[423] J.-Cl.Civ. art. 1146–1155 fasc. VIII (2e cahier) no. 136–137.

[424] *Idem* no. 138.

indeed, the whole topic of mitigation is not well developed in FRENCH law.[425]

The FRENCH rule as to time of abstract assessment is not followed in systems based on FRENCH law, such as those of QUEBEC[426] and LOUISIANA,[427] where the relevant time is that of default. The current FRENCH rule is also contrary to the earlier FRENCH view, which is still sometimes stated, that assessment ought to be made at the time of default.[428]

72. *Other senses of the distinction between "concrete" and "abstract" assessment.* – The distinction between abstract and concrete assessment most naturally bears the sense in which it is used in the preceding discussion. But it is also used in another sense to distinguish between loss occurring in the ordinary course of things and loss resulting from special circumstances peculiar to the aggrieved party. This distinction relates not to the amount of money which the creditor would have to pay for obtaining a substitute for the thing or service contracted for, but to consequential loss, including the amount of gain which the creditor would have been able to make with the subject-matter of the promised performance.

For example, goods may be bought for resale and not delivered to the buyer, who in consequence is unable to satisfy his sub-buyer. Abstract assessment in the sense previously discussed would give the buyer the difference between the contract price and the market price at which he could have *bought* substitute goods; in the different sense used at this point, it would give the buyer the difference between the contract price and the market price at which he could have *sold* the goods if they had been delivered. Concrete assessment, in the sense previously discussed, would give the buyer the difference between the contract price and the price at which the buyer actually made a cover purchase; in the different sense used at this point it would give the buyer the difference between the contract price and the price for which he had resold the goods to the particular sub-buyer.

The distinction just drawn may be compared with statutory provisions in force in some of the UNITED STATES which distinguish between, on the one hand, "value to the seller" (or buyer) and "peculiar value".[429] The first expression is defined in terms of substitute market sales (or purchases) and therefore refers to "abstract" assessment in our first sense. "Peculiar value" is not defined, but it is said that such value is deemed to be the special value of the subject-matter against a person who had notice thereof or against a willful wrongdoer. The reference here seems to be to peculiar value by reason of the use to which the subject-matter was to be put, rather than to the actual cost of a substitute: in other words to "concrete" assessment in our second sense.

The difference between the two senses in which the expressions "abstract" and "concrete" assessment are used is sometimes overlooked;[430] but it deserves to be stressed as the expectation interests to which the two senses respectively refer are quite different.[431] In the first sense, the interest of the aggrieved party which is protected is his expectation of getting the promised subject-matter; in the second sense the interest which is protected is his expectation of making a profit out of the subject-matter. The distinction is comparable to that between "actual loss" and "lost gain" (*supra* s. 51). It is perfectly possible for an aggrieved party to be entitled to concrete assessment in the first sense but only to abstract assessment in the second. This would be the position where a seller of machinery for which there was no market price failed to deliver and the buyer was in consequence unable to perform quite exceptionally lucrative contracts.[432] The buyer's damages for not receiving the machinery could be assessed concretely, by reference to the actual cost of replacement. But his damages for loss of profits would generally under the rules of remoteness be assessed abstractly, that is by reference to the profits which might normally be made by the use of such machinery (*infra* s. 85).

Where a seller fails to deliver and there is a market for goods of the contract description, damages for not getting the subject-matter will often be assessed "abstractly" (in the first sense); and the aggrieved buyer may well be denied damages for loss of the profit which he expected

[425] *Infra* s. 100 ss.; *von Mehren* 511.

[426] *Baudouin* 578.

[427] *Pepper v. Katz*, 77 So.2d 891 (La.C.A. 1955).

[428] Cour d'appel Rennes 28 May 1926, D.P. 1928.2. 161; *Anon., supra* n. 420, no. 76.

[429] These provisions are based on *Field*'s Civil Code s. 1872–1874 (see *supra* s. 31). They are to be found in CALIFORNIAN CC § 3353–3355; NORTH DAKOTA Century Code (*supra* n. 154) § 32-03-31 to 32-03-33; OKLAHOMA Statutes (*supra* n. 187) § 23-91 to 93. In MONTANA and SOUTH DAKOTA these rules were modified on the introduction of the Uniform Commercial Code.

[430] *E.g.* BGB-RGRK § 325 no. 9; *Enneccerus and Lehmann* 227.

[431] *Rabel* I 170–171.

[432] Illustration based on the ENGLISH case of *Victoria Laundry (Windsor), Ltd. v. Newman Industries, Ltd.*, [1949] 2 K.B. 528 (C.A.); *infra* s. 85.

to make out of the subject-matter, or for other loss which he suffered, for example on account of having to pay damages to a sub-buyer. This denial, however, will be based not on the principle of "abstract" assessment (in the second sense) but on the view that the loss is due to the aggrieved party's own failure to mitigate his loss, or on similar reasoning. Certainly ENGLISH law takes the view in such a situation that damages are based on the market price pure and simple; any actual subsales (whether above or below market price) are disregarded.[433] Actual subsales only become relevant when they are of the identical goods to which the original contract related; in which case it is arguable that there is no market for *the goods* which formed the subject-matter of the contract.[434]

Where a buyer refuses to accept and pay for the goods, the seller normally suffers loss only in respect of a single expectation: that of receiving the price, which will of course include his profit. Thus normally the only question is whether damages should be assessed abstractly by reference to the market (as it would be, for instance, in ENGLAND) or concretely by reference to an actual resale (as it would be in the UNITED STATES if the seller exercised his right of resale). If the market or resale price is equal to or greater than the contract price, the seller will normally suffer no loss (or only a loss which he ought to have avoided) and so he will not be entitled to damages. But if the seller is in fact unable to effect a resale or if there are more goods than potential buyers, he will be entitled to recover the profit which he would have made on the transaction if it had been duly carried through.[435] In this situation the seller has a claim for loss of profits which is in principle independent of the market value of the goods but which may nevertheless be assessed abstractly or concretely in our second sense according to the circumstances.

A claim for loss of profits may also be available to a seller who depends on a promised advance payment in order to obtain the contract goods from his supplier.[436] If the buyer fails to make the payment, the seller may suffer loss even though the market rises above the contract price, for the buyer's breach may in fact prevent him from procuring the goods; and so he will not be able to take advantage of the opportunity of selling at or above the contract price, and so avoiding his loss. Here again a question may arise whether the seller's loss should be assessed abstractly or concretely in our second sense. In this context a concrete assessment is one which takes into account the personal circumstances of the seller which *prevented* him from selling in the market: it is *ex hypothesi* not the proceeds of an actual contract to resell, which he was prevented from performing. His claim may, perhaps somewhat loosely, be described as one for loss of profits. The question whether such claims are to be quantified "abstractly" or "concretely" (in our second sense) will be more fully considered in s. 84 below. Here we are only concerned to emphasise the distinction between this question and the question whether damages are to be assessed (concretely) by reference to the actual cost or proceeds of a substitute transaction, or (abstractly) by reference to the market.

iv. "*Difference*" *and* "*Exchange*" *Theories in German Law*

73. *Statement of the theories.* – The expectation interest so far considered has consisted of or been based upon, the creditor's expectation of receiving performance. Where the contract consists of mutual obligations (*i.e.* where it is what FRENCH law calls a synallagmatic contract or what GERMAN law calls a reciprocal contract (*gegenseitiger Vertrag*) the creditor has strictly speaking a double expectation: that of receiving the performance promised to him and that of rendering the performance promised by him. This fact has given rise in GERMAN law, and in related systems such as AUSTRIAN and SWISS law, to a prolonged debate about the proper basis of assessing damages in two cases: first, where the obligations of one party become, through the fault of that party, impossible to perform; and secondly where, because of one party's delay in performance, the other party lawfully gives notice that after the lapse of a fixed time he will refuse to accept performance.[437]

According to the so-called exchange theory (*Austauschtheorie*) the creditor is entitled to the full value of the performance promised to him (and now impossible or overdue) but only on condition of performing his own promise.[438] Thus, to quote a frequently used example,[439] if A agrees to exchange his black horse for B's white horse and B defaults in delivering the white

[433] *Treitel* 789.
[434] *Idem* 780.
[435] *Idem* 794.
[436] *Idem* 793.
[437] *I.e.* in cases falling under GERMAN CC § 325, 326.
[438] *Enneccerus and Lehmann* 208 to 209, 229 to 232.
[439] *Idem* 230.

horse, A is entitled to compensation for the value of the white horse provided that he actually delivers the black horse.

The rival theory is the so-called difference theory (*Differenztheorie*) by which A is on account of B's default released from his obligation to perform his own promise and is entitled to claim the difference in value between the performance which was promised *to* him and that which was promised *by* him. In the above example, A would therefore recover the amount by which the value of the white horse exceeded that of the black horse. Of course if A's performance consists of the payment of money there is no difference in practical effect between the two theories. It is recognised by adherents of the exchange theory that A need not pay over his money in order to recover from B the greater sum representing the value of B's performance;[440] he simply recovers the difference. But even where A's performance does not consist of a payment of money, the GERMAN courts have as a general principle adopted the difference theory; and this theory is also followed in AUSTRIA and SWITZERLAND.[441]

No doubt the exchange theory has a certain theoretical attraction in that it comes closest to giving literal effect to the expectations of the parties; but it has been rejected principally because it would lead to commercially inconvenient results. In particular, it would require a seller in the event of the buyer's default to remain ready to deliver when (particularly in commercial transactions) it would be quite unreasonable to expect him to do this.[442] The difference theory avoids this result. It also enables the court finally to settle the dispute in a single judgment, while the exchange theory might give rise to further questions as to the conformity of the creditor's performance with the contract.[443] The difference theory is also sometimes supported on a more theoretical level by appealing to the language of the Codes. This argument is particularly strong in SWITZERLAND (CO art. 191 par. 2), but in GERMANY it has left scope for considerable difference of academic opinion.[444]

On the other hand there are cases in which the difference theory itself would produce inconvenient results; and in these cases the theory is not followed. The first such case arises where the claimant has an interest in getting rid of the subject-matter of the performance which he has promised. In such a case he is entitled to tender performance and to claim damages on the basis of the exchange theory.[445] In other words, the creditor is entitled, but not bound, to rely on this theory. The second case arises where the claimant has already performed.[446] There the difference theory would strictly require that he should take back his performance and recover the difference between its value and that of the promised performance. In fact he is not bound to do this and the damages are assessed simply by reference to the value of the performance promised by the debtor who retains the performance which he has already received from the creditor. Here again the creditor is not bound to follow this course. He may be entitled[447] *either* to put an end to the contract and to recover back his performance *or* to refuse to accept performance and to recover damages for non-performance which will be based on the difference theory.

The conclusion which may be drawn from these various rules is that the courts will generally apply the difference theory but they will not do so where it leads to inconvenient results; and in some cases they will in effect give the creditor the choice of basing his claim on one or the other theory.

74. *Possible analogies in other systems.* – The conflict between adherents of the exchange and difference theories has no direct parallel in other systems of law. In COMMON LAW countries the basic approach is that of the difference theory in that damages are in principle based on expectation less the amount saved by the aggrieved party in consequence of the breach: this will very often include the expenses saved in consequence of being relieved of the obligation to perform.[448] The provisions as to assessment of a buyer's or seller's damages by reference to the market price expressly state this principle of difference.[449] It is equally clear that, if the aggrieved party has already performed, his recovery will be based on the full value of the performance promised to him.

Where the aggrieved party has not performed there may sometimes be a question whether the

[440] *Idem* 209.

[441] *Klang and Gschnitzer (-Gschnitzer)* IV 1 § 921 no. 1 (where it is assumed that the contract has been terminated); *Guhl* 201.

[442] *Enneccerus and Lehmann* 230-231; *Guhl* 201.

[443] BGB-RGRK § 325 no. 6.

[444] BGB-RGRK § 325 no. 6; *Enneccerus and Lehmann* 230-232.

[445] BGB-RGRK § 325 no. 7.

[446] *Enneccerus and Lehmann* 230.

[447] Under GERMAN CC § 325, 326 (*infra* s. 149, 157).

[448] *Corbin* § 992.

[449] UNITED KINGDOM Sale of Goods Act, 1893 (*supra* n. 312) s. 50(3), 51(3); AMERICAN UCC s. 2-708(1), 2-713(1).

other party's default releases him from his obligation to perform; but such release is assumed in the GERMAN discussions mentioned in s. 73 above. The point of these discussions is not whether the aggrieved party is still *obliged* to perform but whether performance by him is a condition of the assertion of his right to damages. In COMMON LAW countries, this question does not arise once it is established that the aggrieved party is released from his obligation.

COMMON LAW countries have, however, faced a problem which is raised in the GERMAN discussions: namely, that of the aggrieved party who, notwithstanding the other's default, wants to go ahead with his own performance and to claim the full value of the defaulting party's performance. The aggrieved party can in principle take this course of action where the contract is specifically enforceable; but where this is not the case there is, at any rate on the surface, a divergence between ENGLISH and AMERICAN law.

The AMERICAN position is that performance of the aggrieved party's undertaking cannot be forced on the defaulting party: the aggrieved party must not "unreasonably"[450] continue performance but must desist and claim *damages* in which allowance will be made for expenses saved by not completing performance.[451] The ENGLISH position, on the other hand, is that the aggrieved party is entitled to continue performance after default and so to put himself into a position in which he can claim the agreed remuneration.[452] But the ENGLISH rule is subject to the qualifications that the aggrieved party's performance must be such that it can be accomplished without the active co-operation of the defaulting party, that the aggrieved party must have a legitimate interest in continuing with performance, and probably that his continuation should not constitute a breach of the duty to mitigate loss.[453]

In view of these qualifications of the ENGLISH rule, and of the converse qualification of the AMERICAN rule that the aggrieved party is only required not to continue performance "unreasonably" the practical results produced by the two rules may not be as diverse as their fundamentally different starting points suggest. But they do differ in emphasis, particularly where expenses have been incurred by the aggrieved party after repudiation.

The ENGLISH rule therefore comes closer to the GERMAN rule by which a claimant wishing to get rid of his own performance can do so and claim damages on the basis of the exchange theory. But in fact the GERMAN cases cited in support of this rule are cases of contracts which would be specifically enforceable in COMMON LAW jurisdictions,[454] so that on the facts of these cases the same result would be reached in the UNITED STATES.

Where on the other hand the contract is not of the specifically enforceable kind, GERMAN law contains some provisions which reach the same conclusions as AMERICAN law. Thus in the case of a contract to accomplish a particular piece of work (*Werkvertrag*) and of a contract to render services (*Dienstvertrag*), which are types of contract around which the ANGLO-AMERICAN controversy mainly revolves, it is provided that the employer or customer can cancel on payment of the agreed remuneration, subject however to deductions in respect of expenses saved and of any gains which the other party made through otherwise disposing of his working capacity or deliberately or maliciously omitted to make.[455] In the case of the *Werkvertrag* the customer in theory appears to exercise a right to cancel and not to be in default, but the situation is in fact the same as that discussed in the AMERICAN cases; and the result is in financial terms identical with that produced by the AMERICAN rule.

FRENCH law is in principle against any right to cancel a contract except by mutual consent (CC art. 1134 par. 2); so that *prima facie*, if one party purported to cancel, the other could refuse to accept the cancellation, perform and claim the agreed sum. However, the general principle is subject to exceptions one of which again applies to the contract to do a particular piece of work (*contrat d'entreprise*). Here the person for whom the work is to be done can cancel it unilaterally on paying damages to the other party (CC art. 1794). The damages include expenses, and loss of profit, but it seems that they would not be equivalent to the whole price.

[450] Restatement of Contracts (1932) § 338 comment c.

[451] *Corbin* § 1039; the leading case is *Clark v. Marsiglia* (1845), 1 Denio 317 (N.Y.).

[452] *Treitel* 733–735, 833–834; the leading case is *White and Carter (Councils), Ltd. v. McGregor*, [1962] A.C. 413 (H.L.), a decision of the House of Lords on appeal from SCOTLAND. SCOTTISH writers prefer the contrary opinion of the lower courts: *e.g. Walker* I 589.

[453] *Infra* s. 102, 103. *Treitel* 733–735, 833–834.

[454] *E.g.* RG 14 May 1919, RGZ 96, 20; BGH 6 Feb. 1958, BGHZ 26, 337.

[455] See *infra* s. 102. GERMAN CC § 615 (*Dienstvertrag*), § 649 (*Werkvertrag*).

v. *Damages for Non-Performance and for Delay*

75. *The distinction in Civil Law systems.* – In CIVIL LAW countries it is common to distinguish between damages for various kinds of default. Thus FRENCH law draws a sharp distinction between "moratory" and "compensatory" damages available respectively for delay in performance and for other kinds of default. The former are not as a general rule recoverable without a *mise en demeure* (notice putting the debtor in default); while conflicting views have been expressed on the question whether this requirement must be complied with by a party claiming compensatory damages (see *supra* ch. 15). Moratory damages are assessed on the same principles as compensatory damages: this should not be obscured by the fact that often moratory damages are sought for delay in paying money (default in *obligation pécuniaire*) in which case only interest is recoverable.[456] There is no similar limitation on moratory damages for delay in performing some other obligation (default in *obligation en nature*).

The FRENCH CC art. 1147 distinguishes between "*retard dans l'exécution*" (delay in performance), giving rise to moratory damages, and "*inexécution*" (non-performance), giving rise to compensatory damages. Defective performance is treated as a kind of *inexécution*.[457] The distinction is not reproduced in terms in such FRENCH based systems as the Codes of LOUISIANA and QUEBEC,[458] but it exists to some extent in view of the requirement of *mise en demeure* in those countries.

The GERMAN Civil Code also distinguishes between two kinds of default. The first is *Verzug* or delay, giving rise to damages for delay (*Verzugsschaden*). This type of default as a general rule requires a *Mahnung* (notice putting the debtor in default) (see *supra* ch. 15) and a further requirement of a *Nachfrist* (notice setting an extra performance period) (*infra* s. 149) is as a general rule imposed if the creditor wishes to rely on the delay in order to put an end to the contract or to claim damages for non-performance as opposed to damages for delay. A claim for damages for delay may be coupled with one for performance, or for damages for non-performance where the creditor exercises his right to refuse to accept performance on account of the delay.[459] Thus the "delay interest" (*Zögerungsinteresse*) is sharply distinguished from the "performance interest" (*Erfüllungsinteresse*).[460] The former includes gains lost or expenses incurred in consequence of the delay as well as decline in value of the subject-matter during the period of delay. These heads of damage do not differ in principle from those which are allowed in case of impossibility though of course the actual extent of the loss will differ between cases in which performance is not rendered at all and cases in which it is merely delayed.

The second type of default mentioned in the Civil Code is impossibility for which the debtor is responsible: this gives rise to a claim for damages for non-performance. Unlike the claim for *Verzugsschaden*, the claim for damages for non-performance cannot be coupled with one for performance.[461]

A third kind of default, not mentioned in the Civil Code but recognised by writers and the courts, is the so-called *positive Vertragsverletzung* (or *Schlechterfüllung*), which may roughly be said to refer to cases in which performance is rendered in due time, but defectively.[462] There are no special provisions as to damages for this kind of default in the Civil Code, which indeed does not expressly recognize it as a separate concept at all. The concept of *positive Vertragsverletzung* is discussed in ch. 15 above; here it is only necessary to say that damages are in principle assessed on the same basis as damages for impossibility.[463] Once again the actual extent of loss will of course differ between cases in which the debtor does not perform at all or late and cases in which he performs defectively. Defective performance moreover gives rise to a problem which in practice does not arise in cases of impossibility, namely whether the measure of damages is the cost of putting the defect right or the difference in value attributable to the defect (*supra* s. 66).

76. *The distinction in Common Law countries and ULIS.* – COMMON LAW countries do not distinguish, as a matter of legal principle, between damages for delay and non-performance, or between damages for delay, impossibility and defective performance. COMMON LAW systems do distinguish between cases in which time is "of the essence" of

456 CC art. 1153; *infra* s. 115.

457 *Carbonnier* IV 232.

458 LOUISIANA CC art. 1931 - 1933 at the corresponding point draws a distinction between "active" and "passive" violations of contractual duty; QUEBEC CC art. 1071 omits the FRENCH distinction and does not put anything in its place.

459 GERMAN CC § 286, 326; SWISS CO art. 103 par. 1; *infra* s. 119.

460 *Enneccerus and Lehmann* 216, 219.

461 It is only in cases of partial impossibility that a claim for damages for non-performance (in respect of the impossible part) may be combined with one for performance (of the possible part).

462 *Enneccerus and Lehmann* 234-240.

463 *Idem* 237.

the contract and cases in which the time of performance is not of this crucial degree of importance. As a result of this distinction, something like a *mise en demeure* or *Mahnung* or *Nachfrist* may be necessary for some purposes in cases of delay: in particular where the aggrieved party wishes to terminate the contract or to enforce it specifically (*infra* s. 151, 153). But in ANGLO-AMERICAN law the distinction between delay and other forms of default is irrelevant to the entitlement to damages, delay being generally a breach of contract and thus giving rise to a claim for damages if it results in a loss to the aggrieved party.[464] It is true that where the creditor accepts later performance without protest he may be held to have waived the right to damages for delay; but such waiver may occur as well in relation to any other kind of breach.[465] There are no special requirements which have to be satisfied before the right to damages for delay can be asserted.

The statutes relating to sale of goods in ENGLAND and the UNITED STATES (except LOUISIANA)[466] do contain certain special provisions as to the time of performance. But they do not contain any separate provisions which deal with damages for delay. They do, indeed, deal separately with damages for total failure to perform such as non-delivery, and defective performance, such as delivery of defective goods.[467] But these provisions are not based on any distinction in legal principle between the two kinds of breach: they merely reflect the fact that different kinds of breach lead to different practical results and that their consequences in monetary terms must therefore *prima facie* be differently evaluated.

This is equally true of certain rules in COMMON LAW systems which do deal specifically with damages for delay. Thus in some AMERICAN states there is a special statutory provision that damages for delay on the part of a carrier are to be assessed by reference to the depreciation of the goods during the period of delay.[468] But the purpose of such provisions is, again, to state the practical effects of delay in general terms and not to treat delay as in principle different from other kinds of breach of contract. Thus such provisions do not exclude the normal rules as to recovery in respect of consequential loss.[469] COMMON LAW countries have a unified conception of breach of contract; and the result of this is that the conditions of liability in damages, and the principles in which damages are assessed, are the same whatever form the debtor's default may take.

ULIS (*supra* s. 7) occupies an intermediate position. It does distinguish failure to deliver at the agreed time from other breaches (art. 24) and this distinction has certain effects on remedies, in particular on the right to avoid the contract (*infra* s. 170). But its provisions as to damages[470] are perfectly general, applying to all types of breach alike, so that the position is similar to that in COMMON LAW systems. So far as damages are concerned, delay only merits special treatment insofar as it tends to lead to earlier avoidance than other forms of breach, and thus to an earlier time for abstract assessment (*supra* s. 71).

F. METHODS OF LIMITING DAMAGES

77. *General introduction.* – All legal systems agree in placing some limitations on the recoverability of damages for breach of contract. The exact reasons why such limitations exist are hardly ever fully discussed. One possible view is that they can be derived from the fundamental objective of awarding damages for breach of contract which (it is said) is "the prevention of similar breaches in the future and the avoidance of private war."[471] But insofar as this is a deterrent theory it presupposes that liability is based on some degree of fault, which in COMMON LAW systems is not generally the case; and it is also hard to reconcile with some of the actual COMMON LAW rules relating to remoteness: for example, the "prevention of private war" would require one to hold the defendant liable for losses foreseeable by the *plaintiff* but it is generally agreed that the relevant

464 *Corbin* § 1177; INDIAN Contract Act, 1872 (*supra* n. 241) s. 55; in ENGLAND the Law of Property Act, 1925 (25 & 26 Geo.5, c.20) s. 41 appears to have removed any right to damages where time is not "of the essence" of the contract: *Treitel* 724; *infra* s. 153.

465 *Treitel* 723, 707.

466 UNITED KINGDOM Sale of Goods Act, 1893 (*supra* n. 312) s. 10; AMERICAN UCC s. 2-309. The UCC does not apply to LOUISIANA where the Civil Code does contain certain special provisions as to damages for delay: art. 1935 - 1938. In effect these are limited to damages for non-payment of money, as to which see *infra* s. 114-117.

467 UNITED KINGDOM Sale of Goods Act, 1893 (*supra* n. 312) s. 50, 51 (non-performance), s. 53 (defective performance); AMERICAN UCC s. 2-708, 2-713 (non-performance), s. 2-714 (defective performance).

468 CALIFORNIAN CC § 3317; Revised Codes of MONTANA (*supra* n. 137) § 17-316; NORTH DAKOTA Century Code (*supra* n. 154) § 32-03-17; SOUTH DAKOTA Compiled Laws (*ibidem*) § 21-2-10.

469 *Artists' Embassy v. Hunt*, 157 Cal.App.2d 371, 320 P.2d 924 (1958).

470 Art. 82 - 89.

471 *Corbin* § 998; *cf.* § 1006.

foresight is that of the defendant (*infra* s. 88). The more probable view is simply that the full protection of the expectation and reliance interests would operate either as too strong a disincentive to the assumption of contractual obligations, or to an undue raising of charges to cover such unlimited liability. There is, in particular, a reluctance to hold a party liable for heavy damages if the amount of his charges is relatively small in relation to the loss.

Our present concern is with the techniques used by various legal systems to achieve the commonly held aim of limiting damages. Seven principal techniques will be discussed. Under the first, damages are limited by reference to the degree of the debtor's fault. The second requires that damage must be foreseeable. The third relies on the degree of causal connection between the default and the harm. The fourth technique is to give the court a discretion to limit damages. The fifth is based on a number of distinct but related ideas which will be discussed under the heading of mitigation. The sixth is to be found in the requirement that damages must be "certain". There are, seventhly, a number of specific limitations on damages which cannot easily be reduced to any common principle and which are, indeed, not easy to explain or defend. Many legal systems use several of these techniques to deal with various phases of the problem of limiting damages; though it is probably safe to say that no legal system makes use of them all.

i. *Fault*

78. *Relevance to existence or the extent of liability.* – CIVIL LAW systems start with the general principle that some degree of "fault" is a condition of contractual liability. In practice the principle is subject to qualifications which tend to outweigh it in practical effect. The general principle and the qualifications to it are discussed in ch. 15 above and are not our primary concern in the present chapter.

Our concern is rather with the *extent* of liability than with the basic *availability* of a remedy for contractual default. However, if one looks at the remedies available in CIVIL LAW systems through the eyes of a common lawyer the "fault" required as a condition of contractual liability sometimes appears to determine not only the existence of liability but also its extent. This is so because a contracting party may be subject to different types of liability, of varying stringency, only one of which depends on the "fault" which is required as a condition of contractual liability.

The point may be illustrated by taking the case of a seller of specific goods who delivers goods which are defective. In the CIVIL LAW of, for example, FRANCE and GERMANY, the seller is liable in the absence of fault to redhibition and price reduction; but he is only liable on proof of fault to what a common lawyer would call damages for breach of contract. The pecuniary consequences of redhibition and price reduction are in principle different from those of damages (*supra* s. 57, 67). In COMMON LAW countries, "fault" is not a necessary element of contractual liability; and a common lawyer looking at the liability of a seller for defects in CIVIL LAW countries would be inclined to say that the "measure of damages" available to the buyer depended on whether the seller was at "fault".

The degree of "fault" required to hold the seller liable in "damages" in such a situation is in many CIVIL LAW systems greater than that which is required for contractual liability generally, in that (at least in the absence of express warranty) some degree of bad faith on the part of the seller is required. In FRENCH and GERMAN law the seller is liable in damages generally speaking only if he acts in bad faith, *e.g.* by failing to declare defects of which he knows, or by representing that such defects do not exist (*supra* s. 57, 58). Where the buyer claims redhibition he may recover not only any payments he has made but also certain expenses connected with the sale. This right has been discussed in s. 57, 58 above; its existence tends to blur the distinction, based on fault, between redhibition and price reduction on the one hand, and damages on the other. In SWISS law, the seller against whom the remedy of redhibition is asserted is liable to restore the price and expenses and also "direct" damage occasioned to the buyer as a result of delivery of the defective thing; but if he cannot prove that he was in no way at fault he is liable for further damage. Such further damage appears to be capable of including lost gain, so that the seller can be made liable for loss of expectation unless he disproves fault (*supra* s. 59). Under this rule the distinction between redhibition and damages must in practice be a somewhat tenuous one.

79. *Degrees of fault.* – It is possible to relate the extent of recoverable damages directly to the degree of the debtor's fault. This principle is adopted by SWISS law, under which one of the circumstances to be taken into account by the judge in assessing damages is the extent of the debtor's fault.[472]

[472] CO art. 43 par. 1, applied to contract cases by art. 99 par. 3.

AUSTRIAN law recognises a similar principle, though it is not expressed with the same flexibility as that which exists in SWISS law. A distinction is drawn in the AUSTRIAN Civil Code between *Schadloshaltung* and *volle Genugtuung* which is related to the first sense of the distinction between *damnum emergens* and *lucrum cessans* drawn in s. 51 above. *Schadloshaltung* is compensation for the actual loss suffered while *volle Genugtuung* includes in addition compensation for loss of anticipated gains (CC § 1323); it also includes other items which will be discussed in s. 113 below.[473] The Code then goes on to state that normally a plaintiff is entitled only to *Schadloshaltung* but that he is entitled to *volle Genugtuung* if the wrong was done with deliberate intent (*aus böser Absicht*) or with gross negligence (CC § 1324). Under another provision of the AUSTRIAN Civil Code, recompense for damage to property is in cases of mere negligence based on its ordinary value (CC § 1332), but if the damage was caused by an act which was criminal or malicious, special value to the plaintiff in the nature of a *pretium affectionis* (or sentimental value) is recoverable (CC § 1331). The principle of making the extent of recovery depend on degree of fault has been criticised in AUSTRIA on the ground that it confuses punishment with compensation;[474] and there are many exceptions to the principle in AUSTRIAN law; and in particular it does not apply to commercial cases.[475]

It is curious to note that GERMAN law has been criticised for precisely the opposite failing, namely for not recognising a principle whereby the extent of liability is proportioned to the degree of fault;[476] and a recent proposal for the amendment of the GERMAN Civil Code would, if adopted, make the degree of fault a relevant factor for *reducing* damages which otherwise would be exceptionally high.[477] The SWISS and AUSTRIAN rules are not limited in this way: they may result in an *increase* of damages beyond the normal measure (for example so as to include sentimental value) as well as in a reduction.[478]

Under the law of ISRAEL, the position used to be that a defendant was liable for *damnum emergens* without fault and for *lucrum cessans* if he was guilty of wrongful intent.[479] The distinction was criticised as unworkable[480] and it has been abandoned in a recent law which deals with remedies for breach of contract.[481] The present position is that in contractual actions the degree of the defendant's fault is generally[482] disregarded in assessing damages.

Whether or not a legal system adopts a general principle of relating the extent of liability to the degree of fault, it may consider the degree of fault relevant in a number of specific contexts. In some systems the courts have power to reduce amounts made payable under the terms of the contract in the event of default; and the seriousness of the debtor's fault is one factor which the court may take into account in determining the extent of such reduction. This is, for example, the position in GERMAN and AUSTRIAN law (*infra* s. 132). The question whether relief is to be given against forfeiture of a deposit may also be made to depend on the extent of the defaulting party's fault (*infra* s. 139, 140). In FRENCH law the amount at which an *astreinte* is liquidated (*supra* s. 25) may depend on, among other things, the fault of the debtor both in failing to perform the contract and in his unjustified resistance to the order of the court.

80. *Effect of fraud or gross negligence.* – The rule of AUSTRIAN law mentioned in s. 79 above makes recovery in respect of certain losses depend on deliberate wrongdoing or gross negligence; and these factors are also influential in other systems. In FRENCH law the general principle of remoteness, stated in CC art. 1150, is that the debtor is only liable for such damages as he could have foreseen from the time of the contract; but this restriction does not apply where the default in performance is due to the "fraud" (*dol*) of the debtor. It is generally agreed that for this purpose fraud includes gross negligence (*faute lourde*).[483] What is meant by "fraud" in this context is a deliberate breach of contract or one committed in bad faith.[484]

The provisions of CC art. 1150 are reproduced in literal translation in an article of the LOUISIANA Civil Code (art. 1943), but an earlier article of that

473 *I.e.* damages for insult.

474 *Klang (-Wolff)* VI § 1324 no. II 1.

475 *Idem* VI § 1324 no. II 2.

476 *Enneccerus and Lehmann* 71.

477 *Referentenentwurf zur Änderung des Bürgerlichen Gesetzbuchs* (Bundesministerium der Justiz, Bonn 1967), proposal for a new § 255a in the Civil Code.

478 In practice, the SWISS provision operates to reduce damages: thus *Guhl* 78 discusses it under the heading "Grounds for reducing damages."

479 OTTOMAN CCProc. art. 109, 110.

480 *Tedeschi*, Studies in Israel Private Law (Jerusalem 1960) 116.

481 Contracts (Remedies for Breach of Contracts) Law, 5731-1970, 25 LSI 11.

482 It could be taken into account under the Law of 1970, s. 13, which leaves damages "other than pecuniary damage" subject to judicial discretion.

483 *Marty and Raynaud* II no. 471; *Carbonnier* IV 236.

484 *De Page* III no. 113; *Carbonnier* IV 235.

Code provides that the rule limiting liability to such damages as were or might have been contemplated does not apply to a debtor who is guilty of "fraud or bad faith" (art. 1934 par. 1). For this purpose bad faith is defined to mean "a designed breach *from some motive of interest or ill-will*" (*ibidem*). It seems that in FRENCH law it is not necessary to satisfy *both* these requirements: a deliberate breach (*faute intentionelle*) is sufficient, even in the absence of a bad motive.[485]

FRENCH writers are divided on the explanation for the special rule laid down by CC art. 1150 for cases of fraud.[486] According to one view, such cases do not fall under the general rule (discussed in s. 82 below) that the damages recoverable in a contractual action must be foreseeable because that rule is based on implied agreement, and no agreement to limit the damages in this way can be implied to cover cases of "fraud". Another view is that liability in case of "fraud" is really a form of delictual liability, to which the requirement that loss must be foreseeable does not apply. It is however hard to see how delictual liability can be said to arise in a case involving nothing more than a deliberate failure to perform a contractual obligation.

A distinction similar to that contained in CC art. 1150 is drawn in CC art. 1153, which deals with damages for delay in the performance of an obligation to pay money. Here the general rule is that damages are limited to interest at the legal rate (*infra* s. 115); but "prejudice independent of the delay" is recoverable if it is due to the "bad faith" of the debtor. "Bad faith" here has been given a wider meaning than "fraud" in CC art. 1150. The courts at one time tended to interpret "bad faith" to mean lack of that good faith which a contracting party is required to show in the performance of a contract under CC art. 1134 par. 3. Failure to show the spirit of co-operation required by the latter article was regarded as "bad faith" for the purpose of CC art. 1153: for example in the case of an insurance company which "awkwardly" delays in making payments to which a policyholder is entitled.[487] But more recently a somewhat stricter process of interpretation has set in, by which "bad faith" requires at the very least that the debtor should have acted with the knowledge that the delay would in fact cause injury to the creditor.[488]

The phrase "prejudice independent of the delay" is not a happy one.[489] It is in fact prejudice caused by the delay which gives rise to the extra damages: for example if, as a result of the delay, the debtor becomes bankrupt or if his property is seized by his creditors. The phrase simply refers to prejudice of a kind which is not usually suffered by the creditor of a money debt merely as result of delay.

An attempt to introduce a rule similar to that contained in CC art. 1153 has been made in AUSTRIA by a judicial decision to the effect that a debtor is only liable for damages in excess of interest if his delay in payment is due to "gross" fault. But the attempt has been criticised as inconsistent with the relevant provision of the AUSTRIAN Code under which "fault" is not necessary to entitle a creditor to interest by way of damages; from which it is thought to follow that *any* degree of fault, whether "gross" or not, is sufficient to attract the operation of the normal rules as to damages.[490] A similar position is adopted in SWISS law, under which damages for loss suffered in excess of interest are recoverable for delay in payment unless the debtor proves that he was not at fault.[491]

The fact that the defendant has been guilty of deliberate wrongdoing may also affect his liability in depriving him of a defence that would otherwise be available, such as the defence of contributory negligence (*infra* s. 106) or the benefit of a clause excluding liability (see ch. 1).

The rules laid down for the assessment of damages in ULIS (*supra* s. 7) do not apply in cases of fraud. Here the damages are "determined by the rules applicable in respect of contracts of sale not governed by the present law" (art. 89), *i.e.* by the domestic rules of the appropriate system.

81. *Position in Common Law countries.* – In COMMON LAW countries, fault is not in principle an element of contractual liability; nor is the degree of fault normally an element in measuring its extent. Once a breach is established, it makes no difference as a general rule whether the breach was committed deliberately, negligently or innocently, or whether the party in default acted in good or in bad faith. But there are a number of exceptional cases in which a more severe liability is imposed on a party who is guilty of a deliberate breach than on one whose breach is purely innocent.

In ENGLAND and in some AMERICAN states there is a rule (which will be discussed in s. 118 below) that a vendor of land is not liable for expectation

485 *Mazeaud and Tunc,* Traité III (ed. 5) no. 2375.
486 *Idem* III no. 2375-3, 2376; *cf. Baudouin* 580.
487 *Carbonnier* IV 259-260.
488 *Ibidem.*
489 *Mazeaud and Tunc,* Traité III (ed. 5) no. 2340 n. 4.
490 *Klang (-Wolff)* VI § 1332 (p. 170).
491 CO art. 106. *Infra* s. 116.

loss (but only for certain kinds of reliance loss, namely the buyer's costs of investigating the title) if he cannot convey on account of his inability to make title. This rule does not protect a vendor who can make title but will not: in other words, it does not protect one who is guilty of a deliberate breach.[492] A vendor who knows at the time of contracting that he has no title may also be held liable on the ground of fraud for reliance loss generally: in such a case his liability is not restricted to the buyer's cost of investigating the title.[493] But it is by no means clear that a vendor who knew he had no title would be liable for *all* reliance loss, whether or not it was foreseeable. It has indeed been suggested in a recent ENGLISH case that foreseeability is irrelevant in an action based on fraud,[494] but the suggestion is an isolated one and the law cannot be regarded as settled in this sense.

Another suggestion for imposing heavier liability on a party guilty of deliberate default is that the requirement of foreseeability should be applied at the time of breach and not (as is normal) at the time of contracting;[495] but the suggestion is as yet unsupported by authority.

In the UNITED STATES the problem has arisen of the proper measure of damages where a builder in the construction of a house uses materials other than those specified in the contract. One possible view is that the client should recover the difference in value between the house as it is and the house as it would have been if it had been built in accordance with the specifications; another is that he should recover the amount which it would cost to rebuild the house in accordance with the specifications (*supra* s. 66). In most cases the former view would result in a much lower measure of damages against the builder; and in determining which of the two views to apply the courts may have regard to the question whether the builder's breach was deliberate or innocent; or at any rate whether the builder acted reasonably in the circumstances.[496]

As a general rule, COMMON LAW courts will not give damages for mental suffering caused by a mere breach of contract (*infra* s. 110), but there is a tendency particularly in the UNITED STATES, to make exceptions to this rule where the breach was "wanton or reckless."[497] In some COMMON LAW jurisdictions, damages are not recoverable for injury to reputation caused by the wrongful dishonour of a cheque; but this rule is sometimes inapplicable where the dishonour was wilful.[498]

The general rule that punitive damages are not recoverable in a contractual action (*supra* s. 45) is in some COMMON LAW countries subject to a statutory exception in cases in which the defendant is guilty of oppression, fraud or malice.[499] There are, again, statutory provisions making a "wilful" wrongdoer liable for "peculiar" value in the sense discussed in s. 72 above, when an innocent or negligent wrongdoer might only be liable for general value (*supra* n. 429).

But in COMMON LAW countries all these rules are regarded as exceptional. They have not yielded any general principle that fault affects the measure of recovery in a contractual action. Of course that measure may be affected by fault in the inducement of a contract, giving rise to liability in tort for deceit; or by the rules of remoteness which arguably depend on fault by limiting recovery to loss which was foreseeable at the time of contracting. But such rules do not affect the present question, which is whether the extent of liability is affected by fault in the performance of a contract.

ii. *Foreseeability*

82. *Principle of foreseeability in French law.* – The FRENCH CC art. 1150 lays down that a debtor who is not guilty of "fraud" is only liable for damage which he foresaw or which he could at the time of contracting have foreseen. The provision is one of a group which define and limit the extent of the debtor's liability. It must be read together with CC art. 1149 (which indicates that the debtor may be liable for both *damnum emergens* and for *lucrum cessans*, *supra* s. 51), and CC art. 1151 which exonerates him for liability for "indirect" damage. The limitation of liability to "direct" dam-

[492] *Treitel* 816; *Corbin* § 1098; CALIFORNIAN CC § 3306; Revised Codes of MONTANA (*supra* n. 137) § 17-306; SOUTH DAKOTA Compiled Laws (*supra* n. 154) § 21-2-3; NORTH DAKOTA Century Code (*ibidem*) § 32-03-13 gives damages for loss of bargain irrespective of the deliberateness of the breach.

[493] *Treitel* 816.

[494] *Doyle v. Olby (Ironmongers), Ltd.*, [1969] 2 Q.B. 158, 167 (C.A.).

[495] *Corbin* § 1008.

[496] *Jacob and Youngs v. Kent, supra* n. 333, where *Cardozo*, J. stressed (among other factors) that the breach was not a "willful" one; *Corbin* § 1123.

[497] *Corbin* § 1076; Restatement of Contracts (1932) § 341.

[498] *Corbin* § 1020.

[499] CALIFORNIAN CC § 3294; Revised Codes of MONTANA (*supra* n. 137) § 17-208; NORTH DAKOTA Century Code (*supra* n. 154) § 32-03-07; OKLAHOMA Statutes (*supra* n. 187) § 23-9; SOUTH DAKOTA Compiled Laws (*supra* n. 154) § 21-1-4.

age must be kept distinct from that to foreseeable damage though in practice the two are often confused (*infra* s. 84). Even a debtor who is guilty of "fraud" and thus liable for unforeseeable damage is not liable for damage which is "indirect". Where the debtor is not guilty of fraud, the requirements of foreseeability and directness must *both* be satisfied. "Directness" imports a requirement of causation, which will be further discussed in s. 95 below.

The principle of foreseeability has been an exceedingly influential one; it forms one of the comparatively rare instances in which a major doctrine of the CIVIL LAW appears to have been taken over in the nineteenth century by the COMMON LAW. The principle of foreseeability has recently been adopted as the leading test of remoteness in ULIS[500] and in the law of ISRAEL.[501] It is also accepted by the laws of SCOTLAND,[502] SOUTH AFRICA[503] and SRI LANKA[504] though it is hard to say whether it originated in those countries as a CIVIL LAW concept or whether it was accepted in them as a result of COMMON LAW influence. On the other hand the doctrine failed to take root in GERMANY where it is, at least nominally, rejected even at the present day.

83. *Its adoption by the Common Law.* – The principle that foreseeability determines the extent of contractual liability is generally thought to have entered into the COMMON LAW through the leading ENGLISH case of *Hadley v. Baxendale.*[505] In that case the court referred to the FRENCH CC art. 1149 to 1151 and in the course of argument one of the judges described these provisions as "the sensible rule".[506] The facts of the case were that a carrier agreed with a mill owner to carry the broken shaft of the mill to the manufacturer to serve as a pattern for making a new one. Through the carrier's neglect, delivery of the shaft was delayed so that there was a prolonged stoppage at the mill. It was held that the carrier was not liable for the profits lost by the mill owner as a result of the stoppage. In explaining this conclusion the court laid down the rule that "the damages ... should be such as may fairly and reasonably be considered either arising naturally, *i.e.* according to the usual course of things from such breach of contract itself or such as may reasonably be supposed to have been in the contemplation of both parties at the time they made the contract as the probable result of the breach."[507]

Now it is clear that the court did not in fact adopt the whole of the French rules contained in CC art. 1149-1151. There is, for example, no suggestion in the rule in *Hadley v. Baxendale* of any special treatment of a debtor who is guilty of "fraud". But it has been very widely thought, both in ENGLAND and in the UNITED STATES, that *Hadely v. Baxendale* had adopted the test of "foreseeability", and that "natural" consequences were simply foreseeable ones.[508] It has, moreover, been suggested that this requirement of foreseeability was an importation from FRENCH law.[509] The suggestion may well be true, but the history of the matter is a somewhat curious one and suggests that influences other than the FRENCH provision were also at work.

In the first place the court in *Hadley v. Baxendale* did not in its judgment refer to foresight or foreseeability, in spite of the fact that the FRENCH provisions had been drawn to its attention and mentioned by one of the judges in the course of argument. The court in fact referred to damages "arising naturally" or "in the contemplation of the parties" and the most recent decision of the House of Lords on the question lends some support to the view that these concepts may be distinguishable from the test of "foreseeability", or at any rate that they connote an unusually high degree of foreseeability.[510]

Secondly, there are a number of legislative provisions in COMMON LAW countries which purport to give effect to the rule in *Hadley v. Baxendale.* Such provisions are, for instance, contained in the UNITED KINGDOM Sale of Goods Act, 1893, in the INDIAN Contract Act, 1872 and in legislation in force in a number of AMERICAN states, adopting (with variations) some of the provisions of the Civil Code drafted by *Field* for the STATE OF NEW YORK but never enacted in that

[500] *Supra* s. 7; art. 82, 86.

[501] Contracts (Remedies for Breach of Contract) Law 1970 (*supra* n. 481) s. 10.

[502] *Walker* I 589.

[503] *Willie and Millin (-Coaker and Schutz)* 100-102.

[504] *Weeramantry* II § 935.

[505] (1854) 9 Ex. 341, 156 E.R. 145.

[506] (1854) 9 Ex. 341, 346.

[507] *Ibidem* 354.

[508] This was assumed by all the ENGLISH textbooks on the basis of *Victoria Laundry (Windsor), Ltd. v. Newman Industries, Ltd., supra* n. 432, before the decision of the House of Lords in *The Heron II, Koufos v. C.Czarnikow, Ltd.*, [1969] 1 A.C. 350 (H.L.). For the same position in the UNITED STATES, see *Corbin* § 997, 1007.

[509] *Corbin* § 1007; the same point has been made in SOUTH AFRICA where the rule in *Hadley v. Baxendale* is followed: *Willie and Millin (-Coaker and Schutz)* 101.

[510] *The Heron II, Koufos v. C.Czarnikow, Ltd., supra* n. 508.

state (*supra* s. 31). The striking fact is that none of these nineteenth century provisions use the word "foreseeable".

The Sale of Goods Act repeatedly uses the phrase "directly and naturally resulting in the ordinary course of events".[511] The INDIAN Contract Act refers to damage "which naturally arose in the ordinary course of things . . ., or which the parties *knew* . . . to be likely to result";[512] this wording suggests that the defendant must *actually know* that the damage is likely to result and should be contrasted with the more usual COMMON LAW position that foreseeability, and not foresight, is enough to satisfy the test of remoteness.[513] In the UNITED STATES, the legislation based on the *Field* Civil Code refers to "detriment proximately caused (by the breach) which in the ordinary course of things would be likely to result . . .,"[514] and the Uniform Sales Act used language identical with that of the UNITED KINGDOM Sale of Goods Act.[515] The Uniform Sales Act has been superseded by the Uniform Commercial Code, which again does not in terms refer to foreseeability though it comes very close to doing so when it refers to a seller's liability for loss resulting from requirements of the buyer "of which the seller . . . had reason to know" (s. 2-715(2)(a)). The GHANA Sale of Goods Act of 1962 does expressly make a defaulting buyer or seller liable for such damages as could "reasonably have been foreseen"[516] but, as the preceding examples show, the use of such expressions in legislation in the COMMON LAW world is exceptional.

All this is not to say that the concept of foreseeability is not in fact used in relation to these legislative provisions. It has been read into them whether they use the word "foreseeability" or not. Whether the concept was indeed imported into the COMMON LAW through *Hadley v. Baxendale*, or as a result of subsequent interpretations of that case, is a question which it would be hard now to answer. Whatever the historical origins of the matter may be, the subsequent development of the COMMON LAW concept of foreseeability as a test of remoteness in contract owes little or nothing to its FRENCH counterpart. It probably owes more to the analogous concept which in COMMON LAW countries limits liability in tort,[517] an area to which the requirement of foreseeability does not apply in FRENCH law.[518] Recent developments in ENGLAND suggest that the tort analogy may have been pushed too far,[519] but there is no doubt of its influence in the development of the foreseeability test in contract.

84. *Foreseeability and causation.* – The requirements of "foreseeability" and "directness" are sometimes confused in CIVIL LAW countries. This is so even in FRANCE in spite of the fact that there the two requirements are dealt with in separate articles of the Civil Code.[520] The confusion takes the form that the criterion of foreseeability is applied in order to determine whether damage is "direct". The connection between the two concepts is often denied in systems such as GERMAN and AUSTRIAN law, which use the test of causation and reject that of foreseeability for the purpose of limiting damages;[521] but the two concepts may not be as rigidly separated as some of the relevant statements suggest (*infra* s. 93). In SWITZERLAND, it has been suggested that a loss is considered to be caused by an event if the event is appropriate to bring it about and if a third person in the light of general experience and with knowledge of all the facts could have foreseen the possibility of loss;[522] but it is not certain whether the language of the courts actually supports the application of the test of foreseeability here.[523]

In the UNITED STATES too it has been said that "Our only test of causation . . . is foreseeability."[524] Another way of putting the same point, and one which perhaps more accurately reflects the attitude of the courts, is that the COMMON LAW is not greatly concerned with problems of causation in determining the extent of liability for breach of contract. Problems of causation are most frequently raised when it is suggested that there was

[511] Sale of Goods Act, 1893 (*supra* n. 312) s. 50 (2) 51 (2), 53 (2).

[512] INDIAN Contract Act, 1872 (*supra* n. 241) s. 73; the wording of GEORGIA Code (*supra* n. 142) § 20-1407 is very similar.

[513] *Corbin* § 1009.

[514] CALIFORNIAN CC § 3300; Revised Codes of MONTANA (*supra* n. 137) § 17-301; NORTH DAKOTA Century Code (*supra* n. 154) § 32-03-09; OKLAHOMA Statutes (*supra* n. 187) § 23-21; SOUTH DAKOTA Compiled Laws (*supra* n. 154) § 21-2-1.

[515] AMERICAN Uniform Sales Act (ULA (1950) vol. 1 and 1 A) s. 64 (2), 67 (2), 69 (2).

[516] GHANA Sale of Goods Act (*supra* n. 407) s. 48, 54, 56.

[517] See *Corbin* § 997. See this Encyclopedia vol. XI ch. 7.

[518] *Mazeaud and Tunc*, Traité III (ed. 5) no. 2364.

[519] *The Heron II, Koufos v. C.Czarnikow, Ltd.*, *supra* n. 508.

[520] *Carbonnier* IV 317; *De Page* III no. 112B.

[521] *Enneccerus and Lehmann* 73; *Klang (-Wolff)* VI § 1294 no. I 1 e (p. 12). *Infra* s. 92.

[522] *Guhl* 71.

[523] For example, BG 11 Feb. 1954, BGE 80 III 41, 58 refers to the ordinary course of things and experience of life, but not to foresight or foreseeability.

[524] *Corbin* § 1006; *cf.* § 997, 1000.

some extraneous factor, other than the defendant's default, which wholly or partly caused the loss. The tendency of COMMON LAW courts in such cases is simply to apply a test of "foreseeability" and not *in addition* to require a test of "directness" to be satisfied. Even if an extraneous factor did operate so as to cause or augment the loss, the defaulting party may nevertheless be liable in contract if that other factor could have been foreseen by him.

The point may be illustrated by contrasting two ENGLISH cases. In the first, a tort case, the plaintiff failed to recover extra loss suffered by reason of his impecuniousity, as such loss had arisen from a "separate and concurrent cause" and had not been "caused" by the defendant's wrongful act.[525] But in a later contract case, in which the defendant knew of the plaintiff's lack of means, extra loss occasioned by it was held recoverable on the ground that "it might reasonably be expected to be within the contemplation of the parties as likely to flow from a breach of the obligation undertaken."[526] Similar reasoning is often applied where the extraneous factor was the act of a third party or even sometimes where it was the act of the plaintiff himself.[527]

85. *Foreseeability of what.* – There has been considerable dispute in FRANCE as to the factors to which the defendant's foresight must extend. According to one view, it is enough that he should have foreseen the cause of the damage and, in general terms, its kind, but it is not necessary that he should foresee the extent of the damage. This view appears still to be accepted in BELGIUM,[528] but it is now generally rejected in FRANCE on the ground that it would unduly reduce the protection which the Civil Code meant to afford to the debtor by absolving him from liability for unforeseeable consequences.[529]

The FRENCH view of the matter is, in particular, supported by a series of cases concerning the liability of carriers for the loss of parcels containing articles of exceptional value. The general result of these cases is that the carrier is liable for the "normal" value of such things as the parcel might reasonably be expected to contain, but not for the extra loss actually suffered by reason of the exceptional value of the contents of the parcel.[530] The actual results in many such cases are now governed by special regulations limiting the liability of rail carriers to a certain sum for each unit of weight unless excess value is declared.[531]

In COMMON LAW countries the distinction between "cause" or "kind" of damage on the one hand, and its "extent" on the other is indeed drawn in tort cases, in which it is sometimes said that foreseeability of the precise extent of damage is not necessary.[532] Similarly, where a buyer's damages are based on the value of what should have been transferred to him the seller cannot rely on the fact that the property has increased in value to an unforeseeably large extent.[533] The problem in such a case is really one of quantification and not one of remoteness at all (*infra* s. 90). But where a problem of remoteness does arise in a contract case, it seems that a COMMON LAW court would take a view similar to that adopted in FRANCE. An interesting analogy is provided by an ENGLISH case in which a seller of machinery wrongfully delayed its delivery, with the result that the buyer was unable to perform certain quite exceptionally lucrative contracts. It was held that the buyer could not recover in respect of these exceptional profits but that he could claim for loss of the profits which would in the normal course of things have been made by use of the machinery.[534] The principle seems to be similar to that applied in the FRENCH "parcel" cases.

86. *Loss arising naturally and loss due to special circumstances.* – The rule in *Hadley v. Baxendale*[535] refers to two kinds of losses: those "arising naturally" and those which "may reasonably be supposed to have been in the contemplation of the parties." It is usual, in COMMON LAW countries, to use this phraseology as a basis for distinguishing between loss which any reasonable person in the position of the defendant might have foreseen, and extra loss which could have been foreseen by a reasonable person with the same knowledge of special circumstances as the particular defendant had (such as knowledge of the purposes for which the aggrieved party wanted the subject-matter of the contract).

525 *Liesbosch Dredger v. S.S. Edison,* [1933] A.C. 449, 460 (H.L.).

526 *Muhammed Issa el Sheik Ahmed v. Ali,* [1947] A.C. 414 (P.C.), as explained in *Monarch S.S. Co. v. Karlshamns Oljefabriker,* [1949] A.C. 196, 224 (H.L.).

527 *Treitel* 810.

528 *De Page* III no. 112B.

529 *Ibidem*; *Mazeaud,* Leçons II no. 629.

530 *Planiol and Ripert* VII no. 864; *cf. De Page* III no. 112B, citing FRENCH authorities.

531 See this Encyclopedia vol. XII ch. 2 s. 251.

532 *E.g., Smith v. Leech Brain, Ltd.,* [1962] 2 Q.B. 405, 414-415.

533 *Wroth v. Tyler, supra* n. 405.

534 *Victoria Laundry (Windsor), Ltd. v. Newman Industries, Ltd., supra* n. 432; *cf. Corbin* § 1013.

535 (1854) 9 Ex. 341, 156 E.R. 145; *supra* s. 83.

The distinction may be illustrated by a line of AMERICAN cases concerning the liability of telegraph companies for loss resulting from failure in the transmission of messages.[536] If the message is in code the telegraph company is not liable for these losses; but if the message is in plain language and authorises a sale or purchase the telegraph company may (in the absence of a valid limitation of liability) be held liable for losses suffered because the transaction was not effected. However, these cases also illustrate the difficulties inherent in the distinction, for the mere knowledge of the telegraph company of the purpose of the customer in sending the message is not sufficient to fix it with liability.[537] At one time it was thought that the defendant was only liable for loss due to special circumstances if he actually contracted to bear such loss,[538] but this view has been rejected both in ENGLAND and in the UNITED STATES.[539] The exact degree of knowledge which the defendant must have is not easy to formulate. It has been said that the knowledge must be "clear and detailed,"[540] and that liability for loss based on special circumstances depends on "some knowledge and acceptance by one party of the purpose and intention of the other in entering into the contract."[541] A more precise formulation is probably impossible.

If the defendant knows some, but not all, of the special circumstances affecting the plaintiff his liability may be increased while not extending to the full loss. For example in the ENGLISH case mentioned in s. 85 above (*supra* n. 534) the seller of the machinery knew that the buyer wanted it for his business and knew of the nature of the business. He was accordingly held liable for loss of normal profits in that kind of business, and the decision may from this point of view be contrasted with that in *Hadley v. Baxendale* (*supra* n. 505). But the seller was not liable for loss of the exceptional profits as he did not know of the chance that these might be earned. Similar principles would apply where a defaulting seller of goods knew that the buyer wanted them for resale: the seller might be liable for loss of "ordinary" resale profits but not for additional losses suffered because the buyer had made an exceptionally profitable resale.[542] On the same principle the seller would not be liable for penalties which the buyer became liable to pay to a sub-buyer unless he had sufficient notice of the fact that the buyer would be exposed to such liability in consequence of his default.[543]

The distinction between losses which result in the ordinary course of things and those which result from special circumstances known to the defendant is also utilized in CIVIL LAW systems in which the concept of foreseeability is adopted as a means of limiting contractual liability. It appears here as one of the senses of the distinction between "abstract" and "concrete" assessment. In its most common sense, discussed in s. 69 above, that distinction looks at the situation which has arisen as a result of default from the plaintiff's point of view; but in the present context it is rather the defendant's point of view which is taken (*cf. supra* s. 72).

Under the foreseeability test, the general principle is one of "abstract" assessment. The defendant is held liable for such loss as a reasonable person (*un bon père de famille*) could have foreseen. The main point of the rule is that the defendant cannot reduce his liability by showing that he in fact foresaw less.[544] As has been pointed out, FRENCH CC art. 1150 makes the debtor liable for loss "*qu'*ON *a pu prévoir*" – not "*qu'*IL *a pu prévoir*."[545] But there is a considerable body of opinion which holds that "concrete" elements are not wholly excluded. The test has been said to be: what could a reasonable man placed in the circumstances of the debtor have foreseen?[546] These "circumstances" would appear to include known facts about the creditor's position and to this extent "concrete" elements enter into the question of foreseeability.

The distinction between "abstract" and "concrete" elements is less sharply drawn in FRENCH than in ANGLO-AMERICAN law because of the general principle that the assessment of damages is left to the discretion of the judge, with which the *Cour de Cassation* will only interfere if it has been exercised on wrong principles (*supra* s. 56). Decisions on points of the kind here under discussion will rarely be open to attack on grounds of principle; more usually they will simply turn on issues of fact.

[536] *Corbin* § 1018.

[537] *Newsome v. W.Union Telegraph Co.*, 153 N.C. 153, 69 S.E. 10 (1910).

[538] *Horne v. Midland Ry.* (1873), L.R. 8 C.P. 131, 141.

[539] *Treitel* 807; *Corbin* § 1010; UCC s. 2-715 comment 2.

[540] *Corbin* § 1016.

[541] *Weld-Blundell v. Stephens*, [1920] A.C. 956, 980 (H.L.).

[542] *Corbin* § 1015.

[543] *Ibidem.*

[544] J.-Cl.Civ. art. 1146-1155 fasc. VIII (1er cahier) no. 30.

[545] *Mazeaud and Tunc*, Traité III (ed. 5) no. 2381-2.

[546] *Ibidem.*

87. *Degree of foreseeability.* – It is not necessary, in any of the systems of law which use foreseeability as a test, to show that the defendant actually foresaw the loss though of course proof of this fact would normally be sufficient to satisfy the test. If the defendant's capacity for foresight is exceptionally high, he may therefore be liable for consequences for which a reasonable person would not have been liable. The words of FRENCH CC art. 1150 in referring to loss which was foreseen or could have been foreseen make this quite clear; and the position is the same in ANGLO-AMERICAN law.

The exact degree of foreseeability required has received comparatively little discussion. In FRANCE the standard is, as stated in s. 86 above, that of the reasonable man; and AMERICAN discussions of the subject also assume that this is the appropriate standard. The same assumption was widely made in ENGLAND, but the recent decision of the House of Lords in *The Heron II* (*supra* n. 508) has raised a doubt as to its correctness. The question arises because in COMMON LAW countries the test of foreseeability by a reasonable man is also used to limit liability in the law of torts; and in this branch of the law the reasonable man's capacity for foresight is often taken to extend to consequences of a very low degree of probability.[547] We are not here concerned with the question whether the imposition of such a severe standard is justifiable in the law of torts; but the House of Lords has taken the view that in contract cases it is too stringent a test and that it would fail adequately to limit the liability of the defendant.[548]

The imposition of a more severe standard (from the defendant's point of view) in tort than in contract cases may be justified on one of two grounds. The first is that a person injured by a tort is generally an involuntary victim, while a party to a contract is to some extent engaged in conscious risk-taking. The second is that a defendant's liability in contract should be limited at least to some extent by the risks that he may be supposed to have agreed to undertake. It is this very argument which has been advanced as the principal justification for the requirement of foreseeability in FRENCH law.[549]

The present position in ENGLISH law is that the courts tend in the contractual context to refer less and less to consequences which are "foreseeable". Instead, they have (since the decision in *The Heron II*) referred rather to such consequences as were "within the contemplation of the parties;" and this expression is taken to connote a higher degree of probability than foreseeability. The problem of degrees of foreseeability does not appear to have arisen in FRENCH law where the requirement of foreseeability does not exist at all in relation to delictual obligations. As a result it may be assumed that the courts have been able to mould the concept of foreseeability in a fashion appropriate to the contractual context; though in the absence of discussions of the point the degree of foreseeability required in FRENCH law must remain a matter of conjecture.

88. *Whose foreseeability.* – In *Hadley v. Baxendale* the court referred to consequences which arose naturally or such as might "reasonably be supposed to have been in the contemplation of *both parties* . . ."[550] The situation to which these words refer is that in which the plaintiff requires the subject-matter of the contract for some special purpose of which the defendant has notice. It is only in this sense that the consequence is required to be foreseeable by both parties. Where the loss is one which "arises naturally" it is foreseeability by the defendant which is the crucial factor, though in practice foreseeability by the plaintiff will in fact also exist. The main point of requiring "contemplation" by both parties is to emphasise that "contemplation" by the plaintiff is not enough. The position seems to be the same in FRENCH law. It is true that the wording of CC art. 1150 is equivocal; but most of the statements in the reports and in the books refer (if they raise the point at all) to foreseeability by the debtor or by a reasonable man in his position.[551] ULIS (*supra* s. 7) makes it quite clear that foreseeability by a reasonable person in the position of the party in breach is the criterion (art. 82, 86; 13).

89. *When loss must be foreseeable.* – It is necessary to refer yet again to the distinction drawn by the rule in *Hadley v. Baxendale* (*supra* n. 505) between losses which arise "naturally" and those which "may reasonably be supposed to have been in the contemplation of the parties." With regard to losses of the latter kind, the rule explicitly refers to *the time when the contract was made* as the time at which the loss must have been within the contemplation of the parties.

This is also generally considered to be the rele-

547 *Overseas Tankship (U.K.), Ltd. v. Morts Dock & Engineering Co., Ltd. (The Wagon Mound)*, [1961] A.C. 388 (P.C.); *The Wagon Mound (No. 2), Overseas Tankship (U.K.), Ltd. v. The Miller Steamship Co. Pty. and Another*, [1967] 1 A.C. 617 (P.C.).

548 *The Heron II, supra* n. 508.

549 *Mazeaud*, Leçons II no. 629.

550 *Supra* n. 505, p. 354.

551 *E.g. Mazeaud and Tunc*, Traité III (ed. 5) no. 2381–2.

vant time in relation to losses of the first kind, *i.e.* those arising "naturally". It is thought to be unjust to increase the defendant's burden by communicating facts relevant to his potential liability after he has become bound by the contract.[552] For if he had known these facts at the time of entering into the contract he might have charged more, or have limited his liability by an exclusion clause, or in extreme cases have refused to enter into the contract at all; and, as the court said in *Hadley v. Baxendale*, it would be unjust to deprive the defendant of these opportunities.[553] The argument has been criticised as unrealistic:[554] in other words, on the ground that the defendant might not have reacted in any of the suggested ways to the communication of factors increasing the risk. But the criticism is as speculative as the view it seeks to combat; and in any event the rule as to the time of foreseeability is well settled and has proved remarkably resistant to change.

In the UNITED STATES, for example, the original draft of *Field*'s Civil Code (*supra* s. 31) provided that the defendant should be liable for losses of which he had "notice at the time of entering into the contract, or at any time before the breach, and while it was in his power to perform upon his part, would be likely to result from such breach" (s. 1840). This variation of the rule as to time of foreseeability was conspicuously omitted by the legislatures of the various states which have adopted the Code or substantial parts of it.[555] Other statutory provisions in the UNITED STATES and elsewhere expressly adopt the rule as to time of foreseeability laid down in *Hadley v. Baxendale*;[556] and the Uniform Commercial Code likewise makes the seller's liability for "consequential loss" depend on his knowledge of the buyer's needs at the time of contracting (s. 2-715(2)(a)); and ULIS adopts the same rule (art. 82, 86). The question has recently been reconsidered in ISRAEL, where the Contracts (Remedies for Breach of Contracts) Law 1970 again refers to damage which could have been foreseen at the time of contracting.[557]

In the UNITED STATES, a somewhat narrower suggestion has been made that, in the case of a "wilful" breach, foreseeability at the time when the defendant chose to commit the breach should be the criterion.[558] As yet the suggestion has neither been generally accepted nor decisively rejected in COMMON LAW countries. Under FRENCH CC art. 1150 foreseeability at the time of contracting is expressly made the criterion. But in the case just put, of a "wilful" breach, the debtor would probably be held guilty of "fraud" so that he would not be able to rely at all on the defence that a particular loss was unforeseeable.

90. *Scope of the foreseeability test.* – In COMMON LAW countries courts and writers have sometimes shown a tendency to apply the foreseeability test to situations which are in fact outside its scope. In particular, it has sometimes been applied where the question is simply one of quantification, that is, where the question is whether the aggrieved party's loss is to be quantified by reference to market prices or in some other way, and if by market prices at what time. One ENGLISH case, for example, appears to apply the test so as to hold that, although the defendant was in principle liable for a particular item of loss, market fluctuations were to be left out of account in measuring his liability.[559] But the case had been doubted both in ENGLAND and in the UNITED STATES, and it seems unlikely that it will be followed on this point.[560]

ULIS (*supra* s. 7) makes it quite clear that foreseeability is a test of remoteness and not one of quantification. After laying down rules by which damages may be assessed either concretely by reference to an actual substitute contract, or abstractly by reference to market prices (art. 84, 85), it provides that such damages "may be increased by the amount of any loss, including loss of profit, which should have been foreseen by the party in breach . . ." (art. 86). There is no question of applying the foreseeability test to the process of assessing the value of the very thing of which the aggrieved party has been deprived by the breach.

In FRENCH law foreseeability is not mentioned in discussions of such problems whether, and if so at what point of time, market prices are to be taken into account (*supra* s. 69 and 71). The various

[552] *Patterson v. Illinois Central Ry. Co.*, 123 Ky. 783, 97 S.W. 423 (1906).

[553] *Supra* n. 505, p. 355.

[554] *Corbin* § 1008.

[555] See the corresponding provisions in CALIFORNIAN CC § 3300; Revised Codes of MONTANA (*supra* n. 137) § 17-301; NORTH DAKOTA Century Code (*supra* n. 154) § 32-03-09; OKLAHOMA Statutes (*supra* n. 187) § 23-21; SOUTH DAKOTA Compiled Laws (*supra* n. 154) § 21-2-1.

[556] GEORGIA Code (*supra* n. 142) § 20-1407; INDIAN Contract Act, 1872 (*supra* n. 241) s. 73.

[557] Contracts (Remedies for Breach of Contracts) Law 1970 (*supra* n. 481) s. 10.

[558] *Corbin* § 1008, discussing various possible meanings of "wilful" in this context.

[559] *Smeed v. Foord* (1859), 1 E. & E. 602, 120 E.R. 1035.

[560] *Treitel* 789; *Corbin* § 1013; *cf. Wroth v. Tyler*, *supra* n. 405.

"market" rules relate to the method and time of evaluating losses to which the defendant's liability is assumed to extend. The foreseeability test, on the other hand, relates to the definition of the kind or items of loss for which damages are recoverable at all. It is a test of limitation rather than one of evaluation. It applies most frequently where the problem is to what extent a defendant is liable for consequential loss; indeed in the Uniform Commercial Code the test is only explicitly stated in this particular context (s. 2-715 (2) (a)).

All this is not to say that the question whether damages can be recovered for loss due to a fall in the market may not be subject to the foreseeability test. For example, where a carrier is guilty of delay the shipper will not lose *the goods*, but he may lose *the chance of selling them in the market* at the destination at the time when they should have arrived. The carrier will be liable for the resulting loss if *that chance* was something that he could have foreseen.[561] But once it has been held that liability of the carrier is to be assessed on this basis, such questions as the time of assessment and the extent of the loss suffered by reason of the fall in the market do not depend in foreseeability.

iii. *Causation*

91. *General.* – Causation is the principal method of limiting liability in GERMAN law; and it is also used for this purpose, in addition to foreseeability, in FRENCH law and to some extent in ANGLO-AMERICAN law. As the subject is fully dealt with in vol. XI ch. 7 of this Encyclopedia, a comparatively brief survey, stressing the application of the concept in the contractual context, will suffice here.

92. *Theory of "adequate causation" in German law.* – GERMAN law rejects foreseeability as a method of limiting liability for default in the performance of a contract.[562] This fact makes it possible for a GERMAN writer to ask (even if rhetorically) whether a tailor who delays in delivering travelling clothes to a customer who in consequence travels on a later train which crashes is to be made liable to the customer for the personal injuries which he suffers in the crash.[563] In ANGLO-AMERICAN and FRENCH law such injuries would plainly be regarded as unforeseeable. GERMAN law proceeds on the initial assumption that a debtor is liable for loss caused by his default;[564] but in the case put recovery would be denied on the ground that the causal connection between the tailor's default and the customer's personal injury was not sufficiently close or strong.

For this purpose the law rejects the theory that an event is caused by the totality of the conditions which bring it about. Such a theory would insufficiently limit the liability of the party in default. Instead GERMAN law adopts the theory of so-called "adequate" causal connection (*adäquater Kausalzusammenhang; Adäquanztheorie*). The theory does not, any more than the test of foreseeability, lend itself to mechanical application or to the formulation of precise rules. In the last resort, questions of causal connection are often questions of fact which depend to a great extent on the discretion of the judge.[565] But even so there are certain general principles which the judge is bound to observe.

The theory of "adequate causation" holds[566] that a wrongdoer is liable for a loss if his default appreciably increased the objective possibility of loss of a kind that in fact occurred;[567] on the other hand, he is under no liability if his default was, according to the ordinary course of things, quite indifferent with regard to the consequence which in fact occurred, and only became a condition of the occurrence of the loss as a result of unusual or intervening events.[568] In determining whether the default is of the former or of the latter character, the court applies the standard of an experienced observer at the time of the default, or even according to one formulation, that of the most experienced observer (*optimaler Beobachter*). To such an observer the court attributes knowledge of all the circumstances of which a person of that kind could have known, as well as any additional circumstances of which the wrongdoer himself actually knew.[569]

The theory is most frequently applied to tort cases and some of the results of its application in such cases have been extremely favourable to plaintiffs. Thus in one case a person who had suffered personal injury was taken to hospital

[561] *The Heron II, supra* n. 508.

[562] *Enneccerus and Lehmann* 73; AUSTRIA: *Klang (-Wolff)* VI § 1294 no. I 1 e (p. 12).

[563] *Enneccerus and Lehmann* 61; *cf. Larenz* I 318 (A injures B whose journey by air is delayed for a few days and the aeroplane on which B later travels crashes: no adequate causal connection).

[564] The wording of (for example) CC § 286 par. 1 is based on this assumption.

[565] *Enneccerus and Lehmann* 73.

[566] *Idem* 65-75; *Larenz* I 315-325.

[567] BGH 23 Oct. 1951, BGHZ 3, 261 at 267; RG 22 June 1931, RGZ 133, 126.

[568] *Enneccerus and Lehmann* 66.

[569] BGH 23 Oct. 1951, BGHZ 3, 261 at 266-267.

where he was infected with influenza and died. It was held that the person who had caused the original injury was liable for the death.[570] In another case a person lost a leg as a result of an accident for which the defendant was responsible. He accordingly had to wear an artificial limb and 20 years later he fell in consequence of his reduced mobility and suffered further injury. It was held that the original defendant was liable for this further injury.[571] These decisions have been criticised;[572] but even setting such extreme cases aside the efficacy of the theory of adequate causation as a method of limiting a defendant's liability has been doubted.[573] These doubts have led to the formulation of rival theories, additional limitations on recovery, and to proposals for reform, which will be discussed below.

The examples given to illustrate the theory of adequate causation in the field of contract are not so extreme as the tort cases just mentioned. But even in contract cases the loss may be "adequately caused" by a default which is not its immediate cause. Thus where an order to sell shares in a mine is not carried out and subsequently the mine is flooded, so that the owner of the shares suffers financial loss, it is considered that that loss is adequately caused by the failure to carry out the instructions.[574]

There has been much dispute about the relationship between the theory of adequate causation and CC § 252. This paragraph provides that damages may include lost gain; and it goes on in its second sentence to say that lost gain is such gain as could be expected as probable in the ordinary course of things or in the special circumstances, having regard to preparations and provisions made by the aggrieved party. According to one view, lost gain is *only* recoverable if these requirements have been complied with. But the more general view is that CC § 252 is not meant to restrict liability to the circumstances which it specifies. It is only a rule of evidence, intended to facilitate proof that loss of gain has indeed been suffered.[575] The requirement of adequate causation remains in principle both sufficient and necessary, so that it must be found that the plaintiff would, but for the default, indeed have made the gain which he says that he has lost.

In practice it will generally suffice for the plaintiff to show that the circumstances envisaged by the second sentence of CC § 252 exist. Once this is shown the fact that the gain would have been made will normally be presumed. Of course under the test of "adequate causation" the defendant could still limit his liability by showing that the default did not appreciably increase the objective possibility of loss of a kind that in fact occurred. This might be the case, for example, where the loss resulted from the fact that the plaintiff intended to make some highly unusual and exceptionally profitable use of the subject-matter of the contract, of which the defendant did not have notice.

93. *Relations to foreseeability.* – It is said by GERMAN writers that their system does not admit the test of foreseeability for the purpose of limiting liability.[576] The legislative history of the Civil Code shows a deliberate rejection of this test; and some of the cases mentioned in s. 92 above support the same view. And yet some of the expressions used in formulating the theory of "adequate causation" bear a striking resemblance to those used in stating the ANGLO-AMERICAN rules of remoteness in contract.

Both sets of statements refer to losses which occur "in the ordinary course of things", or according to "the common experience of mankind".[577] Both employ the standard of the reasonable man – the GERMAN statements in order to determine what happens in the ordinary course of things and the ANGLO-AMERICAN ones in order to determine what is "foreseeable". A SWISS writer in stating the theory of adequate causation actually uses the concept of foreseeability;[578] while a FRENCH writer regards the GERMAN theory as indistinguishable from the rule of reasonable foreseeability applied by the ENGLISH court.[579] Both the GERMAN and the ANGLO-AMERICAN statements attribute to the reasonable person or observer the knowledge of surrounding circumstances which such a person could normally be expected to have, and also such additional

570 RG 13 Oct. 1922, RGZ 105, 264.

571 RG 5 Dec. 1927, RGZ 119, 204; contrast BGH 24 April 1952, NJW 1952, 1010 where a person who had been made lame in an accident was later killed by artillery fire from which he might have been able to escape, had he been able to run faster.

572 *Enneccerus and Lehmann* 69; *Larenz* I 317.

573 *Ibidem.*

574 *Enneccerus and Lehmann* 68.

575 *Idem* 73-74; *Larenz* I 344-345.

576 *Enneccerus and Lehmann* 73.

577 *Larenz* I 318.

578 *Guhl* 71; but *cf. supra* s. 84 at n. 523.

579 *Carbonnier* IV 320.

knowledge as the defendant in fact had.[580] In practice there must often be a considerable degree of similarity between the two theories;[581] but in the crucial borderline cases the GERMAN theory of adequate causation would lead to results which are more favourable to the plaintiff than the ANGLO-AMERICAN theory of foreseeability.

The point may be illustrated by reference to an example used in GERMAN discussions of liability for lost gain. A vendor of a house fails to convey and in consequence the purchaser is unable to accept an exceptionally high offer which a third party makes for the house. In such a case it is said that the defaulting vendor is liable for loss of the profit which the purchaser could have made on resale to the third party.[582] Under the ANGLO-AMERICAN rules such exceptional "loss of profit" would probably be regarded as unforeseeable; the purchaser could at most recover in respect of an ordinary loss of profit on the transaction.[583] The GERMAN view appears to be that, so long as the "kind" of loss suffered satisfies the "adequate causation" test the defendant is liable to the full "extent" of the loss. This position should also be contrasted with the rule of FRENCH law which requires foreseeability of the "kind" and "extent" of loss. This rule is discussed in s. 85 above, where it is suggested that the FRENCH position is the same as the ANGLO-AMERICAN one. Of course what has been said about the scope of the foreseeability test (*supra* s. 90) must be borne in mind. If the purchaser in our case suffered loss simply because he had to buy a substitute house at a higher price, he could recover such loss even though the extent of the price-rise was unforeseeable. There is no doubt that the seller is liable for the cost of a substitute, whether assessed abstractly or concretely, and the question in the case put is not one of remoteness at all, but of quantification.[584]

A further distinction between these systems and GERMAN law is the time at which the test adopted by each of them is applied. In GERMAN law the relevant time appears to be that of the act or default giving rise to liability.[585] It is true that this rule is stated primarily in relation to tort cases; but no differentiation is made between these cases and cases of breach of contract. In ANGLO-AMERICAN and FRENCH law, the foreseeability test is (as is pointed out in s. 89 above) applied at the time of contracting. In theory this difference could favour either party, but in practice the GERMAN rule on this point is again likely to favour the plaintiff and thus to reduce still further the degree of protection which the test of "adequate causation" affords to a defendant.

94. *Alternative theory: purpose of the contract.* – The practical effect of the theory of "adequate causation" and the rejection by GERMAN law of the principle of foreseeability is often felt to be that insufficient protection is given to the defendant. Attempts have therefore been made to find other methods of limiting his liability. One possibility is to rely for this purpose on the general good faith provision contained in CC § 242; but this approach has rightly been criticised as productive of too much uncertainty.[586]

The most important alternative method of limiting liability is based on the theory that regard should be had to the purpose of the rule of law which imposes the liability.[587] In the contractual context, the criterion becomes the meaning and purpose of the contract under which the liability arises. This theory comes very close indeed to the COMMON LAW rule of foreseeability, which in some cases at least makes the extent of liability depend on the "purpose and intention" (*supra* n. 541) of one party as known to the other.

It has been objected that if the theory depends on the defendant's subjective capacity for foresight it would too severely circumscribe his liability; whereas if the criterion is objective the theory comes close to the theory of adequate causation.[588] One admitted difference, however, is that the present theory takes its stand at the time of contracting and not (like the theory of "adequate causation") at the time of default. Another difference between the two theories would appear to be that even objective foreseeability does not necessarily limit liability under the theory of "adequate causation". The "purpose of the contract" theory would certainly appear to be capable of producing more satisfactory results in limiting liability than the "adequate causation" theory; but it seems that the latter theory is still supported by the courts.

95. *Requirement of "directness" in French law.* – FRENCH law imposes, in addition to foreseeability, the further requirement that the damage must be,

[580] BGH 23 Oct. 1951, BGHZ 3, 267; *Victoria Laundry (Windsor), Ltd. v. Newman Industries, Ltd.* (*supra* n. 432) 539.

[581] *Cf.* RG 5 Dec. 1927, RGZ 119, 204 (*supra* n. 571) with *Wieland v. Cyril Lord Carpets, Ltd.*, [1969] 3 All E.R. 1006 (Q.B.) (where the interval between the two accidents was, however, much shorter).

[582] *Enneccerus and Lehmann* 74.

[583] Under the *Victoria Laundry* case, *supra* n. 432.

[584] *Wroth v. Tyler, supra* n. 405; *supra* s. 85.

[585] *Enneccerus and Lehmann* 68; *Larenz* I 316.

[586] *Enneccerus and Lehmann* 70.

[587] *Larenz* I 318 ss.

[588] *Idem* I 320.

in the words of CC art. 1151, an "immediate and direct[589] consequence" of the non-performance of the contract. The requirement is often illustrated by a famous example given by *Pothier*:[590] if a person sells a cow knowing that it is diseased and conceals this fact, he is guilty of fraud, making him liable not only for the loss of the cow itself but also for the loss of the buyer's other animals which are infected by the disease. But he is not liable for the loss which the buyer suffers through not being able, on account of the loss of the other animals, to cultivate his lands; nor *a fortiori* for the loss which he suffers through not being able, on account of inability to cultivate his lands, to pay his debts so that his creditors levy execution on his property.

The distinction between direct and indirect damage is thus easy enough to illustrate, but much harder to define. The point can be made by reference to another illustration given by *Pothier*[591] of a tenant who is evicted from a house let to him for business purposes. In such a case, it is said, the lessor is liable not only for removal expenses and repayment of rents but also "in some degree" for loss of custom if the tenant cannot find another suitable house in the neighbourhood from which to conduct his business.

Sometimes the distinction between direct and indirect damage is made to depend on foreseeability;[592] but this is clearly regarded by the Civil Code as a separate requirement. Sometimes reference is made to specific factors making damage indirect: for example, to the fact that the damage was the result of an external cause for which the defendant was not responsible;[593] or to the general rule that physical harm to one person causing loss to a second is indirect damage so far as the second is concerned.[594] But obviously these last examples do not exhaust the concept of directness (or rather indirectness), as a comparison of them with *Pothier*'s case of the diseased cow will show; and the view has been expressed that no fixed principles, but only guidelines of a general kind, can be laid down to determine the question of "directness" in particular cases.[595]

There are relatively few decisions which illustrate the requirement of "directness" in contract. Most of the decided cases concern liability in delict: paradoxically, because CC art. 1151 is in terms restricted to contract and has only been extended to the field of delictual liability by judicial interpretation. No doubt the explanation for the scarcity of contract cases illustrating the requirement of directness is that in many such cases the defendant's liability is adequately limited by the test of foreseeability. This fact makes the dispute between the various theories of causation in FRENCH law of relatively small importance in the contractual context.[596]

According to one theory, that of the *équivalence des conditions*, every fact without which the damage would not have occurred is a cause making the actor liable; but the severity of this theory from the defendant's point of view is mitigated in contract cases by the requirement of foreseeability and in tort cases (where it is not so mitigated) it has been rejected.[597] The rival theory, that of *causalité adéquate*, is based on the GERMAN concept discussed in s. 92 above; and in FRANCE at least it has been interpreted to mean very little more than foreseeability.

Most of the contract cases on the requirement of directness deal with the effect of some "extraneous" event, which intervenes between the breach of contract and the damage. Cases of this kind will be discussed in s. 97 below; here it is only necessary to point out that in *Pothier*'s case of the sale of the diseased cow, the buyer is denied recovery in respect of inability to cultivate his land even though there is no intervention of an "extraneous" event. This is equally true of one of the decisions on the issue of "directness" in a contractual context. A carrier in breach of contract caused damage to a piece of agricultural machinery. As a result the consignees were unable to perform a contract which required use of the machinery; and they also claimed damages in respect of further contracts which they might have made with adjoining landowners, had the latter seen the machine in operation. Damages under this second head were disallowed on the ground that such damages were not "immediate and direct" consequences of the breach.[598]

It has been said that the irrecoverable losses in these cases are not "necessary" consequences of the fact that the cow was diseased or the machinery

589 It is not clear what difference, if any, is intended to be conveyed by the use of the *two* words "immediate" and "direct": *cf. De Page* III no. 110.

590 *Pothier*, Traité des obligations (Paris 1761) no. 166–167; *cf. supra* n. 251.

591 *Supra* n. 590, no. 162.

592 *Carbonnier* IV 317.

593 *Idem* IV 317–318.

594 *Idem* IV 305.

595 *Idem* IV 320.

596 *Idem* IV 319–320; *Mazeaud*, Traité II (ed. 6) no. 1438 ss.

597 *Mazeaud*, Traité II (ed. 6) no. 1442–2.

598 Cass.civ. 3 March 1897, D. 1898.1.118.

damaged;[599] but this substitution of "necessary" for "immediate and direct" carries the matter very little further. If in this context "necessary" consequences of the default are to be contrasted with consequences which could equally well have occurred without the default, it is a little hard to see why, in the case of the diseased cow, the loss suffered through the buyer's inability to cultivate his land should not be recoverable.

96. *Position in Anglo-American law.* – The requirement of directness in ANGLO-AMERICAN law is perhaps illustrated by an old case "where a man going to be married to an heiress, his horse having cast a shoe on the journey, employed a blacksmith to replace it, who did the work so unskilfully that the horse was lamed, and, the rider not arriving in time, the lady married another; and the blacksmith was held liable for the loss of the marriage."[600] In a later case from which the above account is taken this result was described as an "absurdity"[601] and there is no doubt that this view would be generally accepted today. But it would almost certainly be explained not on the ground of directness but on the ground of foreseeability; and conversely in COMMON LAW countries the fact that a loss is foreseeable may suffice to make a defendant liable for it even though it is not the "direct" consequence of the defendant's default.

It is interesting from this point of view to compare the techniques used by FRENCH and ENGLISH law in the solution of basically similar problems. We have seen (*supra* s. 84) that in ENGLISH law loss resulting from the plaintiff's own lack of means is considered to arise from a "separate and concurrent cause" and not from the defendant's wrongful act, but that such loss is nevertheless recoverable in a contractual action if it is foreseeable. In the case which supports this rule (*supra* n. 526), the resulting loss was in fact suffered because the impecunious plaintiff's property was subjected to a forced sale which he could have avoided, had the defendant performed his contract. This is precisely one of the kinds of loss which in *Pothier*'s example of the diseased cow (*supra* s. 95) is regarded as "indirect". There is little doubt that an ENGLISH court, if confronted by *Pothier*'s case, would simply apply the foreseeability test and not discuss "directness" or "causation" at all. No doubt the result would generally be the same as that given by *Pothier*, and accepted by modern FRENCH writers, but this would depend on the extent of the seller's knowledge of the buyer's circumstances.

Similar arguments would apply to the FRENCH case discussed in s. 95 above in which a carrier in breach of contract delivered agricultural machinery in damaged condition (*supra* n. 598). The question whether the carrier could be held liable for loss suffered by the consignee on account of his inability to enter into profitable contracts involving the use of the machinery would depend on foreseeability; and under the rule in *Hadley v. Baxendale* (*supra* n. 505) as interpreted in later cases the application of this test would turn on the defendant's capacity for foresight, influenced by factors of the kind discussed in s. 86 above, such as the defendant's knowledge of special circumstances.

Another group of FRENCH cases concerns the liability of a landlord for loss of property stolen from his tenant as a result of the inattention of a porter employed by the landlord.[602] Many of the cases deny liability here on one or both of two grounds: that the landlord is not guilty of "fault" and that, even if he is, the theft is not the direct consequence of the fault. It would seem that the second ground of decision could be overcome by showing that the default had increased the possibility of the loss. In COMMON LAW countries there would likewise be, in general, no duty on the landlord to prevent the theft of his tenant's property, which is equivalent to saying that the theft was not due to the landlord's "fault".[603] But such a duty might be expressly or impliedly undertaken; and given the existence and breach of a duty the COMMON LAW would only enquire whether the theft was the foreseeable consequence of the breach and would not insist on a separate requirement of "directness".[604] There have, it is true, been occasional departures from this principle but they have been criticized precisely on the ground that the loss should be recoverable if it was foreseeable and that if this was the case there was no further requirement of "directness".[605]

599 *Mazeaud*, Leçons II no. 570; *Planiol and Ripert* VII no. 859.

600 Referred to in *British Columbia Saw-Mill Co., Ltd. v. Nettleship* (1868), L.R. 3 C.P. 499, 510.

601 *Ibidem.*

602 Cass.civ. 24 May 1948, D. 1948, 375; Cass.civ. 8 April 1941, D. 1945 J.13, note *Tunc.*

603 *Cf., Edwards v. West Herts Group Hospital Management Committee*, [1957] 1 W.L.R. 415 (C.A.) (there was no relation of landlord and tenant here but the same principle would clearly have applied if there had been such a relationship).

604 *Cf., Stansbie v. Troman*, [1948] 2 K.B. 48 (C.A.).

605 *E.g., Nirdlinger v. American District Telephone Co.*, 245 Pa. 453, 91 A. 883 (1914) (no liability where goods were stolen in consequence of failure to perform contract to keep a burglar alarm set): criticised by *Corbin* § 1000. In an AUSTRIAN case failure to deliver a

The INDIAN Contract Act appears in s. 73 to lay down both requirements in that it first uses words which are meant to reproduce the rule in *Hadley v. Baxendale* and then continues with the words that "compensation is not to be given for any remote or indirect loss or damage sustained by reason of a breach of contract." However, it has been said that s. 73 is only declaratory of the COMMON LAW,[606] and the words just quoted have not in fact been held to impose a requirement of "directness" in addition to that of foreseeability. Another way of putting the same point is that in COMMON LAW countries foreseeability is sometimes said to be the test of causation. This view has already been considered in s. 84 above.

To avoid confusion, it should be pointed out that the requirement of causation is sometimes discussed in cases in which the issue is whether the defendant's conduct contributed in any way at all to the plaintiff's loss. If for example the plaintiff alleges that his animals died as a result of eating allegedly poisonous feeding stuffs supplied by the defendant, the plaintiff will not succeed in a claim for damages if the source of the poisoning is in fact quite different. Or, to take another example, a ship may be technically unseaworthy because she is not carrying a proper medicine chest; but this would not normally be the cause of her foundering in a storm.[607] The foregoing discussion has assumed that there is *some* causal connection between the defendant's default and the plaintiff's loss; the question has been how close or effective that connection must be.

97. *Several causes.* – It is well settled, in all the legal systems under review, that the defendant may be liable although his failure to perform the contract is not the sole cause of the loss. As the point has been put in an ENGLISH case: "If a breach of contract is one of two causes, both co-operating and both of equal efficacy ... it is sufficient to carry a judgment for damages."[608] In the leading *Monarch Steamship* case (*supra* n. 526) a British ship had been chartered for a voyage beginning in April 1939 to carry a cargo from Manchuria to a Swedish port. She was delayed by unseaworthiness. If she had not been delayed she could have reached the agreed destination before the outbreak of war in September 1939, but when that event occurred she was directed by the British authorities to a Scottish port and prohibited from going on to Sweden. In order to get the cargo to the agreed destination, the charterer had to have it transshipped in Scotland to neutral ships. It was held that the charterer could recover damages from the shipowner amounting to the cost of transshipment. The shipowner was liable for this loss even though the unseaworthiness was not the sole cause of the loss. Nor was the loss too remote a consequence of the unseaworthiness as, in the opinion of the House of Lords, the outbreak of war and the embargo were foreseeable events.[609]

In an AMERICAN case it was similarly held that a seller who broke his contract to deliver components to a manufacturer could not escape liability on the ground that the manufacturer also suffered from a shortage of other components. It was not even necessary for the manufacturer to show that the seller's breach was a "chief" cause so long as it was "a substantial factor in bringing about the harm."[610] A very similar example occurs in a GERMAN discussion of the problem: if two suppliers of parts of a machine are guilty of delay in delivery, so that the machine remains idle, each may be liable for the resulting loss,[611] though the owner of the machine cannot of course recover this loss twice over.

The ENGLISH, AMERICAN and GERMAN solutions all assume either that the defendant (whose default constitutes one of a number of causes of the loss) is fully liable, or that he is not liable at all. The possibility of holding him liable to a reduced extent, in proportion to the degree to which his fault contributed to the loss, has not generally been considered. The only situation in which such reduction is regarded as possible in these systems is in the special case where the loss is partly caused by the act of the plaintiff himself: this situation will be discussed in s. 106 below.

In FRANCE, however, a more general principle has been developed of reducing damages where the loss is partly caused by an extraneous event

safety grille was held to have "caused" loss of goods from the premises by theft: *Klang (-Wolff)* VI § 1294 no. I 1 e (p. 10).

606 *Jamal v. Moolla Dawood, Sons & Co.*, [1916] 1 A.C. 175, 180 (P.C.).

607 Example given in *Monarch S.S. Co. v. Karlshamns Oljefabriker* (*supra* n. 526) 226.

608 *Heskell v. Continental Express, Ltd.*, [1950] 1 All E.R. 1033, 1048 (K.B.).

609 An AMERICAN case, *The Malcom Baxter Jr.*, 277 U.S. 323 (1928) was distinguished on the ground that the loss in that case was not foreseeable.

610 *Kraus v. Greenbarg*, 137 F.2d 569, 572 (3 Cir. 1943); *cf. Monarch SS.* case (*supra* n. 526) at 227 ("dominant cause").

611 *Enneccerus and Lehmann* 73; contrast *Hadley v. Baxendale* (*supra* n. 505) 356 (*supra* s. 83) where one reason given for the decision was the supposition that "at the time of the delivery to the carrier the machinery of the mill had been in other respects defective".

for which neither party was responsible. The principle is derived from the famous *Lamoricière* case[612] in which an unseaworthy ship sank in an exceptionally severe storm, and many of the passengers were drowned. In an action brought by the dependants of one of the passengers it was held that the disaster was caused as to 4/5 by the storm and as to 1/5 by the unseaworthiness. Damages were awarded on this basis: that is, the defendants were held liable for 1/5 of the loss. The action was brought in delict, but it seems that the principle would equally apply in a contractual action.

The mathematical division of responsibility has not escaped criticism and even ridicule on account of its arbitrary character.[613] But it is in truth no more or less arbitrary than the division which is undertaken in many jurisdictions in cases where the loss is partly due to the act of the plaintiff, or where the loss is caused by more than one defendant and has to be apportioned between them.[614] In cases of the latter kind the process of apportionment only takes place as between the defendants, each of whom is assumed to be fully liable to the plaintiff. It is arguable that this assumption is inconsistent with the principle of the *Lamoricière* case,[615] and that if the defendant cannot show that the extraneous event is the sole cause of the loss he ought to be held fully liable.[616] Recent decisions of the FRENCH courts have caused considerable doubts as to the correctness of the *Lamoricière* decision.[617] Nevertheless the principle of the case may well provide a more satisfactory solution in cases of this kind than the "all or nothing rule" generally adopted in COMMON LAW countries.

It is interesting to note that a decision very similar to that in the *Lamoricière* case has recently been reached in a contract case in an EAST AFRICAN country whose law is based on COMMON LAW principles.[618] A tenant stored a drum of petrol on premises which had been let to him and thereby committed a breach of the terms of his lease. A fire broke out for which the tenant was not to blame. This fire would have caused severe damage to the premises even if the petrol had not been there. When the fire reached the petrol there was an explosion and the premises were totally destroyed. It was held that the tenant was liable for the value of the premises *less* the amount of the damage which they would have suffered in any event, that is if he had not broken his contract by storing petrol there. Of course such a rule gives rise to difficulties of proof; but where these can be overcome this method of assessment seems in principle to be more satisfactory than one which either denies the plaintiff all recovery or makes the defendant fully liable for consequences only partly caused by his default.

The rule in the *Lamoricière* case is in practice likely to benefit the defendant; and it may be that the need to protect him is more acutely felt in FRENCH law (which does not impose the requirement of foreseeability in tort cases) than in COMMON LAW systems (which do protect the defendant in this way). If this is the justification for the principle it is of course arguable that it should not be applied to contract cases precisely because in such cases the defendant is, in FRENCH law, already protected by the two requirements of foreseeability and directness. Any further reduction of liability for loss caused by extraneous events would (on the basis of the argument) unduly prejudice the plaintiff. But in fact the distinction between delictual and contractual liability has not been relied upon to limit the scope of the *Lamoricière* principle.

Under the foreseeability test (whether applied in contract in FRANCE or in contract and tort in COMMON LAW countries) the plaintiff in the *Lamoricière* case might actually have fared worse; and the same is possibly true under tests of causation applied to similar situations in COMMON LAW countries. In the *Monarch Steamship* case mentioned above, a distinction was drawn between the facts of that case and one in which a ship was delayed by unseaworthiness and then struck by a thunderbolt or by lightning or by a typhoon; and it was said that in such a case the shipowner would not be liable as the unseaworthiness would have no "real" but only a "fortuitous" connection with the destruction of the ship.[619]

[612] Cass.civ. 19 June 1951, S. 1952.1.89; *infra* n. 613.

[613] Note *Ripert* to Cass.com. 19 June 1951, D. 1951, 717; note *Bequé* to Cass. com. 19 June 1951, J.C.P. 1951.II.6426; note *Mazeaud and Mazeaud*, Rev.trim. dr.civ. 1951, 515; *Carbonnier* IV 323.

[614] For example, in ENGLAND under Law Reform (Contributory Negligence) Act, 1945 (8, 9 & 10 Geo. 6, c. 28) and Law Reform (Married Women and Tortfeasors) Act, 1935 (25 & 26 Geo.5, c.30) s. 6.

[615] *Mazeaud and Tunc*, Traité II (ed. 5) no. 1444 n. 2 *bis*; but for the present the FRENCH courts have reaffirmed that each defendant is fully liable: *Mazeaud*, Traité II (ed. 6) no. 1444.

[616] Note *Mazeaud and Mazeaud*, Rev.trim.dr.civ. 1951, 516.

[617] *Mazeaud*, Traité II (ed. 6) no. 1612.

[618] *Rehmtulla Bandali v. Commissioner of Transport*, [1969] H.C.D. (Tanzania) no. 293.

[619] [1949] A.C. 196, 215 (H.L.) approving a statement in the court below: 1947 S.C. 179, 193.

The facts of this hypothetical example are very close to those of the *Lamoricière* case, in which the ship encountered "*une tempête d'une extrême violence, à caractère de cyclone*". It is not clear whether the storm was of a wholly unusual and unforeseeable violence in the area in which the ship went down, but if it was the plaintiff would in a COMMON LAW jurisdiction have recovered no damages at all.

iv. *Judicial Discretion*

98. *Imprecision of rules relating to damages.* – An ENGLISH judge has observed that "the assessment of damages is not an exact science"[620] and this point is reflected in the large degree of discretion left to judges in all legal systems in the performance of this task. The exercise of this discretion is partly necessitated by the imprecise and open-textured nature of the rules which determine the bases of assessment and the limitations on recoverable loss.

In COMMON LAW countries it is, for example, by no means well settled exactly when damages will be based on the expectation as opposed to the reliance or restitution interests, or to what extent one of these bases can be combined with another (*supra* s. 60-62). Nor, when expectation is protected, is there any very clear rule which determines when the plaintiff can recover the cost of cure and when the difference in value resulting from the breach (*supra* s. 66). The power of the court to choose between the various possible methods of assessment obviously gives it a very considerable discretion as to the size of the ultimate award.

Further discretionary elements are introduced by the rules limiting the plaintiff's right of recovery. Under the rules relating to remoteness loss must be "foreseeable" or "within the reasonable contemplation of parties" or "direct and immediate" or such as occurs "in the ordinary course of things" (*supra* s. 82 ss.); and it is obvious that none of these phrases has any very precise meaning. The same is true of the rule that an aggrieved party must (and need only) act reasonably in mitigation (*infra* s. 102). All these factors support the view that "The rules of law governing the recovery of damages for breach of contract are very flexible."[621] Although this view is based on the ANGLO-AMERICAN law, it is equally true of the other systems here under discussion. In all of them the rules which determine the assessment of damages contain a considerable element of vagueness; and this gives the courts a great deal of discretion, though the rules may not overtly recognize this.

99. *Discretion as to damages expressly conferred.* – There is, however, another group of cases in which discretion is more or less expressly conferred. In these cases the judge's discretion is not one that *arises under* the rules governing the extent of recoverable damages but one that exists as a *substitute for* such rules or one that gives the court a power to override or disregard rules even of the low degree of precision mentioned in s. 98 above.

The leading illustration of this technique is SWISS CO art. 43 par. 1, which gives the judge the power to determine the kind and extent of compensation and simply requires him to have regard to the circumstances of the case and to the extent of the debtor's fault. CO art. 44 goes on to provide *inter alia* that if a defendant who was guilty neither of deliberate wrongdoing nor of gross negligence would be placed in a condition of need (*Notlage*) as a result of the duty to make compensation, the court may reduce his liability on this ground. This rule is more likely to be of importance in tort than in contract cases; but a further factor to be taken into account in contract cases is mentioned in CO art. 99 which applies CO art. 43 and 44 to contract cases and provides that the measure of liability is to be more leniently adjudged if the transaction does not secure any advantage for the defendant.

These provisions do give *some* guidance to the judge in the assessment of damages; but they scarcely touch any of the central problems as to damages (except that of fault) which have been discussed in this chapter. One might have supposed, therefore, that the SWISS provisions would have led to an unacceptable degree of uncertainty; but in practice their operation seems to be reasonably satisfactory. SWISS courts and writers in fact make use of concepts and distinctions employed in other jurisdictions such as the theory of adequate causation and the distinction between *damnum emergens* and *lucrum cessans*. But the wide discretion given by CO art. 43 is the overriding principle and seems to be capable of displacing any such judge-made "rules" as to the kind and extent of compensation.

From this point of view the SWISS provision should be contrasted with rules in other systems which are also expressed in terms of giving a discretion as to damages to the courts. One such rule is that stated in GERMAN CCProc. § 287. Under this paragraph a dispute as to whether

[620] *The Heron II, Koufos v. C.Czarnikow* (*supra* n. 508) 425; *cf.* Restatement of Contracts (1932) § 329 comment (a).

[621] *Corbin* § 1002.

damage has occurred, or as to its extent, is to be decided by the court, taking into account all the circumstances, in accordance with its freely formed conviction (*nach freier Überzeugung*). This provision, however, relates to proof of loss and its extent.[622] It has nothing to say about the bases of or limitations on recovery.

A somewhat similar point can be made with regard to FRENCH law in which it is often said that judges of fact have a "sovereign power" (*pouvoir souverain*) to fix the damages; or to evaluate the prejudice and thus the extent of the damages.[623] No doubt this is again true with respect to proof of loss: that is the "sovereign power" extends to a determination whether a particular alleged loss has in fact been suffered and to one as to its extent. But the rule does not protect the judge's decision from review if he has applied the wrong principle, or even if he has misapplied the correct principle.[624] For example, the *Cour de Cassation* can exercise control on the issue whether the loss suffered was foreseeable;[625] and it has been held that the decision of the inferior court as to damages must not be rendered in such imprecise terms as to deprive the *Cour de Cassation* of its power to ensure that the correct principles of law have been observed.[626]

In this respect there is some analogy between the FRENCH rule conceding "sovereign power" to the trial court and the view sometimes expressed in ENGLAND that a question as to the foreseeability of a particular item of loss is "very largely a question of fact."[627] There can however be no doubt that it is the kind of question of "fact" over which an appellate or reviewing court would not hesitate to exercise control even when its power of appeal or review was exercisable only on points of "law". For such purposes a distinction is established between "primary" and "secondary" facts.[628] The former are the physical circumstances of a case; while the latter are inferences drawn from the established physical circumstances so as to bring the situation within one or another legal category. For the purposes of appellate or supervisory jurisdiction questions of "secondary" fact are treated in the same way as questions of law. In the context of damages such questions as foreseeability would certainly be treated as questions of "secondary" fact. Thus in ENGLISH, as in FRENCH, law the decision of a tribunal of first instance which had misapplied the principle of foreseeability would be open to appeal or review. This would of course be true *a fortiori* if the tribunal of first instance had applied the wrong principle of law altogether.

A further group of rules which seems, at least at first sight, to confer considerable discretion on the court in the matter of damages can be found in a statutory provision which is in force in a number of the UNITED STATES.[629] This enacts that damages must be "reasonable", and that where an obligation appears to give rise to unreasonable, grossly oppressive, damages only reasonable damages are to be awarded. The legislative history of this provision suggests that it was intended to provide a safeguard against improvident or harsh bargains.[630] It has in fact been used in situations in which the bargain was perfectly fair but in which one particular method of assessment operated harshly against the defendant without conferring a corresponding advantage on the plaintiff. Thus the provision has been applied to restrict a landlord's claim for damages for breach of his tenant's covenant to repair to the amount by which the breach diminished the value of the property, as opposed to the much higher cost of repair.[631]

A subsection in the Uniform Commercial Code likewise provides that where a buyer accepts goods which do not conform with the contract he is entitled to recover by way of damages the "loss resulting in the ordinary course of events ... *as determined in any manner which is reasonable*" (s. 2-714(1)). It seems that the object of this provision is not to give the court a free discretion. The purpose is rather to make it plain that the court is not tied to any one of a number of recognised bases of

[622] It is therefore to be compared rather with SWISS CO art. 42 par. 2 than 43. The provisions of the new ISRAELI Contracts (Remedies for Breach of Contracts) Law 1970 (*supra* n. 481) s.13 seem to be capable of referring to both phases of the damages problem.

[623] *Mazeaud and Tunc* III (ed. 5) no. 2358; J.-Cl.Civ. art. 1146-1155 fasc. VIII (2e cahier) no. 125.

[624] *Mazeaud and Tunc*, Traité III (ed. 5) no. 2209.

[625] *Ibidem* at n. 4.

[626] J.-Cl.Civ. art. 1146-1155 fasc. VIII (2e cahier) no. 125.

[627] *The Heron II, Koufos v. C.Czarnikow* (*supra* n. 508) 397.

[628] *Benmax v. Austin Motor Co.. Ltd.*, [1955] A.C. 370 (H.L.).

[629] CALIFORNIAN CC § 3359; Revised Codes of MONTANA (*supra* n. 137) § 17-607; NORTH DAKOTA Century Code (*supra* n. 154) § 32-03-37; OKLAHOMA Statutes (*supra* n. 187) § 23-97; SOUTH DAKOTA Compiled Laws (*supra* n. 154) § 21-1-3.

[630] See the notes to *Field*'s Civil Code for NEW YORK (*supra* s. 31) s. 1878, on which the provisions mentioned *supra* n. 629 are based.

[631] *Avery v. Fredericksen and Westbrook*, 61 Cal.App. 2d 334, 154 P.2d 41 (1945); for a similar rule in ENGLAND, see Landlord and Tenant Act, 1927 (*supra* n. 326) s. 18 (1), and *cf. supra* s. 66.

assessment but that it can choose between them. Thus where the goods are defective the court is not bound to award difference in value (even though that is the normal measure); the court may in a proper case base damages on the cost of repair.[632]

The adoption of the principle of a more or less unfettered discretion based on the SWISS model has recently been considered in ISRAEL and in GERMANY. In the former country the Contracts (Remedies for Breach of Contracts) Law 1970 now relies mainly on the test of foreseeability (s. 10); but it is also provided that for non-pecuniary damage the court may award compensation at the rate it deems appropriate in the circumstances of the case (s. 13). It is not clear whether the latter provision relates only to the evaluation of particular items or whether it is intended to give a broad discretion on the SWISS model.

In GERMANY there has been a proposal to introduce a new § 255a into the Civil Code.[633] Under this provision the court would have a power to reduce damages if, having regard to the circumstances giving rise to liability, the damages would be extraordinarily high and if (taking into account the legitimate interests of the claimant) the award would otherwise cause serious injustice to the defendant. In exercising this power of reduction, the court is to have regard to the defendant's degree of fault; but there is to be no reduction if the defendant caused the damage deliberately or through gross negligence.

The proposal has obvious similarities with SWISS CO art. 43 and 44. Like them, it is principally aimed at reducing the very heavy damages which may be awarded in tort cases against a defendant who was only guilty of comparatively slight negligence. In one sense the proposal is narrower than the SWISS provisions under which the court's discretion is not expressly described as one to *reduce* damages (except where a full award would place the defendant into a condition of need), though in practice it is bound to have this effect since CO art. 43 and 44 do not displace the general principle that damages are compensatory.[634] In another and more significant way the GERMAN proposal is broader than SWISS CO art. 44: the proposed power of reduction is not limited to cases in which a full award would place the defendant into a condition of need. Under the GERMAN proposal the court has a broader power to balance the legitimate interests of the aggrieved party against the injustice caused to the defendant by a full award. But the difference is probably more apparent than real since the factors expressly mentioned in the GERMAN proposals could no doubt be taken into account by a SWISS court under the general provisions of CO art. 43.

Although the principal purpose of both the SWISS rules and the GERMAN proposals is to limit liability in tort, they might also be useful in contract cases: for example where the theory of "adequate causation" did not sufficiently limit liability, or where the cost of curing a defect was disproportionate to the increase in the value of the subject-matter which such cure would achieve.

v. *Mitigation*

100. *In general.* – Mitigation involves at least three related ideas.

The first is that the plaintiff cannot recover damages in respect of a loss which he *ought to have avoided.* In this context reference is often made to a "duty" to mitigate damages, but this mode of expression has been justly criticised. There is no sanction for "breach" of this "duty": the only consequence of the plaintiff's failure to mitigate is to reduce the amount of his recovery. He does not incur any liability in consequence of the breach of "duty".

The second idea is that, if the plaintiff actually gains some benefit in consequence of the defendant's breach, he may have to *bring that benefit into account.* Thus damages may be reduced because the plaintiff is, as a result of the defendant's breach, discharged from his obligations to perform and so saves the expense of performing; or because he is enabled in consequence of the breach to obtain some profit or advantage which he would not otherwise have obtained. Under this second notion, the question is not whether the plaintiff was in any sense "bound" to mitigate his loss, but whether in fact his loss was reduced or "mitigated".

In COMMON LAW countries the expression "mitigation" is used in relation to both of the above ideas. GERMAN law distinguishes more sharply between them. It discusses the first situation under the heading of *Mitverschulden* (fault of both parties) and the second under the heading of *Vorteilsausgleichung* (taking into account of compensating advantages).

The third related idea is what in COMMON LAW countries is called contributory negligence. In GERMAN law this is regarded as another aspect of

632 *John Street Auto Wrecking v. Motor Insurance Corp.*, 56 Misc.2d 232, 288 N.Y.S.2d 281 (D.C. Suffolk Co. 1968).

633 *Referentenentwurf* (*supra* n. 477).

634 *Cf. Guhl* 75-76.

Mitverschulden; and in FRENCH law it is discussed under the heading of fault of the victim (*faute de la victime*). These phrases refer to the situation in which loss is caused partly by the fault of the defendant and partly by that of the injured party. The idea can be separated from that of the "duty" to mitigate. It can be said that in the contributory negligence situation the plaintiff is partly responsible for bringing about the event which causes the loss, while in the mitigation situation the plaintiff can only be charged with failing to take positive steps to avoid the harmful effects of an event brought about solely by the defendant's default.

Some such distinction no doubt explains the fact that mitigation and contributory negligence are usually the subject of separate treatment in COMMON LAW countries, in which doubts have occasionally been expressed on the question whether the principle of contributory negligence applies in the contractual situation at all. On the other hand the distinction suggested above is obviously a difficult one to draw in borderline cases and it is of doubtful merit. Both ideas are in GERMAN law worked out under the same provision of the Civil Code (§ 254). The same is true in SWISS and AUSTRIAN law.[635] No distinction of principle is for example drawn between the case where rain damage, caused to the contents of a barn as a result of delay in delivering tiles, could have been avoided by erecting an emergency roof, and the case where damage to goods in transit is caused partly by the default of the carrier and partly by defective packing, for which the shipper is responsible.[636]

Of the three related ideas discussed in this section, the first two are most fully developed in COMMON LAW countries so that most of the ensuing discussion of these ideas will be based on these systems. The same ideas are, however, also well recognized in GERMAN law and in related systems. They are least well developed in FRENCH law where the only one of the three topics which is at all fully dealt with is that of contributory negligence (*faute de la victime*).

101. *Two aspects of the "duty" to mitigate.* – The "duty" to mitigate loss may be said to have two aspects. First, the plaintiff may be bound to take positive steps to minimise the loss which would otherwise flow from the defendant's default. Secondly, he may be bound to refrain from taking steps which but for the default would have been properly taken under the contract, but which in view of the default may unjustifiably augment the loss.

102. *Minimising loss.* – The principle that the victim of a breach of contract cannot recover damages in respect of a loss which he ought to have avoided by taking reasonable steps is clearly recognised by the ANGLO-AMERICAN case law. It is also expressly stated in GERMAN CC § 254 par. 2 and in ULIS art. 88 (*supra* s. 7). The principle applies in a great variety of situations.

One of its applications has already been considered: on a buyer's failure to accept, or a seller's to deliver in accordance with the terms of the contract, the aggrieved party cannot recover loss due to market movements after the time when he ought to have gone into the market to make a substitute contract.[637] As we saw in s. 71 above, ENGLISH, AMERICAN and GERMAN law take different views in the question exactly when it is reasonable for the aggrieved party to make the substitute contract. Only FRENCH law appears not to recognise the existence of any "duty" to make a substitute contract at all.

Another very common application of the principle arises where a contract of employment is wrongfully terminated by the employer: here the employee is bound in COMMON LAW countries to make reasonable efforts to seek other employment of a comparable nature.[638] In determining what other employment the dismissed employee is bound to accept, the courts apply the standard of reasonableness. In particular, the employee is not bound to accept employment which would involve a reduction of status.[639] Nor is he bound to accept an offer of re-employment from the wrongdoer if this would prejudice his rights under the original contract, or if his dismissal took place in circumstances of personal humiliation.[640] In the absence of such factors it has been held in ENGLAND that failure to accept an offer of re-employment may involve reduction of damages; and in cases involving sales and carriage of goods by sea it has been held that even an offer by the defaulting party to perform on terms less advantageous than those contained in the original contract should have been accepted by the aggrieved party.[641] It is doubtful whether this

635 SWISS CO art. 44 par. 1; AUSTRIAN CC § 1304.

636 *Klang (-Wolff)* VI § 1304 no. V (p. 61).

637 *Corbin* § 1039; *Treitel* 817; *Enneccerus and Lehmann* 78, 89; *Oser and Schönenberger* V 1 art. 44 no. 10; *Klang and Gschnitzer (-Gschnitzer)* IV 1 § 220 no. B I 1 b.

638 *Corbin* § 1065; *Treitel* 816–817.

639 *Billeter v. Posell,* 94 Cal.App.2d 858, 211 P.2d 621 (1949); *cf., Edwards v. Society of Graphical & Allied Trades,* [1971] Ch. 354 (C.A.).

640 *Billeter v. Posell, supra* n. 639; *Schisler v. Perfection Milker Co.,* 193 Minn. 160, 285 N.W. 17 (1934).

641 *Treitel* 817.

view would be accepted by the AMERICAN courts.[642]

GERMAN law lays down a very similar rule in CC § 324. This provides that where performance of a reciprocal contract becomes impossible through the fault of one party, the other retains his claim for performance subject to a deduction of (*inter alia*) that which he "*böswillig*" omitted to acquire. The expression "*böswillig*" is not easy to translate, "deliberately" being perhaps too weak and "maliciously" too strong an expression to convey its meaning. It does not seem that an intention to injure the other party is required; it is sufficient if the aggrieved party intends to exploit at the other party's expense the opportunity to remain idle, in a manner which is contrary to good faith.[643]

A special application of the principle of CC § 324 is to be found in CC § 615 which provides that a wrongfully dismissed employee is entitled to his pay less (*inter alia*) the amount which he "*böswillig*" omitted to earn. Here the word "*böswillig*" seems to mean little more than deliberately refusing alternative employment which the employee might reasonably be expected to accept;[644] it seems to come to much the same thing as the COMMON LAW requirement of reasonable conduct. The GERMAN rule does however differ in theory from the COMMON LAW rule in that the basic claim in GERMANY is for the agreed sum, while at COMMON LAW it is for damages (*cf. supra* s. 8). But the practical effect of the two rules is very much the same. A similar AUSTRIAN rule provides that the deduction is to be made in respect of amounts which an employee deliberately (*absichtlich*) failed to earn and that no deductions are to be made for earnings under the wrongfully terminated contract for a period of up to three months (CC § 1162 b).

In contracts of employment, the duty to look for substitute employment is a relatively simple one; but in other situations the notion of a "substitute" requires more elaboration. The point may be illustrated by reference to contracts to provide advertising services or to let advertising space. On breach by the advertiser, the question may arise whether the advertising contractor is bound to dispose of the space which he had reserved for the party in default. This will depend on the relation between supply and demand. If the supply of space exceeds the demand, the contractor will not be bound to let this particular space to a third party, for this would deprive him of the opportunity of making further profitable contracts in respect of other unallocated space at this disposal.[645] It would be different if demand exceeded supply or perhaps if the contract related to specific space.[646] Similar considerations apply where it is alleged that a substitute contract has actually reduced the aggrieved party's loss (*infra* s. 104).

The rule that an aggrieved party must, but need only, act reasonably to avoid loss gives a good deal of flexibility to the mitigation rule. In particular, a party is not bound to take steps to mitigate loss if such steps would be very expensive in relation to the loss to be avoided; he is not bound to engage in complicated litigation with third parties, even though its outcome might have been to reduce the loss; and he is not bound to take steps which are contrary to business ethics and which would tend to lower or ruin his commercial reputation.[647] If the aggrieved party has already paid for the defaulting party's performance, it may be unreasonable to expect him to enter into a substitute contract requiring a second payment.[648] If the aggrieved party acts reasonably in an effort to minimise the loss but in fact thereby increases it he may be entitled to recover the increased loss.[649]

103. *Augmentation of loss; mitigation in claims for an agreed sum.* – We have seen in s. 74 above that there is, or appears to be, a conflict between ENGLISH and AMERICAN law in cases in which a person who is to receive money under a contract for the execution of certain work proceeds to execute the work in disregard of the other party's repudiation of the contract. The present ENGLISH view is that the aggrieved party is, as a general rules, entitled to execute the work in spite of the repudiation and claim the agreed sum; the AMERICAN view is that the aggrieved party should desist and claim damages.[650]

Thus in the advertising cases mentioned above, the advertising contractor is not, in the UNITED STATES, generally entitled to the agreed sum in full *even if* the supply of space exceeded the demand: he would be bound to refrain from displaying the advertisements and to credit the

642 *Corbin* § 1043.

643 BGB-RGRK § 324 no. 8.

644 *Palandt* § 615 no. 4; *cf.* GERMAN CC § 649. These provisions are not strictly concerned with contractual default.

645 *Corbin* § 1041.

646 *Ibidem*.

647 *Corbin* § 1042; *Treitel* 817.

648 Restatement of Contracts (1932) § 336 ill. 10.

649 *Melachrino v. Nicholl & Knight* (*supra* n. 409) 697.

650 The leading cases are *White and Carter (Councils), Ltd. v. McGregor, supra* n. 452 and *Clark v. Marsiglia, supra* n. 451; see *supra* s. 74.

advertiser with the expense which he either saved or should have saved in this way.[651] This conclusion is based on the view that the plaintiff ought to have mitigated by not incurring the expense. This seems to be correct as a general principle; for it may be assumed that the repudiating party no longer desires performance, and generally the aggrieved party will not be prejudiced by following the indicated course of action. There are, however, two possible objections to this line of argument.

One is that the principles of mitigation are only relevant where the claim is one for damages and not where it is one for the price.[652] Certainly the principle of mitigation has been said to be inapplicable where the plaintiff claims specific performance;[653] and it is arguable that a claim for the price is in effect a claim for the specific enforcement of an obligation to pay money. The argument has a parallel in GERMAN law where it is said that the principle of *Vorteilsausgleichung* (*infra* s. 105) does not apply to a claim for performance as opposed to one for compensation, though a very similar principle does in fact apply.[654] Indeed it is clear from GERMAN CC § 324 and 615 (*supra* s. 102) that the principle of reduction in respect of gains which should have been made does apply to an action for the agreed sum. It is true that the same principle is not expressly stated in respect of *expenses which ought to have been but are not* saved; it is simply assumed that the expenses are, and probably that they must be, saved.

The argument that the principle of mitigation *of damage* only applies to an action *for damages* seems to be based rather on an apparent verbal coincidence between "damage" and "damages" than on any sound policy. It is no doubt true that mitigation is irrelevant if the party claiming the price has already done all that it is necessary for him to do to become entitled to the price. But we are concerned with the situation in which further expenditure on his part is required to entitle him to the price; and in this situation the policy of the mitigation rule, which is to prevent needless waste, would in principle seem to apply.

But there may be a second, quite independent, objection to a rule that the aggrieved party can never be justified in continuing with performance after the defendant has repudiated. For the mitigation rule only requires the plaintiff to act reasonably; and it may be reasonable for him to continue with performance for one of a number of reasons. He may be under a duty to third parties to do so;[655] continued performance may enhance his reputation; the damages which he could recover might not fully compensate him, being for example in part too remote. It might even be reasonable for the plaintiff to continue to perform because he reasonably believed that the damages would not fully compensate him.

104. *Aggrieved party benefiting in consequence of breach – Common Law.*[656] – Where an aggrieved party is under a "duty" to mitigate loss and takes the steps required of him in this respect, the gains resulting from such steps are of course taken into account in assessing damages. This follows *a fortiori* from the rule that such gains as he ought to have made are taken into account whether he actually made them or not. It is also clear that the benefits accruing to a party by reason of his being relieved of the obligation to perform are taken into account in reducing his recovery. These rules are well established in COMMON LAW countries[657] and in GERMANY (*infra* s. 105); and although in FRENCH law the "duty" to mitigate damages is not clearly recognised, actual saving of expense would be relevant in determining "the loss suffered" within CC art. 1149. The fact that the necessary calculations are usually left to the discretion of the trial judge probably accounts for the lack of discussion of the topic.

Gains may accrue to a contracting party otherwise than as a result of the performance of his "duty" to mitigate or of saving of expense; and the gains acquired may be different in kind or in amount from those which he ought to have made in performing that "duty". The question whether and if so to what extent gains of these kinds are to be taken into account in assessing damages is one of great difficulty. The basic COMMON LAW principle is that gains made by the aggrieved party are only to be taken into account if they could not have been made, had there been no breach.

Thus earnings in alternative employment are normally deducted from damages claimable by a wrongfully dismissed employee since but for the

651 *Western Advertising Co. v. Mid-West Laundries*, 61 S.W.2d 251 (Mo.App. 1933); similar principle where a seller ships goods after the buyer has countermanded the order: *Edgar v. Grocer's Wholesale Co.*, 298 F. 878 (8 Cir. 1924).

652 *Kunkle v. Jaffe*, 47 Ohio L.Abs. 77, 71 N.E.2d 298 (1946); *Treitel* 833.

653 *Corbin* § 1222.

654 *Enneccerus and Lehmann* 87.

655 *Martin v. Meles*, 179 Mass. 144, 60 N.E. 397 (1901); *cf. Anglo-African Shipping Co. of New York Inc. v. J. Mortner, Ltd.*, [1962] 1 Lloyd's Rep. 80, 94 (Q.B. (Com.Ct.)) (rev'd on another ground, *idem* 610).

656 *Cf. Fleming*, this Encyclopedia vol. XI ch. 11 (Collateral Benefits).

657 *Corbin* § 1038; *Treitel* 816-817.

dismissal he would not have been able to take up the alternative employment. The rule extends to what may be called disguised earnings. In an ENGLISH case[658] an employee took alternative employment with a company at a rate of pay lower than that to which he was entitled under the employment from which he had been wrongfully discharged; and he also bought shares in the company, the value of which increased as a result of his efforts. It was held that this increase in value was to be taken into account in assessing damages for the breach of the original contract of employment. It follows from the principle here under discussion that earnings actually made in alternative employment will be taken into account even if the alternative employment was of a kind which the plaintiff was *not* bound to undertake; though the possibility of *future* earnings in such employment should not be taken into account as this would in effect require the plaintiff to remain in the new employment in spite of the fact that his undertaking it could not have been reasonably required.[659]

The principle of bringing actual gain into account has also been applied to determine the damages recoverable by a seller on account of his buyer's wrongful refusal to accept and pay for goods. In such a case the seller is *prima facie* entitled to damages for loss of the profit which he would have made on the sale; and the question arises whether he must bring into account an equivalent profit which he may make on a substitute sale. He must obviously do so if the goods were unique, since of such goods there can be but one sale, so that the seller could not have sold them both to the original and to the substitute buyer. Similar reasoning applies where the demand for goods of the contract description exceeds the supply; for here the number of profits which the seller can make is limited by the quantity of goods which he can obtain so that he suffers no prejudice (except perhaps some incidental loss: *supra* s. 52) if he sells to a second buyer rather than to the first.[660]

But the position is different where the supply exceeds the demand for in that case the so-called "substitute" sale is not a true substitute as the seller could have supplied both the original and the "substitute" buyer. Hence the seller will recover his full loss of profits on the first sale;[661] though if as a result of the first buyer's default the seller saves some of the expenses (such as delivery costs) which he would otherwise have incurred in relation to the second sale such savings should strictly speaking be taken into account in assessing damages for the first buyer's breach.

Although benefits which could not have been obtained but for the breach *may* be deducted, it does not follow that all such benefits *will* be deducted. A contract of employment may restrict the employee's right to invest in competing companies. On wrongful dismissal, the employee will be freed from the restriction; but it has been held that any profit which he makes from the previously prohibited investments should not be taken into account. Such a profit has been described as "not a direct result of his dismissal" but a "collateral benefit."[662] For the benefit to be taken into account, it must be "one arising out of the consequence of the breach."[663] This requirement can give rise to very difficult questions of causation; and one of the leading ENGLISH decisions on the point has been criticised both in ENGLAND and in the UNITED STATES.[664] Benefits obtained by a plaintiff under a policy of insurance against the losses occasioned by the breach do not need to be brought into account.[665] There are conflicting decisions on social security benefits which have been taken into account in ENGLAND but not in the UNITED STATES.[666]

Where a court is concerned with benefits resulting to the aggrieved party in consequence of the breach, difficulty again arises where the claim is not one for damages but for an agreed sum. As we saw in s. 103 above, the rules as to mitigation do not apply where the claimant has already done everything which it is necessary for him to do to become entitled to the price or other agreed remuneration. That rule is based on the assumption that the claimant has performed all his obligations under the contract; but of course the price or other agreed remuneration may be payable in advance of performance. In such a case

[658] *Lavarack v. Woods of Colchester, Ltd.*, [1967] 1 Q.B. 278 (C.A.).

[659] *Cf., Edwards v. Society of Graphical & Allied Trades, supra* n. 639.

[660] *Treitel* 795.

[661] *Idem* 796.

[662] *Lavarack v. Woods of Colchester, Ltd.* (*supra* n. 658) 290; a contrary CANADIAN decision in *Cockburn v. Trusts and Guarantee Co.* (1917), 33 D.L.R. 159 (S.C. Ont.), 37 D.L.R. 701, 704 (S.C. Can.) is criticised by *Corbin* § 1095.

[663] *British Westinghouse Electric & Manufacturing Co., Ltd. v. Underground Electric Railways Co. of London, Ltd.*, [1912] A.C. 673, 690 (H.L.).

[664] *Treitel* 818; *Corbin* § 1039.

[665] *Treitel* 818; ISRAELI Contracts (Remedies for Breach of Contracts) Law 1970 (*supra* n. 481) s. 16.

[666] *E.g., Foxley v. Olton*, [1965] 2 Q.B. 306; *Billeter v. Posell, supra* n. 639.

there is the possibility that the claimant may be entitled to the price but that he may in fact not render the performance due from him by reason of the other party's default. For example, a seller of goods may be entitled to payment in advance of delivery but he may be prevented from making delivery by the buyer's breach of contract. It is clear that the aggrieved party cannot in such situations both recover the price and retain his own performance; and various techniques are used to reach this result.

In the case just put, the Uniform Commercial Code generally avoids the problem by providing that the seller cannot bring the action for the price where resale is possible,[667] the normal remedies in such a case being resale or damages for non-acceptance. Even if the seller can sue for the price, he must hold the goods for the buyer or give him credit for the proceeds of resale (s. 2-709(2); for example where that course of action *subsequently* becomes possible).

The position under ULIS is broadly similar. The seller is not entitled to "require payment" (*i.e.* he cannot sue for the price) where it is in conformity with usage and reasonably possible for him to resell the goods (art. 61(2)). Again the seller's normal remedies will be resale (the contract being *ipso facto* avoided: *infra* s. 178) and damages.[668]

Where a case of this kind is not covered by an express statutory provision, the correct position would seem to be that a payment due in advance of performance is recoverable in full; but that, if such a payment is claimed notwithstanding repudiation, the claimant thereby affirms the contract so that he would be bound to render performance (or to pay damages for non-performance) if this should subsequently be claimed from him.

105. *"Vorteilsausgleichung" in German law.* – The GERMAN principle of *Vorteilsausgleichung* covers much the same ground as the COMMON LAW rules outlined above. The general principle of CC § 324, stated in s. 103 above in relation to gains which *should have been* made, is also expressed to apply to savings and gains which *actually were* made in consequence of the fact that the aggrieved party was freed from his obligation to perform. The same is true of the provisions of CC § 615, which applies the general principle of CC § 324 to contracts for services and of employment. Under both provisions, the benefits must accrue to the aggrieved party "in consequence" of his relief from the obligation to perform his part of the contract; and this requirement raises problems of causation similar to those which have faced COMMON LAW courts.

The general principle governing *Vorteilsausgleichung* in GERMAN law is that there must be an "adequate causal connection" between the defendant's default and the gain or saving of expense to the plaintiff.[669] Insurance payments are (as in ENGLISH law) disregarded; so are voluntary payments by third parties, employers' pensions and (by statute) state pensions.[670] Gains which are due to the voluntary acts of the aggrieved party are likewise disregarded if the acts were not done in performance of the "duty" to mitigate loss or if they did not have a sufficiently close causal connection with the act causing the loss.[671] Both the presence and the absence of a sufficient causal nexus may be illustrated by reference to the following situations.

If as a result of a seller's default a buyer has to make a number of cover purchases, some above and some below the contract price, the expenses saved by buying below the contract price will be set off against the loss made by buying above it. But if he subsequently sells the whole of the goods thus acquired at a further profit, he is not bound to bring this into account.[672] If a creditor acquires pledged securities at a price below their market value on the debtor's default, he must bring this gain into account, but not any further gain which he makes out of a subsequent rise in the market value of those securities.[673] Sums which a dismissed employee earned in addition to those earned under his new employment by working in his *spare* time are not to be taken into account. But if in part of the time covered by the original employment the employee earns an exceptionally large amount, the whole of that amount is to be taken into account in assessing damages against the original employer.[674] So far as saving of expense is concerned, the GERMAN provisions refer to savings made in consequence of being freed from the obligation to perform. In SWITZERLAND a broader view has been taken: thus it has been said that storage charges saved by a buyer in consequence of a seller's failure to deliver will be

[667] UCC s. 2-709 (1); *cf.* ULIS (*supra* s. 7) art. 61 (2); in ENGLAND the price can be sued for even though resale is possible if the property has passed or if the price is payable "on a day certain irrespective of delivery": Sale of Goods Act, 1893 (*supra* n. 312) s. 49.

[668] ULIS art. 61 (2), 63 (1).

[669] *Enneccerus and Lehmann* 85.

[670] *Idem* 85–86.

[671] *Idem* 86–87.

[672] *Idem* 86.

[673] *Idem* 87.

[674] BGB-RGRK § 615 no. 3.

taken into account even though the buyer is under no contractual duty to the seller to incur the storage charges.[675] Of course in cases of this last kind it might well be difficult to establish a sufficiently strong causal connection between the buyer's saving of expense and the seller's default.

106. *Loss partly caused by victim's fault.* – The principle governing cases in which the loss is partly caused by the fault of the victim is most clearly stated in GERMAN CC § 254.[676] This provides that if the fault of the injured party contributed to his loss, the existence and extent of the duty of compensate depends on the circumstances and in particular on the question how far the loss was preponderantly caused by, or was due to the fault of, one or the other of the parties. This principle is expressly stated to apply to two special situations: first where the "fault" of the injured party is limited to failure to warn the other party of the risk of an exceptionally high loss; and secondly where the injured party has omitted to take steps to avoid or reduce the loss.

The second situation is one in which there is a "duty" to mitigate, which is discussed in s. 102 above. Just as that "duty" has no sanction other than a reduction in damages, so the "fault" here under discussion is not of a kind that is necessarily actionable. It amounts merely to a failure on the part of the injured party to take reasonable steps to safeguard his own interests. In determining what steps are reasonable, however, the courts in GERMANY apply much the same criteria (see *supra* ch. 15) as they apply to the definition of actionable fault. The basic test of "fault" under CC § 254 is accordingly that of foreseeability of harmful consequences.[677]

The wording of CC § 254 refers without distinction to two bases on which the court can dismiss or reduce the plaintiff's claim, namely the extent to which the loss was *caused* by, or due to the *fault* of, (*verursacht oder verschuldet*) the injured party. But it has been held that causation is the primary factor and fault or responsibility only secondary.[678] Perhaps it could be said that causation is the more important test where the injured party is partly responsible for the event giving rise to the loss while the expression "*verschuldet*" is particularly apt to refer to the situation in which the injured party failed to take steps to minimise loss.

The great majority of the decisions under CC § 254 concern cases of tort, but there is no doubt that the paragraph also applies in cases of contractual default; indeed CC § 254 is, as was pointed out in s. 100 above, the basis of the "duty" to mitigate in contract cases. It is particularly interesting to note that failure to notify the defendant of the risk of a special loss is regarded as a ground for excluding or reducing damages under CC § 254. In COMMON LAW jurisdictions much the same result would be reached on different reasoning. The plaintiff's failure to notify would make the loss too remote as the special loss would not be within the contemplation of the defendant under the second part of the rule in *Hadley v. Baxendale.*[679]

Most of the cases falling within CC § 254 would in COMMON LAW countries be described as cases of "contributory negligence". The COMMON LAW doctrine of contributory negligence once again applies primarily to tort cases. Under it a plaintiff who contributed to his own injury was in some cases wholly denied the right to recover damages, while in other cases he recovered in full, his contribution to the injury being totally disregarded. More recently legislation has been introduced in many COMMON LAW jurisdictions enabling the courts in such cases to reduce damages in proportion to the effect which the plaintiff's and the defendant's fault had in causing the injury.[680]

There has, at least until recently, been relatively little discussion of the problems whether the doctrine of contributory negligence or the legislation modifying its effects applied to contract cases. In such cases, the mitigation rules, which were well developed in COMMON LAW jurisdictions, covered most of the same ground and covered it more satisfactorily since they enabled the court to reduce the plaintiff's claim, while under the COMMON LAW rules of contributory negligence the court only had the choice of allowing the claim in full or of dismissing it altogether. It is only the recent legislation, giving the courts the power to reduce claims on the ground of contributory negligence, which has led to discussions of the questions whether the doctrine of contributory negligence and the amending legislation apply to contract cases.[681]

It seems clear that the answer to both questions is affirmative where the same set of facts constitutes

675 *Guhl* 72.

676 *Cf.* SWISS CO art. 44 par. 1; AUSTRIAN CC § 1304.

677 *Enneccerus and Lehmann* 77-78.

678 *Idem* 81.

679 *Supra* n. 505; see *supra* s. 86.

680 *E.g.* in ENGLAND under the Law Reform (Contributory Negligence) Act, 1945 (*supra* n. 614). Similar legislation is in force in many COMMONWEALTH countries and in some of the UNITED STATES: see this Encyclopedia vol. XI ch. 7 s. 147.

681 *Williams*, Joint Torts and Contributory Negligence (London 1951) § 59.

both a breach of contract and a tort: for example where a passenger who is being carried for reward, or an employee suffers injury partly because of the carrier's or employer's breach of duty and partly because of his own carelessness for his own safety.[682] Where the defendant's duty of care is based solely on contract, it has been held in AUSTRALIA that neither the doctrine of contributory negligence nor the amending legislation applies;[683] though dicta in ENGLISH cases can be cited in support of the opposite view.[684] It seems unlikely that the amending legislation can, on its wording, be held to apply to cases in which liability for breach of contract arises (as it commonly does) quite irrespective of fault.[685] But in all contract cases it is open to the defendant to show that the plaintiff's injury was in fact caused by the plaintiff's own act. If the defendant succeeds in showing this, he will not be liable at all; and it is arguable that this rule is simply the Common Law (*i.e.*, unamended) doctrine of contributory negligence under another name.

In FRENCH law, there is no provision in the Civil Code which in so many words expresses a doctrine of contributory negligence. But the courts have developed a notion which serves the same purpose: that if the loss is due to the act or fault of the victim (*fait ou faute de la victime*) the liability of the defendant may be extinguished or attenuated. It is extinguished if the act of the victim can be said to be the sole cause of the loss, and attenuated if the fault of both parties has contributed to the loss.[686] In the latter case there is sometimes said to be common fault (*faute commune*),[687] the effect of which is that the plaintiff's damages will be reduced in proportion to the degree of his responsibility for the loss.[688]

The main application of these principles is, as in GERMANY and in COMMON LAW countries, to tort cases; so much so that it was at one time thought that the principles were not applicable in cases of contractual liability at all.[689] But this view is now generally rejected in FRANCE. Reliance is placed, in particular, on the fact that the principle of *faute de la victime* is often invoked in cases of personal injury to passengers even though the responsibility of the carrier is considered to be contractual.[690] It is interesting to note that this is a situation in which the liability would in COMMON LAW countries be characterised as either contractual or tortious,[691] so that both the doctrine of contributory negligence and the amending legislation would no doubt apply.

FRENCH writers do not consider that the doctrine is limited to cases of this kind. They regard it as applicable to "pure" contract cases. It is considered to explain such rules as that a debtor is not responsible for delay which is due to the act of the creditor;[692] and that a carrier is not liable for loss due to inherent vice in the thing carried.[693]

The fault of the victim is also sometimes regarded as a kind of extraneous cause (*cause étrangère*) so as to bring the case within CC art. 1147, which exonerates the contracting party from liability for loss due to an extraneous cause not imputable to him.[694] This view has, in turn, given rise to a difficulty. If the fault of the victim is a *cause étrangère* should it not logically free the debtor from all liability, instead of operating sometimes merely to reduce liability? Indeed, in many of the cases total release of the debtor has been the consequence of the application of the doctrine of *faute de la victime*, but this is probably because the courts have generally taken the view that the fault of the victim was the sole cause of the injury. Where injury is caused partly by the fault of the defendant and partly by that of the victim, reduction of liability so as to take account of both parties' responsibility seems to be a possible solution.

It has been suggested that CC art. 1147 does not exclude this view, for it deals with the situation in which the failure in performance is due to (*provient de*) the extraneous cause.[695] This language seems to leave open the possibility of distinguishing between cases where the loss is due solely to the fault of one party and those where it is due partly to the fault of each party. Indeed it

682 *Treitel* 830.

683 *Belous v. Willetts*, [1970] V.R. 45.

684 *Quinn v. Burch Bros. (Builders), Ltd.*, [1966] 2 Q.B. 370, 380–381 (C.A.).

685 *Treitel* 831–832.

686 *Marty and Raynaud* II no. 497 to 498.

687 *Mazeaud*, Traité II (ed. 6) no. 1505.

688 *Ibidem; Mazeaud*, Leçons II no. 594, 598. There is much controversy as to the exact basis of reduction in FRENCH law: see *Mazeaud*, Traité II (ed. 6) no. 1509 ss.

689 See *Mazeaud*, Traité II (ed. 6) no. 1457.

690 *Ibidem.*

691 *Cf.* Cass.req. 30 Jan. 1929, S. 1929.1.191 (fraud of agent).

692 Cass.req. 7 Jan. 1929, Gaz.Pal.1929.1.575; *Mazeaud*, Traité II (ed. 6) no. 1457.

693 See Cass.civ. 17 July 1930, Gaz.Pal.1930.2.456; *Mazeaud*, Traité II (ed. 6) no. 1457 n. 760.

694 *Mazeaud*, Leçons II no. 572; *idem*, Traité II (ed. 6) no. 1446; Cass.civ. 11 Nov. 1941, D.C. 1942 J.153.

695 *Mazeaud*, Traité II (ed. 6) no. 1521.

would seem that the principle of reduction applied in the *Lamoricière* case[696] could be applied by analogy.

The notion of *faute de la victime* is thus fairly well developed in FRENCH law in cases in which the victim's conduct has positively contributed to bring about the injury. In some tort cases it has also been applied to fault in failing to avoid the consequences of a wrongful act, or their aggravation: for example if the victim of personal injuries neglects them or refuses reasonable medical treatment.[697] There seems to be no logical distinction between this situation and cases falling under the "duty" to mitigate loss arising from a breach of contract (*supra* s. 101-103); but there is no indication that the principle has been extended to such cases. Indeed the view (discussed *supra* s. 71) that "abstract" assessment of damages is by reference to the market price *at the time of judgment* (and not at a time when the aggrieved party might have been expected to enter into a cover transaction) suggests that the extension has not been made.

vi. "*Certainty*" *of Damage*

107. *Civil Law approach.* – Most systems of law impose some requirement as to "certainty" of damage, but the requirement is not in any of them regarded as an absolute one. The general approach is rather that the degree of uncertainty may be a ground for reducing the amount recoverable. Only uncertainty of a very high degree will utterly defeat the aggrieved party's claim.

FRENCH law starts with the principle that there is no right of recovery in respect of *dommage éventuel*,[698] an expression which may be translated as hypothetical future damages. For example there is no right to damages (though there may be a right to an injunction) in respect of the danger of possible damage to premises due to the proximity of a high-tension electric cable. But such hypothetical future damage has been distinguished from the loss of a chance which can be presently valued.

In some of the older cases recovery in respect of loss of a chance was denied:[699] for example where a racehorse was prevented from taking part in a race, it was considered impossible to value the chance that it might gain a prize as the probability of the horse's winning could not be forecast with sufficient certainty.[700] But the modern tendency, supported by both writers and the courts, is to allow damages for loss of a chance. Such damages will be assessed not by reference to the whole gain which the plaintiff hoped to make or the whole loss which he hoped to avoid, but by reference to the degree of probability of the chance's turning out in the plaintiff's favour. For example, a lawyer may fail in his contractual duty to act diligently in his client's interests, so that the client in consequence loses a lawsuit. In such a case the client will be entitled to damages based, not on the amount of the judgment actually awarded against him, but on the chance of his position having been improved if the lawyer had not failed in the performance of his duty.[701] The principle that damage may be recovered for loss of a chance can also be said to underlie the well-established rule (recognised by CC art. 1149) that damages for loss of a gain of which the aggrieved party has been deprived are recoverable in a contractual action.

Such lost gains are also recoverable under GERMAN CC § 252; and it has been said that in order to recover such loss the claimant must show that it is "certain" that the gain would have been made.[702] But this requirement is in fact qualified by the presumption created by the second sentence of CC § 252, to the effect that a gain will be deemed to have been lost if it is one which would have been made in the ordinary course of things (*supra* s. 92). Here again loss of a chance, such as the chance of winning a prize in a lottery, is in principle a loss in respect of which damages can be recovered.[703] Another type of chance in respect of which recovery has been allowed in AUSTRIA is an employee's chance of earning tips.[704]

108. *Common Law approach.* – COMMON LAW countries follow very similar principles. Damages are of course frequently recovered for loss of businesss profits even though these may depend on chances which are more or less conjectural. Damages have likewise been recovered for loss of the chance of taking part in the final stages of a beauty contest; for loss of the chance of earning tips; for loss of the chance to earn a commission; for loss of a season's catch of seals and whales; and

696 *Supra* n. 612; see *supra* s. 97.

697 *Lalou* (*-Azard*), Traité pratique de la responsabilité civile (ed. 6 Paris 1962) no. 336 and 337.

698 *Carbonnier* IV 304.

699 *Idem* IV 312.

700 *Ibidem*.

701 Cour d'appel Paris 16 May 1963, J.C.P.1963.II. 13372.

702 *Enneccerus and Lehmann* 73.

703 BGB-RGRK § 252 no. 8.

704 *Klang and Gschnitzer* (*-Adler and Höller*) V § 1162 b no. I c.

for loss of a crop where a warranty to the quality of seeds was broken.[705] AMERICAN courts have been somewhat reluctant to award damages for the loss of the chance to win a prize in a competition, but this is at least partly due to the fact that the plaintiffs in the relevant cases have tended to claim *the full prize*, as opposed to the value of the chance of winning it.[706] Obviously a claim for the full prize is excessive.

In cases of this kind the court must take into account the number of contingencies on which the plaintiff's chance depends, and the likelihood of their being satisfied in the plaintiff's favour.[707] It is only if the contingency is entirely within the discretion of the defaulting party, who exercises the discretion to prevent the contingency from occurring, that damages for loss of a chance may be irrecoverable. Thus in an ENGLISH case an employee was remunerated by a fixed salary and a bonus at the discretion of the employer. The employee was wrongfully dismissed before the end of the agreed period of employment, and it was held that he was not entitled to damages for loss of the chance of earning the bonus.[708]

A plaintiff who claims damages for loss of a chance normally bases his claim on loss of expectation interest. The court may hold that the chance is too uncertain to found a claim of this kind but nevertheless award damages on some other basis: for example it may allow the plaintiff to recover on a reliance basis for expenses incurred by him in preparation to perform or in part performance of the contract, or for expenses which have become useless in consequence of the defendant's breach. Cases illustrating this principle have been discussed in s. 60 above.

vii. *Specific Limitations*

109. *Introduction.* – Most systems of law contain further restrictions on the right to recover damages which cannot be explained on the basis of the general principles which underlie the six limitations discussed above. Of these further restrictions two which are fairly commonly found relate to injury to feelings and to default in the performance of an obligation to pay money. A third restriction, which is peculiar to the COMMON LAW and which is increasingly being abandoned in the UNITED STATES, relates to default of a vendor of land in being unable to make title.

a. Injured Feelings

110. *The Common Law position.* – We have seen in s. 45 above that COMMON LAW courts do not generally award "punitive" or "exemplary" damages in a contractual action. Such damages must be distinguished from damages for injured feelings. The object of "punitive" damages is to punish the defendant, irrespective of the plaintiff's loss, while the object of damages for injured feelings is to compensate the plaintiff for an injury which he has actually suffered, although it is not a material one. In practice the distinction is hard to draw,[709] particularly as damages for injured feelings (where they are recoverable) are at large, so that there may be a temptation to assess them at a high level as a way of indirectly punishing the defendant.[710]

ANGLO-AMERICAN law starts with the rule that damages cannot be recovered in a contractual action for injury to feelings.[711] The rule has been applied to deny recovery to a servant for the injury to his feelings which he suffered as a result of being dismissed in a manner that was "harsh and humiliating";[712] to a client for the anxiety which she suffered as a result of her lawyer's failure to take proper steps to safeguard her interests in matrimonial proceedings;[713] to a guest at a hotel who was refused accommodation which he had previously reserved;[714] and to a bride for the anguish which she suffered in consequence of her dressmaker's failure to deliver her wedding dress and bridal veil in time for her wedding.[715] Similarly the sentimental value of the subject-matter of a contract will not be taken into account in assessing damages for breach of contract,[716] though the presence of a *pretium affectionis* may be

[705] *Treitel* 795; *Corbin* § 1025, 1026.

[706] *Corbin* § 1028, 1030; for an AMERICAN case in which a claim for *damages* (as opposed to one for *the prize*) was upheld, see *Wachtel v. National Alfalfa Journal Co.*, 190 Iowa 1293, 176 N.W. 801 (1921).

[707] *Treitel* 796.

[708] *Lavarack v. Woods of Colchester, Ltd., supra* n. 658.

[709] *Corbin* § 1076, 1077.

[710] *E.g., Chelini v. Nieri, supra* n. 211.

[711] *Asher v. Reliance Insurance Co.*, 308 F.Supp. 847, 852 (N.D.Cal. 1970).

[712] *Addis v. Gramophone Co., Ltd., supra* n. 213 (*contra : Scheps v. Giles, supra* n. 218, where the employee was publicly called a liar).

[713] *Cook v. Swinfen*, [1967] 1 W.L.R. 457 (C.A.).

[714] *Constantine v. Imperial Hotels, Ltd.*, [1944] K.B. 693 (where there was a contract but no claim was based on it); *Jockie v. Meyer*, (1945) A.D. 354. Special statutory provisions apply in the UNITED STATES and in GREAT BRITAIN where the refusal is based on grounds prohibited by civil rights or race relations legislations.

[715] *Seidenbach's Inc. v. Williams*, 361 P.2d 185, 88 A.L.R.2d 1360 (Okla. S.Ct. 1961).

[716] *Corbin* § 1004.

a ground for ordering specific relief (*supra* s. 31). There are conflicting decisions in the UNITED STATES on the liability of telegraph companies for delay in delivering personal messages (*e.g.* relating to the death of a relative); the preponderant view is against allowing damages for injured feelings in such cases.[717]

There are, however, many exceptions to the general COMMON LAW rule.

In the first place, damages for injured feelings are recoverable in actions for breach of promise of marriage in jurisdictions which still recognize this form of action.[718] Secondly, a person who is personally injured can recover damages for "pain and suffering" and this may include the mental suffering resulting from (for example) the loss of a limb or an eye. Such damages are of course most frequently recovered in tort, but in principle the COMMON LAW attaches them to the nature of the injury (injury to the person) irrespective of the legal category of the wrong (breach of contract or tort) giving rise to the injury.[719] Such damages are, for example, recoverable by a buyer of goods who suffers personal injury on account of a defect in them, even though the seller could not be made liable in tort.[720]

Thirdly, damages for breach of contract may include compensation for "inconvenience"[721]; and the "inconvenience" suffered by a person as a result of being wrongfully ejected from a train or refused admission to a hotel is obviously hard to separate from his humiliation and anxiety.

There is, fourthly, an increasing tendency to allow damages for mental suffering where the breach was wanton or reckless or where the contract was of such a nature that mental suffering could have been contemplated as a result of its breach. Such damages have been allowed, in particular, for breaches of contracts by carriers of passengers, innkeepers, holiday tour operators and funeral undertakers.[722] The tendency of these cases seems to be sound, for the view that damages cannot be recovered in a contractual action for deliberately inflicted humiliation or for disappointment seems hard to support. The denial of damages for "anxiety" stands on a different footing and can be justified by the argument that some anxiety is an almost inevitable incident of contractual expectations, so that the plaintiff may be assumed to take the risk of it.[723]

The general COMMON LAW rule denies damages not only for injury to feelings but also for injury to reputation so that, for example, a wrongfully dismissed servant cannot recover damages merely because the fact of his dismissal makes it harder for him to secure other employment.[724] But there seems to be no sound basis for this rule and there is a tendency both in ENGLAND and in the UNITED STATES to restrict its scope. In particular, it does not apply where the injury is to the commercial reputation of a trader;[725] and where the whole purpose of the contract is to increase the reputation of the aggrieved party or his capacity to secure employment.[726]

111. *French law.* – FRENCH law, like the COMMON LAW, hesitated to award compensation for *dommage moral* or *préjudice moral.* This notion is hard to define, but basically it refers to a form of injury that does not consist of or lead to any patrimonial loss. It includes such injuries as attacks on a person's honour or reputation; and also certain kinds of physical harm which do not entail any pecuniary consequences. Thus it includes a disfiguring scar which does not impair the injured party's earning capacity.[727]

At one time a difficulty was felt in giving money compensation for loss which was, by its nature, non-pecuniary.[728] But the concept of damages for *préjudice moral* is now expressly recognised by the Civil Code;[729] and in cases of delictual liability FRENCH law awards compensation for non-pecuniary loss to a far greater extent than the COMMON LAW.[730] The older writers, however, took the view that, in a contractual action, only pecuniary prejudice could be compensated.[731] Their view has remained influential so that even at the present time the availability of a contractual remedy for *préjudice moral* remains in dispute.[732]

The better view, however, is that such a remedy is available.[733] One commonly cited

717 *Idem* § 1076.

718 *Ibidem.*

719 *Treitel* 813-814.

720 *E.g., Godley v. Perry,* [1960] 1 W.L.R. 9 (Q.B.).

721 *Treitel* 813.

722 *Corbin* § 1076, citing Restatement of Contracts (1932) § 361; *cf., Chande v. East African Airways Corp.,* [1964] E.A. 78 (K) (damages for "disappointment" for breach of a contract to fly a wedding party to places at which receptions were to be held); *Treitel* 813 n. 61; *Jarvis v. Swans Tours, Ltd.,* [1973] 1 Q.B. 233 (C.A.).

723 *Corbin* § 1076; *Treitel* 814.

724 *Addis v. Gramophone Co., Ltd., supra* n. 213.

725 *Corbin* § 1077; *Treitel* 814.

726 *Dunk v. George Waller & Son, Ltd.,* [1970] 2 Q.B. 163 (C.A.).

727 *Mazeaud and Tunc,* Traité I (ed. 5) no. 293.

728 *Carbonnier* IV 306.

729 *E.g.* CC art. 301 par. 2.

730 See *Mazeaud and Tunc,* Traité I (ed. 5) no. 301 ss.

731 See *idem* no. 299.

732 *De Page* III no. 115.

733 *Carbonnier* IV 323.

illustration is that of the passenger who is injured in an accident caused by the carrier's breach of contract: he is entitled to damages in the same way as the victim of a tort. This is of course the type of case in which damages for injured feelings could be recovered at COMMON LAW simply because they flowed from a physical injury to the person; and it is also a situation in which COMMON LAW systems would allow the victim to bring his action either in contract or in tort.

In FRENCH law the right to claim compensation for *préjudice moral* in a contractual action now extends far beyond situations of this kind.[734] It has, for example, been upheld in a case in which a butcher committed a breach of contract which offended his customer's religious susceptibilities;[735] where breaches of contracts by funeral undertakers caused mental anguish to the relatives of the deceased;[736] where a passenger suffered distress as a result of mere delay by a carrier;[737] and where a workman broke his contract and at the same time abused his employer so as to undermine the latter's authority.[738] Damages for injury to feelings have even been awarded to the owner of a horse which was killed as a result of the negligence of the person who had contracted to look after it;[739] though in this case liability could have been based either on contractual or on tortious principles. These cases have been supported on the ground that the Civil Code does not expressly restrict damages in contractual actions to material loss: CC art. 1149 refers quite generally to loss suffered and not to pecuniary loss;[740] and it is said that there is no justification for treating the problem of *dommage moral* differently according to whether the action is based on contract or on tort.

There is no doubt that the result of these FRENCH decisions is to give a greater scope to *dommage moral* in contractual actions than the COMMON LAW gives, in such actions, to damages for injured feelings. If an employer can recover damages because a workman's abusive breach of contract has undermined his authority, he would no doubt be liable in the converse case of injuring the workman's feelings by an abusive dismissal – a situation in which such a remedy is denied in ANGLO-AMERICAN law.[741] Again, we have seen that in a COMMON LAW jurisdiction a bride failed to recover damages for injury to her feelings which she suffered when her wedding dress was delivered after the day of her wedding (*supra* n. 715). In an almost identical case recovery of damages for injury to feelings was allowed in LOUISIANA,[742] a state whose legal system is based on FRENCH law. The decision is based on an interesting provision of the LOUISIANA Civil Code which expressly provides that damages for non-pecuniary loss may be recovered "where the contract has for its object the gratification of some intellectual enjoyment, whether in religion, morality or taste" (art. 1934(3)). This is somewhat narrower than the rule supported by the FRENCH decisions which bases the right to recover *dommage moral* not so much on the object of the contract as on the effects of its breach.

There is, finally, no doubt that damages are recoverable in FRENCH law for loss of reputation, *e.g.* where an architect is wrongfully discharged or where an actress does not have her name displayed on advertisements with the agreed measure of prominence.[743] Here the difference between FRENCH and ANGLO-AMERICAN law is probably more apparent than real, for these are cases in which ANGLO-AMERICAN courts would probably make exceptions to the general rule that damages cannot be recovered for loss of reputation in a contractual action. In ENGLAND it has for example been held that an actor who had wrongfully been refused employment could recover damages for loss of the opportunity to enhance his reputation, though not for injury to his existing reputation.[744]

112. *German law.* – The general rule in GERMAN law is laid down in CC § 253: in cases of non-pecuniary damage, compensation in money is only available in cases where this is expressly provided by law. It should be emphasised that CC § 253 only refers to compensation in money and not to other forms of relief. Thus where the defendant wrongfully copied a letter addressed to the plaintiff, a claim for damages failed but the court ordered the destruction of the copies.[745]

Provisions in the Civil Code which envisage

734 See *Mazeaud and Tunc*, Traité I (ed. 5) no. 334.

735 Trib.com. Lyon 18 Sept. 1936, Gaz.Pal.1936.2. 893.

736 Cour d'appel Paris 25 May 1950, D. 1950, 439; Trib.Seine 20 Dec. 1932, S. 1933.2.44.

737 Cass.com.et fin. 7 Oct. 1953, Gaz.Pal.1953.2. Somm.19.

738 Cour d'appel Marseille 20 Dec. 1929, Gaz.Pal. 1930.1. 426.

739 Cass.civ. 16 Jan. 1962, D. 1962, 199.

740 *Mazeaud and Tunc*, Traité I (ed. 5) no. 330.

741 *Addis v. Gramophone Co., Ltd., supra* n. 213. See *supra* s. 110.

742 *Lewis v. Holmes*, 109 La. 1030, 34 So. 66 (1903); *cf.* in SCOTLAND *Diesen v. Samson*, 1971 S.L.T. (Sh.Ct.) 49 (breach of contract to take wedding photographs).

743 *Mazeaud and Tunc*, Traité I (ed. 6) no. 334.

744 *Treitel* 813.

745 RG 31 Oct. 1918, RGZ 94, 3.

compensation for non-pecuniary loss are contained in the part of the Code which deals with tortious liability. CC § 823 provides for compensation where the defendant deliberately or negligently and unlawfully causes injury to the life, limb, health, liberty of another or his property or some other right (*Eigentum oder ein sonstiges Recht*). It has been held that a person's honour is not a *sonstiges Recht*;[746] but the phrase has been held to include certain rights of personality which will be discussed below.

Damages for injured feelings are specifically provided for by CC § 847, under which a reasonable compensation in money is available for non-pecuniary loss in cases of injury to the plaintiff's person or health, in cases of deprivation of liberty, and at the suit of a female plaintiff in certain cases of seduction. Such damages are also available under CC § 1300 at the suit of a female plaintiff who has allowed the defendant to cohabit with her on the strength of a promise of marriage which is subsequently broken. The damages recoverable under CC § 847 are not limited to the bodily pain flowing from the injury but can include the distress suffered by the plaintiff:[747] they resemble damages for "pain and suffering" in ANGLO-AMERICAN law.

Although CC § 847 refers to bodily harm, *etc.* in general terms, it has been held that the provision only applies where the plaintiff has a cause of action in tort, and not where the harm arises solely from a breach of contract.[748] If the harm is inflicted in circumstances giving rise to liability both in contract and in tort, *Schmerzensgeld* may be awarded under CC § 847.[749] The result of these rules is to reduce liability for injury to feelings arising from a breach of contract to within very narrow bounds; and this state of the law in GERMANY has not escaped criticism.[750]

It is, perhaps, arguable that the provisions of the Civil Code do not restrict recovery for non-pecuniary loss in contract cases within quite such narrow bounds as the foregoing discussion may suggest. The GERMAN courts have in a number of decisions awarded damages for non-pecuniary injury, basing themselves on constitutional provisions which are said to give rise to a general right of personality (*allgemeines Persönlichkeitsrecht*). The leading case is one in which the plaintiff's picture was without his consent used in advertisements for a preparation said to have certain aphrodisiac qualities. It was held that the plaintiff was entitled to damages on the ground that the *Persönlichkeitsrecht* was a *sonstiges Recht* within CC § 823; and that damages were recoverable under CC § 847 as the plaintiff had at least metaphorically been deprived of his liberty.[751]

The case has aroused acute controversy[752] which is beyond the scope of this chapter;[753] and it has never been applied to an injury due solely to a breach of contractual duty. Such extension is theoretically possible: for example in a situation analogous to that which occurred in the FRENCH case mentioned in s. 111 above, where the defendant's breach of contract caused *dommage moral* by offending the plaintiff's religious susceptibilities (*supra* n. 735). But so far there is no sign that the principle will be extended in this direction in GERMAN law.

113. *Austrian and Swiss law.* – The narrow scope of damages for injured feelings in GERMAN law may be contrasted with the position in AUSTRIAN law. Reference has already been made in s. 79 above to the AUSTRIAN distinction between *Schadloshaltung* and *volle Genugtuung* (CC § 1324). The latter concept includes compensation not only for lost gains but also for *Beleidigung*[754] (insult), so that damages for injured feelings are in principle available in cases of deliberate wrongdoing (*supra* s. 79). The right to recover such damages exists even though the cause of action is purely contractual. Damages for *Beleidigung* can, for example, be recovered where a wedding party finds a hotel room which it has booked occupied by other guests.[755]

The AUSTRIAN Civil Code also provides for damages for pain and suffering (*Schmerzensgeld*) in cases of personal injury (CC § 1325); and such damages are recoverable even though the cause of action is purely contractual.[756] Special provision is also made for cases of disfigurement, particularly of a female plaintiff (CC § 1326): in such a case the defendant is liable to the extent that the plaintiff's advancement is hindered thereby. It is assumed that the harm is not caused deliberately. If it is so

[746] BGB-RGRK § 823 no. 26, where other methods of protecting a person's honour are enumerated.

[747] *Palandt* § 847 no. 3.

[748] RG 8 Jan. 1926, RGZ 112, 294.

[749] BGH 27 Feb. 1952, BGHZ 5, 321.

[750] *Enneccerus and Lehmann* 94.

[751] BGH 14 Feb. 1958, BGHZ 26, 349.

[752] See BGB-RGRK § 847 no. 2, and in particular *Larenz*, Das "allgemeine Persönlichkeitsrecht" im Recht der unerlaubten Handlungen: NJW 1955, 521.

[753] See this Encyclopedia vol. XI ch. 8 s. 95.

[754] CC § 1323; *cf.* also CC § 1330.

[755] *Klang* (-*Wolff*) VI § 1324 no. II2 (p. 127); *cf. supra* n. 722.

[756] *Klang* (-*Wolff*) VI § 1325 no. III4.

caused, the principle of *volle Genugtuung* applies.

SWISS law draws a distinction between *Schadenersatz* and *Genugtuung*. The former expression refers to compensation for material loss while the latter refers to money payments which may be claimed in cases of death, personal injury or injury to personality.[757] The purpose of a *Genugtuung* is not so much to compensate the plaintiff for loss as to provide him with some "satisfaction" for injury to his feelings.[758] The idea is that although money will not compensate the plaintiff it may provide him with alternative sources of enjoyment which will in a sense make up for the injury to his feelings.[759]

The SWISS concept is basically similar to the FRENCH notion of *dommage moral*, on which it appears to be based. The provisions for *Genugtuung* are contained in the part of the Code of Obligations which deals with torts; but these provisions are made applicable to contracts (CO art. 99 par. 3). It follows that a *Genugtuung* can be recovered in a contractual action: for example, by an employee injured at work as a result of the employer's breach of contract.[760] The possibility of recovery of *Genugtuung* has even been envisaged in a case in which a person who had been engaged as a salesman repudiated the engagement on the day after it was made, though in this case the claim failed since no injury to the employer's personality was in fact shown to have occurred.[761]

b. Non-Payment of Money

114. *Interest as damages in Anglo-American law.* – The original rule of ENGLISH law was that if a debtor failed to perform an obligation to pay a fixed sum of money he could be sued for that sum and no more. He was not liable even to pay interest unless the debt arose out of a mercantile security, or unless there was a special agreement to pay interest.[762] The ENGLISH courts have however long had a power by statute to award interest on overdue debts;[763] and the general position in ANGLO-AMERICAN law now is that interest is recoverable by way of damages for non-payment of money.

It is also the general rule that interest constitutes the sole damages for a default of this kind.[764] The explanation for this rule is sometimes said to be that the creditor could have mitigated his loss by going into the market to borrow an equivalent sum; or that extra loss resulting from his failure or inability to do so is not foreseeable.[765] But the rule is in fact more general than these explanations would suggest. It applies even though it was not reasonably possible for the creditor to raise money elsewhere and even though the debtor could perfectly well foresee that his failure to make the payment would lead to the ruin of the creditor.[766] The rule, though well established, has been strongly criticised as it may leave the aggrieved party uncompensated for a loss which he in fact suffered, which he could not in fact have avoided, and which was not on any of the normal tests too remote.[767] It seems that the rule serves no useful purpose that could not be equally well accomplished by the principles of remoteness and mitigation.

Courts and legislatures in COMMON LAW countries have therefore created many important exceptions to the rule. It does not, for example, apply where a banker wrongfully fails to honour a customer's cheque; where a person who has agreed to subscribe for debentures in a company, or perhaps to make any other loan, fails to do so; where a buyer fails in his obligation to provide a letter of credit in accordance with the requirements of a contract of sale; and where a hirer of goods not only fails to make payments already due but repudiates his obligation to make future payments under the contract.[768] This list of exceptions should be regarded as illustrative and not as exhaustive. It would seem to be capable of extension to cover any case in which the court could find some other way of describing the defendant's obligation than one simply to pay a fixed sum of money.

Where interest is recoverable the rate is at the discretion of the court; and that interest may be awarded irrespective of proof of any loss to the plaintiff.[769]

115. *Interest as damages in French law.* – In

757 CC art. 28; CO art. 47, 49.

758 *Guhl* 68–69.

759 *Oser and Schönenberger* V 1 art. 47 no. 4–5.

760 BG 7 Sept. 1954, BGE 80 II 256.

761 BG 27 Nov. 1928, BGE 54 II 481.

762 *Treitel* 814.

763 See now Law Reform (Miscellaneous Provisions) Act, 1934 (24 & 25 Geo. 5, c. 41) s. 3.

764 *Corbin* § 995; *Treitel* 814; CALIFORNIAN CC § 3302; Revised Codes of MONTANA (*supra* n. 137) § 17-303; NORTH DAKOTA Century Code (*supra* n. 154) § 32-03-10; OKLAHOMA Statutes (*supra* n. 187) § 23-27; SOUTH DAKOTA Compiled Laws (*supra* n. 154) § 21-2-2.

765 *Corbin* § 995; *Treitel* 814.

766 INDIAN Contract Act, 1872 (*supra* n. 241) s. 73 ill. (n).

767 *Wallis v. Smith* (1882), 21 Ch.D. 243, 257 (C.A.).

768 *Treitel* 815; UCC s. 4-402.

769 So, for example, the ENGLISH provision cited *supra* n. 763.

FRANCE the law starts with a rule similar to that of ANGLO-AMERICAN law. CC art. 1153 lays down the general rule that in obligations which are limited to the payment of money, damages resulting from delay in payment are never to consist of anything except interest at the legal rate. This rate is fixed by the *Conseil d'État*.[770] Some exceptions to this rule are stated in CC art. 1153 itself: it is subject to special rules governing certain commercial transactions and suretyship; and it does not apply where the debtor is guilty of bad faith.

The last of these exceptions has already been discussed in s. 80 above; while the others are illustrated by CC art. 2028 and 1846. CC art. 2028 provides that a surety who has been compelled to pay the principal debt is entitled not only to reimbursement of the principal sum, interest and expenses but also, in a proper case, to damages. Under CC art. 1846 a partner who fails to make an agreed contribution of money to the "civil company" is liable for interest and in addition for extra loss suffered by the firm in consequence of his default.

It appears, moreover, that the creditor may be entitled, in addition to interest, to expenses incurred in compelling the debtor to pay, for example to the expense of issuing a *mise en demeure* (notice putting the debtor in default; see ch. 15).[771] There is furthermore nothing to prevent the parties from varying the rule laid down in CC art. 1153, for example by making an agreement for the payment of interest above the legal rate.[772] Such interest, however, would appear to be contractual interest rather than interest which is payable by way of damages.

CC art. 1153 provides that interest at the legal rate is recoverable without proof of loss. It therefore constitutes a minimum, as well as a normal maximum measure of recovery.

116. *Interest in German law and other systems.* – In GERMANY CC § 288 provides for interest at four per cent in the case of delay in the payment of a money debt; if the debt arises out of a commercial transaction the rate is fixed by Comm.C § 352 at five per cent. GERMAN law differs from the systems so far discussed in that these rules lay down the minimum but *not* the maximum measure of recovery. That is, the rates prescribed by the Codes are recoverable irrespective of any proof of loss;[773] but CC § 288 provides that a claim for further damage is not excluded.[774] If further loss has been suffered (for example, if higher interest has to be paid by the aggrieved party to his creditor) it may be recoverable as damages for delay under the general provisions governing such damages in CC § 286. The position is the same under ULIS.[775] The AUSTRIAN Civil Code likewise provides that the loss suffered by a creditor as a result of a delay in payment is compensated by payment at the rate determined by law (CC § 1333); but this provision does not exclude the possibility of recovering further loss if it has in fact been suffered and if it is recoverable in accordance with the general principles relating to the existence and extent of liability.[776] In this connection it should be recalled that lost gains are not (except in commercial transactions) recoverable unless the defendant is guilty of deliberate wrongdoing (*supra* s. 79). The SWISS Code of Obligations is generally similar in effect to the GERMAN and AUSTRIAN rules: that is, it provides for interest for delay in payment and for the recovery of further damages if additional loss has been suffered.[777] Once again it is of course assumed that the general rules as to the existence and extent of liability are satisfied. In this connection it should be noted that under SWISS law the burden of disproving fault in the type of case here under consideration is expressly placed on the debtor (CO art. 106).

117. *Conclusion.* – As a matter of general policy, the systems of law which in principle allow damages beyond interest for the failure to perform an obligation to pay money would seem to offer the preferable solution. The systems which in principle confine the creditor to interest do so on the basis of assumptions about the availability of credit and the stability of currencies which in modern conditions are of very questionable validity. They therefore feel bound to engraft exceptions onto their general rule, and these often give the law an inelegant and illogical appearance, without adequately ensuring that desirable results are reached in all situations. The debtor of an obligation to pay money can be adequately protected by the general rules limiting damages; any further limitation is liable to cause undue prejudice to the creditor.

c. Failure to Make Title

118. *Rule limiting damages to certain types of*

[770] *Mazeaud and Tunc*, Traité III (ed. 5) no. 2335.

[771] *Idem* III no. 2338.

[772] *Idem* III no. 2041.

[773] RG 4 March 1918, RGZ 92, 284; BGH 29 Oct. 1952, NJW 1953, 337.

[774] *E.g.* for loss of profits: *Enneccerus and Lehmann* 225.

[775] *Supra* s. 7; art. 82, 83.

[776] *Klang (-Wolff)* VI § 1333, 1334 no. II 4 (p. 179).

[777] CO art. 104, 106.

reliance. – It is well settled in ENGLISH law that where a vendor of land is unable to show good title, so that the contract cannot be completed by conveyance, the purchaser is not entitled to damages for loss of his bargain, that is for loss of his expectation interest. The only damages which he can recover are the costs of investigating the vendor's title.[778] He is not (it seems) entitled to other items of reliance loss. The rule does not apply where the vendor could show a good title by taking certain steps and refuses to do so; or where the defect in his title consists simply of a charge which he fails to pay off.[779] Moreover, if the vendor knows that his title is defective he is liable in tort for misrepresentation, so that he can recover in respect of items of reliance beyond the costs of investigating the vendor's title.[780]

Various attempts have been made to justify the rule but none of them is really successful. One argument is that, in view of the complexities of ENGLISH land law, the purchaser takes the risk that the vendor may not be able to show good title; but the rule is applied even in cases in which the vendor's failure is not due to these complexities but simply due to the failure of a superior landlord to give a required consent to the transaction.[781] Another argument is that transactions in land are generally completed in a fairly short space of time and that during this time the land is not likely to fluctuate very much in value.[782] But one or both of these assumptions may be false; and in any event the argument ignores the simple possibility that the buyer may have made a good bargain.

The rule appears simply to be an anomaly, and many COMMON LAW jurisdictions have recognized this fact and have accordingly refused to follow the rule. It has, for example, been held not to apply in INDIA and PAKISTAN, whose law of contract is based on an Act which was passed before the rule was finally established in ENGLAND.[783] Many of the UNITED STATES OF AMERICA also refuse to follow the rule.[784] In other states the rule exists in a statutory form which, however, expressly entitles the purchaser to recover the difference between the price and the value of the land in cases of bad faith.[785] In one state a statutory provision of this kind has been amended so as to allow the buyer damages for loss of expectation irrespective of bad faith, thus reversing the original ENGLISH rule.[786]

There appears to be no parallel to the rule in the CIVIL LAW; nor does there seem to be any cogent reason for limiting reliance and excluding expectation loss in cases of this kind.

G. PAYMENTS STIPULATED BY THE CONTRACT[787]

119. *Terminology.* – A contract may contain a stipulation providing for the payment of a fixed amount of money by the debtor in the event of his default. Such a clause is known as a *clause pénale* in FRENCH law and as a *Vertragsstrafe* in GERMAN law. In principle such provisions are valid in FRENCH and GERMAN law, though they are not always literally enforced. In ANGLO-AMERICAN law the literal translation of the FRENCH and GERMAN terms (penal clause; contractual penalty) is normally used to refer to an *invalid* stipulation for the payment of a fixed sum in the event of default. Where the clause is valid, it is referred to as a "liquidated damages" clause. This difference in terminology gives rise to some awkwardness in a comparative discussion of the institution. In the following sections, such expressions as "penalty clause" will be used in the CIVIL LAW sense (of a valid provision) when rules are under discussion which apply in CIVIL LAW countries alone, or both in CIVIL LAW and in COMMON LAW countries. The COMMON LAW distinction between penalty clauses and liquidated damages clauses will be used only in discussions restricted to COMMON LAW rules; or if it is used in other contexts attention will expressly be drawn to this fact.

778 *Treite* 815-816.

779 *Idem* 816.

780 *Ibidem.*

781 As in the leading case of *Bain v. Forthergill* (1874), *supra* n. 362.

782 See *Corbin* § 1098.

783 *Pollock and Mullah*, The Indian Contract and Specific Relief Acts (ed. 5 London and Bombay 1924) 410; *Dutt*, 677-678; *Mahmood* 538-542. The INDIAN Contract Act (*supra* n. 241) was passed in 1872, two years before *Bain v. Forthergill* (*supra* n. 362).

784 *Corbin* § 1098.

785 CALIFORNIAN CC § 3306; Revised Codes of MONTANA (*supra* n. 137) § 17-306; OKLAHOMA Statutes (*supra* n. 187) § 23-27; SOUTH DAKOTA Compiled Laws (*supra* n. 154) § 21-2-3.

786 NORTH DAKOTA Century Code (*supra* n. 154) § 32-03-13.

787 *Lindacher; Marsh*, Penal Clauses in Contracts – A Comparative Study: 32 J.Comp.Leg. (1950) III-IV 66; *Benjamin*, Penalties, Liquidated Damages and Penal Clauses in Commercial Contracts – A Comparative Study of English and Continental Law: 9 I.C.L.Q. 600 (1960). Important changes to FRENCH CC art. 1152 and 1231 (*infra* s. 129, 130) have been made by the Law of 9 July 1975 (JO 10 July 1975 p. 7076), giving the courts power to modify manifestly excessive or derisory penalties.

i. *Nature and Purposes of Penalty Clauses*

120. *Nature of penalty clauses.* – A penalty clause normally takes the form of requiring the debtor to pay a fixed sum of money in the event of his default. In the case of an obligation to do an act the debtor may be required to pay a single lump sum on his failure to do the act; in the case of an obligation to forbear he may be required to make such a payment on his doing the act from which he promised to forbear. Where the debtor is required to do an act within a fixed time, it is common to find a penalty clause which obliges him to make, not a single lump sum payment but a series of payments for each stipulated period of delay. Even where the penalty is payable for non-performance or defective performance, it may be expressly proportioned to the seriousness of the default, *e.g.* where a contract of sale provides for penalties for short delivery at a rate proportioned to the degree of shortage.

Penalty clauses are not, of course, always as explicit as the foregoing account may suggest. They may simply provide for the payment of a certain sum or sums on default, without specifying exactly which of many possible kinds of default they are intended to cover; and this looseness of drafting is one source of difficulty in relation to such clauses.

Almost always a penalty clause requires the debtor to make a payment of money; but in principle this does not appear to be essential. A provision requiring a seller to deliver more goods for the same price on his failure to deliver the agreed quantity at the agreed time would in principle be a penalty clause. The GERMAN Civil Code indeed begins by defining a penalty clause as one providing for the payment of a sum of money (CC § 339); but it goes on to recognise the fundamentally similar character of a provision for a performance other than the payment of money.[788] The INDIAN Contract Act similarly refers in s. 74 to two cases: "if a sum is named in the contract as the amount to be paid in case of such breach or if the contract contains any other stipulation by way of penalty". The Illustrations to the Act make it clear that a stipulation for a performance other than the payment of a sum of money is intended to be included.[789] The FRENCH definition of a penal clause as one by which the debtor binds himself to "something" in case of nonperformance (CC art. 1226) is obviously broad enough to include things other than the payment of a sum of money.

121. *Penalty clauses distinguished from analogous provisions.* – Penalty clauses must be distinguished from a number of analogous types of provisions which share one or more of their purposes (*infra* s. 122).

First, they must be distinguished from clauses which limit the liability of the defaulting party to a certain sum. The effect of a valid limitation clause is that the plaintiff can recover his actual loss to the extent to which it does not exceed the amount specified. Under a penalty clause, on the other hand, the plaintiff in principle recovers the full stipulated sum even though his actual loss is less, and in some systems at least even though he cannot prove that the default actually caused him any loss at all (*see infra* s. 127).

Secondly, penalty clauses must be distinguished from stipulations for the payment of money on events other than default, such as the death or bankruptcy of the debtor, the lawful termination of the contract or some other event.[790] In the ENGLISH case of *Alder v. Moore*[791] a professional footballer received a sum of money from an insurance company on account of a personal injury which was supposed to have disabled him; and he undertook to repay that sum in the event of his again playing professional football. This was not a penalty since the footballer made no promise not to play again and committed no breach by so doing. An undertaking of this kind is known as a *selbständiges Strafversprechen* (independent penal promise) in GERMAN law.[792]

An analogous but distinguishable institution in the COMMON LAW was the so-called penal bond under which a person promised to pay a fixed sum of money unless he performed a certain act within a fixed time. Such bonds differed from the agreement in *Alder v. Moore* in that their principal purpose was to secure the performance of the stipulated act; and an early ENGLISH statute provided that the creditor, though he might recover judgment for the sum named in the bond, could only levy execution for the loss which he had sustained as a result of the non-performance of the act.[793] The statute is no longer in force in ENGLAND where such penal bonds are not now in

[788] CC § 342; *cf.* AUSTRIAN CC § 1336.

[789] INDIAN Contract Act, 1872 (*supra* n. 241) s. 74 ill. (e).

[790] *Treitel* 824.

[791] [1961] 2 Q.B. 57 (C.A.); contrast INDIAN Contract Act, 1872 (*supra* n. 241) s. 74 ill. (b).

[792] *Enneccerus and Lehmann* 160.

[793] The Administration of Justice Act, 1696 (8 & 9 Will. 3, c. 11); see *Wall v. Rederiaktiebolaget Luggude*, [1915] 3 K.B. 66.

common use, though similar legislation is still in force in some of the UNITED STATES.[794] The modern tendency in the UNITED STATES is to regard penal bonds as contracts to perform the stipulated act and thus in substance to treat them as contracts containing penalty clauses.

The expression penalty clause covers clauses which provide for an additional payment in the event of default. A clause is therefore a penalty if it provides that an increased rate of interest is to be paid by a debtor on failure to pay at the agreed time.[795] But a clause providing for reduction in the rate of interest on punctual payment is not generally regarded as penal;[796] though it has been suggested in the UNITED STATES that such a clause might sometimes be regarded as penal[797] and there are conflicting decisions on the question whether a provision for a "discount" on punctual payment is penal in nature.[798] A similar distinction exists in the case of contracts (such as contracts for the execution of works or for the delivery of goods) to be performed within a fixed time. A provision for the payment of certain specified sums by the contractor in the event of delay in performance is regarded as penal; and the same would appear to be true of a provision for a reduction of the injured party's counter-performance (*i.e.* of the price) on such on event. But a bonus payable in the event of early completion is not regarded as a penalty.[799]

A clause accelerating the liability of a party in case of, for example, default in payment is generally held to be not penal since it does not actually increase the amount payable;[800] though if the deferred payments do not bear interest it is arguable that their acceleration compels the debtor to pay more than the present value of payments not originally due until a future date.[801] It is also arguable that an acceleration clause may have a purpose very similar to that of a penalty clause (see below s. 122); and acceleration clauses have sometimes been held penal on this ground.[802]

A penalty clause is one by which the parties at the time of making the contract provide for certain consequences of default. If they make such a provision *after* the default has already occurred, it is not in principle a penalty. This point is made particularly clear by statutory provisions which refer to penalties as provisions determining *in advance* the amount payable on breach;[803] and by the reference in FRENCH CC art. 1152 to an agreement providing for the payment of a certain sum if he "will fail" (*manquera*) to perform his part of the contract. The corresponding provisions of the GERMAN Civil Code[804] use the present tense (*nicht ... erfüllt*) which equally excludes agreements made after default has already occurred.

Considerable difficulty exists in distinguishing between penalty and forfeiture clauses. The expression forfeiture clause itself has no clear, single meaning but refers to a variety of different types of provisions.

It refers first to a provision by which a party is to forfeit payments which he has made under the contract in the event of his default. Some such provisions are in some systems regarded as penal, or at any rate as governed by the same principles as penalty clauses.[805] In ENGLAND the preponderant view is that such provisions are not to be regarded as penal,[806] while in the UNITED STATES there is considerable conflict of judicial opinion on the point.[807] The law with respect to such payments also depends on a number of further distinctions to be discussed in s. 137 ss. below. The expression forfeiture clause also refers to provisions extinguishing certain claims of a party in the event of his default. Here a subdivision has to be made between a clause purporting to deprive the defaulting party of all his rights and one purporting to deprive him of some of his rights only. GERMAN terminology neatly expresses the distinction by describing the former provision as a *Verfallklausel* and the latter as an *Einzelverfallklausel*. A clause of the first kind may be one which purports to

[794] *E.g.* MASSACHUSETTS General Laws Annotated – M.G.L.A. – Ch.235 § 9; General Laws of RHODE ISLAND (1956) 1969 Reenactment, § 9-27-1 and 4.

[795] INDIAN Contract Act, 1872 (*supra* n. 241) s. 74 ill. (a), (b).

[796] *Pollock and Mullah* (*supra* n. 783) 434; *Mahmood* 579.

[797] *Corbin* § 1065.

[798] *Idem* § 1058.

[799] *Idem* § 1072, 1073; *cf.* in GERMANY RG 28 Feb. 1908, RGZ 68, 41 at 42.

[800] *Corbin* § 1059; *cf.*, *White and Carter (Councils), Ltd. v. McGregor, supra* n. 452.

[801] *Corbin* § 1059; *cf. Treitel* 821.

[802] *E.g.*, *Commissioner of Insurance v. Massachusetts Accident Co.*, 310 Mass. 769, 39 N.E.2d 759 (1942). Such clauses may also be the subject of specific statutory control: *e.g.* GERMAN *Abzahlungsgesetz* (Instalment Sales Act) of 16 May 1894 (RGBl. 450) § 4 par. 2.

[803] CALIFORNIAN CC § 1670; Revised Code of MONTANA (*supra* n. 137) § 13-084, 085; NORTH DAKOTA Century Code (*supra* n. 154) § 9-08-04; OKLAHOMA Statutes (*supra* n. 187) § 15-214; SOUTH DAKOTA Compiled Laws (*supra* n. 154) § 53-9-5.

[804] CC § 339; *cf.* AUSTRIAN CC § 1336; SWISS CO art. 160.

[805] *E.g.* SOUTH AFRICAN Conventional Penalties Act (no. 15 of 1962) s. 4.

[806] *Treitel* 826-828.

[807] *Corbin* § 1063.

regulate the right to terminate the contract;[808] such a clause is not considered penal and its effect will be discussed in s. 149, 157, 172 below. A clause of the second kind, though not literally within the statutory definitions, is treated in the same way as a penalty clause in GERMANY.[809] There is some support for the same view in the UNITED STATES and in ENGLAND: for example where a builder in default forfeits a sum due or to become due to him under the contract.[810]

Clauses of the last kind make it necessary to distinguish between provisions under which rights which *have* accrued under the contract are forfeited and provisions which determine *when* rights accrue. Provisions of the latter kind (for example, a provision that a person must work for a stipulated time before he is entitled to his pay, or one that goods must be carried to their destination before freight is earned) are not generally regarded as penal,[811] though provisions of the former kind (for example, a provision that an employee shall forfeit wages accrued due if he departs without due notice) are sometimes so regarded.[812]

The SWISS Code of Obligations, when dealing with sums retained under contracts of service, lays down that they are not to be regarded as penalties, but as security for claims of the employer resulting from the employment relationship.[813]

122. *Purposes of penalty clauses.* – The primary purpose of penalty clauses is to fix in advance the damages payable in the event of default. This is in itself a perfectly legitimate and indeed laudable purpose. It obviates the often difficult tasks of assessing the aggrieved party's loss and of determining how much of that loss is legally recoverable. A clause which serves this purpose may even be advantageous from the point of view of the defaulting party in enabling him with some degree of certainty to know in advance what his liability will be in the event of default.

A second object of penalty clauses is precisely to limit a defaulting party's liability; and this is true in spite of the fact that penalty clauses are distinct in their legal nature from limitation clauses (*supra* s. 121). This second object of penalty clauses is not always achieved; we shall see that in many legal systems a contracting party is not necessarily limited to the amount of the payment stipulated.

A third object of penalty clauses is to provide a means of pressure on the debtor so as to coerce him into performing his principal undertaking. Indeed, in FRANCE penalty clauses have been described as a sort of *astreinte*[814] (*supra* s. 24), an analogy which is particularly apt where the penalty clause provides for a series of payments for each designated period of delay. It is obvious that the use of penalty clauses for this purpose is a potential source of abuse in that it may enable the creditor to exert an amount of pressure on the debtor which a particular legal system regards as excessive. It may at the same time enable the creditor to recover a sum of money which manifestly and very considerably exceeds the amount of his loss; and there is a natural reluctance on the part of the courts to make awards which drastically cut across the rules of law which determine the assessment of damages.

Such considerations have led to restrictions on the enforceability of penalty clauses in many legal systems: as a SCOTTISH judge has said, "the law will not let people punish each other."[815] This represents the attitude of ANGLO-AMERICAN law in which certain kinds of penalty clauses are wholly invalid, and indeed are sometimes said to be contrary to "public policy" or to be "unlawful" contracts;[816] it is also the basis of the rule adopted by GERMAN law and certain other systems by which the courts have a power to reduce the amount of a disproportionately high penalty. These solutions are of course open to the objection that they tend to subvert the first and legitimate purpose of penalty clauses; and it is on this view that the general principle of FRENCH law, giving literal effect to penalty clauses, is based. What is at stake here is the perennial conflict between certainty and justice; and in fact some degree of compromise is to be found in all the legal systems under consideration. The various solutions will be considered in greater detail in s. 128 ss. below after we have discussed a number of rules relating to penalties on which the various legal systems are (subject to a few minor variations) in basic agreement.

808 And hence governed by GERMAN CC § 360.

809 *Enneccerus and Lehmann* 159; *Palandt* no. 2b before § 339; BGH 22 May 1968, NJW 1968, 1625.

810 *Corbin* § 1073; *Gilbert-Ash (Northern), Ltd. v. Modern Engineering (Bristol), Ltd., supra* n. 337.

811 *Corbin* § 1058.

812 *E.g., Schrimpf v. Tennessee Mfg. Co.*, 86 Tenn. 219, 6 S.W. 131 (1887).

813 CO art. 323a par. 3 as amended by the Law of 25 June 1971 (AS 1971, 1465).

814 *Carbonnier* IV 264.

815 *Robertson v. Driver's Trustees* (1881), 8 R. 555, 562.

816 See the legislation referred to *supra* in n. 803; *Corbin* § 1057.

ii. *Effects of Penalty Clauses in General*

123. *Accessory nature of penalty.* – A penalty is a sum payable in the event of default and is recoverable only in that event. The penalty clause does not give rise to an independent obligation but to one which is accessory to the obligation to perform the principal obligation. The point is very clearly put in the LOUISIANA Civil Code (art. 2117): "A penal clause is a secondary obligation entered into for the purpose of enforcing performance of a primary obligation."

Thus if "fault" on the part of a debtor is an essential ingredient of contractual liability, it must exist before the penalty can be exacted;[817] if a *mise en demeure* or similar notice is required for the purpose of putting the debtor in default it must equally be given to sustain a claim for the penalty;[818] if the principal obligation is null, so is the penalty;[819] if performance of the principal obligation becomes impossible as a result of an event for which the debtor is not responsible or if the debtor has some other excuse for non-performance of the principal obligation, liability to pay the penalty is likewise discharged;[820] termination of the contract normally deprives the penalty clause of its effect;[821] assignment of the principal obligation involves assignment of the penalty;[822] and the time at which a penalty becomes due depends on the time at which performance of the principal obligation is due, either under the terms of the contract or under any relevant rules of law.[823]

Of course none of the above rules apply to "independent penal promises" of the kind described in s. 121 above; and it is also possible for a debtor to undertake to pay a certain sum in the event of his failure to bring about a certain state of affairs whether or not that failure is due to factors for which he is contractually responsible.[824] But such exceptional bargains do not derogate from the general principle that a penalty clause contains a merely accessory obligation.

124. *Penalty not alternative.* – The general rule is that a contract with a penalty clause does not create an alternative obligation: that it is not open to the debtor to discharge himself by paying the penalty instead of performing his principal obligation. It is true that statements can be found in the AMERICAN authorities to the effect that the debtor has a "right" to break the contract on payment of the penalty;[825] but such statements no longer command general acceptance.[826] The view that the debtor has no right to discharge himself by paying the penalty is most clearly supported by cases in which the availability of specific enforcement of the principal obligation is recognised in spite of the fact that the contract contains a penalty clause.[827] The rule that the debtor does not have the right to discharge himself by paying the penal sum is expressly stated in the AUSTRIAN Civil Code (§ 1336 par. 1).

The converse question also arises: to what extent is the creditor free to choose, assuming that he cannot claim both the penalty and performance (*infra* s. 125, 126), between these two methods of relief? GERMAN law does give him such a choice: CC § 340 par. 1 provides that he can sue for the penalty instead of performance. The FRENCH Civil Code contains an apparently similar provision in art. 1228, which lays down that, instead of demanding the penalty, the creditor may sue for performance, but the conception differs from that of the GERMAN provision. The penalty is regarded not as something which the creditor can claim at his option instead of performance, but as an evaluation of damages.[828] The point of CC art. 1228 is not to give the creditor an option but rather to emphasise the fact that the presence of a penalty clause does not exclude the claim for performance.[829]

Where the principal obligation is one that cannot be specifically enforced and the penalty clause amounts in effect to a valid limitation of liability, it might be thought that there was no substantial difference between saying that the penalty clause determined the amount payable in the event of

[817] *Carbonnier* IV 264.

[818] FRENCH CC art. 1230; unless the clause is construed as as stipulation dispensing with the requirement of *mise en demeure*: *Mazeaud and Tunc*, Traité III (ed. 5) no. 2281.

[819] FRENCH CC art. 1227 par. 1; GERMAN CC § 344; SWISS CO art. 163 par. 2.

[820] *Enneccerus and Lehmann* 160; SWISS CO art. 163 par. 2 (unless the contrary is agreed); LOUISIANA CC art. 2120.

[821] *De Page* III no. 121 *bis* (unless the clause provides for damages on termination). On the question whether termination has retrospective effect, see *infra* s. 179.

[822] *Enneccerus and Lehmann* 160, 319.

[823] *Idem* 160, 161.

[824] SWISS CO art. 163 par. 2; LOUISIANA CC art. 2121.

[825] *Lattimore v. Harsen*, 14 Johnson (N.Y. Superior Court) 330 (1817).

[826] *Corbin* § 1070; *cf.* in SCOTLAND: *Gloag and Henderson* 134.

[827] *Stokes v. Moore*, 262 Ala. 59, 77 So.2d 331 (1955); ALABAMA Code (*supra* n. 137) § 9-54; *cf.* UCC s. 2-719 (1) (b).

[828] See FRENCH CC art. 1152, 1229; *De Page* III no. 119.

[829] *Planiol and Ripert* VII no. 872.

breach and that it expressed an alternative obligation. But even in such a case this would not necessarily be true. It is possible for a party to be deprived of the benefit of a limitation clause because of the nature of his default: for example because he deliberately failed to perform his undertaking. In that event the party who refused to perform and simply tendered the penal sum might find himself liable in damages for a larger amount.

All this is not to say that a contract might not be expressed in such a way as to give the debtor the option of either performing an act or forbearance *or* paying a fixed sum.[830] But in the absence of a clear indication of intention to that effect penalty clauses will not normally be construed in this way.[831]

125. *Can more than the penalty be claimed?* – The fact that a creditor's claim for performance is not excluded by the presence of a penalty clause gives rise to two problems. The first is whether the creditor can recover more by claiming "performance" than by claiming the penalty. The second, to be discussed in s. 126 below, is in what circumstances he can combine a claim for performance with one for the penalty.

A creditor may obviously recover "more" than the penalty where he seeks and obtains actual performance *in specie* of the obligation undertaken by the debtor. But in CIVIL LAW countries a claim for "performance" may include a claim for the cost of *substitute* performance which may amount to a claim, or at any rate may result in a judgment, for a sum of money by way of what a common lawyer would call damages (*supra* s. 9). At this point the distinction drawn in s. 124 above between the different conceptions of the nature of a penalty again becomes relevant.

If the penalty is regarded simply as an assessment of the damages payable on default, then (assuming the validity of the penalty clause) it follows that no more than the penalty can be recovered by way of substitutionary relief. This is the position in FRENCH law, where CC art. 1152 provides that where the agreement stipulates for the payment of a certain sum by way of damages no more can be recovered. The question arises, however, whether the same rule would apply where the aggrieved party claimed substitute performance, *e.g.* the right to have something that was done in contravention of the agreement destroyed at the expense of the debtor. A successful claim of this kind would result in a money judgment, but not in one for damages. It is not at all clear whether CC art. 1152 would apply to such a claim.

GERMAN law adopts a wholly different principle. CC § 340 par. 1 provides that where the penalty is promised for non-performance the creditor may claim the penalty instead of performance; and if he demands the penalty his claim for performance is excluded. But CC § 340 par. 2 goes on to provide that where the creditor claims compensation for non-performance, he is entitled to the penalty as a minimum sum, and that a claim for further damages is not excluded.[832] The GERMAN conception of a penalty is, therefore, not that of an assessment of damages but of an arbitrary sum, a true "penalty" for non-performance.

In COMMON LAW countries, the answer to our question turns on the distinction, discussed in s. 135 below, between liquidated damages clauses (which are valid) and penalty clauses (which are invalid). If the clause is a valid liquidated damages clause no more than the stipulated sum is recoverable by way of damages:[833] the COMMON LAW conception of a valid liquidated damages clause is from this point of view the same as the FRENCH. If, on the other hand, the clause is an invalid penalty clause it is totally disregarded and the plaintiff recovers his actual loss (subject to the normal limitations).[834] Under the INDIAN Contract Act, 1872 (*supra* n. 241) however, it appears that the stipulated sum cannot in any event be exceeded (s. 74). That Act rejects the COMMON LAW distinction between penalty and liquidated damages clauses and makes the stipulated sum the upper limit of recovery except where the clause is a limitation clause and is invalid as such.

126. *Can penalty be claimed together with performance or damages?* – So far it has been assumed that the penalty is payable simply on total non-performance of the principal obligation. In such a case it is clear that the aggrieved party cannot claim both the penalty and performance, or both the penalty and damages.[835] This may be called the general rule. It is however possible and indeed more common for the penalty to be payable for some partial failure in the promised performance,

[830] *Enneccerus and Lehmann* 163; *cf.* SWISS CO art. 160 par. 3.

[831] *Corbin* § 1070.

[832] See *Enneccerus and Lehmann* 162; *cf.* SWISS CO art. 161 par. 2; contrast the position under AUSTRIAN CC § 1336: *Klang* (-*Wolff*) VI § 1336 no. II6 b, c.

[833] *Corbin* § 1061; *Treitel* 822-823.

[834] *Treitel* 823.

[835] FRENCH CC art. 1229. The position is the same under GERMAN CC § 340 par. 1 where in such a case the penalty is claimable "in place of performance"; *cf.* SWISS CO art. 160 par. 1; AUSTRIAN CC § 1336 par. 1 sent. 1; SOUTH AFRICAN Conventional Penalties Act (*supra* n. 805) s. 2(1).

such as delayed or incomplete or defective performance, or failure to perform only one or more out of a greater number of duties incumbent on the defaulting party. In such situations all the systems under discussion recognise an exception to the general rule, by which it is often possible to claim both the penalty for the particular breach and either performance or compensation for non-performance in respect of other breaches.

Thus FRENCH CC art. 1229, after laying down the general rule that the creditor cannot demand both performance of the principal obligation and the penalty states an exception: "unless the penalty was provided for simple delay." The SWISS and AUSTRIAN Codes also recognise the general rule but state the exception more broadly:[836] it extends to cases where the penalty was provided for the case of failure to perform either at the agreed time or at the agreed place. A still broader statement of the exception can be found in GERMAN CC § 341 par. 1, under which the exception extends to cases where the penalty was provided for failure to perform properly (*gehörig*), that is in accordance with the contract.[837] Special reference is indeed made to failure to perform within the agreed time, but simply by way of illustration of the more general statement of the exception. There is, however, an exception to the exception: if the penalty clause provides for something to be performed by the debtor other than the payment of money, the creditor cannot demand this kind of penalty and also claim compensation.[838] There seems to be no doubt that in COMMON LAW jurisdictions a clause liquidating damages on one breach would not affect the damages recoverable on another breach;[839] the question which breach the clause was intended to cover would depend on the construction of the clause.

The wide scope of the exceptions in many of these systems gives rise to the question whether the narrower exception stated in FRENCH CC art. 1229 is in fact exhaustive or illustrative of a more general principle. If a penalty is stipulated for some default other than delay (*e.g.* shortage) could it be recovered in FRENCH law in addition to damages for some other breach (*e.g.* a qualitative defect)? It seems that in such a case both the penalty and damages could be recovered, even though there is no express warrant for this in the Civil Code.[840]

127. *Whether loss must be proved.* – It is generally agreed that judgment may be given for the amount of the penalty even though the aggrieved party does not show the amount of his loss. Sometimes the more extreme position is taken that the aggrieved party can recover the penalty without proving any loss at all. Indeed the law is expressly stated in this way in SWISS CO art. 161 par. 1.

In the absence of such express legislative statements some scepticism has been expressed with regard to the alleged rule.[841] This is particularly true in the context of systems of law which in principle require proof of loss to establish a cause of action for contractual default. The view that no loss at all need be proved in an action for a penalty has been criticised in AUSTRIA (though it is supported by decisions in that country). But at the same time it is admitted that proof of "immaterial" loss is sufficient and that such loss includes the worry occasioned by non-performance.[842] This admission seems to deprive the criticism of most of its force.

An interesting development has taken place in INDIA where the Contract Act, 1872, s. 74 provides for enforcement of penalty clauses (subject to a judicial power of reducing the stipulated amount to a reasonable sum) "whether or not actual damage or loss is proved to have been caused" by the breach of contract. The courts have seized on the word "actual" to support the view that neither the penalty nor any smaller sum should be awarded where "no legal injury at all has resulted";[843] though on the other hand they have also taken the view that the breach of contract is itself evidence that a loss has occurred.[844]

This sort of formulation would fit the common case in which a ship is detained for loading or unloading beyond the time allowed by the contract so that provisions for demurrage become operative. Here the fact of the ship's detention is sufficient damage; there is no need for a shipowner claiming demurrage to prove affirmatively that he would have had profitable (or any) employment for the ship during the period of her detention.[845]

Even where loss does not need to be proved,

[836] SWISS CO art. 160 par. 2; AUSTRIAN CC § 1336 par. 1 sent. 3.

[837] *Enneccerus and Lehmann* 162.

[838] *Idem* 163; CC § 342.

[839] *E.g., Akt.Reidar v. Arcos,* [1927] 1 K.B. 532.

[840] *Anon.,* Clause pénale. Généralités...: J.-Cl.Civ. art. 1226-1233 no. 119.

[841] *Corbin* § 1062.

[842] *Klang (-Wolff)* VI § 1336 no. II 6 a.

[843] *Fateh Shand v. Balkistan Dass,* A.I.R. 1963 S.C. 1405.

[844] *Mahadeoprasad v. Siemens (India), Ltd.,* A.I.R. 1934 Cal. 285; *Mahmood* 589.

[845] See *Suisse Atlantique Société d'Armement Maritime S.A. v. N.V. Rotterdamsche Kolen Centrale,* [1967] 1 A.C. 361, 395, 421, 435-436 (H.L.).

there are a number of reasons why it will often be advisable for the aggrieved party to show that he did in fact suffer loss and what the extent of the loss was. Where the courts have a discretion to reduce the amount payable under the penalty clause (*infra* s. 131), they will no doubt have regard to the amount of loss actually suffered. This factor will also be of some weight under the ANGLO-AMERICAN distinction between penalties and liquidated damages (*infra* s. 134-135). It is true that that distinction turns on the genuineness of the *pre*-estimate of loss; but the extent of the loss actually suffered will often be relevant (though it will not of course be decisive) to the question whether the pre-estimate was indeed genuine.

iii. *The Enforceability of Penalty Clauses*

128. *Introduction.* – The policy arguments for and against enforcing penalty clauses have been considered in s. 122 above, where the three principal methods of dealing with this problem were also outlined. These methods will now be considered in greater detail. Most of the rules which limit the enforceability of penal clauses are concerned with clauses which stipulate for the payment of too *high* a sum, that is a sum which exceeds the creditor's actual loss. These rules are not particularly suitable for dealing with the converse problem of clauses which stipulate for too *low* a sum so that they operate in practice (though not in legal theory) as limitation clauses. This problem is fully dealt with in ch. 1, and will only be briefly touched upon here (*infra* s. 136).

a. Literal Enforcement

129. *The French principle of literal enforcement.* – The general principle of FRENCH law is stated in CC art. 1152: when an agreement provides for the payment of a certain sum by way of damages in case of non-performance by one party, the other may not be awarded either a larger or a smaller sum. The courts have no general power to *reduce* the stipulated sum on the ground that it is excessive; nor is there any general principle under which a penalty clause may be *held invalid* on the ground that it stipulates for an excessive amount.[846]

It is sometimes said that the general principle of CC art. 1152 is a corollary of CC art. 1134 which enshrines the principle of freedom of contract.[847] But the principle of freedom of contract is nowhere an absolute one;[848] most WESTERN systems recognise it to some extent but nevertheless control the operation of penalty clauses by general rules and not (as FRENCH law does) by specific exceptions to a general principle of literal enforceability. The general principle of CC art. 1152 may also be supported on the ground that interference with penal clauses would destroy their principal, or at least their most easily justifiable purpose which is to obviate the difficulties of assessing damages.[849] But again the argument is not wholly convincing, for the experience of other systems suggests that it is possible to preserve this advantage of penalty clauses within a framework of rules designed to ensure that parties do not in fact stipulate for or recover excessive penalties.

The general principle of CC art. 1152 is in fact a surprising one, particularly in a system which is more solicitous than most to afford protection to the debtor. Perhaps this need is less acutely felt when the performance sought from the debtor is simply the payment of money. Similar reasoning no doubt helps to justify the *astreinte* and it has been suggested that a penalty clause is in fact analogous to this institution (*supra* s. 122). But if the *astreinte* is open to criticism on the ground of bringing undue pressure to bear on the debtor (*supra* s. 28) this objection is, if anything, stronger in the case of a penalty clause since the amount payable under such a clause is (unlike the *astreinte*) not subject to reduction. It is, however, interesting to note that legal systems based on FRENCH law, such as those of BELGIUM, LOUISIANA and QUEBEC, have, while rejecting the *astreinte*, accepted the general FRENCH principle of the irreducibility of penalty clauses.[850]

130. *Exceptions to the principle of literal enforcement.* – Exceptions to the principle of literal enforcement in FRENCH law are of two kinds. In some cases the court has a power to reduce the penalty. In others the penalty is wholly disregarded. For the most part the exceptions are based on specific legislative provisions.

The most important provision for reduction is contained in FRENCH CC art. 1231, under which the penalty may be modified where the contract has been performed in part. This power of reduc-

[846] *Planiol and Ripert* VII n. 869. But see *supra* n. 787.
[847] *De Page* III no. 124 *bis*.
[848] *Carbonnier* IV 265.
[849] *De Page* III no. 124 *bis*.

[850] The BELGIAN Civil Code, which generally follows the FRENCH, makes no departure from it at this point; LOUISIANA CC art. 1934 par. 5; QUEBEC CC art. 1076.

tion may be excluded by contrary agreement.[851] In QUEBEC this power of reduction only exists if the time for (full) performance is not material and if the part performance is beneficial to the creditor (CC art. 1076 par. 2). The power of reduction may also be conferred by special statutory provisions relating to certain types of contract, for example to instalment sales.[852]

A number of statutory provisions invalidating penalty clauses exist in the law of employment.[853] A disproportionately large penalty imposed on an employee has also been held invalid as tending to deprive the employee of his liberty to depart from his service.[854] A clause which had this effect would contravene the spirit of CC art. 1780 which gives the employee a power to leave even though the exercise of the power may make him liable in damages.

A clause raising the rate of interest on late payment beyond the rate permitted by law is also invalid.[855] A provision that the debtor is to pay interest on interest may be invalid as contrary to CC art. 1154, which provides that interest on interest can only become due if the latter interest is due for at least one year.

It has been suggested that penalty clauses might also be held void under a more general doctrine, such as the doctrine of abuse of rights or *fraude à la loi*;[856] and the case of the employee who is prevented from leaving his employment by an excessive penalty clause may be cited in support of this view. According to a BELGIAN decision a penalty clause may be attacked as "immoral and illicit" if it is not only excessive in amount but was also obtained by taking advantage of the gullibility and ignorance of the other contracting party.[857] This principle was applied where an agent, by exaggerating the value of a property, induced the owner to instruct him to sell the property for a commission of 10000 francs, and the contract provided that if the owner sold the property himself without informing the agent within 48 hours he was to pay the agent 6 per cent of the proceeds of sale, a sum which amounted to 16500 francs.

In cases in which the penalty clause is invalid under any of the preceding rules, this nullity does not affect the validity of the principal obligation.[858]

b. Enforcement Subject to Reduction

131. *The principle of enforcement subject to judicial discretion to reduce the amount.* – In GERMAN law, the general principle is that a penalty clause is valid and enforceable; but CC § 343 provides that if the penalty is unreasonably high it can be reduced by the court to a reasonable sum. This provision applies not only to penalty clauses *stricto sensu* but also to independent penal promises;[859] and it may even in some cases be applied to forfeiture clauses such as clauses providing for excessive reduction in wages or in the agreed price in the event of default.[860] The principle of reduction further applies whether the penalty consists of a sum of money or of some other performance (see CC § 343 par. 2).

Similar provisions for the reduction of unreasonably high penalties exist in many other countries, for example in AUSTRIA (CC § 1336 par. 2), ISRAEL,[861] ITALY (CC art. 1384), SWITZERLAND (CO art. 163 par. 3) and SOUTH AFRICA.[862] A substantially similar power exists under the INDIAN Contract Act s. 74 under which the court can award a reasonable compensation not exceeding the stipulated sum. A SCOTTISH case is sometimes cited in support of the proposition that the court may "modify" an exorbitant penalty;[863] but this seems in practice to mean little more than that the court may disregard the penalty, which is the same position as that reached under the ANGLO-AMERICAN distinction between penalties and liquidated damages. A power of reduction in ANGLO-AMERICAN law only existed and in some jurisdictions still exists in the special case of penal bonds (see *supra* s. 121), where it affected the amount of execution and not of judgment. Under the Uniform Commercial Code an unreasonably *small* stipulated sum may be regarded as unconscionable and thus become subject to modi-

851 Cass. civ. 4 June 1860, D.P. 1860. 1.257; the right to exclude the power of reduction is expressly conferred by LOUISIANA CC. art. 1934 par. 5 sent. 2 and QUEBEC CC art. 1076 par. 2. And see *supra* n. 787.

852 *De Page* III no. 125.

853 FRENCH *Code du travail* (Labour Code) Book I art. 22b, 290.

854 *Carbonnier* IV 265; *Mazeaud and Tunc*, Traité III (ed. 5) no. 2634.

855 *Mazeaud and Tunc*, Traité III (ed. 5) no. 2634.

856 *Carbonnier* IV 265.

857 Cass. 9 July 1936, Pas.1936.I.345.

858 FRENCH CC art. 1227 par. 2.

859 CC § 343 par. 2; *Enneccerus and Lehmann* 164. See *supra* s. 121.

860 *Ibidem*.

861 Contracts (Remedies for Breach of Contracts) Law 1970 (*supra* n. 481) s. 15.

862 SOUTH AFRICAN Conventional Penalties Act (*supra* n. 805) s. 3.

863 *Forrest and Barr v. Henderson* (1869), 8 M. 187 (C.S. Scotland).

fication;[864] but there is no corresponding power to vary a stipulation for an unreasonably *large* sum. Such a stipulation is simply void (s. 2-718 (1)).

In FRENCH law, a stipulation for an unreasonably small sum may be disregarded, but on a different theory. The test is not whether the stipulation was unconscionable, but whether the defendant was guilty of *dol* or *faute lourde*.[865] There is a power to *reduce* the stipulated sum only where the principal obligation has been performed in part.[866]

It will be seen that ANGLO-AMERICAN and FRENCH law are distinctly in a minority in refusing to recognise the principle of judicial reduction of unreasonably high penalty clauses.

132. *Grounds on which the power of reduction is based and exercised.* – Two questions arise in connection with the judicial power to reduce the amount of a penalty clause. In what circumstances does the power arise? And, assuming that it exists, on what principles will the reduction be made?

With regard to the first question, the legislative provisions which authorise reduction (*supra* s. 131) do so where the penalty is "disproportionately high" or "excessively high" or "excessive" or "unreasonable". Whether this requirement is satisfied is clearly a question of proportion between the stipulated sum and something else; but most of the legislative provisions do not make it clear with exactly what the stipulated sum is to be compared.

The only statutory provisions in which this is explicitly stated are those of SOUTH AFRICA and ISRAEL. Under the SOUTH AFRICAN legislation, the power of reduction exists if it appears to the court that the penalty is "out of proportion to the prejudice suffered by the creditor by reason of the act or omission in respect of which the penalty was stipulated."[867] Under the ISRAELI legislation, the court may reduce the penalty if it finds that it was fixed "without any reasonable relation to the damage which could be foreseen, at the time the contract was made, as the probable consequence of the breach."[868] Under both systems the question is one of proportion and not one of exact correspondence,[869] so that a penalty will not be regarded as too high merely because it exceeds the loss. But the two systems differ in that the SOUTH AFRICAN provision refers to the "prejudice suffered" (which seems to mean the *actual* loss) while the ISRAELI provision refers to foreseeable damage, that is, to the *recoverable* loss.

The distinction will be of practical importance where the actual prejudice exceeds the loss recoverable under the relevant rules as to (for example) remoteness. In systems which are not committed by legislation to one or the other of the criteria just stated, it would seem desirable to have regard to the proportion between the stipulated sum and the *actual loss*. There is nothing unfair or oppressive about stipulating for a payment which is reasonably related to the actual loss; particularly as the extent to which this loss will ultimately be held to have been foreseeable by the defendant, or adequately caused by the breach (and thus recoverable) will often be unknown by the parties at the time of contracting. Certainly it is hard to justify a reduction *below* the loss actually suffered where part of it would be too remote.[870] If, however, the actual loss is in part irrecoverable because the plaintiff ought to have *mitigated* or because he partly caused the loss, the better rule would seem to be one which looked to the relationship between the stipulated sum and the recoverable loss, *i.e.* that part of it for which the plaintiff did not, in a sense, share responsibility.

It is also possible for the actual loss to fall short of the loss that might have been recoverable: *e.g.* in a system in which foreseeability is the test of remoteness the loss suffered may be less than that which could have been foreseen; while the stipulated sum may be greater than both these amounts. Here again it would seem that the power of reduction, where it exists, should be exercised by reference to the actual loss. This should certainly be so where the stipulation is for a lump sum and the failure in performance is only partial. It follows that the general power of reduction would be exercisable in the circumstances in which the special power of reduction which exists in FRENCH law may be exercised, *i.e.* where the debtor had performed in part. Of the legislative provisions here under consideration, only the ITALIAN expressly states this rule (CC art. 1384), but the result would be the same under the other systems as part performance would normally reduce the prejudice to the creditor.

The SOUTH AFRICAN Act states that in assessing

864 Under UCC s. 2-302: see comment 1 to UCC s. 2-718.

865 Cour d'appel Paris 1 Feb. 1936, D.H. 1936, 242.

866 CC art. 1231; *supra* s. 130.

867 SOUTH AFRICAN Conventional Penalties Act (*supra* n. 805) s.3.

868 Contracts (Remedies for Breach of Contracts) Law 1970 (*supra* n. 481) s. 15.

869 *Cf.* the GERMAN view: BGB-RGRK § 343 no. 6; and the AUSTRIAN view: *Klang* (-*Wolff*) VI § 1336 no. II 10.

870 *Klang* (–*Wolff*) *ibidem*.

the prejudice "the court shall take into consideration not only the creditor's proprietary interest but every other rightful interest which may be affected by the act or omission in question."[871] The same criterion has been said to govern in GERMANY;[872] though on a literal reading of CC § 343 it seems to be relevant to the *exercise* rather than to the *existence* of the power of reduction.

With regard to the exercise of the power of reduction, most of the legislative provisions are extraordinarily vague. They simply leave the amount of reduction to the discretion of the judge or to his sense of what is equitable. Only the GERMAN provision expressly directs the judge to take into account every legitimate interest (and not only the financial interest) of the creditor.[873] Since legitimate non-financial interests do not always constitute items of recoverable loss, it seems to follow that it is the *actual* rather than the *recoverable* loss which is relevant to the exercise (no less than to the existence) of the power of reduction. Thus a creditor may quite probably recover more by way even of a reduced penalty than he would have recovered by way of damages in the absence of a penalty clause. The GERMAN courts are not restricted to taking into account the interests of the creditor which are mentioned in CC § 343. They may also take into account such factors as the debtor's degree of fault, any benefit which accrues to him as a result of the default, and his general financial situation.[874] In AUSTRIA the difficulty of finding a substitute and the size of the loss which could have occurred (as opposed to that which actually did occur) have also been regarded as relevant factors.[875]

In GERMAN law CC § 343 provides that there can be no reduction of the penalty after it has been paid. SOUTH AFRICAN law would probably reach the same conclusion as the power of reduction is given to the courts "upon the hearing of a claim for a penalty."[876] The position in the other systems under discussion is not explicitly stated but is probably the same since money paid over under a valid contract cannot normally be recovered back.

133. *Exceptions to the general principle.* – Exceptions to the general principle of enforcement subject to reduction are of two kinds.

In some cases the penalty clause is not enforceable at all. In GERMAN law, for example, the penalty cannot be enforced if it is contrary to a law specifically prohibiting penal promises in certain types of contracts;[877] or if it is contrary to good morals within CC § 138; or if it can be impeached on grounds which a common lawyer would describe as economic duress.[878] The penalty clause is not invalid on any of these grounds merely because the sum payable is disproportionate to the prejudice, though it may be struck down if it exceeds all reasonable bounds. This was, for example, held to be the position in a case decided in 1908 in which an employee whose annual salary was under 3000 M entered into a covenant not to compete and promised to pay the employers a penalty of 100000 M for each infraction.[879]

In other cases the principle of reduction does not apply. The most important of these in GERMAN law is contained in Comm.C § 348 which makes CC § 343 inapplicable to commercial transactions entered into by *Vollkaufleute*, an expression which may roughly be translated as "full merchants".[880] The principle of Comm.C § 348 may also in exceptional circumstances be applied to cases which fall outside the letter but within the spirit of this provision.[881] This exception of course goes far to serve the needs of certainty in the area where these needs are most acute and thus secures an important part of the advantage which is claimed for the FRENCH principle of literal enforcement. Even in commercial cases, however, a penalty may be reduced on some ground apart from GERMAN CC § 343: for example on the ground of error as to a fundamental assumption underlying the contract.[882]

The principle of reduction, moreover, only

[871] SOUTH AFRICAN Conventional Penalties Act (*supra* n. 805) s. 3 proviso.

[872] *Enneccerus and Lehmann* 164.

[873] CC § 343 par. 1 sent. 2; similar language in the SOUTH AFRICAN provision (*supra* n. 871) appears to refer to the assessment of the prejudice and not to the actual process of reduction.

[874] *Enneccerus and Lehmann* 164; BGB-RGRK § 343 no. 6.

[875] *Klang* (- *Wolff*) VI (*supra* n. 869).

[876] SOUTH AFRICAN Conventional Penalties Act (*supra* n. 805) s. 3.

[877] This follows from CC § 134.

[878] BGB-RGRK § 343 no. 4.

[879] RG 7 April 1908, RGZ 68, 229.

[880] They are contrasted with *Minderkaufleute* or minor merchants defined in Comm.C § 4; the provisions of Comm.C § 348 are by Comm.C § 351 made inapplicable to the contracts of such persons.

[881] BGH 13 Feb. 1952, BGHZ 5, 133 where the defendant was a "full merchant" at the time of the principal promise but had ceased to be so at the time of the penal promise by reason of having been incorporated.

[882] BGH 24 March 1954, NJW 1954, 998; see *supra* ch. 11.

applies to a penalty clause in the GERMAN sense of a true penalty (*supra* s. 125) as opposed to an attempt to make a pre-estimate of damages. A stipulation of the latter kind (or *Schadenersatzpauschalierung*) is in principle valid and not subject to reduction; though in standard form contracts the courts have shown a strong inclination to strike down a clause of this kind (*e.g.* as being contrary to CC § 138) where its literal enforcement would lead to the enrichment of the party relying on it. The distinction between the two types of provision is of fairly recent origin and the exact line between them remains uncertain.[883] It has obvious affinities with the ANGLO-AMERICAN distinction between penalties and liquidated damages (*infra* s. 134).

c. Distinction Between Penalties and Liquidated Damages

134. *General principle of Anglo-American law.* – ANGLO-AMERICAN law[884] divides stipulations for the payment of a sum of money in the event of breach (and other similar clauses) into two kinds: penalty clauses and liquidated damages clauses. The distinction is, in principle, based on the purpose of the clause, though it has become overlaid with technicalities.

If the clause is "stipulated as *in terrorem* of the offending party",[885] that is, if it is intended as a means of coercing him into performing the principal obligation, it is a penalty clause. Such a clause is disregarded for all purposes.[886] The aggrieved party cannot recover the stipulated sum but only his actual loss or so much of it as is recoverable in accordance with the principles discussed earlier in this chapter (*supra* s. 77-118). This is true whether that loss was smaller or greater than the stipulated sum. On the other hand, if the clause is a genuine attempt to estimate in advance the loss which was likely to result from the breach it is a liquidated damages clause. Such a clause is valid and is literally enforced. The aggrieved party is entitled to the stipulated sum whether his actual (or recoverable) loss amounted to more or to less.[887] There is (with a possible exception which will be discussed in s. 136 below) no judicial power to modify valid liquidated damages clauses.

The distinction between penalties and liquidated damages is one of substance so that the mere fact that the contract refers to a stipulated payment as a penalty or as liquidated damages does not conclusively determine its character.[888] This depends on the purpose of the clause, but the courts and in some cases the legislatures have laid down a number of rules which are intended as aids to determining that purpose.[889] Some of these rules are soundly based on the policy underlying the distinction. Others are very hard to justify, though they may be explained historically as evidencing the desire of the courts to escape from the principle of literal enforcement of liquidated damages clauses and to deter bargains which they regarded as highly unfair ones.

135. *Specific rules.* – The first and most important rule has been stated in ENGLAND as follows: that a stipulation will be a penalty if it is "extravagant and unconscionable in amount in comparison with the greatest loss that could conceivably be proved to have followed from the breach."[890] An illustration, given in an ENGLISH case, is a promise by a builder to pay £ 1 million if he failed to do work worth only £ 50.[891] This is of course just the sort of situation in which the clause would be invalid also in GERMAN law under CC § 138.[892] In the UNITED STATES the rule is sometimes said to be that a stipulation will be a penalty unless it is "reasonable".[893] The emphasis may be different from that of the ENGLISH statement, but the practical effect would almost always be the same.

The second rule is that a stipulation will be regarded as a valid liquidated damages clause if the circumstances were such that an accurate or precise pre-estimate of damages was impossible,

883 *Lindacher* esp. ch. 4 and 6; *Beuthien*, Pauschalierter Schadenersatz und Vertragstrafe: Festschrift Karl Larenz (Munich 1972) 495-516.

884 The same principles applied in the Roman Dutch law of SOUTH AFRICA before the Conventional Penalties Act (*supra* n. 805), and they still apply in SRI LANKA: *Weeramantry* II § 942. The principles also apply in SCOTLAND (subject to the possible qualification mentioned *supra* at n. 863: *Gloag and Henderson* 554-556).

885 *Dunlop Pneumatic Tyre Co., Ltd. v. New Garage and Motor Co., Ltd.*, [1915] A.C. 79, 86 (H.L.).

886 *Corbin* § 1062; *Treitel* 819, 823.

887 *Corbin* § 1061; *Treitel* 819; UCC s. 2-718 (1).

888 *Corbin* § 1058; *Treitel* 819.

889 See, in particular, *Dunlop Pneumatic Tyre Co., Ltd. v. New Garage and Motor Co., Ltd.* (*supra* n. 885) 87-88; *Corbin* § 1063.

890 *Dunlop Pneumatic Tyre Co., Ltd. v. New Garage and Motor Co., Ltd.* (*supra* n. 885) 87.

891 *Clydebank Engineering Co. v. Don Jose Ramos Yzquierdo y Castaneda* (*supra* n. 226) 10.

892 *Supra* s. 133. For analogous AMERICAN cases, see *Metz v. Clay*, 101 Kan. 45, 165 P. 809 (1917); *May v. Young*, 125 Conn. 1, 2 A.2d 385 (1938).

893 Restatement of Contracts (1932) § 339; UCC s. 2-718 (1).

and if the stipulated sum was in fact a genuine attempt to make a reasonable pre-estimate.[894] This would be the case, for example, where the stipulated sum was payable for breaches which would be likely to cause general disruption of the aggrieved party's business,[895] or for delay in beginning to drill an oil well.[896] In such cases the actual loss is obviously speculative.

In some AMERICAN states legislation is in force under which stipulations for a fixed sum are valid *only* "when from the nature of the case it would be impracticable or extremely difficult to fix the actual damage."[897] This is probably a more rigorous requirement than the COMMON LAW would generally impose. The difficulty of pre-estimating would be the typical, but not the only, case in which a valid stipulation could be made. There would appear to be no reason in principle why a valid pre-estimate should not be made for the case of short delivery of goods even though there is generally no special difficulty of pre-estimation in such a case.[898]

The question whether a sum was a genuine pre-estimate must be determined by reference to the time of contracting and not to the time of breach. It is possible (for example because of changing market conditions) for a sum to exceed a genuine pre-estimate and yet to fall short of the actual loss. It is this possibility which gives point to the rule that a penalty is disregarded for all purposes, so that the aggrieved party can in such a case recover more than the penalty.

The two rules so far discussed are soundly based on the purposes of the distinction between penalties and liquidated damages; but it is more questionable whether this is true of the third rule which has been evolved in this context. This rule deals with the situation in which a single sum is payable on one or more or all of several breaches which may occasion different amounts of damage. In such a case there is a presumption, but no more than a presumption, that the sum is a penalty, the argument being that it cannot be a genuine pre-estimate of damage for all the breaches.[899] The argument is most easily understood by reference to a case in which a tenant farmer promised to pay "the additional rent of £ 3 per ton by way of penalty for every ton of hay or straw which shall be sold off the premises during the last twelve months of the tenancy." This was held to be a penalty as hay was more valuable than straw.[900]

Similarly, where a contract provides for a lump sum which is to be paid on *any* breach it is likely to be penal[901] since it covers at the same time major and minor breaches A lump sum payable for breach of an undertaking not to compete for a fixed period would be open to this objection since a breach committed near the beginning of the period would almost certainly cause greater loss than one committed near its end. In this context it should be noted that COMMON LAW courts do not have even the limited power of apportionment which the FRENCH courts have under CC art. 1231 in cases of partial performance.[902] Such a power sometimes exists by virtue of special statutory provisions, for example in ENGLAND in the case of certain hire-purchase transactions.[903] Apart from such statutory provisions, the power of apportionment only exists if it has been created by the contract itself. In practice draftsmen often do create it by proportioning the sum payable to the seriousness of the breach.[904] If they do this, they also considerably reduce the risk of the clause being invalidated under the present rule.[905]

In some cases the rule, at any rate in ENGLAND, produces results which look incongruous. If a clause provides for the payment of a single sum on several breaches, it may be struck down on the ground that the sum *might* have become due on a trifling breach, even though the breach which *actually* occurred was quite a serious one, and one

894 *Corbin* § 1060; *Treitel* 822.

895 As in *Dunlop Pneumatic Tyre Co., Ltd. v. New Garage and Motor Co., Ltd., supra* n. 885.

896 See *Corbin* § 1064.

897 CALIFORNIAN CC § 1671 and other provisions cited *supra* n. 803; see also GEORGIA Code (*supra* n. 142) § 20-1043.

898 *Corbin* § 1064 cites *Russell Miller Mill Co. v. McLean*, 48 S.D. 198, 203 N.W. 498 (1925) and *Betts v. Burch* (1859), 4 H & N. 506, 157 E.R. 938 *contra*. But in the former case the stipulation was excessive and the latter was complicated by the fact that the penalty was payable on (*inter alia*) failure to pay a smaller sum, as to which see *infra* at n. 910.

899 *Corbin* § 1060; *Treitel* 821.

900 *Willson v. Love*, [1896] 1 Q.B. 626 (C.A.).

901 *Kemble v. Farren* (1829), 6 Bing. 141, 130 E.R. 1234; *Betts v. Burch*, *supra* n. 898.

902 *Supra* s. 130. *Corbin* § 1071 argues that there should be such a power.

903 *Hire-Purchase Act* 1965 (c.66) s. 28(2); *cf. supra* s. 130 at n. 852.

904 *Corbin* § 1072; *Treitel* 821.

905 It may of course still be invalid if it provides for payments which are excessive: *e.g., Christopher Founding Co. v. Steininger Construction Co.*, 200 Mo. App. 33, 205 S.W. 278 (1918). A clause providing for payment of so much per day of delay will not apply in cases of total abandonment of the contract (since otherwise the payments would have to go on in perpetuity): *British Glanzstoff Mfg. Co., Ltd. v. General Accident etc. Corp., Ltd.*, [1913] A.C. 143 (H.L.).

for which the sum could be regarded as a genuine and reasonable pre-estimate. This rule was no doubt intended to deter parties from stipulating for harsh penalties; but it can also invalidate perfectly fair (if badly expressed) bargains.[906] The courts will do their best to avoid such results by construing the contract so as to make the sum payable only on major breaches, for which the stipulated sum can be regarded as a genuine pre-estimate.[907]

The rule is not generally followed in the UNITED STATES, where the stipulation is normally enforced if it is a reasonable pre-estimate of the loss resulting from the breach which has actually occurred.[908] An AUSTRALIAN court has similarly suggested that the validity of the clause should depend on its normal or usual operation, and not on the possibility that, in extraordinary circumstances, the stipulated sum might greatly exceed the plaintiff's loss.[909] The ENGLISH courts could also follow this rule where the losses likely to result from the various breaches were sufficiently speculative to make it impossible to say that one *must* be considerably more serious than another; but even with this modification the ENGLISH rule perhaps places an undue premium on draftsmanship.

The fourth of the COMMON LAW rules is that a stipulation is a penalty "if the breach consists only in not paying a sum of money, and the sum stipulated is a sum greater than that which ought to have been paid."[910] This rule is well established both in ENGLAND and in the UNITED STATES.[911] It is obviously related to the rule (*supra* s. 114) that damages other than interest cannot be recovered for failure to perform an obligation to pay money.

The assumption underlying our fourth rule is that an express stipulation to pay more must exceed the loss and that it therefore cannot be a genuine pre-estimate. In fact this assumption is as questionable as those which underly the rule limiting the damages for non-payment of money to interest; and, just as the courts have been anxious to limit that rule, so they have been reluctant to apply our fourth rule for distinguishing between penalties and liquidated damages. This is particularly true where the third and fourth rules have been combined. In one such case the court held a stipulation penal merely because *one* of the events on which the sum was payable was the non-payment of a smaller sum; but the court was clearly reluctant to reach this conclusion, the result of which was to strike down a perfectly fair bargain.[912] In other cases the courts have managed to evade the rule, which in fact serves no useful purpose since unfair stipulations of this kind could be dealt with under our first rule.[913]

The COMMON LAW rules for distinguishing between penalties and liquidated damages manage to get the worst of both worlds. They achieve neither the certainty of the FRENCH rule, since there is always some doubt as to the category into which the clause will fall, nor the flexibility of the GERMAN rule, since there is no judicial power of reduction. On the other hand, they place an undue premium on draftsmanship. It is probably true to say that there are no reasonable business needs which a skilful draftsman cannot satisfy under ANGLO-AMERICAN rules. The chief danger is to "home-made" clauses which may be invalidated even though they are not intrinsically unfair.

iv. *Penalty Clauses as Limitations of Liability*

136. *Penalty and limitation clauses.* – As was pointed out in s. 122 above, one of the objects of penalty clauses may be to limit a defendant's liability. As a general rule, the law gives effect to this purpose. If the defendant undertakes to pay, in the event of breach, a sum which is intended to be, and in fact is, less than the loss suffered, the aggrieved party can recover only the stipulated sum. But most systems of law impose some restrictions on limitation clauses; and it is generally said that these restrictions or at least some of them apply to penalty clauses which stipulate a low amount and are intended to operate so as to limit liability.[914] The problem does not arise in cases in which the aggrieved party can claim the cost of substitute performance or compensation for non-performance instead of the stipulated sum (*supra* s. 125). In such cases the aggrieved party

[906] *Cf., Betts v. Burch, supra* n. 898 (where the fourth rule of construction was also involved).

[907] *E.g., Webster v. Bosanquet,* [1912] A.C. 394 (P.C.).

[908] *Corbin* § 1066.

[909] *International Leasing Corp. (Vic.), Ltd. v. Aiken* (1967), 85 W.N. (Pt.1.) (N.S.W.) 766.

[910] *Dunlop Pneumatic Tyre Co., Ltd. v. New Garage and Motor Co., Ltd.* (*supra* n. 885) 87.

[911] *Corbin* § 1065; *Treitel* 820-821.

[912] *Betts v. Burch, supra* n. 898.

[913] *Treitel* 820-821.

[914] *E.g. Mazeaud,* Leçons II no. 641; *Mazeaud and Tunc,* Traité III (ed. 5) no. 2628; *De Page* III no. 212 *ter*; UCC s. 2-718 comment 1.

can, if his loss exceeds the agreed sum, recover it by claiming such cost or compensation for non-performance.

The operation of penalty clauses as limitation clauses is discussed in ch. 1. Here it is only necessary to repeat that a penalty clause differs in legal nature from a limitation clause in that it is capable of benefiting either party while a limitation clause is capable of benefiting only the debtor (*supra* s. 121). It may be entirely a matter of chance which party is in fact benefited by a penalty clause. For example, a demurrage clause in a charterparty will benefit the shipowner if, during the period for which his ship was detained, he could not in fact have found any employment for her, or if he could only have found employment for her at a rate below the stipulated demurrage. On the other hand such a clause will (and generally does) benefit the charterer if by reason of the detention the shipowner suffers a loss of earnings in excess of the payments due under the clause.[915] It may be quite impossible at the time of contracting to foretell which of these eventualities will occur. This aspect of the matter has led the House of Lords to express doubts on the question whether the rules governing limitation clauses should indeed be applied to penalty clauses which stipulate for a low amount.[916] In the UNITED STATES and FRANCE these rules are in certain cases applied to such clauses (*supra* s. 131). More generally it would seem that such rules should only apply to clauses of this kind if it is quite clear that their purpose was indeed restricted to limiting liability; or, to put the point in another way, if the possibility of their operating in favour of the plaintiff was nothing more than a remote and theoretical one.

v. *Deposits and Part Payments*

137. *General.* – One party to a contract may make to the other a payment in advance of full performance either of his own or of the other party's principal obligation; and either the contract or a rule of law may provide for the disposal of the payment in the event of default by either party. As in the case of penalties, the "payment" usually consists of a sum of money but it may equally well consist of some other performance, such as a deposit in kind.[917] Where a system of law refuses to give literal effect to penalty clauses, the question arises whether any powers of the courts which exist in relation to such clauses apply also to contractual provisions for the forfeiture of payments already made under the contract.

All the legal systems under consideration agree on the broad principle that one relevant factor in determining the effects of such a payment is the intention with which it was made. The intention may be to provide evidence of the conclusion of a contract; or to reserve a right of withdrawal; or to provide for the forfeiture of the payment on default; or to do neither of these things, so that the payment may have to be restored even to a defaulting party, though without prejudice to his liability to make compensation for his default.

Although they agree broadly on the relevance of the intention with which the payment was made, the various legal systems take widely differing views as to the extent to which they will give effect to that intention; and as to the effects of a payment in respect of which no intention is clearly expressed. Indeed much of the difficulty which arises in this area of the law is due to the failure of the parties to specify the nature of the payment or to make clear their intention with respect to its disposal in the event of default. But the problems which arise in determining the validity of such provisions as the parties do make are by no means negligible; and the difficulties of comparison are increased by the bewildering variety of terminology which exists in this branch of the law.

138. *French law.* – The leading FRENCH distinction is between earnest (*arrhes*) and part payment (*accomptes*). Earnest may be further subdivided according to whether it does or does not give rise to a right of withdrawal on certain terms as to forfeiture (*faculté de dédit*).

The general rule with regard to an agreement for sale on the conclusion of which earnest is paid is laid down in CC art. 1590. Each party has the right to withdraw. If the payor withdraws, he forfeits the payment; if the payee withdraws, he has to restore double the amount. In such a case it has been said that the earnest provides a reciprocal *faculté de dédit*.[918] There is no further liability on either party; and it seems that the rule is not regarded as imposing a "penalty". In FRENCH law a "penalty clause" is regarded as an estimation of damages payable on default (*supra* s. 124), and in the case put neither party is liable in damages. There is no default but simply an exercise of a contractual right (or of one conferred by law) to withdraw from the contract on certain terms. As was pointed out in s. 124 above, a

[915] *Suisse Atlantique Société d'Armement Maritime S.A. v. N.V. Rotterdamsche Kolen Centrale* (*supra* n. 845) 395, 421, 435-436.

[916] *Ibidem.*

[917] GERMAN CC § 336 allows for this ("*etwas*").

[918] *Mazeaud*, Leçons II no. 806.

penalty clause does not give rise to an alternative obligation, while a payment of earnest with *faculté de dédit* has precisely this effect.

The position would be different if the contract stipulated for the payment of earnest without *faculté de dédit*.[919] In such a case there would be no *right* to withdraw from the contract on forfeiting the earnest or restoring double the amount. If one of the parties withdrew from the contract without lawful excuse he would be in default and could in appropriate cases be sued for performance. The stipulation with regard to earnest would, on such wrongful withdrawal, operate as a penal clause. In many cases the effect of such "penal earnest" would not differ in money terms from that laid down in CC art. 1590; for the general rule of FRENCH law is that the court cannot award either more or less than the amount stipulated in a penalty clause (*supra* s. 129). But there are exceptions to this rule and where they operate (*supra* s. 130) the distinction between "penal earnest" and earnest with a *faculté de dédit* could have practical consequences so far as the amount of retention or recovery is concerned. The *faculté de dédit* may exist quite independently of the giving of earnest; and the contract may, where earnest has been given, reserve the *faculté de dédit* to one party but not to the other.

Part payment does not have any of the principal consequences of earnest. It is simply a payment on account of the price. It does not give either party the right of withdrawal; it is not in principle forfeited nor restored double on default of either party; and it does not determine either the lower or the upper limit of the aggrieved party's recovery on a claim for damages. Often the parties will fail to make it clear whether a payment is intended by them as earnest or as part payment. They may indeed use the word "earnest" when they mean part payment; and conversely. Nor is it always clear whether the parties have intended to modify the rule laid down in CC art. 1590, *e.g.*, by giving the *faculté de dédit* to one party but not to the other. Such problems turn on the construction of the contractual provisions in each case.

The discussion of the effect of payments of these various kinds is always found in relation to agreements to sell. No doubt the principles have their most common application in this area; but it seems that they are capable of applying to other contracts as well. In the other systems to be discussed below, the relevant rules are not restricted to any one kind of contract but are of general application. It is, however, perhaps open to question whether the presumption in effect created by CC art. 1590, of the existence of a reciprocal right of withdrawal, would be readily extended outside the area of sale. The terms of the article are restricted to such contracts.

139. *German law.* – GERMAN law has nothing that corresponds precisely to the FRENCH institution of earnest. The Civil Code distinguishes between something given by way of deposit (*Draufgabe*) and a sum to be paid, or forfeited as the case may be, on the exercise of a contractual right to withdraw (*Reugeld*). Both of these concepts are distinguishable from part payment (*Anzahlung*) which is not specifically dealt with in the Civil Code.

Draufgabe under CC § 336 has a strictly evidentiary function; it is described as an indication of the conclusion of the contract. In case of doubt it is not regarded as *Reugeld:* in other words, it is not to be assumed that one or both of the parties have any right to withdraw from the contract. To give the payment this effect, the contract must so provide. There is no provision in the Civil Code obliging the recipient to restore double the amount, though no doubt it is possible for a contract expressly so to provide. The expression *Reugeld* is not restricted to deposits forfeited on withdrawal by virtue of a contractual provision to that effect; it applies to and indeed primarily refers to sums *to be paid* on the exercise of a contractual right to withdraw (CC § 359). If the expression *Reugeld* is to be taken literally, it is confined to a payment of, or promise to pay, *money*. *Draufgabe* is not so restricted: CC § 336 simply refers to the situation in which on the conclusion of the contract "something" is given by way of *Draufgabe*.

The effect of a *Draufgabe* is regulated by the following rules.

On performance of the contract, the *Draufgabe* is, wherever possible to be deducted from the price, or if this is not possible (for example because it consists of a non-fungible thing whose value cannot readily be estimated in money) it must be returned (CC § 337 par. 1). In the absence of an express provision to that effect, the creditor is not entitled to the *Draufgabe and* the price.

If the contract is brought to an end, whether by mutual consent or by the act of one party, the *Draufgabe* is to be returned (CC § 337 par. 2); again this rule can be excluded by agreement. However, if the reason for the termination is the fault of the payor, then the payee is entitled to retain the *Draufgabe;* and the same rule applies if

[919] *Ibidem.*

performance becomes impossible on account of circumstances for which the payor is responsible (CC § 338 sent. 1). A distinction therefore has to be drawn between cases in which termination occurs because of a contractually reserved right and those in which it occurs on account of the fault of the payor. In the former case the *Draufgabe* must be returned; in the latter case it may be retained. Of course it must also be returned if the contract is terminated on account of the fault of the payee. And the same is true where the payee is under some liability though he may not be technically at "fault": *e.g.*, if he delivers defective goods and so is liable to *Wandelung*.[920]

If the payee claims compensation for non-performance the position of the *Draufgabe* is the same as it would be if he obtained performance. That is the payee is not entitled to both compensation *and* the *Draufgabe* unless the contract expressly so provides. The *Draufgabe* is deducted from the compensation, or, where this is impractical, it must be returned.[921] Once again this rule only applies in cases of doubt, so that it is possible to stipulate for the retention of the *Draufgabe* in cases of this kind.

Draufgabe is to be distinguished from *Anzahlung*, which is simply a part payment.[922] The rules relating to *Draufgabe* do not as such apply to part payment. In particular there is in principle no right to retain a part payment, though no doubt in practice it may be deducted not only from the price but also from compensation for non-performance. But if it exceeds the loss the balance would have to be returned, whereas under the rules stated above the whole of a *Draufgabe* may be retained irrespective of the size of the creditor's actual loss.

The assumption which underlies the GERMAN provisions as to *Draufgabe* is that it is a small, token sum; and if this assumption is accepted problems as to the relationship between *Draufgabe* and penalty clauses will not in practice arise. But it is theoretically possible for the *Draufgabe* to be of a substantial amount which would operate in the nature of a penalty where it was forfeited either under the terms of the contract, or under the provisions of the Civil Code entitling the payee in certain events to retain the payment. In such a case the question could arise whether the principle of CC § 343 could *mutatis mutandis* be applied so as to enable the court to "reduce" the *Draufgabe*, *i.e.* in effect order the repayment of part of it to the payor.

One view is that the principle should not be applied because *Draufgabe* refers to something which *has been* paid while a penalty is something *to be* paid. But this distinction seems to have little merit in that either kind of payment can be used as a means of undesirable coercion. The distinction can also be controverted by referring to the rule that an *Einzelverfallklausel* (*supra* s. 121) is considered to be a penalty for the purposes of the power of reduction conferred by CC § 343. The SOUTH AFRICAN legislation on penalties, which in basic principle resembles the GERMAN provisions on this subject, expressly subjects stipulations for the forfeiture of deposits to the judicial power of reduction.[923] This seems to be the sensible solution though it does not seem to be explicitly recognised in the GERMAN Civil Code.

No doubt where the payment is substantial it will often be possible to avoid the problem by regarding the payment not as a *Draufgabe* but rather as an *Anzahlung*, which is not subject to forfeiture at all, and which has to be restored in the event of termination of the contract by the payee. An express provision entitling the payee to retain such a payment, contrary to the general rules governing termination, is undoubtedly penal.[924] In the case of instalment sales of moveables the law goes further and provides that a seller who exercises the right to terminate the contract is bound to restore payments made by the buyer: any contractual provision to the contrary is not merely penal but void.[925] In other cases of hardship it could no doubt be argued that an aggrieved party attempting to forfeit a large deposit would be acting contrary to good faith.

140. *Austrian and Swiss law.* – These systems contain an interesting combination of elements found in FRENCH and GERMAN law, as well as some original solutions of their own.

AUSTRIAN and SWISS law agree with the basic GERMAN idea that a deposit is only a sign of the conclusion of the contract;[926] they reject the FRENCH idea that a deposit *prima facie* affords a *locus poenitentiae* to both parties. In AUSTRIAN law such a deposit is known as *Angeld*. In SWISS law a distinction is drawn between *Angeld* and *Draufgeld*: the former is a payment which is

920 *Supra* s. 58; *infra* s. 157. BGB-RGRK § 338 no. 1.

921 *I.e.* CC § 338 sent. 2 applies.

922 *Enneccerus and Lehmann* 157 n. 1.

923 SOUTH AFRICAN Conventional Penalties Act (*supra* n. 805) s. 4.

924 *Enneccerus and Lehmann* 172.

925 GERMAN *Abzahlungsgesetz* (*supra* n. 802) § 1.

926 This is expressly stated in AUSTRIAN CC § 908 and seems to be implied in SWISS CO art. 158.

ultimately to be deducted from the price, while the latter is retained by the payee in addition to the price.[927] Both systems distinguish between deposits having this evidentiary function and *Reugeld*, which (as in GERMAN law) refers to a sum paid or payable on the exercise of a contractually reserved right of withdrawal.[928] The AUSTRIAN Civil Code provides that if an *Angeld* is paid and a right to terminate is included in the contract, the *Angeld* takes the place of *Reugeld* (CC § 910). This probably goes beyond the GERMAN provision which would require the contract to provide expressly or by implication for the forfeiture of the deposit if it were to count as *Reugeld* (CC § 336 par. 2).

The AUSTRIAN and SWISS rules on the other hand adopt the FRENCH principle whereby in certain events the payee is entitled to retain the sum paid or bound to restore double the amount; while GERMAN law of course rejects the principle of double restoration. In AUSTRIAN law the principle applies to *Angeld* against a party through whose fault the contract is not performed, though without prejudice to the aggrieved party's right to claim performance or compensation for non-performance (CC § 908). It also applies, where *Angeld* has been paid and a right to put an end to the contract has been reserved, in two cases: against a party who exercises the contractual right toterminate the contract, and against one who can no longer exercise this right because performance has as a result of his fault and at a time when the right still existed become impossible.[929] Where the deposit is forfeited as *Reugeld* there is no further liability to perform or to pay damages. The SWISS Code of Obligations states the principle of forfeiture and restoration of double only in relation to *Reugeld* (CO art. 158 par. 3).

Both systems assume that if the contract is invalid or if it is terminated by mutual consent the deposit is to be returned;[930] and this also seems to be the case if performance becomes impossible without fault of either party.[931] The principle of forfeiture and restoration of double is also inapplicable to a part payment; and a substantial payment is assumed to have this character.[932] Neither system makes it clear whether the judicial power to reduce penalties applies to deposits. In AUSTRIA it has been said that *Angeld* is distinguishable from a penalty in that it imposes a potential liability on *each* party (in view of the principle of double restoration).[933] But a penalty clause may likewise stipulate for a sum to be paid by either party on breach by the other.[934] The arguments which have been considered in relation to the GERMAN position with respect to this question (see *supra* s. 139) are also relevant at this point.

141. *Common Law.* – The COMMON LAW differs from the CIVIL LAW in two striking respects. First, it does not recognize a general legal principle corresponding to the FRENCH *faculté de dédit* or to the GERMAN *Reugeld*. A deposit is not considered to give either party a *locus poenitentiae* unless the contract expressly so provides; and in practice contractual provisions of this kind are rare. Secondly, there is no trace in the COMMON LAW of any rule requiring the recipient of the payment to restore double in certain events.

The giving of something by way of earnest was formerly of some evidential value since it would suffice to make an oral contract for the sale of goods above a certain value enforceable, by way of substitute for the normal requirement of written evidence. But this requirement has been abolished in ENGLAND;[935] and the provision of the Uniform Commercial Code which retains it in the UNITED STATES no longer permits earnest as an alternative to written evidence of the contract.[936] The ROMAN concept of *arra*, on which the present CIVIL LAW rules are largely based, has played very little part in the development of the COMMON LAW.

A distinction is however drawn between a part payment and a deposit.

A part payment is similar to the corresponding FRENCH and GERMAN conception (*supra* s. 138, 139). It is simply a payment on account of the price. In principle it is recoverable if for any reason the

927 *Von Tuhr and Siegwart*, Allgemeiner Teil des Schweizerischen Obligationenrechts (ed. 2 Zürich 1944) 732.

928 AUSTRIAN CC § 909, 910; SWISS CO art. 158 par. 3.

929 AUSTRIAN CC § 910, 911; *Klang and Gschnitzer (-Gschnitzer)* IV 1 § 911 note.

930 *Klang and Gschnitzer (-Gschnitzer)* IV 1 § 908 no. B III 2 a, b; *von Tuhr and Siegwart* (*supra* n. 927) 732-733.

931 *Klang and Gschnitzer (-Gschnitzer)* IV 1 § 908 no. A III 3, B III 2 b.

932 *Idem* IV § 908 no. A III 3.

933 *Idem* IV 1 § 908 no. A III 2.

934 See, for example, the penalty clause in the ENGLISH case of *Kemble v. Farren, supra* n. 901.

935 Law Reform (Enforcement of Contracts) Act, 1954 (2 & 3 Eliz.2, c. 34) repealing Sale of Goods Act, 1893 (*supra* n. 312) s. 4. The 1954 Act applies to GREAT BRITIAN but similar provision was made for NORTHERN IRELAND by the Law Reform (Miscellaneous Provision) Act, 1954 (Northern Ireland 2 & 3 Eliz. 2, c. 26), so that the position stated in the text obtains in the whole UNITED KINGDOM.

936 UCC s. 2-201, replacing Uniform Sales Act s. 4.

contract is not carried out, unless the contract validly provides the contrary;[937] the validity of such provisions will be considered below. Of course if the contract is not carried out by reason of one party's breach he will be liable in damages, but there is no necessary relationship between such damages and the amount of the part payment.

A deposit on the other hand is a payment of money (or some other performance) as "a guarantee that the contract shall be performed."[938] It must of course be paid back by the payee if he fails to perform; but if the payor fails to perform in circumstances amounting to a breach of contract he cannot recover the deposit unless the contract otherwise provides.[939]

Two difficult questions which arise in COMMON LAW countries are whether a deposit or a provision for the forfeiture of a part payment may be invalid as a penalty.

In an ENGLISH case where a deposit was paid on express terms as to forfeiture these terms were held valid on the ground that the loss caused by the payor's breach was such that it could not be precisely estimated in advance.[940] This is of course exactly the reasoning which is used to distinguish between penalties and liquidated damages (*supra* s. 134-135) and it suggests that if the loss *had* been capable of precise pre-estimation and if the deposit had been excessive the payee might not have been allowed to retain the whole of it. As deposits no less than penalties may be means of exerting undue pressure this would seem in principle to be a desirable state of the law, particularly in view of the rule that a deposit which has been promised but not paid can be sued for.[941] The distinction between claiming a penalty and suing for a deposit which has not been paid is one that wholly lacks substance. Since in practice deposits are generally reasonable in amount, they would not often be held penal if the rules as to penalties were applied to them.

But the applicability of those rules in the present situation is very much in doubt because of another line of ENGLISH cases which concern the right of a seller to enforce contractual provisions for the forfeiture of instalments on a buyer's default. In such a case the court may allow the buyer extra time to pay. But if he fails to pay even within the extended time the seller can enforce the forfeiture: according to one view he can do so provided that he was not guilty of any "unconscionable" conduct in inducing the contract; while according to another he can only enforce the forfeiture provision if it is not "unconscionable" for him to rely on that provision.[942] The restrictions imposed on his right to forfeiture under the latter view are not necessarily the same as those which prevent the enforcement of a penalty clause; for a stipulation may be held to be penal even though it is in no way unfair (*supra* s. 134-135). The view that forfeiture provisions are not penal is also adopted by a number of CIVIL LAW systems which have been exposed to the influence of ENGLISH law, such as those of SCOTLAND and SRI LANKA.[943]

In the UNITED STATES there is a general tendency to regard forfeiture provisions as penal. This tendency has been applied to provisions for the forfeiture of rights which have accrued under the contract such as a right to be paid;[944] and the same principle has been applied to the forfeiture of a deposit.[945] Although there is considerable division of opinion on the point, the prevailing view appears to be that a stipulation entitling a vendor of land to retain instalments of purchase price on the buyer's default may be struck down as penal.[946] Under the Uniform Commercial Code a buyer is entitled to restitution of payments made by him, if the seller justifiably withholds delivery, to the extent to which the payment exceeds the sum for which the seller might have stipulated by means of a valid liquidated damages clause.[947] Thus in principle the same factors which make a clause invalid as a penalty will also deprive a forfeiture clause of its full legal effect. This principle is however subject to an exception in the case of certain small payments which may be retained in any event.[948]

937 *Treitel* 826.

938 *Howe v. Smith* (1884), 27 Ch.D. 89, 95 (C.A.).

939 *Ibidem*. In ENGLAND the Law of Property Act, 1925 (*supra* n. 464) s. 49 (2) gives the court power to order the return of a deposit paid under a contract for the sale or exchange of an interest in land, but this power is not normally exercised in the ordinary case of a purchaser's default: *James Macara, Ltd. v. Barclays Bank, Ltd.*, [1944] 2 All E.R. 31, 32 (K.B.), *aff'd* [1945] K.B. 148 (C.A.).

940 *Pye v. British Automobile Commercial Syndicate, Ltd.*, [1906] 1 K.B. 425.

941 *Treitel* 826.

942 *Idem* 827-828.

943 *Gloag and Henderson* 134; *Weeramantry* II § 944.

944 *E.g., Corbin* § 1073.

945 *Idem* § 1074; *Ashurst v. Rosser*, 275 Ala. 163, 153 So. 2d 240 (1963).

946 *Corbin* § 1075.

947 UCC s. 2-718(2). An express clause purporting to deprive the buyer of his right to restitution could perhaps be modified or struck down under UCC s. 2-302 or held to contravene the requirement of good faith in enforcement (UCC s. 1-203).

948 UCC s. 2-718(2)(b).

The principles relating to penalties have also been applied to forfeiture provisions in a number of other countries such as INDIA,[949] ISRAEL[950] and GHANA.[951] It would seem that if interference with penalty clauses is justified, it is equally justified in the present context, for both types of provisions are means of exerting undue pressure on the debtor and they are both liable to lead to the unjust enrichment of the creditor.

142. *Conclusion.* – The various solutions adopted by different legal systems with regard to deposits present an unusual degree of variety. Two points in particular stand out for comment: the presence in some systems and the absence in others of a rule giving the deposit the function of a *locus poenitentiae;* and the difficulties which all the systems have had in relating the rules as to deposits with those as to penalties. On the first point, it may be doubted whether the institution of the deposit as a *locus poenitentiae* at the present time serves any strongly felt commercial need. On the second point it is suggested that the principles relating to penalties should generally be applied to provisions for the forfeiture of deposits.

949 *Fateh Shand v. Balkistan Dass, supra* n. 843.

950 Contracts (Remedies for Breach of Contracts) Law 1970 (*supra* n. 481) s. 15(c).

951 GHANA Sale of Goods Act, 1962 (*supra* n. 407) s. 57.

IV. TERMINATION OF THE CONTRACT

A. INTRODUCTORY

143. *Concept.* – A party who is aggrieved as a result of not obtaining the performance for which he bargained may wish, in a general sense, to put an end to further performance of the contract and also so far as possible to put matters back into the position in which they were before performance on either side was begun. There are at least three different processes by which effect may be given to this desire.

First, the aggrieved party may refuse to pay (or to render whatever counter-performance he has promised) for the defective performance which he has received or on the ground that he has not received any performance at all. Secondly, he may refuse to accept further performance from the party in default, but be content to allow matters to remain in the state in which they are at the time of refusal so far as past acts of performance are concerned. This is a particularly common solution where a contract calls for the performance of reciprocal duties over a period of time. Thirdly, the aggrieved party may already have performed his part and seek restitution of his own performance. If the other party has not completed performance on his side, some combination of the second and third courses of action will be involved. In addition to taking one or more of these steps the aggrieved party may further wish to claim compensation for loss which he has suffered as a result of the other party's default.

The various courses of action outlined above are not by any means confined to cases of contractual default. They may be available where the contract suffers from some degree of invalidity (for example, because it was induced by misrepresentation or made under the influence of a mistake); or where the parties are excused from further performance on some ground such as supervening impossibility for which neither party was responsible, or supervening illegality.[952]

Generally speaking, the ensuing discussion will be limited to cases of contractual default. Since, however, the systems of law to be discussed often do not agree on what constitutes contractual default, a broad view will be taken of this question. In particular the discussion will cover problems which arise out of the delivery of defective goods under contracts of sale, such delivery being regarded as contractual default in COMMON LAW countries, while in CIVIL LAW countries it may only give rise to "guarantee" liabilities (*supra* s. 7). One of the remedies used for enforcing such liabilities, that of redhibition or ***Wandelung***, is so closely analogous to remedies available by way of termination for contractual default that the two kinds of remedy are conveniently discussed together.

In addition it will be convenient to refer from time to time to consequences of the exercise of powers to terminate contracts conferred by law irrespective of default,[953] and to the exercise of powers to terminate conferred by the contract itself.[954] Usually powers of the latter kind refer to termination in case of the other party's default but they are not necessarily limited in this way.

144. *Terminology.* – A party wishing to follow the first of the three courses of action outlined in s. 143 above will in CIVIL LAW countries do so by pleading the *exceptio non adimpleti contractus*, which is discussed in ch. 15 above. In COMMON LAW countries no sharp doctrinal distinction is drawn between cases in which the aggrieved party seeks to follow this course of action and those in which he seeks to follow one (or both) of the other two. Indeed authorities which relate to one of these courses of action are commonly cited in cases concerning another.[955] There is, moreover, a common terminology which covers all three

[952] This is what is known in FRENCH law as *résolution* (termination) on the theory of risks (see *Carbonnier* IV 278 ss.); it must be distinguished from *résolution* for contractual default, which is the subject-matter of the ensuing discussion.

[953] *E.g.* to powers such as those given by GERMAN CC § 626 to terminate certain contracts on an "important ground".

[954] The AMERICAN UCC s. 2-106(3) uses "termination" in this narrow sense and distinguishes it from "cancellation" which means termination for breach in the sense of the present chapter: see UCC s. 2-106(3) and (4). The GERMAN CC deals in § 346 to 356 with contractually reserved rights to terminate; but the chief importance of these provisions lies in the fact that they apply "correspondingly" to termination for contractual default by virtue of CC § 280 par. 2, 286 par. 2, 325 par. 1 and 326 par. 1.

[955] See the citation of *Boone v. Eyre* (1789), 1 Hy.Bl. 273 n., 126 E.R. 160 (refusal to pay) in *Hongkong Fir Shipping Co., Ltd. v. Kawasaki Kisen Kaisha, Ltd.*, [1962] 2 Q.B. 26 (Q.B.) and 41 at 58 (C.A.) (refusal to accept performance).

courses of action. They are often referred to indiscriminately as "rescinding" the contract.

This use of the same word in several senses has been justly criticised[956], but it remains deeply rooted in judicial usage. In ENGLAND, for example, the Sale of Goods Act, 1893 makes some attempt to distinguish between "rejection" and "rescission";[957] but in one of the decisions on the point it has nevertheless been said that "a right to reject is merely a particular form of the right to rescind."[958] In the UNITED STATES, the Uniform Commercial Code draws an elaborate set of distinctions between termination, cancellation, rejection and revocation of acceptance (see *infra* s. 169).[959] The purpose was to get away from the vague term "rescission"[960] but judicial usage of it remains inveterate.[961] Moreover, even the Uniform Commercial Code does not distinguish sharply between the first and the other two of the courses of action here under discussion.

That is not to say that the distinction is completely without effect in COMMON LAW countries. The courts may be more ready to allow a party to put an end to a contract if it remains partly unperformed than if it has been completely performed on both sides;[962] and in this sense they may be said to favour the first course of action more than the other two.[963] But they treat the distinction as one of degree only, and therefore the general attitude of favouring the first course more than the second or third may be counterbalanced by others, such as the desire to avoid unjust enrichment or the reluctance to allow redistribution of commercial risks on the pretext of default.

In this subchapter an attempt will be made to follow the CIVIL LAW approach and to discuss the second and third courses of action open to the aggrieved party. A further terminological difficulty, however, arises from the fact that the GERMAN expression *Rücktritt* seems to refer strictly speaking only to the third course of action. The second is referred to as *Ablehnung der Leistung* (CC § 286 par. 2), but it is in fact closely related to *Rücktritt*. The most important practical effect of the distinction relates to the creditor's right to damages where he puts an end to the contract. Here GERMAN law faces a problem which does not exist in FRENCH or probably in ANGLO-AMERICAN law; and this fact probably accounts for the fact that in GERMAN law the distinction between the second and third course is more sharply drawn than elsewhere. In GERMAN law *Rücktritt* deprives the aggrieved party of his right to damages for non-performance; while termination in the second sense leaves this right, and in particular the right to claim compensation for loss of expectation unimpaired.

In FRENCH and probably in ANGLO-AMERICAN law the right to damages is not lost merely because the aggrieved party adopts the third course of action. Therefore these systems, and indeed most legal systems, refer to the second and third courses of action indiscriminately by the same name – as *résolution* (termination) in FRENCH law and as rescission in COMMON LAW. They are content to assert that the aggrieved party may terminate the contract but leave the particular legal remedy consequent on termination to be moulded according to the circumstances of the particular case. In doing this they may take into account such factors as the extent to which performance has gone and the loss caused by the default. But they do not bar the right to damages merely because the aggrieved party seeks to recover back the performance that he himself has rendered under the contract. The precise relationship between termination and damages is more fully discussed in s. 183 ss. below.

From time to time in the ensuing discussion it will be convenient to use a single word or phrase to refer to the various processes which have just been described. For this purpose the word "termination" will be used. It has the advantage of being fairly colourless and of not having acquired a technical meaning in any except one[964] of the legal systems under discussion. It should be stressed that the phrase is not intended to carry any connotations as to the legal consequences of the various remedies to which it refers.

145. *Practical effects and legal limitations.*[965] – The practical effects of terminating a contract can best be appreciated by referring to the conflict of interest between the parties with regard to the

956 *E.g.* by *Corbin* § 1105.

957 See for example s. 11(1)(b), 48(1) and (2).

958 *Kwei Tek Chao v. British Traders, Ltd.*, [1954] 2 Q.B. 459, 480.

959 UCC s. 2-106(3) and (4) (*supra* n. 954), s. 2-601, 2-608.

960 See comment 1 to UCC s. 2-608.

961 *E.g.*, *Dailey v. Holiday Distributing Corp.* (*supra* n. 303) 482 ("Rescission is the unmaking of a contract").

962 This distinction underlies a number of legislative provisions such as that between subsections (2) and (4) of CALIFORNIAN CC § 1689: see *Conlin v. Osborn*, 161 Cal. 659, 120 P. 755 (1911).

963 *Corbin* § 1119.

964 *I.e.* under AMERICAN UCC s. 2-106(3), *supra* n. 954.

965 *Honnold*, Buyer's Right of Rejection: 97 U.Pa. L.Rev. 457 (1949).

availability of this particular remedy. In discussing this conflict, it is assumed that the aggrieved party undoubtedly has *some* remedy. The question is why he should wish to pursue, and the aggrieved party to resist, the particular remedy of termination.

The most obvious reason which the aggrieved party has for terminating the contract is the hardship which he may suffer in having to accept or retain (as the case may be) a performance different from that for which he bargained. But in practice the right to terminate is often asserted for quite different reasons. One such reason, which holds good in many systems of law, is that termination is a speedier remedy than a suit for performance or damages, in that it does not require the judgment of a court;[966] though such a judgment may still be required to work out the effects of termination. Another, and perhaps in practice the most important, reason for seeking termination is that this remedy may yield a more favourable result in money terms. This will be so where the aggrieved party has made a bargain which would have been a bad one even if the contract had been duly performed; or where the loss which he has suffered is wholly or partly irrecoverable, *e.g.* because it is unforeseeable.[967] Finally, termination may in principle favour the aggrieved party in the event of the other party's insolvency, though in practice this advantage of termination is severely curtailed by special rules which exist in most systems of law for the purpose of protecting an insolvent person's property for the benefit of his creditors generally.[968]

On the other hand, the party in default may have equally obvious reasons for wishing to resist termination. If the effect of this remedy is to throw the subject-matter of the contract back to him on a falling market, he may be made to bear a risk which by the terms of the contract, or by its very nature, was one which had been undertaken by the other party. In addition, he may have incurred expenses in his attempts to perform the contract which will be wholly or largely wasted as a result of termination. He may, in short, suffer financially to an extent going beyond the loss actually caused by his default, and *a fortiori* beyond that which would be legally recoverable.

146. *Legal limitations.* – All legal systems have to achieve some balance between the conflicting interests discussed in s. 145 above. On the one hand they protect the interests of the aggrieved party by recognising in principle the existence of the right to terminate. On the other hand, they have developed a number of techniques for protecting the party in default. First, they may insist on the use of certain machinery such as obtaining a judgment for termination, or giving a formal notice of termination. Secondly, they may restrict the grounds on which a contract can be terminated. For this purpose it is often not sufficient to show merely that the debtor was in default: the default may have to be of a certain degree of seriousness. Thirdly there are rules which restrict the right to terminate a contract: in other words, rules which assume the exercise of such a right but limit its exercise. In the following discussion we shall consider these various techniques, the effects of termination, and certain analogous remedies.

B. THE MACHINERY OF TERMINATION

i. *Termination by Act of the Court*

147. *The French principle: requirement of a judgment.* – The general principle of FRENCH law is stated in CC art. 1184.[969] This provides first that a resolutive condition is implied in all synallagmatic contracts in case one party fails to perform his undertaking; secondly that in such a case the contract is not "resolved" by operation of law (*de plein droit*) and that the aggrieved party can claim *either* performance *or résolution* (termination) and damages; and thirdly that termination must be sought in legal proceedings (*en justice*).

CC art. 1184 does not specify the grounds for termination; it does not on the one hand require the aggrieved party to show total non-performance, nor on the other hand say that any non-performance will suffice. It prescribes how termination must be *sought* – not *when* it will be granted. That is a matter for the court before which the claim for termination comes. In determining whether to grant the remedy the court will have regard to various factors such as the defendant's degree of fault and the seriousness of the defect in performance.

A court in disposing of a claim for termination can follow one of three courses of action: it can grant the claim, or reject it, or grant the defendant

966 FRENCH law constitutes the exception here: *infra* s. 147.

967 See, for example, in GERMAN law, *Enneccerus and Lehmann* 210; in ENGLISH law, *Treitel* 673.

968 See this Encyclopedia vol. XVI ch. 14.

969 For an important specific application of the principle see FRENCH CC art. 1654 (termination of sale for failure to pay the price).

a period of grace (*délai de grâce*) within which to perform his obligation.[970] At any time before termination has been ordered the party in default can prevent termination by offering to perform; indeed he can even do this while an appeal against an order for termination is pending.[971] Conversely, the aggrieved party is not barred from claiming performance merely because he has put in a claim for termination; nor is he barred from claiming termination merely because he has put in a claim for performance.[972] Termination is regarded as an extraordinary remedy, performance or damages being generally preferred.

The effect of the general requirement that a judgment for termination must be obtained is two-fold. Until such a judgment has been pronounced, the party in default is not deprived of his right to perform nor is the aggrieved party justified in refusing to perform his part, or in putting it out of his power to perform. These points are also true of the special remedy of redhibition which is available to a buyer of goods which are defective (even though the existence of the defect does not amount to contractual default). This remedy is considered to be a kind of termination and therefore in principle requires a judgment.[973] A judgment is of course required for termination on account of the seller's failure to deliver and for termination on account of the buyer's refusal to pay.[974] But termination for the buyer's failure to take delivery is governed by a different rule (*infra* s. 148).

The requirement of a judgment for termination of a contract is not confined to FRENCH law. It exists in the law of LOUISIANA by virtue of express provisions in the Civil Code of that state (art. 2046); and in QUEBEC it exists as a result of judicial decision although the Civil Code is silent on the point.[975] There are traces of a similar requirement in other systems; though the point of certain somewhat equivocal statements may simply be that the aggrieved party *can* get a judgment cancelling the contract – not that he *must* get such a judgment if he wishes to cancel.[976] Such a judgment will be useful, for example, where there is a doubt on the question whether *grounds* for termination exist: here the judgment will protect the aggrieved party from the risk of terminating wrongfully even in a system in which termination does not, as a matter of machinery, require a judgment. Statutory provisions are in force in a number of COMMON LAW countries which envisage a judgment for rescission or cancellation of a contract but they are all permissive: they say that such a judgment *may* be given,[977] without derogating from the principle that termination is the act of the parties, or of one of them, and not that of the court.

148. *Exceptions to the requirement of a judgment.* – The general principle of FRENCH law is no doubt effective for the purpose of protecting the debtor; but on the other hand the principle can lead to commercially inconvenient results.[978] The requirement of a judgment inevitably imposes delays and creates uncertainty as it is hard to know in advance whether the court will grant termination, or refuse it, or adopt some intermediate solution such as giving the debtor extra time to perform. To meet this objection, FRENCH law has developed a number of exceptions to the rule that termination requires an order of the court.

The most important of these exceptions arises where the contract contains an express provision for termination. There is no doubt as to the general validity of such provisions. CC art. 1184 is not considered to contain a principle of public policy, so that the parties are (subject to statutory exceptions) free to provide that in certain events the contract will be terminated by operation of law (*de plein droit*).[979] Some care is, however, needed in drafting express provisions of this kind as the FRENCH courts tend to construe them strictly

[970] For a similar, but more limited, provision as to period of grace in cases of sale, see FRENCH CC art. 1655 par. 2.

[971] *Carbonnier* IV 272; the rule is criticised by *Marty and Raynaud* II no. 301.

[972] *Zweigert and Kötz* 197 (pointing out that ITALIAN law is different in that under ITALIAN CC art. 1453 par. 2 and 3 performance can no longer be claimed after an action for termination has been brought).

[973] *Mazeaud*, Leçons III no. 987.

[974] See CC art. 1610, 1654.

[975] *Baudouin* 736.

[976] See *Willie and Millin (-Coaker and Schutz)* 93.

[977] See, for example, INDIAN Specific Relief Act, 1877 (*supra* n. 136) s. 35, 41. These provisions remain in force in PAKISTAN but in INDIA they have been superseded by Specific Relief Act, 1963 (*ibidem*) s. 27, 33. The above provisions were (at least in their 1877 version) based on *Field's* Draft New York Civil Code § 1903 (referring to § 839) and § 1906 (*supra* s. 31). See now as to rescission Revised Codes of MONTANA (*supra* n. 137) § 17-905; NORTH DAKOTA Century Code (*supra* n. 157) § 32-04-21; OKLAHOMA Statutes (*supra* n. 187) § 15-233; SOUTH DAKOTA Century Code (*supra* n. 154) § 21-12-1 (CALIFORNIAN CC § 1689 contains no reference to a judgment for rescission). As to cancellation see the above Codes of CALIFORNIA (§ 3412); MONTANA (§ 17-1001); NORTH DAKOTA (§ 32-04-24); SOUTH DAKOTA (§ 21-13-1).

[978] *Zweigert and Kötz* 199.

[979] *Carbonnier* IV 273-274, 277.

against parties seeking to take advantage of them.[980] A provision that in certain events the contract will be terminated is considered to operate simply as a reminder of CC art. 1184 and not to dispense with the requirement of a judgment.[981] Nor is a mere provision requiring performance within a fixed time (subject to CC art. 1657, which is discussed below) sufficient for this purpose.[982] On this point FRENCH law differs strikingly from GERMAN and ANGLO-AMERICAN law (*infra* s. 150, 153).

If the contract provides that it will be terminated by operation of law, the aggrieved party need not obtain a judgment but he may still have to give a formal notice of default (*sommation*). In the case of sales of land there is an express provision to this effect in CC art. 1656. In the case of other contracts it is a question of construction whether a provision for termination by operation of law dispenses the aggrieved party from all formalities, though it is common to insert an express statement to this effect.[983] A properly drafted provision of this kind may literally appear to permit termination of a contract for some relatively minor default;[984] but an attempt to use it in this way may fail on the ground that it is contrary to good faith.[985] Moreover, even an express provision will not entitle a seller to terminate the contract after the buyer's bankruptcy so as to obtain the return of property delivered to the buyer and thus in effect to secure a priority over the buyer's other creditors.[986] Thus qualified, the express provision does seem to overcome the inconvenience of the requirement of a judgment, while providing safeguards against the most serious of the possible abuses of the right to terminate.

A second exception to the general rule that termination requires a judgment is contained in CC art. 1657. This deals with the contracts for the sale of commodities or other moveables of which delivery is to be taken within a fixed time. The article provides that at the end of the agreed time (*i.e.* if the buyer has not taken delivery) the contract may be regarded as terminated by operation of law at the option of the seller. The purpose of this rule is to enable the seller to take prompt measures to safeguard his position in the event of the buyer's default. He can dispose of the goods at once and so free his storage space and also protect himself against any fall in the market price of the goods. He can do this only if the contract specifies a date by which the buyer must take delivery.

If there is no term of this kind, CC art. 1657 does not apply so that normally a judgment is necessary for termination on the ground of failure to take delivery. A judgment is also necessary where the buyer's default takes the form of failure to pay, unless the seller has protected himself by stipulating expressly for termination by operation of law in the event of such default (CC art. 1654). In the case of the seller's delay in making delivery a judgment for termination must again be sought in the absence of an express contrary provision in the contract (CC art. 1610). It is not at all easy to see why the one case of failure of the buyer to take delivery within the agreed time has been singled out for special treatment; and in practice it appears that sellers rarely exercise the right of *peremptory* termination which CC art. 1657 confers upon them. That is to say, they normally give notice of intention to terminate, though they do not of course sue for termination.[987]

A third exception to the requirement of a judgment for termination has been established by the courts to deal with certain particularly grave breaches of duty. The authorities on this subject originate with cases in which employees committed such breaches and it was held that the employers were justified in dismissing such employees without prior court order at their "risk and peril".[988] In other words, the dismissal was not wrongful merely because it had been effected without a prior judgment; but it still might have to be justified in subsequent proceedings in which it would have to be shown that the breach was sufficiently grave to have warranted a judgment for termination, had such a remedy been sought. The principle of these cases has been applied to other types of contracts, as well as to cases of declared refusal of the debtor to perform.[989]

In view of the terms of CC art. 1184, it is not easy to justify this line of cases. Possible explanations are that it is based on necessity brought about by the urgency of the situation, on the

980 *Mazeaud*, Leçons II no. 1105.

981 *Carbonnier* IV 274.

982 This appears from the contrast between failure to pay and failure to take delivery at the stipulated time, discussed *infra* under CC art. 1654; and indeed from the general provisions as to *délai de grâce* (period of grace).

983 *Mazeaud*, Leçons III no. 1011; *Carbonnier* IV 274.

984 *Mazeaud*, Leçons III no. 947.

985 *Carbonnier* IV 277.

986 Law no. 67-563 of 13 July 1967 (JO 14 July p. 7059) art. 61 par. 1. *Mazeaud*, Leçons III no. 1011.

987 *Houin* (*supra* n. 92) 16, 28.

988 *Carbonnier* IV 272, 276-277.

989 *Ibidem*.

"*fraud*" of the debtor, or on a subsequent agreement of the parties to terminate the contract. But these explanations do not cover all cases in which the rule applies; nor do they substantially resolve the conflict between the rule and CC art. 1184.[990] The cases show that CC art. 1184 does not contain an absolute value, in that its prohibition of "private justice" may have to yield to more pressing interests. It could, indeed, be said that CC art. 1184 extends the principle that "*nul ne peut faire justice à soi-même*" beyond all reasonable bounds for it applies the maxim to cases in which the acts of the creditor do not physically affect the defaulting party or any property in his possession. All this amounts to no more, however, than to a criticism of the policy of CC art. 1184, and one which may be well founded. It does not really help to reconcile the cases here under discussion with the wording of the article.

ii. *Requirement of Formal Notice*

149. *Requirement of "Nachfrist" in German law.* – The general principle of GERMAN law is that the mere failure of the debtor to perform does not entitle the creditor either to refuse to accept performance if later tendered or to terminate the contract so as, for example, to recover back his own performance. So long as performance remains possible the creditor must first give the debtor a notice requiring him to perform within a stated time (*Nachfrist*). This principle is stated with regard to obligations to make reparation in CC § 250; with regard to cases in which a judgment for performance has been rendered against the debtor in CC § 283; and with regard to reciprocal contracts in CC § 326.[991]

The notice does not have to be in any particular form but it must in effect contain two statements. First, it must require the debtor to perform his obligations and generally specify a reasonable time within which he is required to do so. If the creditor sets too short a time for performance the notice is, however, not invalid: a reasonable time will begin to run unless the creditor has deliberately set a time which is so short that it indicates lack of good faith.[992] The creditor need not actually specify any time at all but simply ask for performance within a reasonable time.[993] To get over the uncertainty which may result from such a notice and the difficulty of determining what length of time is reasonable, the claimant can apply to the court to fix a time for this purpose (CCProc. § 255). The notice must, secondly, contain a statement to the effect that at the end of the period designated in the notice the creditor will refuse to accept performance.

If performance is not rendered within the period a number of consequences follow. First, and most obviously, the creditor is no longer bound to accept performance. In the case of a reciprocal contract it is necessary to go further and to provide, secondly, for the creditor's release from the obligations which he has undertaken and for the recovery by him of any performance which he may have rendered. CC § 326 accordingly provides that in the case of such contracts the creditor has a further option: instead of claiming compensation after the expiry of the term he has the right to terminate the contract (*von dem Vertrage zurückzutreten; Rücktritt*). Thirdly, on expiry of the term the creditor loses the right to claim performance. Instead he is entitled to compensation (*supra* s. 11).

This third consequence is not stated in the corresponding provision of the AUSTRIAN Civil Code (§ 918); and SWISS CO art. 107 expressly provides the contrary, *i.e.* that after expiry of the term set for performance the creditor still has the option of claiming performance or terminating the contract.[994] Once again it is assumed that the creditor is not *bound to accept* late performance: he is merely *entitled to claim* it. This aspect of the SWISS rule is open to the criticism[995] that a debtor from whom performance is claimed after the expiry of a *Nachfrist* might well be taken by surprise, at least unless the notice expressly reserves the creditor's rights (*supra* s. 11). The GERMAN rule, excluding this possibility, seems to be the preferable one.

The main purpose of the requirement of a *Nachfrist* is obviously to protect the debtor by giving him a further period of grace within which to perform, even after the time when he has been put formally in default. To put him in default, a *Mahnung* may be necessary (see *supra* ch. 15); but

[990] *Ibidem.*

[991] *Cf.* AUSTRIAN CC § 918; SWISS CO art. 107.

[992] *Enneccerus and Lehmann* 93.

[993] *Ibidem.*

[994] The debtor can ask the creditor to declare his option: *Guhl* 200. In the absence of such a declaration, SWISS CO art. 107 par. 2 creates a presumption that the creditor will still accept performance; in the case of commercial transactions, on the other hand, there is a presumption under CO art. 190 par. 1 that he will claim damages. Neither CO art. 107 nor CO art. 190 creates a presumption in favour of termination.

[995] In the case of a commercial sale, the criticism is met by CO art. 190 par. 2 (requiring the buyer to give immediate notice after the end of the term if he wants to claim performance).

even where this is so and the *Mahnung* has been given, a *Nachfrist* is in principle also necessary before the creditor is entitled to terminate the contract. In practice the two notices are often combined and it has been held that this practice is legally valid.[996]

The requirement of a *Nachfrist* may also protect the debtor in other ways than by giving him extra time to perform. In GERMAN law it forces a creditor who wishes to terminate the contract to declare his intentions well in advance and it deprives him of the right to claim performance at the end of the designated period. The debtor is thus protected by not having to hold himself ready to perform after that time; he will know that thereafter his sole liability will be one to make compensation. This protection is carried further by CC § 355, which is one of a group of provisions dealing with the situation in which a right to terminate the contract is reserved to the creditor by the contract; most of these provisions have been extended to cases in which the right to terminate arises by operation of law.[997] CC § 355 provides that if no time is set by the contract for the exercise of the right to terminate, the debtor is entitled to demand that it be exercised within a limited time. If it is not exercised within that time, the right to terminate is lost. Moreover, it seems that in all cases of termination good faith requires the aggrieved party to act with reasonable promptness.[998] Further rules which exist for the purpose of relieving the debtor from uncertainty as to whether performance will be required of him will be considered in s. 150 below (see also *supra* s. 11).

The protection which is afforded to the debtor by the requirement of a *Nachfrist* is thus considerable, but it is not so great as that afforded by the FRENCH requirement of a judgment. In GERMAN law, termination remains the act of the creditor, and not that of the court. It is effected by the creditor's declaration (CC § 349), even though he may have to go through rather elaborate motions in order to be entitled to exercise the right. Its actual exercise may call for yet a further declaration by the creditor after the expiry of the *Nachfrist* to the effect that he now does terminate the contract. The one important respect in which the creditor's position is worse in GERMAN than in FRENCH law is that he is in GERMAN law bound to choose between termination and damages. Under FRENCH CC art. 1184 these two remedies are not mutually exclusive (*infra* s. 183, 184).

150. *Cases in which a "Nachfrist" is not required.* – The German requirement of a *Nachfrist* is in its nature inapplicable to certain kinds of default; and it is also relaxed in a number of cases in which it is considered to cause inconvenience or injustice.

So far as the nature of the default is concerned, it is clear that the object of a *Nachfrist* is simply to give the debtor extra time to perform. It follows that the requirement is inapplicable where the default does not consist of delay but of impossibility. It has similarly been held to be inapplicable in cases of *positive Vertragsverletzung*.[999] By a process of further extension, the requirement has also been held to be inapplicable where performance is still possible but there is in fact no hope of receiving it because the debtor has unequivocally declared that he will refuse to perform. In such a case no useful purpose would be served by the *Nachfrist*.[1000] The debtor may also waive the requirement of a *Nachfrist* expressly or by implication.[1001]

In some situations, the distinction between delay and impossibility becomes blurred. These are cases in which delayed performance, though physically possible, is in fact useless to the creditor. CC § 326 par. 2 provides that termination is possible without *Nachfrist* if in consequence of the delay performance of the contract is of "no interest" to the aggrieved party.[1002] What is required to be of no interest is the performance of the contract: that is (as CC § 326 deals with reciprocal contracts) the *exchange of* performances (*infra* s. 165). A *very sharp* decline in the value of the subject-matter may therefore have the effect of making it of no interest to the aggrieved party to acquire that subject-matter for the counter-performance which he had promised,[1003] though a *mere* fall in value would not normally have this effect.[1004] A typical illustration of the rule laid down in CC § 326 par. 2 would be provided by late performance of a contract having a seasonal element.[1005] In AUSTRIAN, but not in GERMAN, law there is in some cases a further requirement that the lack of interest must be

[996] RG 28 June 1918, RGZ 93, 181.

[997] CC § 280 par. 2, 286 par. 2, 325 par. 1 sent. 2, 326 par. 1 sent. 3.

[998] *Palandt* § 325 no. 5.

[999] *Supra* s. 75. *Enneccerus and Lehmann* 229, 239; *Palandt* § 326 no. 6 a.

[1000] *Enneccerus and Lehmann* 229; *Palandt* § 326 no. 6d.

[1001] *Enneccerus and Lehmann* 229.

[1002] *Cf.* also CC § 286 par. 2.

[1003] *Enneccerus and Lehmann* 228.

[1004] *Palandt* § 326 no. 11.

[1005] *Ibidem.*

known to the party in default if the requirement of *Nachfrist* is to be avoided.[1006]

The most important case in which a *Nachfrist* is not required is that of the so-called *Fixgeschäft*.[1007] This is a contract under which the obligations of at least one party have to be performed at or within a stipulated time. It is necessary to distinguish between three situations. First, there is the situation in which performance outside the stipulated time may be so different from that contemplated that it cannot properly speaking be said to be performance of the contract at all.[1008] If performance is not rendered within the stipulated time the case is one of impossibility and there is no need to resort to the special rules relieving the creditor from the obligation to set a *Nachfrist* on the ground that the transaction is a *Fixgeschäft*. Secondly, and at the other extreme, a contract may state a date or period of performance without imposing an unqualified duty on the debtor to perform within that time.[1009] In such a case there is no *Fixgeschäft* merely because the contract contains a stipulation as to time. Thirdly, the contract may state a time which is regarded as one of the bases of the contract:[1010] for example where a contract of sale stipulates for the time of shipment.[1011] It is this third situation which is dealt with by the Code provisions discussed below.

The distinction between the second and third of the above situations is obviously a hard one to draw. It depends on the construction of the contract; it is similar to that drawn in COMMON LAW countries between stipulations as to time which are, and those which are not, "of the essence" of the contract (*infra* s. 153).

CC § 361 provides that if a reciprocal contract contains a stipulation as to time (falling into the third of the above categories) and that stipulation is not complied with, then it is to be presumed that the aggrieved party is entitled to terminate the contract. In the case of commercial sales Comm.C § 376 lays down a positive rule (and not a mere presumption) to the same effect. No requirement of *Nachfrist* is stated; in the SWISS Code of Obligations the requirement is expressly excluded in such cases (art. 108 no. 3). Lapse of the fixed time does not deprive the aggrieved party of his claim to performance. He has the option of asserting this claim or of terminating the contract.

The existence of this option is obviously a source of potential prejudice to the party in default who may as a result of it, be left in doubt on the point whether performance of the contract will still be required of him (supra s. 11). In GERMAN law the problem is confined to *Fixgeschäfte*[1012] but in SWISS law the problem is a more general one, since under CO art. 107 even the expiry of a *Nachfrist* in cases not involving a *Fixgeschäft* does not deprive the aggrieved party of the right to claim performance.

In GERMAN law Comm.C § 376 provides that if the aggrieved party wishes to claim performance he must notify the party in default immediately, once the time or period fixed for performance has gone by:[1013] if he fails to do this he loses his claim to performance and is confined to his rights to terminate the contract or claim compensation for non-performance. Although this is not expressly stated, it seems clear that in such a situation the aggrieved party is not bound to accept performance either. CC § 361 contains no corresponding provision; but it is generally agreed that the right to terminate the contract must be exercised without excessive delay. If it is not so exercised it will be deemed to have been waived, or it will be lost by lapse of time, or its exercise will be regarded as contrary to good faith.[1014] The result is of course the exact opposite of that laid down in Comm.C § 376. Under the Civil Code it is the right to terminate which is lost by delay in notifying the debtor; under the Commercial Code what is lost is the right to claim performance.

A similar distinction exists under SWISS CO art. 107 and 190. The general rule, stated in CO art. 107 par. 2, is that the aggrieved party can either claim performance or terminate the contract. If he wishes to terminate the contract he must give notice to that effect immediately the debtor is in default. This rule is of general application and is not restricted to *Fixgeschäfte*. In the case of a commercial sale with a fixed delivery date CO art. 190 lays down a presumption that the buyer will not claim delivery after the fixed date has gone by; if he does wish to claim delivery he must immediately notify the seller to that effect. CO art. 190 does not expressly refer to the right to terminate the contract, but it may be assumed that this right is also available in cases

1006 AUSTRIAN CC § 919 sent. 2.

1007 See GERMAN CC § 361; SWISS CO **art.** 108 no. 3; AUSTRIAN CC § 919 sent. 1.

1008 BGB-RGRK § 361 no. 1.

1009 *Idem* § 361 no. 2.

1010 *Ibidem*; *cf. Guhl* 188.

1011 BGB-RGRK § 361 no. 3.

1012 Since in other cases a *Nachfrist*, requiring a declaration that performance will be refused, is normally required.

1013 *Cf.* AUSTRIAN CC § 919.

1014 BGB-RGRK § 361 no. 4; § 346 no. 2.

falling within that article. It may also be assumed (though this, too, is not expressly stated) that once the delivery date has gone by the buyer is no longer bound to accept delivery.

151. *Analogous rules in other systems.* – The requirement of a *Nachfrist* may be compared with the power of a FRENCH court, when considering a claim for termination, to grant the debtor a further period of time (*délai de grâce*) within which to perform. The power to grant such a *délai* is within the discretion of the court: CC art. 1184 par. 3 simply says that the court must have regard to the circumstances in deciding whether to grant it. In the case of sales of land one restriction is imposed by CC art. 1655: no *délai* can be granted on a claim for termination if it puts the seller in danger of losing the subject-matter of the sale and the price.

Under CC art. 1244 a court can grant a *délai* of up to one year for the payment of a debt, having regard to the position of the debtor, the economic situation and other circumstances; but this provision is not concerned with the powers of the court on a claim for termination. On the contrary, the underlying assumption is that the creditor is claiming payment, *i.e.* performance rather than termination. No similar period of grace is allowed when a seller who is guilty of delay is sued for performance,[1015] though it may be granted where the seller is sued for termination:[1016] thus a buyer who is sued for payment may be treated more leniently than a seller who is sued for performance of his obligation to deliver.

CC art. 1244 may further be contrasted with CC art. 1184 and 1655 in that there is no statutory time limit to the *délai* which can be granted under the latter provisions. CC art. 1655 provides that if by the end of the *délai* the purchaser has not paid termination must be adjudged. There is no corresponding directive in CC art. 1184, but the result would usually be the same though perhaps the court could in its discretion grant a further *délai*.

The *délai de grâce* could be regarded as a kind of judicially imposed *Nachfrist*,[1017] though obviously the two institutions differ in a number of respects. The most important of these is that the *délai* can only be granted by the judge while the *Nachfrist* must be set by the creditor; and that the *délai* is discretionary while the *Nachfrist* is a mandatory requirement.

The requirement of a *Nachfrist* may also be compared with a number of rules of ANGLO-AMERICAN law. The most obvious comparison is with the rules which determine the effects of stipulations as to the time of performance. These rules and their comparison with the requirement of a *Nachfrist* will be discussed in s. 153 below. They are not exclusively nor even primarily concerned with the right to terminate the contract.[1018]

Under analogous COMMON LAW rules a party may be granted relief against an express provision for termination of the contract on terms of making good a defect in his performance (*infra* s. 172). For example a tenant may be given extra time to pay off arrears of rent or to perform an undertaking to repair; and in the meantime the landlord will not be entitled to enforce a forfeiture clause in the lease.[1019] The landlord is required in the first place to give a notice requiring the tenant to make good his default; and this notice certainly has affinities with the *Nachfrist*. But the court can grant a further period of grace, and in this respect relief against forfeiture is more closely analogous to the FRENCH *délai de grâce*.

Where relief is granted against forfeiture, the defaulting party is in effect given a liberty to cure his default. This liberty also exists in other areas of the COMMON LAW (*infra* s. 174) where it in no way depends on the issue of any notice resembling a *Nachfrist* by the aggrieved party; it arises, on the contrary, from an offer by the party in default. A similar liberty sometimes exists in GERMAN law[1020] and is not discussed in connection with the requirement of a *Nachfrist*. The liberty to cure should of course be carefully distinguished from a duty to cure. The question whether such a duty exists is discussed in s. 7 above; generally there is no such duty. The possibility of cure may also affect the question whether the default is sufficiently serious to warrant termination: this question is discussed in s. 174 below. In COMMON LAW countries, failure to object to defective performance may amount to acquiescence or waiver depriving the aggrieved

[1015] *Mazeaud*, Leçons III no. 946.

[1016] Under the general principle of CC art. 1184 par. 3.

[1017] *Cf. Zweigert and Kötz* 198.

[1018] The main purpose of a notice making time of the essence is to pave the way for a claim to performance: in this respect it is more closely analogous to a *Mahnung* than to a *Nachfrist*. An incidental consequence of failure to comply with the notice is that it justifies rescission and forfeiture of the buyer's deposit.

[1019] *E.g.* in ENGLAND under Law of Property Act, 1925 (*supra* n. 464) s. 146.

[1020] *E.g.* where the subject-matter of the sale suffers from minor curable defects: *Enneccerus and Lehmann* 452.

party of the right to terminate or even sometimes of all remedies.[1021] But the notice that is required to avoid this consequence is quite different from the *Nachfrist*. It need not set a term for due performance or call for such performance at all; nor is it exclusively concerned with the situation in which the default consists of delay.

There is some superficial resemblance between the *Nachfrist* and the COMMON LAW rule which governs the termination of contracts of indefinite duration.[1022] Such termination is effected by giving reasonable notice; but this process has nothing to do with default nor is the notice one that calls for performance. It is simply a notice of termination given in the exercise of a power conferred by law.

A final rule of AMERICAN law which may be compared with the *Nachfrist* is that laid down by UCC s. 2-609 with regard to "adequate assurance of performance". There is some resemblance to the *Nachfrist* in that the giving of a notice entitles a party to terminate the contract if no assurance is given by the end of a fixed time; but there are also important differences between the two institutions. The principle of adequate assurance is not confined to (or even primarily intended for) cases of delay; and adequate assurance may be (and generally will be) sought before there has been any contractual default at all. UCC s. 2-609 is more closely analogous to the principle of GERMAN CC § 321, which in certain cases entitles a party to a reciprocal contract to suspend his performance until the other party has either performed or given security for his performance. The two provisions and the differences between them are discussed in s. 189 below.

iii. *No Formal Machinery*

152. *General position in Anglo-American law.* – The general principle in ANGLO-AMERICAN law is that termination of a contract on the ground of default may be effected simply by a notice to that effect given by the aggrieved to the defaulting party. No prior formal notice in the nature of a *Nachfrist* is normally required; nor does the process of termination involve the need to go to court. Of course it is sometimes possible for the creditor to obtain a judgment to the effect that the contract is or has been terminated; indeed it may be desirable for him to do so in order to clarify the legal position (*cf. supra* n. 977). It is also true that a judgment must often be obtained to give effect to the consequences of termination, in the sense that a party seeking restitution of his own performance is not normally entitled to self-help.

The notice by which the right to terminate is exercised does not have to be in any particular form. It need not as a general rule even specify the ground on which the contract is terminated. If the ground stated in the notice does not in law justify termination, the notice may nevertheless be valid so long as a ground which does justify termination actually exists.[1023] A notice of termination which fails to state the correct ground of termination is however invalid if the effect of the failure is to deprive the defaulting party of an opportunity to cure the defect to which he was entitled under any relevant rules of law.[1024]

153. *Exception: stipulations as to time.* – So far as damages are concerned, the COMMON LAW draws no sharp distinction between delay and other forms of contractual default (*supra* s. 76). To some extent this is also true in relation to the right to terminate a contract: thus the question whether delay gives rise to such a right may be determined simply in accordance with the general principle that the breach must be of the required degree of seriousness (*infra* s. 161 ss.). For example, in shipping cases the question whether termination is justified by delay in loading, or in prosecuting a voyage, has been discussed in terms of this general principle.[1025] It has not been considered to fall into a special category concerned with delay as such. Certainly there has not been any suggestion that, where delay is sufficiently serious, a notice calling for performance within a specified time is necessary to give rise to a right to terminate the contract; nor, where the delay is not serious enough, would such a notice be sufficient for this purpose.[1026] The most that can be said is that failure to comply with such a notice may be

[1021] UNITED KINGDOM Sale of Goods Act, 1893 (*supra* n. 312) s. 11 (1) (a); AMERICAN UCC s. 2-607 (3) (a).

[1022] *Carnegie*, Terminability of Contracts of Unspecified Duration: 85 L.Q.R. 392 (1969); UCC s. 2-309 (2).

[1023] *Boston Deep Sea Fishing and Ice Co., Ltd. v. Ansell* (1888), 39 Ch.D. 339 (C.A.) (employment); *Taylor v. Oakes, Roncoroni & Co.* (1922), 38 T.L.R. 349 (K.B.) and 517 (C.A.) (sale of goods); *Corbin* § 762; *Treitel* 728.

[1024] UCC s. 2-605; *Panchaud Frères S.A. v. Etablissement Général Grain Co.*, [1970] 1 Lloyd's Rep. 53 (C.A.).

[1025] *E.g.*, *Universal Cargo Carriers Corp. v. Citati*, [1957] 2 Q.B. 401; *Hongkong Fir Shipping Co., Ltd. v. Kawasaki Kisen Kaisha, Ltd.*, *supra* n. 955.

[1026] *Eshun v. Moorgate Mercantile Credit Co.*, [1971] 1 W.L.R. 722 (C.A.).

evidence of intention to repudiate the contract and that it may therefore justify termination of the contract on that ground.

There are, however, cases in which ANGLO-AMERICAN law does accord special treatment to delay, probably for historical reasons. A distinction was drawn, and probably applied originally only to contracts for the sale of interests in land, between those stipulations as to the time of performance which did, and those which did not, "go to the essence" of the contract. The present effect of the distinction is as follows.[1027] If a stipulation as to time goes to the essence of the contract, failure by one party to perform it within the stated time generally gives the other party the right to terminate the contract; though the exercise of this right may be limited by other rules: for example those relating to relief against forfeiture. If on the other hand the stipulation does not go to the essence of the contract, failure by one party to perform within the stipulated time does not give the other the right to terminate the contract though it does at least in theory give him a right to claim damages. In ENGLAND however, the right to damages for failure to comply with a non-essential stipulation as to time appears to have been taken away by legislation,[1028] except in cases of negligent or wilful default.[1029]

The question whether a stipulation as to time goes to the essence of the contract depends first on the terms of the contract, which may expressly specify that time is to be of the essence. Secondly, it depends on the nature of the subject-matter: for example time will be regarded as of the essence of a contract for the sale of a short leasehold interest as this is likely to depreciate rapidly. On similar grounds the time for taking delivery of goods, though not normally regarded as of the essence, will be so regarded if the goods are perishable. Thirdly, the character of a stipulation as to time depends (at any rate *prima facie*) in some cases on rules of law: for example in ENGLAND the Sale of Goods Act, 1893 s. 10 provides that in a contract for the sale of goods stipulations as to the time of payment are not deemed to be of the essence of the contract.

Even where time is not of the essence of the contract, the party aggrieved by delay can in effect make it of the essence *ex post facto* by giving notice to the other party calling upon him to perform within a specified period (which must be reasonable). Once such a notice has been given, *either* party can terminate, and claim damages, if the other does not perform within the time set by the notice.

These rules have obvious affinities with the GERMAN rules discussed in s. 149 and 150 above. The notice making time of the essence can be compared with the *Nachfrist*, while the cases in which time is of the essence *ab initio* could be regarded as the ANGLO-AMERICAN equivalent of the *Fixgeschäft*. But although there is considerable force in the comparison, there are also important differences between the two sets of rules.

In the first place, the expiry of a notice making time of the essence *ex post facto* only has the effect of giving the party who fails to receive performance within that time the *option* of terminating: unlike a *Nachfrist*, the notice need not say that performance after that time will be refused, nor does it deprive the aggrieved party of the right to claim performance of the contract. On the contrary, the giving of the notice is often a preliminary step to a claim for specific performance.

Secondly, the notice binds both parties so that if the party who gave the notice fails to perform his part within the time stated in the notice the other party can equally terminate the contract.[1030] A similar point can be made with regard to the case where time is of the essence of the contract *ab initio*. There is no rule of ANGLO-AMERICAN law corresponding to that contained in GERMAN Comm.C § 376 which requires a party wishing to claim performance after the fixed time has gone by to give immediate notice to that effect to the other party. The importance of this distinction is of course to some extent reduced by the fact that specific enforcement is less readily available in ANGLO-AMERICAN than in GERMAN law; so that very commonly the only option of the aggrieved party would be the same as in GERMAN law, *viz.* to terminate or claim damages. But this would not be so where the contract was for the disposition of an interest in land.

Finally, and perhaps most important, the categories of "contracts in which time is of the essence" and *Fixgeschäfte* do not in practice appear to have the same content. Although this is a matter on which it is difficult to generalise, it does seem that the GERMAN courts are much more reluctant

[1027] *Corbin* § 1177; *Treitel* 720–724; *cf.* INDIAN Contract Act, 1872 (*supra* n. 241) s. 53.

[1028] Law of Property Act, 1925 (*supra* n. 464) s. 41, re-enacting provisions formerly contained in Judicature Act, 1873 (36 & 37 Vict., c.66) s. 25 (7). However, even before this legislation a court of equity might restrain an action for damages in such cases: *Treitel* 724.

[1029] *Treitel* 724.

[1030] *Idem* 722.

to hold that a transaction is a *Fixgeschäft* than the ANGLO-AMERICAN courts are to hold that time is of the essence of the contract.[1031]

All these differences favour the aggrieved party and lend support to the view that the ANGLO-AMERICAN courts are, in the matter of termination, less concerned with the protection of the debtor than either GERMAN or FRENCH law. Their emphasis tends on the contrary to be on speedy and convenient remedies for the creditor; and the cases in which he has to give a notice in the nature of a *Nachfrist* are regarded as somewhat exceptional (see also *infra* s. 172).

iv. *A Mixed Approach*

154. *"Avoidance" under ULIS.* – The machinery of termination under ULIS (*supra* s. 7) (which refers to the process as "avoidance" in the ENGLISH and as "*résolution*" in the FRENCH text) owes nothing to FRENCH law. There is no requirement of a judgment; and the notion of a period of grace is expressly rejected.[1032] ULIS does, however, show an interesting combination of GERMAN and COMMON LAW ideas. Sometimes a notice in the nature of a *Nachfrist* (*supra* s. 149) is required. Sometimes there is no formal requirement for termination at all. Here ULIS goes beyond the COMMON LAW in occasionally treating failure to affirm as equivalent to termination: this is known as "*ipso facto* avoidance" (for criticism see *infra* s. 178).

Where the breach is "fundamental" (*infra* s. 162 ss.) termination takes place without any preliminary formal steps. A distinction is drawn between cases in which the defaulting party has not performed at all (*e.g.* the seller has failed to deliver on the agreed day) and those in which he has performed defectively (*e.g.* the seller has delivered late, or he has delivered non-conforming goods). In the former case there is "*ipso facto* avoidance".[1033] In the latter case, the contract may be avoided by a declaration of the aggrieved party;[1034] this is the COMMON LAW position.

Where the breach is not fundamental, the aggrieved party can give a notice in the nature of a *Nachfrist*, requiring performance. Failure to perform at the end of the period may lead either to "*ipso facto* avoidance" if the defaulting party is a seller who has not performed at all,[1035] or to avoidance by declaration of the aggrieved party if the defaulting party is a seller who has performed defectively[1036] or if he is a buyer who has failed to pay the price.[1037] Where the seller delivers non-conforming goods, the buyer must also give a notice of non-conformity (art. 39); but this is not a special requirement of termination. It is a prerequisite to the exercise of *any* remedy.

C. THE GROUNDS FOR TERMINATION

i. *Fault*

155. *Requirement of "fault".* – In many legal systems "fault" is at least in certain cases an element of contractual liability.[1038] This requirement of fault is generally stated to exist in connection with liability in damages; but to some extent it must also be satisfied where the remedy sought is the termination of the contract.

156. *French law – requirement of fault and exceptions.* – In FRENCH law fault is relevant for two purposes. First, the remedy of termination available under CC art. 1184 depends on the presence of fault:[1039] indeed this seems to be clear from the fact that CC art. 1184 provides for termination and damages. Fault is clearly a requirement for the second of these two remedies and no distinction is drawn between them so far as the basis of liability is concerned. Secondly, termination is in principle a judicial remedy, available at the discretion of the court. In exercising that discretion, one of the principal factors which the court will take into account will be the degree of the defendant's fault. For example, the court may be influenced by the fact that the defendant acted in bad faith: termination is more likely to be granted against one who knew of defects in the subject-matter of the contract than against one who did not.[1040]

All this is not to say that dissolution of the contract may not take place where failure of performance is not due to the defendant's fault. If performance of one party's obligation becomes impossible through *force majeure*, the other party's obligation may well be extinguished. But such extinction takes place under the so-called theory

[1031] *Enneccerus and Lehmann* 108; *cf. Zweigert*, Aspects of the German Law of Sale: Some Comparative Aspects of the Law Relating to Sale of Goods (*supra* n. 92) 1, 12.

[1032] Art. 24 (3), 64.

[1033] *E.g.* art. 26 (1), 30 (1), 62 (1).

[1034] *E.g.* art. 26 (3), 30 (3), 43.

[1035] Art. 27, 31 (2).

[1036] Art. 26 (3), 30 (3), 44 (2).

[1037] Art. 62 (2); *cf. infra* s. 178.

[1038] See *supra* ch. 15.

[1039] *Marty and Raynaud* II no. 300.

[1040] *Carbonnier* IV 272, 276.

of risks.[1041] It is not, like termination, based on the theory of an implied resolutive condition. Moreover its effect is different from that of termination in that it operates only prospectively and not retrospectively; and in that it excludes a claim to damages.[1042]

A further case of what amounts to termination without fault arises where the subject-matter of a sale suffers from defects which justify redhibition. The presence of such defects does not constitute contractual default (*supra* s. 7, 57) but the remedy of redhibition is very similar in its effects to termination, except of course that it cannot be coupled with a claim for damages.

Finally, it is no doubt possible for the parties to include in their contract an express resolutive condition providing for termination in the event of non-performance irrespective of fault.

157. *German law – delay and impossibility; legal and contractual powers of termination.* – In GERMAN law the provisions relating to the requirement of "fault" in cases of termination are complex so that the task of stating the law is unusually difficult. It is based on two distinctions. The first relates to the kind of default for which termination is sought: this may be either impossibility (*Unmöglichkeit*) or delay (*Verzug*). The second is the distinction between cases in which the right to terminate is conferred by law and those in which the right is expressly reserved by the contract. Moreover, the notion of "fault" in the present context is (as will appear below) a wider one than the corresponding notion in relation to liability for damages.

So far as impossibility is concerned, the GERMAN Civil Code deals with three situations. In the first, impossibility is due to the fault of neither party. Here CC § 323 provides that both are released from their obligations to perform and any performance already rendered must be restored in accordance with the principles of unjust enrichment. This situation is not our concern in the present chapter, since the impossibility provides a lawful excuse for non-performance (*supra* n. 1); it is considered in ch. 15 above. In the second impossibility is due to the wrongful failure of one of the parties to *accept performance.* This situation has already been discussed. The basic rule is that the party so refusing to accept remains liable to render the counter-performance which he has promised, subject to certain deductions.[1043] In the third situation, impossibility arises from the wrongful failure of one party to *render* performance. Where the contract is reciprocal, the other party may wish to terminate with a view to reclaiming his own performance. It is in this situation alone that rights to "terminate" in the sense of the present chapter arise;[1044] and the following discussion is restricted to it.

The effect of impossibility in our third situation on a reciprocal contract is governed by CC § 325. This gives the aggrieved party a choice. He can either claim damages or terminate the contract (*von dem Vertrage zurücktreten*). These rights exist if the impossibility is due to a circumstance for which the other party is responsible (*den er zu vertreten hat*). Alternatively he can reclaim his own performance on the principles of unjust enrichment instead of claiming damages or terminating.[1045] Where the contract is not reciprocal, the aggrieved party will not be seeking recovery of anything performed by him. His only claim will be for damages (CC § 280 par. 1) and no question of termination arises.

In cases of partial impossibility, the question arises whether the aggrieved party is bound to accept the part remaining possible. CC § 280 par. 2 provides that the creditor can refuse to accept performance if the part remaining possible has no interest for him and claim damages for non-performance of the entire obligation. The requirement of "fault" (in the above sense of legal responsibility) is not expressly stated here but it must clearly be implied. CC § 280 par. 2 follows on from CC § 280 par. 1 which deals with total impossibility due to a circumstance for which the debtor is responsible; and the fact that CC § 280 par. 2 confers on the creditor a right to damages also shows that the contemplated situation is one in which the usual conditions as to damages (including "fault") have to be complied with. CC § 325 applies the rule stated in CC § 280 par. 2 to cases of reciprocal contracts where performance of the contract is in view of the partial impossibility of no further interest to the party claiming termination. The test is therefore not whether the performance due from the debtor is of no further interest to the creditor, but whether he still has an interest in the exchange of performances under the contract (*cf. supra* s. 150). Under CC § 325, "fault" is expressly made a requirement of termination.

The phrase used to describe the requirement of "fault" in this context is "for which he is responsible". This refers primarily to "fault" in the sense of deliberate wrongdoing or negligence

[1041] *Idem* IV 271-272, 278 ss.; *supra* n. 952. See *supra* ch. 15.

[1042] *Carbonnier* IV 271-272, 278 ss., *supra* n. 952.

[1043] CC § 324; *supra* s. 102.

[1044] *Cf. supra* s. 143, 144.

[1045] CC § 325 par. 1 sent. 3.

(CC § 276): fault in this sense is referred to as *Verschulden*. However, a person may be "responsible" even in the absence of "fault" in cases of so-called *Unvermögen*, an expression which may be translated as subjective impossibility (see *supra* ch. 15). For example a seller of generic goods is "responsible" for failure to deliver even though he personally could not obtain goods of the contract description, and even though he did not act deliberately or negligently in this respect, so long as goods of that description were available somewhere (CC § 279).

A person may be "responsible" for the purpose of being liable to termination even though he is not at fault for the purpose of liability in damages. For example, a seller may not be liable in damages merely because the subject-matter of the sale is defective (*supra* s. 7, 57), but he may nevertheless be "responsible" in the sense of being liable to the special remedies of *Wandelung* and *Minderung*.[1046] It is therefore "responsibility" in this extended sense rather than "fault" in the sense of *Verschulden* which is a condition of termination on the ground of impossibility.

The same principle applies where the contract is terminated on the ground of delay (*Verzug*), the debtor having failed to perform after the setting of a *Nachfrist* (*supra* s. 149). The right to terminate a reciprocal contract on this ground is conferred by CC § 326; and it is true that that provision contains no reference to responsibility or fault. But such a reference must be implied by reason of the definition of *Verzug* in CC § 285, which provides that the debtor is not in *Verzug* if his omission to perform is due to a circumstance for which he is not responsible. It is, finally, possible to terminate a contract on the ground of *positive Vertragsverletzung* (*supra* s. 75). Since the very concept of this kind of breach connotes "fault", it is clear that "fault" is required for termination on this ground.

These rights to terminate the contract which arise by operation of law must be contrasted with the right to terminate which arises by express contractual reservation.[1047] In such cases there is as a general rule no requirement of "fault" or "responsibility". The right to terminate simply depends on the contractual stipulations to that effect and the only questions are whether the circumstances for which the right has been reserved have indeed arisen, and whether the stipulated conditions (if any) have been complied with. The point emerges particularly clearly from CC § 359 which deals with the reservation of a right to terminate on payment of *Reugeld* (*supra* s. 139). The only requirement for termination here is the payment or tender of the stipulated sum. If indeed "fault" or "responsibility" can be attributed to one of the parties the other party can terminate without payment of *Reugeld*,[1048] a rule which clearly indicates that the right to terminate under CC § 359 exists irrespective of fault.

There is, however, an exception to the general principle that a contractually reserved right of termination exists irrespective of fault. CC § 360 deals with the case of a contract containing a so-called *Verwirkungsklausel* under which the debtor is to lose his rights under the contract if he does not perform his obligations. In the event of such failure to perform, the creditor is entitled to terminate the contract. CC § 360 does not specify any requirement of fault for the exercise of this right to terminate; and the decisions are in apparent conflict on the question whether there is such a requirement in cases of this kind. The correct view probably is that there is no single answer to this question but that the solution depends in each case on the construction of the contractual provision by virtue of which the right to terminate arises.[1049]

So far, then, two general principles are fairly clear: that "responsibility" is a requirement for the exercise of the right to terminate which arises by operation of law, but that there is in general no such requirement where the right to terminate the contract arises by virtue of an express contractual provision. A liability to make restitution in accordance with the principles of unjust enrichment may also arise where neither party is responsible; but this is a case of excused non-performance and hence not our primary concern in this chapter (*supra* n. 1).

Considerable difficulty is, however, caused in this context by the obscure wording of CC § 327. This paragraph in its first sentence provides that the rules laid down in CC § 346 to 356 for the contractually reserved right to terminate shall correspondingly apply to the right to terminate by operation of law arising under CC § 325 and 326. One of the rules thus made applicable for the

[1046] See CC § 462 which refers to a defect for which the seller is responsible (*den er zu vertreten hat*).

[1047] This right is governed by CC § 346-356. That these provisions apply primarily to the contractually reserved right to terminate appears from (*inter alia*) CC § 280 par. 2, 286 par. 2 and § 327 which apply § 346-356 "correspondingly" to the rights to terminate which arise by operation of law. In addition § 357-359 clearly apply to the contractually reserved right.

[1048] *Enneccerus and Lehmann* 173.

[1049] BGB-RGRK § 360 no. 3; *Enneccerus and Lehmann* 172.

purposes of CC § 325 and 326 is the rule requiring mutual restoration of performances received by each party to the contract which has been terminated (*infra* s. 181 ss.). CC § 327 then goes on to provide that if termination occurs on account of circumstances for which the "other party" is not responsible, then that party is only liable in accordance with the principles of unjust enrichment. This may considerably alleviate the liability of the "other party" since instead of having to restore what he received, and certain other benefits (*infra* s. 181) he will only be obliged to restore such benefits as he still retains.[1050]

The question remains who the "other party" is, whose liability is thus alleviated. The difficulty is that he is the *only* party referred to in CC § 327. It seems clear that the "other party" cannot be the party against whom the right to terminate the contract is asserted, for if that party is not "responsible" for the circumstances on which an alleged right to terminate is asserted then the right will not exist, "responsibility" being a requirement of termination under CC § 325 and 326 to which (alone) CC § 327 refers. The "other party" must therefore be the party who is asserting the right to terminate and who accordingly comes under a liability to make restitution of the performance he has received. This is the sense in which the expression "other party" (*der andere Teil*) is used in CC § 325 and 326, and the reference to those paragraphs in CC § 327 would appear to support the view that the expression refers to the same party in all three paragraphs, even though only one party is expressly mentioned in CC § 327. The purpose of CC § 327 then is to alleviate the position of the party claiming termination who will normally not be "responsible" for the circumstances giving right to termination.[1051] CC § 327 carries no implication that the right to terminate by operation of law may be exercised in circumstances for which the person *against whom* the right is asserted is not responsible. Such a party is at most liable to make restitution under the principles of unjust enrichment.[1052]

158. *Austrian and Swiss law.* – AUSTRIAN law draws a distinction between cases in which performance is delayed and those in which it is prevented (*vereitelt*). In the former case the contract can be terminated without any reference to fault;[1053] in the latter case the contract can only be terminated if the prevention is due to the fault of the debtor or to an accidental cause (*Zufall*) for which he was responsible (CC § 920). Accidental impossibility operates as an automatic release, subject however to a requirement to make restitution so as to prevent unjust enrichment (CC § 1447). In SWISS law no requirement of fault or "responsibility" is stated for the termination of the contract;[1054] though the presence of fault will of course be relevant to the right to damages[1055] which the party claiming termination may be able to assert together with the right to terminate the contract.[1056]

159. *Anglo-American law – no general requirement of "fault".* – In ANGLO-AMERICAN law "fault" is not generally a condition of contractual liability;[1057] and this principle is as true in relation to a claim to terminate a contract as it is in relation to a claim for damages. The right to terminate under ULIS (*supra* s. 7) similarly does not depend on "fault". There are, it is true, certain statutory provisions in the UNITED STATES under which the right to terminate is in some circumstances said to depend on the "fault" of one of the contracting parties.[1058] But "fault" here does not mean anything more or less than breach of contract. This does not normally require "fault" in the sense of deliberate or negligent wrongdoing. Nevertheless there are two points at which ANGLO-AMERICAN law bears some resemblance to the CIVIL LAW rules (*supra* s. 155-157).

The first is that the manner of breach may be relevant to the existence of the right to terminate. Generally the existence of that right depends on the seriousness of the breach (*infra* s. 161 ss.); but the right to terminate may exist even where the breach is not of a particularly "serious" kind, so far as its effects are concerned, if the breach is a deliberate one.[1059] A deliberate breach may amount to fraud: for example where a seller of

1050 Under CC § 818 par. 3; *cf. Enneccerus and Lehmann* 166.

1051 BGB-RGRK § 327 no. 2; *cf. Larenz* I 297, 298.

1052 CC § 323 par. 3; *supra* at n. 1050.

1053 CC § 918; *Klang and Gschnitzer (-Gschnitzer)* IV 1 § 918 no. AII, BII 1.

1054 *I.e.* in CO art. 107, 108, 190. The definition of *Verzug* in CO art. 102 again contains no reference to "fault"; while CO art. 103 par. 2 makes absence of fault a defence only to a claim for compensation (and not to termination). See *Guhl* 74.

1055 Under CO art. 109 par. 2.

1056 *Supra* s. 57, 58, 78; *infra* s. 184.

1057 See *supra* ch. 15.

1058 *E.g.* UCC s. 2-305 (3); CALIFORNIAN CC § 1689 (2); Revised Codes of MONTANA (*supra* n. 137) § 13-903 (2); NORTH DAKOTA Century Code (*supra* n. 154) § 9-09-02 (2); OKLAHOMA Statutes (*supra* n. 187) § 15-233 (2); SOUTH DAKOTA Compiled Laws (*supra* n. 154) § 21-12-1 (2).

1059 See Restatement of Contracts (1932) § 275 (e).

land *deliberately* overstates its area.[1060] In such a case the purchaser can terminate the contract, even though he would not have been entitled to do so, had the misstatement been innocent. Again, the fact that a breach is deliberate may secondly be relevant as showing "an intention no longer to be bound by the contract"[1061] and as justifying termination on that ground. There was, moreover, at one time some support in ENGLISH law for the proposition that wilful disobedience of *any* lawful order justified the summary dismissal of a servant; but it is clear that this view would no longer be accepted today.[1062] The relevance of "fault" in this sense in ANGLO-AMERICAN law may be compared with the FRENCH principle under which the *degree* of the defendant's fault is taken into account by the court in determining, not whether the minimum conditions for termination exist, but whether the remedy should actually be granted (*supra* s. 156).

The second point is that the right to terminate may arise in ANGLO-AMERICAN law on account of a failure in performance which does not amount to a breach at all. A contract may of course be terminated under the doctrine of frustration; and in such cases it is not strictly correct to talk of a right to terminate, since termination occurs automatically by operation of law and not at the election of one or other of the contracting parties. But there may be a right to terminate for failure in performance which is due to circumstances providing an excuse for non-performance though the contract is not frustrated. This was the situation where a singer who had been engaged to take a leading part in a new opera was unable through illness to perform on the opening nights.[1063] The court said that she was not in breach and it seems clear that the contract was not frustrated either in the sense of being automatically terminated. The singer could have been held to the rest of her engagement (which was to run for some months) after the end of her illness. It was nevertheless held that the employer was entitled to terminate the contract.

In GERMAN law there is a similar right of *Kündigung* which may be exercised for an important reason (*aus wichtigem Grund*)[1064] but this right must be distinguished from *Rücktritt* on a number of grounds: in particular it has no retrospective operation.[1065] In ANGLO-AMERICAN law there is no such sharp distinction between the right to terminate for breach and for excused failure in performance, though of course it is clear that damages cannot be recovered in the latter case.

160. *Conclusion.* – As a matter of general principle, the requirement that there must be "fault" before a contract can be terminated is not easy to defend. Even granted that such a requirement is justifiable before damages (or certain kinds of damages) can be claimed, it by no means follows that the same requirement should be imposed on a claim for termination. The remedies are quite different in their *consequences;* and there is, accordingly, no necessary connection between the *conditions* in which they can respectively be claimed. The point is well illustrated by the relevant provision of ULIS which, in cases of excused non-performance, protects the party who has not performed from liability in damages; but it does not prevent the other party from avoiding the contract if the failure in performance is of the degree of seriousness required by other provision of the Law.[1066]

It is, of course, not hard to see how the requirement of fault has become associated with the remedy of termination. FRENCH CC art. 1184 provides that in certain conditions the aggrieved party can claim termination *and* damages. As the conditions specified are the same for both remedies, and as it is established that fault must exist if a claim for damages is to succeed, the same requirement is naturally supposed to exist also for the purpose of termination. In GERMAN law, a similar argument could be advanced. Admittedly CC § 325 and 326 only provide that the aggrieved party can in certain conditions claim compensation *or* terminate the contract; but still no distinction is drawn in the Code between the conditions required for the availability of the two remedies.

Such arguments, however, are merely attempts to justify the requirement of fault (for the remedy of termination) on the wording of the Codes. They do not meet the objection that there is no necessary connection between the requirements for damages and for termination. The argument is particularly strong in view of the power of legislatures and of the courts to mould each remedy in accordance with the degree of fault of the defendant. This point is illustrated in

1060 *Treitel* 702.

1061 *Freeth v. Burr* (1874), L.R. 9 C.P. 208, 213; *cf.* INDIAN Contract Act, 1872 (*supra* n. 241) s. 39, making refusal to perform a separate ground of termination.

1062 *Treitel* 704; in GREAT BRITAIN such a dismissal would now seem to be an "unfair" dismissal within the Industrial Relations Act 1971 (*supra* n. 21) s. 28.

1063 *Poussard v. Spiers* (1876), 1 Q.B.D. 410.

1064 CC § 626; *cf.* CC § 723 par. 2.

1065 *Enneccerus and Lehmann* 165.

1066 ULIS art. 74 (3). In the ENGLISH version, "include" is an obvious mistake.

relation to damages by the discussion in s. 79 above; and in relation to termination by the provision of GERMAN CC § 327 (*supra* s. 157). In COMMON LAW countries it is of course true that in the great majority of cases a person who is entitled to terminate will also be entitled to damages (though there may be restrictions on the extent to which he can pursue both remedies at once: see s. 184 below). But in principle the right to terminate may exist in ANGLO-AMERICAN law even though the conditions for recovery of damages do not exist. This is also the SWISS position; and it seems to be preferable to the general principle adopted by FRENCH and GERMAN law.

ii. *Seriousness of Default*

a. In General

161. *Introduction.* – As we saw in s. 145 above, a claim to terminate a contract gives rise to a considerable conflict of interests between the parties. Even assuming that *some* remedy is admittedly available against him, the defaulting party may have good reasons for resisting termination and taking the view that his only liability should be in damages (or, where appropriate, to performance). In particular, and the importance of this point can hardly be overemphasised, the effect of termination may be to throw back on the defaulting party a risk which, having regard to the nature of the contract, was clearly intended to be borne by the aggrieved party. This will generally be the position when a buyer seeks to terminate a forward sale on a falling market, or when a seller seeks to terminate such a sale on a rising market. The problem is not, of course, confined to sales; it arises just as much in other contexts, for example in the case of charterparties whose commercial value is affected by fluctuations in freight rates.[1067]

The most important single principle used to control the remedy of termination in these and other similar situations is that the remedy is only available if the default attains a certain minimum degree of seriousness. This principle exists in one form or another in all the legal systems under discussion.[1068] It is usually stated in very vague general terms; and any attempt at precision is certainly foredoomed to failure. The delicate balancing of interests that is required in this area is pre-eminently a matter for judicial discretion, and not one that can be determined in advance by fixed rules. On the other hand judicial discretion has its obvious dangers in this as in other parts of the law. Where the default offends the susceptibilities of the court there is a danger that open-textured rules of law may simply conceal judicial indignation;[1069] and if termination is allowed (or recognised as effective) in such circumstances it may lead to serious injustice to the defaulting party.

It is therefore both useful and necessary to make some attempt to determine in a general way what principles *guide* judicial discretion in this area; and this can best be done by considering a number of specific applications of the requirement of seriousness of default for the purposes of termination. After this attempt has been made, some exceptional cases will be considered in which termination is in principle available even though the default may not reach the degree of seriousness normally required. The hardship that may be caused in these cases to the defaulting party has in turn led to qualifications of the exceptions.

162. *General statements of the principle.* – Various expressions are used to describe the seriousness of default (or other failure in performance) required to justify termination. The failure must, it is said, be "vital",[1070] or "total"[1071] or "fundamental"[1072] or "essential";[1073] it must "go to the root"[1074] of the contract; it must be such that, had the aggrieved party known of it at the time of contracting, he would not have entered into the contract;[1075] it must deprive him of the "substance" of what he bargained for;[1076] it must "frustrate" his purpose in entering into the contract;[1077] it must amount to a "repudiation" of

[1067] For a striking illustration of an attempt to terminate being motivated by such factors, see *Empresa Cubana de Fletes v. Lagonisi Shipping Co.*, [1971] 1 Q.B. 488 (C.A.).

[1068] *Zweigert and Kötz* 214-215.

[1069] As, for example, in *Bright v. Ganas*, 171 Md. 493, 189 A. 427 (1936).

[1070] *Willie and Millin (-Coaker and Schutz)* 94.

[1071] *Corbin* § 1104.

[1072] An expression used throughout ULIS (*supra* s. 7): *e.g.* art. 26(1), 30(1), 43. And see *infra* n. 1075.

[1073] This expression occurs most commonly in cases in which time is said to be "of the essence" of the contract.

[1074] A very frequently used expression in COMMON LAW countries. It goes back at least to *Glaholm v. Hays* (1841), 2 M. & G. 257, 268, 133 E.R. 743, 747.

[1075] FRENCH CC art. 1636; ULIS art. 10.

[1076] *Hongkong Fir Shipping Co., Ltd. v. Kawasaki Kisen Kaisha, Ltd.*, *supra* n. 955, at p. 70.

[1077] *Universal Cargo Carriers Corp. v. Citati*, *supra* n. 1025.

the contract;[1078] it must be such that further performance is of "no interest" to him;[1079] it must constitute an "important ground" for termination;[1080] it must go to the whole and not to part only of the consideration;[1081] it must be material.[1082] None of these expressions is particularly helpful; nor, on the other hand, are most of them particularly misleading. There are, however, two of them which are open to some criticism.

The first is the COMMON LAW statement that the failure in performance must go to the whole and not to part of the consideration. This mode of expression is taken from a famous, if sketchily reported ENGLISH eighteenth century case[1083] which was in fact concerned with what CIVIL LAWYERS would call the *exceptio non adimpleti contractus* (see *supra* ch. 15) and not with termination in the sense of the present chapter. However, the expression is often carried over into discussions of termination in our present sense, since COMMON LAWYERS do not distinguish at all sharply between the *exceptio* and termination, or between the various senses of termination. Subsequent cases make it clear that the failure need not, either for the purpose of the *exceptio* or for the purpose of termination, go to the *whole* of the consideration. In other words, termination may be available notwithstanding the fact that some small part of the contract has been duly performed.[1084] Legislation in force in some of the UNITED STATES makes the point by providing for termination where the consideration "fails in whole or in part".[1085] This formulation is of course open to the opposite criticism that it might suggest that failure in *any* part (however insignificant) opens the way to termination; but the phrase has in fact been interpreted restrictively so that the partial failure is required to be one which "goes to the root" of the contract.[1086]

Criticism can secondly be levelled at the statement that, in order to justify termination, the failure in performance must be "material". This expression is misleading on account of its ambiguity. A "material" failure may simply be one of *some* commercial significance;[1087] and if that is all it is insufficient to give rise to the right to terminate. On the other hand "material" may simply mean the same as "essential" or "fundamental". It is in this sense that the expression should be understood in the present context. It is indeed sometimes truly said that an "*immaterial*" failure does *not* justify termination; and this is often true in the sense that termination is not allowed if the failure causes no, or no serious, prejudice to the aggrieved party. But it does not of course follow from this that a failure *does* justify termination merely because it is "material" in the first of the two senses here distinguished.

163. *Wide discretion in French law*. – FRENCH CC art. 1184 simply lays down that, as a general rule, a judgment for termination must be sought. Under this provision, it is within the discretion of the trial judge whether he will order termination, grant a period of grace, or uphold the contract.[1088] The court may even decide not to terminate the contract completely but only in part, for example with respect to part of the goods due under a contract of sale but not delivered at the time when the buyer seeks termination.[1089] There is nothing in CC art. 1184 which indicates how the discretion is to be exercised; and very little control is exerted by the reviewing courts.[1090]

No doubt here, as elsewhere, the judges of fact are subject to control if they apply wrong principles. But it is probably true to say that fewer "principles" control the exercise of discretion here than in relation to damages.[1091] Certainly some of the grounds which are said to control the remedy of termination in other systems have been held not to be grounds for controlling a decision to allow termination. It is, for example, generally not necessary to show that the failure in performance was such that the aggrieved party would, had he been able to foresee it, not have entered into the contract at all.[1092] On the other hand a decision which disregarded a provision in the Civil Code directing such a factor to be taken

[1078] *Mersey Steel and Iron Co. v. Naylor Benzon & Co.* (1884), 9 A.C. 434 (H.L.).

[1079] GERMAN CC § 280 par. 2, 286 par. 2, 325 par. 1 sent. 2, 326 par. 2.

[1080] GERMAN CC § 626.

[1081] *Boone v. Eyre, supra* n. 955.

[1082] Restatement of Contracts (1932) § 274(1).

[1083] *Boone v. Eyre, supra* n. 955.

[1084] *Treitel* 690–691.

[1085] See the legislation referred to *supra* n. 1058 (except for UCC s. 2-305(3)).

[1086] *Wilson v. Corrugated Kraft Containers*, 117 Cal. App.2d 691, 256 P.2d 1012 (1953).

[1087] The ENGLISH version of ULIS (*supra* s. 7) art. 33(2) uses "not material" in this sense. In the FRENCH version, the corresponding phrase is *sans importance*.

[1088] *Carbonnier* IV 272–273.

[1089] Cass.req. 21 Dec. 1927, Gaz.Pal.1928.1.521. The court may also suspend the contract: *Marty and Raynaud* II no. 301.

[1090] *Carbonnier* IV 276.

[1091] *Supra* s. 99; *Mazeaud*, Leçons III no. 1101.

[1092] Cass. req. 20 Nov. 1929, Gaz.Pal.1929.2.978.

into account[1093] would clearly be subject to control by the reviewing courts. Normally, the evaluation of the seriousness of the default and the decision whether it is serious enough to justify termination is one with which these courts will not interfere. In other systems of law, greater attempts are made to formulate more specific principles as to the seriousness of default required for termination; and these principles will be discussed in the following sections.

b. Illustrations of the Principle

164. *"Total" non-performance.* – Relatively little difficulty arises where the party in default wholly fails to perform his obligations: in such a case there is no doubt that the aggrieved party is entitled to terminate. Total failure to perform may, however, consist not only in complete inactivity in relation to the contract (or in outright contravention of an obligation to forbear) but also in a purported performance which is wholly different from that contracted for. To take an example given in an ENGLISH case,[1094] a person who contracted to sell beans and delivered peas instead would be guilty of a "total" or "fundamental" failure to perform in our present sense. Such a case can be contrasted with one in which the seller had contracted to sell beans equal to a certain sample and delivered beans of a different quality.[1095] It is true that even in the latter case the buyer would generally be entitled to terminate the contract. His right, however, would not be based on the principle of "total" non-performance but on the principle stated in s. 167 below. The difference between the two principles is important, not in considering the circumstances in which the right to terminate *arises*, but those in which it *may be lost* (*infra* s. 185 ss.).

Where some attempt at performance has been made by the defaulting party, it is often disputed whether what he has actually done is "totally" different from what he contracted to do. This depends in the first place on the construction of the contract. The case of the buyer who receives peas when he ordered beans has been contrasted with the plight of "an anxious hostess (who) is late in the preparation of a meal", and who says to her supplier: "'Send me peas or if you haven't got peas, send me beans; but for heaven's sake send something.' That would be a contract for peas, beans or anything else *ejusdem generis* and is a perfectly sensible contract to make."[1096]

It is, similarly, a question of construction whether failure to perform a contract at or within a stipulated time amounts to a "total" failure to perform. It will have this effect if performance outside that time entirely defeats the purpose of the aggrieved party (see *supra* s. 161, 162). Again it should not be supposed that failure to perform in time *only* gives rise to a right to terminate if it has this drastic effect. But the result of the failure will be governed by different considerations according to whether the breach is regarded as "total" or not. In GERMAN law, for example, a "total" failure in respect of time will make the case one of impossibility and not one of delay (*supra* s. 150).

It is obvious that the questions of construction and degree which can arise in determining whether the default is "total" are often much more difficult than the simple illustrations given above might suggest. The question whether a breach is "total" or "fundamental" tends in fact to merge into the various other factors on which the right to terminate depends, and which are discussed in the following sections. In these sections we shall assume that the performance is not "totally" different from that contracted for, but differs from it in quality or quantity or as to time; or in that the defaulting party has failed to perform only some of his obligations under the contract. The effects of such failures in performance on the right to terminate are worked out in some detail in the GERMAN Civil Code and in the ANGLO-AMERICAN case law.

165. *Performance "of no interest".* – GERMAN law in a number of cases provides for termination where, on account of the default, performance is of "no interest" for the aggrieved party. This principle is stated in the Civil Code both in relation to delay and in relation to partial impossibility.

The general rule with regard to delay is stated in CC § 286 par. 2. If in consequence of the delay the performance has no interest for the creditor, he can refuse to accept performance (which is one sense in which "termination" is used in this chapter) and claim compensation for non-performance. In the case of reciprocal contracts the relevant provision is CC § 326. Here the right to terminate is not in principle dependent on the

[1093] *E.g.* FRENCH CC art. 1636.

[1094] *Chanter v. Hopkins* (1838), 4 M. & W. 399, 404, 150 E.R. 1484, 1487.

[1095] *Smeaton Hanscomb & Co. v. Sassoon I. Setty & Co.* (No. 1), [1953] 1 W.L.R. 1468, 1470 (Q.B.).

[1096] *Lord Devlin*, The Treatment of Breach of Contract: 1966 C.L.J. 192 at p. 212.

aggrieved party's having no interest, but on the satisfaction of the requirement of *Nachfrist* (*supra* s. 149). But under CC § 326 par. 2 this requirement is dispensed with where the performance of the contract has in consequence of the delay no interest for him. What must be lacking, for the purpose of this rule, is interest in the performance of the contract, that is in the exchange of the aggrieved party's performance for that of the defaulting party.[1097] Under CC § 286 par. 2, on the other hand, what must be lacking is interest simply in receiving the defaulting party's performance, there being no exchange performance due from the aggrieved party in a case within this paragraph.

Under both CC § 286 par. 2 and CC § 326 par. 2 the lack of interest must arise *in consequence of* the delay (*infolge des Verzugs*). This rule excludes the possibility that the aggrieved party may use delay as an excuse for peremptorily terminating a contract the performance of which has ceased to be of interest to him for some quite different reason:[1098] for example because the market has moved against him.

Similar principles with regard to partial impossibility are stated in CC § 280 and 325. CC § 280 states the general rule that the creditor can refuse to accept the part of the performance which remains possible if this is of no interest to him and instead claim damages for non-performance of the whole obligation. CC § 325 par. 1 sent. 2 states the corresponding rule for reciprocal contracts: where partial performance of the contract has no interest for the creditor, he can either claim damages for non-performance of the whole contract in accordance with CC § 280 par. 2 or terminate (*zurücktreten*) the contract. A claim for damages in accordance with CC § 280 par. 2 depends on the aggrieved party's refusing to accept performance; the termination referred to in CC § 325 also depends on this; and it involves the additional consequences of liberating the aggrieved party from his obligations to perform his part and of giving rise to mutual obligations of restoration. In the case of a reciprocal contract the aggrieved party's lack of interest must, again, be, not simply in receiving the part of the performance promised to him which remains possible, but in the partial performance *of the contract*. Here, as in CC § 326 par. 2, the reference is to his lack of interest in exchanging his performance for the partially possible performance on the other side.[1099]

Analogous principles apply to cases of so-called *positive Vertragsverletzung* (*supra* s. 75), for which no express provision is made in the Civil Code. Here again the aggrieved party is entitled to terminate if further performance is of no interest to him. Thus termination was held justified where a seller of building materials made defective deliveries and the buyer in the process of buying against the seller bought other materials which could not be combined with those still due under the contract.[1100] Termination is also said to be justified on the further (and apparently separate) ground that the creditor cannot reasonably be expected to accept the defective performance.[1101] This principle applies particularly in cases in which the default gives rise to uncertainty as to future performance and in which the creditor cannot reasonably be expected to wait until this uncertainty is resolved.[1102] The same principle has been applied in cases of delay, for example where a charterer was guilty of such delays in loading as to make it unreasonable to expect the shipowner to adhere to the contract.[1103] Such cases suggest that the requirement that further performance of the contract must be of "no interest" is in fact interpreted somewhat liberally in favour of the aggrieved party.

166. *Frustrating or substantial breach.* – The GERMAN principles discussed in s. 165 above have their counterpart in the ANGLO-AMERICAN rule that a breach will justify termination if it "frustrates" the aggrieved party's purpose in entering the contract or if it "substantially" deprives him of what he bargained for.[1104] This rule is not normally expressed in terms as strict as the GERMAN rule in cases of impossibility or delay: *total* lack of interest in receiving the defective performance or in the performance of the contract is not generally said to be required in order to justify termination. The rule is more like the second branch of the GERMAN rule in cases of *positive Vertragsverletzung*, the test being whether it can reasonably be expected that the aggrieved party will accept or continue to accept performance. There is a striking analogy between the reasoning of the GERMAN cases mentioned at the end of s. 165 above and a number of ENGLISH cases in which uncertainty caused

[1097] *Enneccerus and Lehmann* 228; *supra* s. 150.

[1098] BGB-RGRK § 326 no. 14 where a different example is given: the rule does not apply where the lack of interest arises, not from the delay but from the fact that the buyer has already bought elsewhere. For exceptional market declines see *supra* s. 150.

[1099] *Palandt* § 325 no. 7c.

[1100] *Enneccerus and Lehmann* 238.

[1101] *Idem* 239.

[1102] *Ibidem.*

[1103] *Zweigert and Kötz* 196; *cf. Guhl* 192.

[1104] *Corbin* § 1104; *Treitel* 690-702.

by the other party's default is put forward as a justification for termination.[1105]

This factor of uncertainty as to future performance is the main basis for distinguishing between a famous pair of nineteenth century ENGLISH cases in which singers failed on account of illness to present themselves on the dates stipulated in their contracts. In the first case the leading soprano for a new opera was unable to appear on the opening night and did not regain her health and voice until the piece had run for some time. It was held that in these circumstances termination was justified.[1106] In the second case, the illness of a leading tenor only prevented his attendance at some of the rehearsals; he was available for the opening of the season for which he had been engaged. There was nothing to show that his failure to attend punctually at rehearsals in any way affected the opening performances and, as all uncertainty as to his future availability had been removed by the time these took place, the termination of his engagement was held to be unjustified.[1107]

The same factor of uncertainty underlies many shipping cases in which delay on the part of either the shipowner or the charterer has been put forward as a ground for termination.[1108] It appears, again, in cases of instalment contracts where the likelihood that a breach may recur (either by the seller in making defective delivery or by the buyer in failing to pay in accordance with the contract) is a factor which is often stressed as one justification for terminating the contract.[1109]

Another factor which is of importance in instalment contracts and in other contracts which require performance over a period of time is the quantitative ratio which the breach bears to the performance as a whole. Thus defects in one out of a large number of instalments of goods will not generally justify termination; and the same is true where a ship under time charter is by reason of the shipowner's breach of his undertaking as to seaworthiness unavailable only for a relatively small part of the chartered period.[1110]

Although it is thus possible to isolate a number of factors relevant to the issue whether a particular breach is of a "frustrating" or "substantial" kind, the subject is one that defies exhaustive analysis. One reason for this is that COMMON LAW courts, when faced with problems of this kind, are very much influenced by the practical effects of their classifications. Thus in some cases the decision whether to hold termination justified is clearly influenced by the court's view on the question whether or not an award of damages would adequately protect the aggrieved party.[1111] In other cases the decision may be influenced by the reluctance of the court to throw back on the defaulting party a risk which by the terms or nature of the contract was manifestly undertaken by the aggrieved party.[1112] In a nineteenth century ENGLISH case in which a cargo arrived damaged owing to the shipowner's breach of contract, and also much reduced in value by reason of market fluctuations, this policy is stated very clearly: "It would be unjust and almost absurd that . . . the risk of a mercantile adventure should be thrown upon the shipowner by the accident of the value of the cargo being a little more than the freight."[1113]

The factors so far mentioned as relevant to the right to terminate can be explained, even if they cannot always be precisely analyzed, in terms of the balancing of interests on which that right depends (*supra* s. 145). There are, however, cases to which it is difficult to extend such explanations and in which the right to terminate has nevertheless been upheld. These are cases in which the breach is of a particularly dramatic character and in this way impresses the court with its "seriousness". Thus in an AMERICAN case termination of a contract to deliver milk to state institutions (including hospitals) for one year was held to be justified on the ground that on 3 out of the first 14 days the milk had been contaminated with dead flies and live maggots.[1114] Again, in an ENGLISH case termination of an advertising contract extending over a period of up to nine months was held to be justified on the ground that on a single occasion the contractor displayed an ad-

1105 *Cf.* BGH 13 Nov. 1953, BGHZ 11, 80 with *Universal Cargo Carriers Corp. v. Citati, supra* n. 1025.

1106 *Poussard v. Spiers, supra* n. 1063.

1107 *Bettini v. Gye* (1876), 1 Q.B.D. 183.

1108 *Bradford v. Williams* (1872), L.R. 7 Ex. 259; *Universal Cargo Carriers Corp. v. Citati, supra* n. 1025; *Hongkong Fir Shipping Co., Ltd. v. Kawasaki Kisen Kaisha, Ltd., supra* n. 955.

1109 See *Maple Flock Co., Ltd. v. Universal Furniture Products (Wembley), Ltd.*, [1934] 1 K.B. 148 (C.A.); *Plotnick v. Pennsylvania Smelting and Refining Co.*, 194 F.2d 859 (3 Cir. 1952) (in these cases the courts held that there was in fact no likelihood of recurrence).

1110 See the *Hongkong Fir* and *Maple Flock* cases (*supra* n. 955, 1109).

1111 *Treitel* 693-695.

1112 *Idem* 700. *Cf. supra* s. 161.

1113 *Dakin v. Oxley* (1864) (*supra* n. 338) 667-668. The case was concerned with a simple refusal by the aggrieved party to pay, but COMMON LAW courts do not distinguish between this situation and termination in the sense of the present chapter: *supra* s. 143.

1114 *Hershey Farms, Inc., v. State*, 202 Misc. 105, 110 N.Y.S.2d 324 (S.Ct. 1952).

vertisement in a way that seriously offended many members of the public and so tended to diminish the client's share of the market.[1115] Such decisions are not necessarily wrong merely because they cannot be logically explained in terms of the policies governing the right to terminate; but their unprincipled nature is a regrettable even if unavoidable feature of this branch of the law (*cf. supra* s. 161).

c. Exceptions to the Principle.

167. *Conditions and warranties.* – In a number of cases the law may allow termination in spite of the fact that the default is not substantial. One reason why this possibility arises is that the right to terminate may depend simply on the *nature* of the obligation which is not performed rather than on the *effect* of the failure in performance. No doubt the legal classifications of obligations for this purpose are based on the assumption that the effect of non-performance of some obligations is more serious than the effect of non-performance of others; but the classifications inevitably introduce an element of rigidity and tend to distract attention from the effects of non-compliance in individual cases.

The most conspicuous illustration of this process is to be found in the ENGLISH distinction between "conditions" and "warranties",[1116] particularly in contracts for the sale of goods. A "condition" is an important term of the contract of sale, the breach of which gives rise to a right to terminate the contract; while a "warranty" is a subsidiary term, the breach of which gives rise only to a right to damages and not to a right to terminate the contract.[1117]

The basic idea behind the distinction thus reflects the principle that only a "substantial" breach gives rise to a right to terminate; but the practical result of the distinction may be to give a right to terminate in respect of a breach which, in terms of its effect, is not substantial at all. The main reason for this is that some of the terms of a contract of sale are classified as "conditions" by statute; and when such a term is broken a right to terminate arises even though the breach causes the buyer only very slight prejudice, or no prejudice at all. This is, for example, the case where there is a breach of the "implied condition" that the goods must correspond to the "description" given in the contract.[1118]

The alleged justification for the rule lies in the needs of commerce: a buyer who has bought under a particular description may have resold under it and be faced with a claim to terminate from his sub-buyer (to whom the breach may have caused serious prejudice).[1119] Of course this hypothetical hardship may not actually exist at all, and the right to terminate on the ground that there has been such a breach of condition may be exercised solely for the purpose of escaping from a bad bargain. This situation arises most commonly in relation to sales of goods; but it is not by any means confined to such contracts. Thus in contracts for the carriage of goods by sea statements as to the situation of the ship and as to the date of sailing are regarded as "conditions" and their breach gives rise to a right to terminate irrespective of actual prejudice to the charterer.[1120] Similarly, a statement that a ship is "expected ready to load" at a named port at or about a designated time gives rise to a right to terminate if such expectation is not honestly held on reasonable grounds.[1121]

There is again a right to terminate irrespective of actual prejudice where a ship deviates, *i.e.* departs without justification from the agreed route. Here the right to terminate is based on the hypothetical hardship that the deviation is likely to deprive the shipper of the benefit of any insurance which he may have on the goods.[1122] In ENGLAND the right exists irrespective of the fact whether such or any hardship has actually resulted from the deviation;[1123] though the contrary has been suggested in the UNITED STATES.[1124]

[1115] *Aerial Advertising Co. v. Batchelors Peas, Ltd.*, [1938] 2 All E.R. 788 (K.B.).

[1116] *Treitel* 683-690.

[1117] The UNITED KINGDOM Sale of Goods Act, 1893 (*supra* n. 312) only defines "warranty" (s. 62 (1)) and leaves the definition of "condition" to be inferred *e.g.* from s. 11 (1). The INDIAN Sale of Goods Act, 1930 (*supra* n. 408) defines both terms: s. 12 (1) and (2). In ENGLAND a warranty may give rise to terminate if it originated as a misrepresentation inducing the contract, and perhaps in certain other cases: *Treitel* 687-688.

[1118] *E.g., Arcos, Ltd. v. Ronaasen, supra* n. 311.

[1119] *Re Moore and Landauer*, [1921] 2 K.B. 519 (C.A.).

[1120] *Treitel* 686, 688-689.

[1121] *Maredelanto Compania Naviera S.A. v. Bergbau-Handel G.m.b.H.*, (*The Mihalis Angelos*), [1971] 1 Q.B. 164 (Q.B.) and 183 (C.A.).

[1122] *Hain S.S. Co. v. Tate and Lyle, Ltd.* (1936), 155 L.T. 177, 179 (H.L.).

[1123] *Cf., Joseph Thorley, Ltd. v. Orchis S.S. Co., Ltd.*, [1907] 1 K.B. 660 (C.A.).

[1124] *Gilmore and Black*, The Law of Admiralty (Brooklyn 1957) 156, relying on clauses by which the insured is "held covered" during deviation. But *cf., Vincentelli v. Rowlett* (1911), 105 L.T. 411 (K.B.), which reveals the weakness of such provisions in ENGLAND.

On the other hand the mere failure of a shipowner to provide a seaworthy ship and the mere failure of a charterer to load within the time stipulated by the charterparty will not justify termination; such breaches will only have this effect if they in fact frustrate the aggrieved party's purpose in entering into the contract.[1125]

Like the distinction between conditions and warranties in sale of goods, these rules relating to carriage introduce an element of rigidity: the right to terminate is sometimes attached to breach of a particular term without regard to the effect of the breach in an individual case.

168. *Quantitative defects.* – The distinction between conditions and warranties in contracts for the sale of goods is at any rate based on hypothetical hardship to the aggrieved party. Even this cannot be said of the rules which apply in ENGLISH law to quantitative defects in the performance of such contracts. The rule is that *any* quantitative defect (unless so minute as to fall within the principle *de minimis non curat lex*) justifies termination.[1126] There is no need to show that the defect was the source of any prejudice, actual or hypothetical, to the buyer. The rule is not followed in contracts for the sale of land, which cannot be terminated unless the shortage is substantial: if it is not, the only remedy is a price reduction, assessed under the rules of specific performance with "compensation" (*supra* s. 68). The requirement that the shortage must be substantial also exists in the case of sales of land under GERMAN (CC § 468) and SOUTH AFRICAN[1127] law and apparently in FRENCH law.[1128]

169. *Uniform Commercial Code.* – The sharp distinction drawn by ENGLISH law between qualitative and quantitative defects in contracts for the sale of goods is hard to support in principle; and the same is true of the rigid distinction between conditions and warranties. Both distinctions tend to lose sight of the fundamental principle that a default should be serious in order to justify termination.

The distinctions have therefore not been adopted by the AMERICAN Uniform Commercial Code, s. 2-601 of which gives rise to a right to terminate "if the goods or the tender of delivery fail *in any respect* to conform to the contract". This rule at first sight gives rise to a very wide power to terminate, regardless of the seriousness of the non-conformity. But in fact the appearance is deceptive as the requirement of seriousness is reintroduced by a number of other provisions which must be read together with UCC s. 2-601.

Thus once the buyer has "accepted" the goods he can only terminate ("revoke his acceptance") if the non-conformity of the goods "substantially" impairs their value (UCC s. 2-608(1)). In practice the courts appear rather readily to hold that the buyer has "accepted" the goods so as to restrict the right of termination to cases of "substantial" impairment.[1129] A similar requirement is stated in cases of anticipatory breach and in cases of instalment contracts (but the requirement does not apply where the non-conformity is a defect in the required documents).[1130] Moreover, there will be no right to reject if the seller is able to cure the non-conformity and gives adequate assurance that he will do so (UCC s. 2-508). It is possible, finally, that a buyer who sought to terminate on the pretext of a non-conformity which was not "substantial" when his real motive for terminating was to escape from a bad bargain would be held to have contravened the obligation of good faith in the "enforcement" of the contract.[1131]

A similar good faith provision is contained in the ISRAELI Sales Law of 1968.[1132] This law rejects the ENGLISH distinction between conditions and warranties and at first sight creates very wide rights of termination. But it has been said that the good faith provision would preclude termination where the goods were not of the contract description but the breach was not "material".[1133]

170. *ULIS.* – Like the Uniform Commercial Code, *ULIS* (*supra* s. 7) does not distinguish between qualitative and quantitative defects: both amount simply to "lack of conformity" (art. 33). But ULIS does draw a distinction (not used for the present purpose in the Uniform Commercial Code) between failure to deliver at the agreed time or place and failure to deliver conforming goods. Moreover, ULIS starts with the principle that only a *fundamental* breach[1134] justifies termination. This is in sharp contrast to the starting

1125 *Treitel* 687.

1126 Sale of Goods Act, 1893 (*supra* n. 312) s. 30.

1127 *Celliers v. Papenfus & Roth*, 1904 T.S. 73 (S.Ct. Transvaal).

1128 *Mazeaud*, Leçons III no. 938. For details of these rules, see this Encyclopedia vol. VIII ch. 6.

1129 *E.g., Rozmus v. Thompson's Lincoln Mercury Co.*, 209 Pa.Super. 120, 224 A.2d 782 (1966) (buyer who had driven car home not entitled to revoke acceptance on account of easily curable defects).

1130 UCC s. 2-610, 2-612 (2) and (3).

1131 UCC s. 1-203; it is perhaps arguable that termination is not "enforcement".

1132 ISRAELI Sales Law 1968 (*supra* n. 352) s. 6.

1133 *Aranovsky*, Comments on the New Law of Sale: 4 Israel L.Rev. 141, 145 (1969).

1134 *Supra* s. 162 at n. 1075.

principle laid down in UCC s. 2-601 (*supra*). But the ULIS principle, like that of the Uniform Commercial Code, is subject to important qualifications; so that the practical results reached under the two Codes will not be as strikingly different as their fundamentally opposed starting principles might suggest. The main qualifications to the ULIS principle are as follows.

First, it is open to the buyer to turn a non-fundamental into a fundamental breach by giving the seller a notice (resembling the GERMAN *Nachfrist*) calling on him to cure the breach within a reasonable time.[1135] Termination can then follow if at the end of that time the seller has not performed. A similar notice may, with like effect, be given by the seller where the buyer has failed to pay or to take delivery in circumstances not amounting *ab initio* to a fundamental breach.[1136]

Secondly, failure to deliver at the date fixed "shall amount to a fundamental breach whenever a price for such goods is quoted on a market where the buyer can obtain them" (ULIS art. 28). This provision makes failure to deliver at the date fixed a ground for termination in the majority of commercial sales. If, however, the buyer complains of lack of conformity, he can only terminate if there is a double fundamental breach: *i.e.* if both the non-conformity and the failure to deliver (conforming) goods on the date fixed amount to fundamental breaches (ULIS art. 43). The second of these requirements will be satisfied if there is a market, but not the first. To this extent ULIS favours the seller, who will normally wish to resist avoidance.

Thirdly, ULIS deals in art. 25 with the situation in which the seller has failed to deliver at the date or place fixed and it is reasonably possible for the buyer to purchase goods to replace those to which the contract relates. In such a case the buyer cannot claim specific enforcement (*supra* s. 39) but art. 25 goes on puzzlingly to provide that the contract is "ipso facto avoided as from the time when such purchase should be effected". The purpose of this rule is, no doubt, to fix the damages by reference to that time. But it applies even though the breach is not fundamental under the general definition and even though there is no quoted market price. Hence the result (probably unintended) is that, even though the buyer has not bought a substitute, the contract is terminated on account of a non-fundamental breach. A similar provision leads to an equally strange result where the buyer has failed to pay on the date fixed (ULIS art. 61(2)).

171. *Civil Law*. – In CIVIL LAW systems, the right to terminate a contract of sale on account of qualitative defects in the subject-matter is not usually said to be restricted to cases in which the defect is of a serious nature. It may in practice be so restricted in FRENCH law in the sense that termination in principle requires a judgment; and if the defect is not of a serious nature the court may refuse to order termination and instead order a price reduction (*cf. supra* s. 163). In GERMAN law the choice between termination and price reduction is in principle that of the buyer (CC § 462); though machinery is provided whereby the seller can force the buyer to declare his election within a set time of his alleging that the thing is defective (CC § 466). It is true that the defect must remove or reduce the utility of the thing for its normal or intended use and that insignificant defects are to be left out of account (CC § 459 par. 1 sent. 2). But this requirement applies equally to the remedies of termination and price reduction; there is no provision in the Civil Code to the effect that the defect must be more serious for the one purpose than for the other.

The distinction between a serious defect (*Hauptmangel*) and a minor defect (*Nebenmangel*) is, however, one of the bases for distinguishing between the availability of the two remedies in AUSTRIAN law.[1137] Under the AUSTRIAN Civil Code termination is available only if the defect cannot be cured (*cf. infra* s. 174) and prevents the normal use of the thing; if it does not have this effect only price reduction (or where possible cure) can be demanded.[1138] Lack of expressly warranted qualities constitutes a serious defect for this purpose.[1139] The result of these restrictions on the right to terminate is to make it hard in AUSTRIAN law for the buyer to use a defect which has not caused him substantial prejudice as a pretext for terminating a contract which has turned out to be a bad bargain.

There may indeed at first sight appear to be some analogy to the AUSTRIAN rule in the GERMAN distinction between defects in the principal thing sold (*Hauptsache*) and in some accessory or subsidiary part of the subject-matter (*Nebensache*) (CC § 470). A defect in the latter does not justify termination in respect of the *Hauptsache*, but only

1135 ULIS art. 27 (2), 31 (2), 44 (2).

1136 ULIS art. 62 (2), 66 (2).

1137 This distinction should not be confused with that between principal and subsidiary *duties* which is discussed *infra* s. 165.

1138 CC § 932; *cf.* CC § 1167; *Klang and Gschnitzer* (*-Gschnitzer*) IV 1 § 932 no. AII 1-3.

1139 *Klang and Gschnitzer* (*-Gschnitzer*) IV 1 § 932 no. AI2; CC § 1167.

in respect of the *Nebensache* itself. But in GERMAN law, *any* defect in the *Hauptsache* justifies termination though it is possible that termination for an obviously oblique motive would be disallowed as contrary to good faith.

A similar argument has been advanced in GERMAN law in relation to failure to perform at the agreed time. The rules in this respect have been stated in s. 149, 150 above. Here it is only necessary to consider their relation to the requirement of "substantial" default. Generally speaking, that requirement need not be satisfied; it is at the most necessary to comply with the machinery of a *Nachfrist*, and even this is not necessary in the case of a *Fixgeschäft*. However, in either case it appears that an attempt to terminate may be resisted as contrary to good faith if the delay (beyond the expiry of the *Nachfrist* or the period within which the *Fixgeschäft* must be performed) is insignificant, not due to the "fault" of the debtor, and causes no prejudice to the aggrieved party.[1140] A defect may be significant for this purpose without being "substantial" or serious in the sense discussed in s. 161-166 above.

The COMMON LAW (lacking a general principle of good faith)[1141] has no general rule against termination for a commercially insignificant delay. Once time is of the essence *any* failure to perform in time justifies termination. It should however be stressed that the COMMON LAW rules as to the time of performance are more closely linked than the GERMAN rules to the requirement of substantial default. The principle which underlies the distinction between stipulations as to time which do, and those which do not, go to the essence of the contract is basically that breach of the former is, while breach of the latter is not, likely to cause serious prejudice to the aggrieved party. In GERMAN law this principle does not govern the right to terminate for delay, but only the need to set a *Nachfrist*: hence there is greater need to have a further limitation (in the nature of a good faith requirement) on the right to terminate.

172. *Express provisions for termination.* – Express provisions for termination give rise to a further category of cases in which the requirement of "substantial" or "serious" default need not be satisfied. This is for example the position in FRENCH law, where the principal purpose of such provisions is to do away with the need to obtain a judgment for termination.[1142] This point is discussed in s. 148 above where attention is drawn to the strict construction often adopted of express resolutive clauses. This process of construction is also relevant at this point as it tends to mitigate the hardship which the defaulting party may suffer as a result of the literal enforcement of such provisions.[1143]

Such hardship may further be prevented by making the enforcement of express resolutive clauses subject to the requirement of good faith.[1144] No doubt the same technique could be used in GERMAN law. It is not in principle available in COMMON LAW countries, but these have a number of other techniques for mitigating the hardship which can arise from express provisions for termination. One of these is to construe such an express provision strictly against the party relying on it, and to insist on exact compliance with its terms.[1145] Another is the rule that, in certain contracts, formal notice of intention to terminate must be given, calling on the debtor to cure his default, coupled with the power of the courts to grant him "relief against forfeiture". This power is of particular importance in the law of landlord and tenant though it is by no means restricted to that relationship.[1146] The power may be compared with that of the FRENCH courts to grant a *délai de grâce;* but that power exists by virtue of the need as a general rule to obtain a judgment for termination. The COMMON LAW power to grant relief against forfeiture exists precisely where the need to obtain a judgment for termination does not exist in FRENCH law: it is a power to give relief against the effect of an express resolutive clause.

173. *Main and subsidiary duties.* – A distinction is drawn in GERMAN law between failure to perform a principal duty (*Hauptpflicht*) and failure to perform a subsidiary duty (*Nebenpflicht*).[1147] Only a failure to perform a duty of the former kind, it is said, gives rise to a right to terminate the contract. The point is most commonly illustrated by contrasting a seller's duty to deliver with a buyer's duty to accept delivery. The former is a *Hauptpflicht*, while the latter is generally a *Neben-*

[1140] BGB-RGRK § 361 no. 3 and 4; *Palandt* § 326 no. 7.

[1141] See *Margaronis Navigation Agency, Ltd. v. Henry W. Peabody & Co. of London, Ltd.*, [1965] 1 Q.B. 300.

[1142] *Mazeaud*, Leçons II no. 1096, 1104.

[1143] *Cf.* the distinction in SCOTS law between "legal irritancies" and "conventional irritancies". The latter are strictly enforced, without regard to hardship to the defaulting party: *Smith* 856 (though subject to the rules relating to penalties: *Gloag and Henderson* 131).

[1144] *Carbonnier* IV 277.

[1145] *E.g.* the *Empresa Cubana* case, *supra* n. 1067; *The Mihalis Angelos*, *supra* n. 1121.

[1146] *Treitel* 704.

[1147] *Enneccerus and Lehmann* 213.

pflicht.[1148] However, this is not invariably the case: if the seller's principal object in making the contract is, for example, to clear his storage space or to get rid of an accumulation of rubble (which forms the subject-matter of the sale) then the buyer's duty to take delivery will be a *Hauptpflicht.*[1149] Similarly, where the sale is of goods to be taken from a ship and the obligation to collect them is on the buyer that obligation is a *Hauptpflicht,* since failure to perform it can obviously prejudice the seller's position in relation to the shipowner.[1150]

ENGLISH law similarly recognises that the buyer's failure to take delivery at the agreed time does not give rise to a right to terminate the contract as a general rule, but that it may have this effect in exceptional cases.[1151] The exceptions have a somewhat wider scope in ENGLISH than in GERMAN law. This is probably the case because they have to cover situations which in GERMAN law would be more appropriately dealt with by the institution of *Selbsthilfeverkauf,*[1152] an institution which is less well developed in ENGLISH than in GERMAN law.

These rules of GERMAN and ENGLISH law stand in striking contrast to the provisions of FRENCH CC art. 1657 (*supra* s. 148). Under this article a contract for the sale of commodities and other moveables may be determined "*de plein droit*" (that is, without the usual requirement of a judgment) at the option of the seller "after the expiration of the time agreed for taking delivery." It is true that the article does not expressly say that termination is allowed for failure to take delivery: the reference could be to failure to perform some other obligation (*e.g.* to pay the price) within the time fixed for delivery. But such an interpretation of CC art. 1657 would be strained and does not appear to have been adopted. Thus a FRENCH writer has said that failure to take delivery is subject to a more severe sanction than failure to pay the price (which is not a ground for termination *de plein droit* but only one for seeking a judgment for termination).[1153] Clearly this supports the view that CC art. 1657 refers to the obligation to take delivery, and not merely to the time at which that obligation should have been performed in relation to some other obligation. The failure to take delivery is thus not only a ground for termination, but one in respect of which the aggrieved seller is placed in an exceptionally favourable position. The reason for this rule is (as was suggested in s. 148 above) by no means obvious; and the policy of the rule is all the more puzzling when contrasted with the GERMAN and ENGLISH rules considered in the present section.

The distinction between principal and subsidiary duties in GERMAN law has been compared with the ENGLISH distinction between conditions and warranties;[1154] but the GERMAN distinction is less rigid than the ENGLISH at least in relation to sale of goods. In that context the ENGLISH distinction not only produces the result that a breach of condition *always* justifies termination. It may also lead to the consequence that a breach of warranty (other than one based on a statement of fact made before the contract)[1155] *never* justifies termination. Whether it has this effect depends on the meaning of certain provisions of the Sale of Goods Act, 1893, a matter which still awaits judicial determination.[1156] In GERMAN law the classification of a duty as principal or subsidiary is more flexible, depending on the importance to be attached to the performance of the duty in the light of the particular contractual context.

From this point of view the distinction is more closely comparable to a number of rules which in ENGLISH law govern the right of termination in contracts for the carriage of goods by sea.[1157] Here the breach of certain obligations, *e.g.* as to the route, position of the ship, time of sailing, and time of expected readiness to load always give rise to a right to terminate on the ground that they are principal duties (*supra* s. 167). But in the case of other obligations *e.g.* as to seaworthiness or time within which the charterer must load there is no fixed rule one way or the other: the question whether breach of such obligations gives rise to a right to terminate depends on whether it frustrates the aggrieved party's purpose in entering into the contract (*supra* s. 166). These obligations are thus similar to the buyer's obligation to take delivery in GERMAN law. Failure to perform them does not normally give rise to a right to terminate

1148 *Idem* 247, 422; *Zweigert and Kötz* 194-195.

1149 *Zweigert and Kötz, ibidem; Enneccerus and Lehmann* 246.

1150 *Enneccerus and Lehmann* 422.

1151 *Treitel* 720. ULIS (*supra* s. 7) applies the ordinary distinction between fundamental and non-fundamental breach to the buyer's failure to take delivery: art. 66.

1152 See *supra* s. 70. *E.g.* cases in which the goods are perishable: *cf.* UNITED KINGDOM Sale of Goods Act, 1893 (*supra* n. 312) s. 48 (3).

1153 *Mazeaud,* Leçons III no. 1025.

1154 *Zweigert and Kötz* 208.

1155 Misrepresentation Act 1967 (*supra* n. 312) s. 1 (a); *Treitel* 687.

1156 *Treitel* 687-688.

1157 *Idem* 686-687.

the contract; but it will give rise to such a right when its effects are of a particularly serious kind.

174. *Curable defect in performance.* – The possibility that a defect in performance can be cured may be important for a number of purposes. It may give the aggrieved party a right to have the defect actually cured or a right to the cost of such cure (*supra* s. 7, 9, 66). At this point, however, we are concerned with cure, not as a duty, but as a liberty accorded to the party in default: he may be entitled to an opportunity to cure the defect so as to avoid termination of the contract.[1158]

ENGLISH law recognises a general principle of liberty to cure in the sense that a person who has made a bad tender under a contract is not thereby deprived of the opportunity of making a further, good tender if he can do so within the time allowed by the contract for performance.[1159] However, the defaulting party does not always have this right. If the defective tender shows an intention to perform only in that way, it may be regarded as a repudiation which the aggrieved party can "accept" as an anticipatory breach; and if he does so accept it the defaulting party will be deprived of his liberty to cure.[1160] The liberty to cure is regarded as a liberty to substitute a conforming tender for a bad one; there is no authority to support the view that a seller of a specific thing is entitled to a liberty to cure as to avoid termination;[1161] nor is there any such liberty *after* the time fixed for performance of the contract has gone by (except in the special cases considered in s. 172 above).

The possibility that the defect might have been (even if it was not) cured may also be relevant in other ways to the right to terminate. One situation in which this is the case is the common one in which each party alleges wrongful repudiation by the other. If a buyer repudiates on the ground that the seller's tender is defective, the buyer's repudiation will be wrongful if the seller was still entitled to make a good tender,[1162] while the seller will be relieved from making such a tender by the buyer's wrongful repudiation.[1163] Again, as a general rule a party can terminate a contract so long as a ground for termination in fact exists, even though he does not state it when he exercises his right to terminate (*supra* s. 152); but this rule does not apply where the default is one which could have been cured had attention been drawn to it at the time of termination.[1164]

The AMERICAN Uniform Commercial Code gives a seller of goods a right, similar to that which exists in ENGLAND, of curing a non-conforming tender by making a conforming one within the contract period[1165] and even outside the contract period where he had reasonable grounds for believing that it would be accepted (UCC s. 2-508(2)). In this last respect the liberty to cure in the UNITED STATES is wider than it is in ENGLAND.

The same is true of the seller's liberty to cure under ULIS (*supra* s. 7). Where the seller fails to deliver goods at the agreed place or delivers non-conforming goods, the breach can only lead to termination if that breach *and* failure to deliver (in accordance with the contract) at the date fixed amount to a fundamental breach.[1166] This requirement of a *double fundamental breach* in effect gives the seller a liberty to cure which may be exercised even after the agreed delivery date, until the delay in delivery becomes fundamental. Of course if the contract is one in which the time of delivery is of the essence of the contract (*supra* s. 153) failure to deliver at the date fixed is a fundamental breach as soon as it occurs, and there is no subsequent liberty to cure. The seller also has a liberty to cure non-fundamental defects (ULIS art. 44(1)) but, as these do not give rise to a right to terminate in the first place, this liberty is relevant to his liability in damages rather than to termination.

In CIVIL LAW systems the defaulting party's liberty to cure is often recognised, but rather as a feature of particular contracts than as a general contract principle. The GERMAN Civil Code, for example, states the principle in relation to a *Werkvertrag*, that is, a contract for the execution of certain work such as a building contract. Here the customer has both a right to have the defect cured and a right to terminate (or to a price reduction) if cure is not effected; but before he can exercise the latter right he must afford the contractor an opportunity of making good the

[1158] The seller may also in this way be able to avoid, or at any rate to reduce, his liability in damages.

[1159] *Treitel* 668; *cf. Willie and Millin (-Coaker and Schutz)* 192 for the same rule in SOUTH AFRICA.

[1160] *Cf.* the explanation of *Braithwaite v. Foreign Hardwood Co.*, [1905] 2 K.B. 543 (C.A.) given in *Taylor v. Oakes, Roncoroni & Co., supra* n. 1023.

[1161] Indeed there is SOUTH AFRICAN authority to the ntrary: *Willie and Millin (-Coaker and Schutz)* 192.

[1162] See authorities cited *supra* n. 1160.

[1163] *British and Beningtons, Ltd. v. North Western Cachar Tea Co.*, [1923] A.C. 48 (H.L.).

[1164] AMERICAN UCC s. 2-605 (1) (a); *Panchaud Frères S.A. v. Etablissement Général Grain Co., supra* n. 1024.

[1165] UCC s. 2-508 (1); *cf.* UCC s. 2-612 (2).

[1166] ULIS art. 30, 43.

defect.[1167] For this purpose the customer must set a *Nachfrist* within which cure must be effected (§ 634). A recent addition to the FRENCH Civil Code gives a similar liberty to cure to a person who agrees to build and sell a house.[1168]

In the case of a simple sale, no corresponding liberty to cure is stated in the general provisions of the FRENCH Civil Code which deal with the guarantee liability of a seller though such a liberty can probably be accorded by virtue of the court's discretion where termination or redhibition is sought judicially.[1169] In GERMANY it has been suggested that a seller may be entitled to a liberty to cure a minor defect (such as a broken watch-spring);[1170] and that where the sale is of generic goods it might be contrary to good faith for a buyer to refuse a seller's offer to cure a defective tender by making a fresh conforming tender, or even by curing a defect in goods which have been appropriated to the contract.[1171] Much greater prominence is given to the possibility of cure in the provisions of the AUSTRIAN Civil Code relating to defects in the subject-matter of a sale. Here it is expressly provided that termination is available only in respect of a defect which is both a *Hauptmangel* (*supra* s. 171) and which cannot be cured.[1172] It seems that here too the liberty to cure may exist at least for a limited time after the period fixed for the performance of the contract.

All these provisions for cure seem to be eminently reasonable where the purpose of the contract is to make or transfer a thing for use (whether privately or commercially) by the aggrieved party. Where on the other hand defective goods are delivered to a dealer who buys for resale, the seller's liberty to cure, especially if exercisable after the period designated for performance, might well give rise to an undesirable element of uncertainty. In such a situation the aggrieved party might reasonably wish to terminate and to exercise the remedy of making a cover purchase. Under the AMERICAN Uniform Commercial Code the liberty to cure after the end of the contract period is restricted to cases in which the seller has reasonable grounds to believe that his tender, though not a conforming one, would in fact be accepted (s. 2-508(2)). This provision should enable the courts to limit the liberty according to the needs of the different commercial situations outlined above.

175. *Partial default.* – The expression "partial default" is capable of referring to any case in which the performance rendered is not strictly in accordance with the contract. Thus it may refer to cases in which performance differs from that promised in quantity, quality or in respect of the time of performance. In the present section the expression will, however, be used in a narrower sense to refer to the situation in which a part of the performance quantitatively speaking is not in accordance with the contract. The defect may be that performance of that part is not rendered at all, or that it is rendered late, or that the part in question is defective in some other way. Thus a seller who only delivers part of the goods sold, or a buyer who pays only part of the price is in partial default; and the same is true if only part of the goods is delivered, or only part of the price is paid, within the agreed time; or if part of the goods delivered is defective.

So far as the right to terminate a contract is concerned, such partial default may give the aggrieved party an option. It may either justify termination of the whole contract, or it may justify termination in relation only to the part of the contract which is defectively performed. Termination of the whole contract will be justified where the partial default is "substantial" or where it justifies termination of the whole contract on one of the grounds specified in s. 168 above. Even in such situations however, the aggrieved party may sometimes be entitled to opt for partial termination.

In ENGLISH law, this is the position where a seller delivers goods of the contract description mixed with goods which are not of the contract description: the buyer is entitled to terminate the whole contract or (at his option) to terminate it with respect to the goods which are not of the contract description.[1173] In the UNITED STATES a similar but not identical rule prevails: the buyer can terminate either *in toto* or with respect to "any commercial unit".[1174] In theory this is not the same as the right to terminate with respect to the defective part; though in practice there will be little difference between the operation of the two rules.

In GERMAN law the buyer to whom a partly defective delivery is made does not as a general rule have the option discussed above. He is only

1167 CC § 633, 634.

1168 CC art. 1646-1 par. 4.

1169 The *délai de grâce* constitutes a sort of liberty to cure.

1170 *Enneccerus and Lehmann* 452.

1171 *Idem* 458.

1172 CC § 932; *cf.* CC § 1167.

1173 Sale of Goods Act, 1893 (*supra* n. 312) s. 30 (3).

1174 UCC s. 2-601 (a), (c).

entitled to terminate in respect of such goods as are defective.[1175] This is so even if the sale was for a lump sum: in such a case the effect of such termination is a price reduction in the proportion which the value of the whole subject-matter would have had (if it had not been defective) to the value of that part of the subject-matter in respect of which the right to terminate is asserted (CC § 471). Partial termination may however not be available if the things were sold as a unit and cannot be separated without prejudice to either party. In such a case *either party* may demand that termination should be in respect of the entire subject-matter (CC § 469 sent. 2). This should be contrasted with the rule of ENGLISH and AMERICAN law where the possibility of total termination depends simply on the choice of the buyer.

ULIS (*supra* s. 7) resembles GERMAN law in allowing only partial termination where there is a partial defect in quantity or quality (art. 45(1)). Termination of the whole contract is allowed only where the defect is a fundamental breach of the contract as a whole (art. 45(2)). As in ANGLO-AMERICAN LAW, termination depends on the choice of the buyer.

ENGLISH and AMERICAN law again give the aggrieved party the option of total or partial termination in certain cases of contracts which provide for delivery in instalments. Here the fact that one or some instalments are defective may give rise to a right to terminate with respect to those instalments and may also give rise to terminate the whole contract.[1176] However it seems clear that, although the right is expressed to be to terminate "the whole contract",[1177] this is not in fact to be taken quite literally. There appears to be no right of termination in respect of conforming deliveries made before the breach in respect of which termination is exercised. In GERMAN law, the position is made clear by judicial decisions: in cases of this kind the right to terminate (even the "whole contract") only operates with respect to future deliveries, *i.e.* those due after the defective one is tendered.[1178] ULIS lays down a similar rule, except that the buyer can terminate in respect of past conforming deliveries where these would be worthless to him "by reason of their interdependence with the non-conforming ones" (art. 75).

The GERMAN rules are based on a general contract principle which is stated by or deducible from the provisions of the Civil Code with respect to partial impossibility and delay as to part.[1179] We have seen in s. 165 above that if such circumstances render the debtor's performance (or performance of the contract in the case of a reciprocal contract) of no interest to the creditor, then the latter may terminate the whole contract. If there is no such total lack of "interest" partial impossibility, or partial failure to perform by the expiry of the *Nachfrist*, gives rise only to a right to terminate in respect of the part that remains unperformed. Even this right only exists if it does not defeat the purpose of the contract.[1180] This is the general contract principle underlying the rule stated in cases of the sale of things as a unit which cannot be separated without prejudice to either party. Obviously the application of this principle to other factual situations gives rise to difficult factual distinctions, and to decisions which are not always easy to reconcile.[1181]

In FRENCH law, there is little authority on the question of partial termination but, in spite of early hesitations, the present position seems to be that the courts have a power to allow partial termination in cases of partial default.[1182] In cases in which part of the subject-matter of a sale is defective, this remedy would take the form of a proportionate price reduction, which is available even though the sale was for a lump sum. This is referred to as *réfaction*, as it involves some "remaking" of the contract.[1183]

In COMMON LAW countries partial termination may also be possible by virtue of the distinction between entire and severable obligations. This distinction is usually drawn in situations which in CIVIL LAW systems would be dealt with under the *exceptio non adimpleti contractus;*[1184] but it could be used equally for the purpose of termination within the present chapter.[1185] A contract is said to be

[1175] CC § 469 sent. 1: he cannot terminate in respect of the part of the goods which do conform to the contract.

[1176] UCC s. 2-612(2) and (3); the same principles are applied to a case of buyer's breach by UCC s. 2-703, which cross-refers to UCC s. 2-612. The UNITED KINGDOM Sale of Goods Act, 1893 (*supra* n. 312) s. 31 (2) does not expressly give the first of the options mentioned in the text, but there can be little doubt that it exists.

[1177] See references *supra* n. 1176.

[1178] *Palandt* § 326 no. 13.

[1179] *I.e.* in particular GERMAN CC § 280 par. 2, 325 par. 1 sent. 2, 326 par. 1 sent. 3; *Enneccerus and Lehmann* 212, 224; *Larenz* I 250, 251.

[1180] *Enneccerus and Lehmann* 232.

[1181] *Von Mehren* 815-818.

[1182] *Idem* 815; *Marty and Raynaud* II no. 301. See *supra* s. 163.

[1183] *Mazeaud*, Leçons III no. 947.

[1184] This is true, for example, of the cases discussed in *Treitel* 678-683.

[1185] *E.g.*, *Morgan v. McKee*, 77 Pa. 228 (1874).

entire where the whole of a party's obligations under it must be performed before he can base a right of action on it.[1186] The contract is said to be severable where the remuneration of a party is fixed at a certain rate per unit, in which case partial remuneration for partial performance is recoverable.[1187] No doubt partial refusal to accept and partial recovery back by the aggrieved party of his own performance could be justified on similar reasoning where the obligation is divisible.[1188] It is assumed in cases of this kind that the aggrieved party's counter-performance is simply a payment of money and thus "divisible" in the sense of being readily apportionable to the parts of performance rendered. If the counter-performance were not divisible in this latter sense (*e.g.* if A delivered a single car to B in exchange for 100 bicycles, of which only some were delivered by B) there could be not partial termination.[1189] There is no COMMON LAW authority on this type of situation, but it seems clear that the availability of total termination in such a case would depend on the question whether B's default was "substantial" within s. 166 above. If it was, B could reject the bicycles delivered and recover his car or its value.

Other situations regarded in CIVIL LAW systems as cases of partial non-performance would in COMMON LAW countries be dealt with by different techniques and with different results. For example, a landlord might undertake to heat or repair premises which he had let. Failure in the performance of these obligations might be regarded in CIVIL LAW countries as partial default giving rise to a right of partial termination: *i.e.*, in effect to a reduction of rent.[1190] In COMMON LAW countries such failure would almost certainly be regarded as a failure to perform an "independent" covenant, giving rise to no right to terminate but only to a right to damages.[1191] If on the other hand performance of the term which is not performed is held to be a "condition precedent" or "concurrent condition" failure to perform it gives rise to a right of total (and not merely partial) termination.[1192]

176. *Anticipatory breach.* – The COMMON LAW doctrine of anticipatory breach has no precise counter-part in CIVIL LAW. The most important effect of the doctrine is to enable an aggrieved party to claim damages even before performance has actually become due. Similarly, an aggrieved party who "accepts" an anticipatory breach thereupon generally becomes entitled to terminate the contract. This is always assumed in ENGLISH discussions of the doctrine;[1193] and the rule to this effect is stated in the AMERICAN Uniform Commercial Code.[1194] The right of the aggrieved party to terminate on "acceptance" of the anticipatory breach does not of course arise *merely* because the breach is anticipatory. Other requirements of termination may have to be satisfied. The Uniform Commercial Code, for example, requires that the breach must "substantially impair the value of the contract" (s. 2-610) to the aggrieved party. An analogous provision in ULIS (*supra* s. 7) likewise requires the breach to be "fundamental" (art. 76). In ENGLISH law "substantial" impairment may not be necessary where the defaulting party shows a clear intention not to perform the contract according to its terms;[1195] and the fact that this requirement is almost always satisfied in cases of anticipatory breach probably accounts for the absence of discussion of the general requirements for termination in the relevant authorities. If the repudiation contained an element of equivocation or ambiguity, a question might arise as to whether termination was indeed justified.[1196]

CIVIL LAW systems do not appear to recognise the possibility that anticipatory breach may render a defendant liable in damages or to termination before the time at which performance under the contract was actually due.[1197] But they nevertheless do give certain special effects to what a COMMON LAWYER would call anticipatory breach. So far as termination is concerned, those special

[1186] *Treitel* 678-680.

[1187] *Idem* 680-681.

[1188] *Ebrahim Dawood, Ltd. v. Heath (Est. 1927), Ltd.*, [1961] 2 Lloyd's Rep. 512 (Q.B.).

[1189] *Cf.* the example given by *Larenz* I 251.

[1190] *Carbonnier* IV 280 (the author at this point discusses termination under the "theory of risks" and not for non-performance: *cf. supra* s. 156 and n. 952.

[1191] *Cf. Treitel* 677.

[1192] *Idem* 675-676; Restatement of Contracts (1932) § 250, 251. The COMMON LAW distinction referred to in the text is most commonly applied in situations which in CIVIL LAW fall under the *exceptio non adimpleti contractus* and is therefore more fully discussed in ch. 15 above.

[1193] The argument of the leading case of *Hochster v. De la Tour* (1853), 2 E. & B. 678, 118 E.R. 922 makes no sense unless this assumption is made.

[1194] UCC s. 2-610(b), cross-referring to the rights to "cancel" conferred by UCC s. 2-703(f) and UCC s. 2-711(1).

[1195] *Withers v. Reynolds* (1831), 2 B. & Ad. 882, 109 E.R. 1370.

[1196] *Universal Cargo Carriers Corp. v. Citati, supra* n. 1025, at p. 436.

[1197] *Houin* (*supra* n. 92) 27, discussing the FRENCH law of sale.

effects are apparent in relation to the machinery of termination.

In FRENCH law a creditor may treat a contract as discharged without getting a prior judgment for termination in cases of declared refusal by the debtor to perform.[1198] He runs the risk that his course of action may be treated as wrongful if the court subsequently finds that it was unjustified (see *supra* s. 148); but it will not be wrongful merely because he acted without first getting a judgment. In GERMAN law it has similarly been held that an unequivocal declaration of refusal to perform entitles the aggrieved party to exercise his rights under CC § 326 without complying with the normal requirements of *Mahnung* or *Nachfrist*.[1199] The position is the same in SWISS and AUSTRIAN law.[1200] It should be stressed that in all these systems the "anticipatory breach" *only* affects the *machinery* of termination. It does not (as in COMMON LAW countries) entitle the aggrieved party to terminate before performance has become due.

D. THE OPTION TO TERMINATE

177. *Termination generally depends on the election of the aggrieved party.* – In this division we are concerned with termination as a remedy for contractual default. Where this remedy is available, the aggrieved party is not bound to make use of it. He can, if he prefers it, sue for performance or damages (assuming, again, that those remedies are, in principle, available). In other words, breach by one party does not automatically terminate the contract, but gives the other party an option to terminate it. This principle is universally accepted; a recent suggestion in ENGLAND that sometimes breach may automatically terminate a contract[1201] has not been accepted in that country.[1202] The reason behind the principle is obvious: the contract may contain provisions highly favourable to the aggrieved party, and it would be unjust to allow the other party by breaking the contract to bring about an automatic termination and so to deprive the aggrieved party of those beneficial provisions.

Granted, however, that the contract can only be terminated at the option of the aggrieved party, the question remains: how must that option be exercised? In most systems there is no doubt on this point: termination requires some positive declaration or act of the aggrieved party. The contract is not terminated merely because of the failure of the aggrieved party to declare it subsisting or to require performance or to institute proceedings for its specific enforcement. Such failure to act may lead to loss of the remedy of specific enforcement; but it does not lead to termination, with the consequences of relieving both parties of their primary obligations to perform or of giving rise to reciprocal duties of restitution.

178. *Failure to affirm as termination.* – ULIS, however, departs from the generally accepted view by introducing a concept of "*ipso facto* avoidance". This applies where a seller has committed a fundamental breach by failing to deliver at the date fixed, or within an extended period (in the nature of a *Nachfrist, supra* s. 149) set by the buyer[1203] and where a buyer has committed a fundamental breach by failing to pay the price at the date fixed (ULIS art. 62(1)). In all these cases, the contract is "*ipso facto* avoided" unless, within a reasonable time (of the breach, or of its becoming fundamental) the aggrieved party informs the defaulting party of his intention to claim performance.

The purpose of the notion of "*ipso facto* avoidance" appears to be twofold: to fix the time by reference to which damages are assessed, which is often under ULIS the time of avoidance (*supra* s. 71), at a comparatively early point; and to protect the defaulting party against the hardship of being ordered to perform specifically after long delay (*supra* s. 11). Both these purposes could be, and in the other systems considered are, served by quite independent rules; and to achieve them by a process of "*ipso facto* avoidance" seems inelegant and unnecessary. It may lead to the result that the defaulting party is actually in a better position as a result of a fundamental than of a non-fundamental breach; for "*ipso facto* avoidance" only follows from a breach of the former kind.

E. THE EFFECTS OF TERMINATION

i. *Whether Retrospective or Prospective*

179. *General principle.* – The general principle

[1198] *Carbonnier* IV 272.

[1199] *Palandt* § 326 no. 6d.

[1200] *Guhl* 197, 200; Swiss CO art. 108 no. 1; *Klang and Gschnitzer (-Gschnitzer)* IV § 918 no. II 2b (p. 458).

[1201] *Harbutt's "Plasticine", Ltd. v. Wayne Tank and Pump Co., Ltd.* (*supra* n. 67) 465.

[1202] *E.g., Decro-Wall International S.A. v. Practitioners in Marketing, Ltd.* [1971] 1 W.L.R. 361, 368, 375, 381 (C.A.).

[1203] ULIS art. 26(1), 27(3); *cf.* ULIS art. 30(1) as to failure to deliver at the place fixed.

is that termination can operate not only prospectively but also retrospectively. This principle is expressly stated by FRENCH writers in relation to *résolution*[1204] and by GERMAN writers in relation to *Rücktritt*,[1205] though doubts have recently been expressed as to the scope of the principle of retroactivity in GERMANY.[1206] The assumption that termination can operate retrospectively also underlies some COMMON LAW discussions of the subject, in which it is said that the purpose of termination is to place each party into the situation into which he would have been if the contract had never been made.[1207]

What is meant by saying that termination can operate prospectively and retrospectively is that its basic effects are (or may be) twofold. It liberates the parties from their obligation to perform in future and it imposes on them reciprocal duties of restoration (*infra* s. 181, 182) in respect of any performance already rendered.[1208] An obligation to perform before the date of termination may likewise be discharged.[1209] So far as the defaulting party is concerned, it is only his obligation *to perform* which is discharged by termination. It should not be assumed that this liability *in damages* is extinguished merely because termination operates retrospectively.[1210]

There is, however, considerable divergence between the different legal systems as to some of the legal effects of the retrospective operation of termination. In GERMAN law, the principle only operates on the contractual rights of the parties. It creates a personal duty of restoration and has no proprietary effects with regard to the rights of third parties who have acquired an interest in the subject-matter of the contract.[1211] In FRENCH law, on the other hand, retrospective operation has not only a "personal" but also a "proprietary" effect, so that termination is capable of affecting the rights of third parties and of giving (for example) an unpaid seller a real security in the subject-matter of the sale.[1212] In ANGLO-AMERICAN law, termination by a seller on account of the buyer's breach would similarly create only a personal duty to restore: it would not revest property in the seller to the prejudice of third parties or of the buyer's general creditors. Rejection by the buyer does however have the effect of revesting property in the seller both under ENGLISH law[1213] and under the AMERICAN Uniform Commercial Code.[1214]

180. *Special rules for "continuing" contracts.* – In CIVIL LAW countries it is common to distinguish sharply between contracts performed by single acts of performance on each side ("instantaneous" contracts), and those which require continuing acts of performance over a period of time ("successive" contracts), such as leases or instalment contracts. In relation to these contracts the principle of retroactive operation does not apply, or at least only applies subject to extensive modifications. In FRENCH law, the termination of these contracts is referred to by the distinctive term *résiliation*: unlike *résolution*, this operates only so as to terminate the contract for the future.[1215] In GERMAN law, a similar principle is established by judicial decisions; however the operation of termination has some retrospective operation in that it affects performance which was due but not yet rendered at the time of termination.[1216] In this respect it must be distinguished from termination by notice (*Kündigung*) irrespective of default in performance, which only operates in respect of performance not yet due at the time of termination.[1217]

The assumption which underlies these special rules as to "successive" contracts is that a substantial amount of performance on both sides has taken place so that the mutual restoration required on retrospective termination is impossible or very difficult. Where termination is sought before performance has begun there is no objection to allowing it to have its normal retrospective operation.[1218] The same would in principle appear to be true where performance has not gone very far: for example where the first delivery under an

[1204] *E.g., Marty and Raynaud* II no. 303.

[1205] *E.g., Enneccerus and Lehmann* 232.

[1206] See *Larenz* I 294.

[1207] *E.g., Corbin* § 1102; the point also occurs in cases in which the impossibility of restitution is said to be a bar to termination: see *infra* s. 182.

[1208] *Cf.* ULIS art. 78.

[1209] See the discussion of the *exceptio non adimpleti contractus, supra* ch. 15.

[1210] *Cf.* the criticism of the GERMAN position (*infra* s. 184) in *Larenz* I 294-295.

[1211] *Enneccerus and Lehmann* 167

[1212] *Carbonnier* IV 273, 275 (criticising the FRENCH position). *Cf.* also CC art. 2102 no. 4, but this right is subject to several restrictions there stated.

[1213] *Kwei Tek Chao v. British Traders, Ltd.* (*supra* n. 958) 487.

[1214] UCC s. 2-401(4); *cf.* UCC s. 2-602(2)(a), making acts of ownership by the buyer after termination (in the sense of the present chapter) wrongful.

[1215] *Carbonnier* IV 273, 280; however *Marty and Raynaud* II no. 303 note some tendency to apply termination even to "successive" contracts.

[1216] *Palandt* § 326 no. 13.

[1217] *Enneccerus and Lehmann* 232; *cf. idem* 165.

[1218] See *Klang and Gschnitzer* (-*Gschnitzer*) IV 1 § 918 no. III 2 b (p. 447-448).

instalment contract is so seriously defective as to justify not only its own rejection but the termination of the whole contract.

COMMON LAW systems do not distinguish sharply between "instantaneous" and "successive" contracts in the context of termination; but in cases involving contracts of this kind they reach results which are very similar to those reached in the CIVIL LAW. There seems for example, to be little doubt that such a result would be reached under an instalment contract which, after running satisfactorily for some time, is then so seriously broken as to justify termination. As was suggested in s. 175 above, the right to terminate would only operate in such cases with respect to the defective instalment and to future instalments, and not with respect to earlier conforming instalments accepted and paid for under the contract. This rule is, admittedly, hard to extract from the relevant legislative provisions; but since it is not expressly excluded by them and is also obviously convenient, there is little doubt that it would be applied by the courts.

ii. *Requirement of Restoration*

181. *Benefits to be restored by aggrieved party.* – A party who seeks to terminate a contract for the purpose of recovering back his own performance[1219] is bound to restore to the defaulting party any performance received from the latter.[1220] This general principle is recognised by all the systems under discussion; but its precise scope gives rise to difficult questions.

The duty of the aggrieved party is often referred to as a duty to "restore" benefits received from the defaulting party.[1221] Literal restoration is normally required where the aggrieved party has received some physical thing; but often the nature of the performance received will be such that it cannot in this sense be restored. This will be the case, for example, where the aggrieved party has received the benefit of the defaulting party's services under the contract; or where, under a contract for the use of a thing belonging to the defaulting party, the aggrieved party has had the benefit of such use. GERMAN CC § 346 provides that in such cases the aggrieved party is to recompense the defaulting party for the value of such benefits; or, if the contract stipulated a counter-performance in money, to pay that sum. Under the latter part of this rule, payment by way of "restoration" is at the contract rate. CC § 346 seems to apply most naturally to the case in which the aggrieved party seeks to "terminate" in the sense of putting an end to the primary obligations of the contract. But it seems to apply equally where he terminates in order to recover back an advance payment after part of the performance promised to him has been rendered.

COMMON LAW systems distinguish between cases in which physical restoration of the defaulting party's performance is possible, and cases in which this is not possible. In cases of the first kind such restoration is necessary to sustain a claim by the aggrieved party for the return of an advance payment. Where such restoration is not possible, *e.g.* because the aggrieved party has had the benefit of services or the use of a thing, ENGLISH and AMERICAN law diverge.

In ENGLISH law, the aggrieved party can only recover back an advance payment if there has been a "total failure of consideration" – *i.e.* if he has not received any part of what he bargained for.[1222] Thus in an old case[1223] a tenant went into possession under an agreement for a lease, but terminated it and vacated the premises a few days later on account of the landlord's breach. It was held that he could not get back an advance payment of £ 10 as he was not in a position to "restore" the benefit derived from his temporary possession of the premises. However, the rule is not strictly applied where it is easy to apportion the part of the performance which has been duly rendered to the whole: *e.g.* where goods are sold at so much per unit paid in advance and only part of the agreed quantity is delivered or only part of the amount delivered is in accordance with the contract.[1224] Even with this qualification, the ENGLISH rule is often regarded as unduly rigid.

In the UNITED STATES, the rule is not followed. The aggrieved party is entitled to get back his payment on making allowance for the reasonable value of what he has received either by way of part performance or by way of the benefit of intermediate possession.[1225] Except in cases of

1219 The principles discussed in the following part of the text do not necessarily apply where termination takes the form of refusal to accept further performance; nor where the aggrieved party refuses to perform under what civil lawyers call the *exceptio non adimpleti contractus*.

1220 *Cf.* ULIS (*supra* s. 7) art. 79(1).

1221 See, for example, *Corbin* § 1115, 116; GERMAN CC § 346; *Mazeaud*, Leçons III no. 947.

1222 *Fibrosa Spolka Akcyjna v. Fairbairn, Lawson, Combe Barbour, Ltd.*, [1943] A.C. 32, 48 (H.L.).

1223 *Hunt v. Silk* (1804), 5 East 449, 102 E.R. 1142; criticised by *Corbin* § 1115.

1224 *Ebrahim Dawood, Ltd. v. Heath (Est. 1927), Ltd.*, *supra* n. 1188.

1225 *Corbin* § 1114, 1115.

partial termination (*supra* s. 175) the allowance will not be at the contract rate but at a reasonable rate.[1226] It may, however, be taken for granted that the allowance made to the defaulting party will never exceed payment at the contract rate.[1227]

In all the above cases, the benefit in respect of which restoration must be made is the very performance bargained for under the contract. The duty to restore may, however, extend further to include certain benefits derived from the performance received. The most obvious illustration of this principle is that the aggrieved party is bound to restore not only the thing itself but any "fruits" which he derived from it, or which he negligently failed to derive from it.[1228] There is a similar duty of restoration in respect of benefits derived from the use of the thing. Here GERMAN law distinguishes between the case in which the contract was actually one to allow the aggrieved party to use the thing, and cases in which the use of the thing was not the principal object of the contract.[1229] In the former case "restoration" may be at the contract rate under the provisions of CC § 346, discussed above; in the latter case restoration can only be at a reasonable rate.[1230] A troublesome ENGLISH case suggests that a buyer aggrieved by reason of the seller's lack of title is entitled to recover back the price without making any allowance for use of the subject-matter of the sale.[1231] The result is closely related to the ENGLISH requirement that failure of consideration must be total if recovery of the price was to be allowed at all. For this purpose it was necessary to assert that mere possession without title was no part of what the buyer had bargained for, which was a good title to the thing bought. Once this is accepted, it follows logically that the buyer should not have to make an allowance for use of the thing.[1232] The possible liability of the buyer to the true owner for such use may also, in some cases, be a ground for holding that he should not be liable in this respect to the seller as well. Finally it is possible to explain the actual decision in the ENGLISH case on the ground that it was in fact very doubtful whether there was any unjust enrichment of the buyer in that case.[1233]

No doubt in a general sense the object of the requirement of restoration is to prevent such unjust enrichment; but GERMAN law draws a sharp distinction between restoration of benefits on termination and restoration on the principle of unjust enrichment. Under the former heading *all benefits* obtained must be restored; under the latter only *benefits retained* (and not those of which the restoring party has been deprived by subsequent events) must be restored.[1234] In GERMAN law the first principle is applied against a person exercising a contractually reserved right to terminate, and against one on account of whose fault the right to terminate is exercised. A party who is not a fault can limit his liability to restore according to the principles of unjust enrichment where he exercises a right of termination conferred by law.[1235]

182. *Supervening impossibility of restoration.* – Here we are concerned with the situation in which literal or physical restoration was at one stage possible but has ceased to be possible because the thing which should have been restored by the aggrieved party has perished or deteriorated or because its nature has been changed. The question whether such impossibility deprives the aggrieved party of the right to terminate depends on a number of distinctions.

The most important of these distinctions is between cases in which the impossibility is due to the fault of the defaulting party and those in which it is due to the "fault" of the aggrieved party, who is seeking to terminate the contract. In the former case it is generally agreed that the right to terminate is unaffected: for example if the thing sold perishes because of the defect on account of which termination is sought;[1236] or if the buyer's inability to restore is due to the seller's want of title.[1237]

1226 *Idem* § 1125, 1127.

1227 Restatement of Contracts (1932) § 357 (1).

1228 *E.g., Mazeaud*, Leçons III no. 1015; *Enneccerus and Lehmann* 166.

1229 *Palandt* § 346 no. 3.

1230 Under CC § 347 sent. 2.

1231 *Rowland v. Divall, supra* n. 316, criticised by the Law Reform Committee (*supra* n. 317) par. 36, but see Law Com. Paper no. 24 and Scot. Law Com. Paper no. 12 (*ibidem*) par. 16. Contrast the GERMAN case cited *infra* n. 1237.

1232 *Argens v. Whitcomb*, 20 Wash.2d 371, 147 P.2d 501, 504 (1944).

1233 *Treitel*, Some Problems of Breach of Contract: 30 M.L.R. 146-148 (1967). None of the above arguments however justify the extension of the principle to the case of *Butterworth v. Kingsway Motors*, [1954] 1 W.L.R. 1286 (Liverpool Ass.); *Treitel* 862.

1234 *Enneccerus and Lehmann* 165-166.

1235 CC § 327; *supra* s. 157.

1236 FRENCH CC art. 1647 par. 1; SWISS CO art. 207 par. 1; ULIS art. 79(2) (a); *cf. Treitel* 320; the provisions of the GERMAN Civil Code do not deal directly with the point, but the position seems to be the same: see *Enneccerus and Lehmann* 445.

1237 BGH 28 March 1952, JZ 1952, 527; *Ernst Wolf*, Rücktritt, Vertretenmüssen und Verschulden: AcP 153 (1954) 97; *Rowland v. Divall, supra* n. 316. In GERMAN law there would in such a case be a claim under CC § 347 sent. 2.

On the other hand, if the aggrieved party's inability to restore is due to his own "fault" the right to terminate is generally lost.[1238] For this purpose, inability to restore a substantial part of the subject-matter is equivalent to total inability to restore; but inability affecting only a relatively minor part of the subject-matter would not generally lead to a loss of the right to terminate.[1239] "Fault" on the part of the aggrieved party probably is not restricted to an actionable breach of duty; misuse of the subject-matter or such use as would not have been made of it by a reasonable person appears to suffice.[1240]

Where the destruction or deterioration is not due to the fault of either party but to some accidental cause a greater variety of solutions is encountered. In GERMAN law, the right to terminate is not excluded merely because the thing which the aggrieved party has received is destroyed or deteriorates accidentally.[1241] This rule is made applicable to cases of sale (CC § 467), in apparent derogation of the rule that risk passes on delivery (CC § 446) which is here subordinated to the right to terminate. In ENGLISH law it has been held that accidental destruction or deterioration does not deprive the buyer of the right to terminate, at any rate where a right to terminate is expressly reserved by the contract for a limited period and the destruction or deterioration takes place within that period; and it is generally assumed that the rule applies even apart from such express reservation.[1242] In AMERICA, the Uniform Commercial Code provides that the risk in non-conforming goods remains on the seller until cure or acceptance, and even thereafter to the extent to which the buyer is not effectively covered by insurance (s. 2-510). FRENCH law differs fundamentally from all these systems in laying down that accidental destruction deprives the buyer of the right to terminate (CC art. 1647 par. 2). This is of course in accordance with the general FRENCH rule that risk passes with ownership (CC art. 1138); but the justice of applying this rule where the thing was, after all, defective appears to be questionable.

There are, finally, cases in which the supervening impossibility of restoration cannot very sensibly be ascribed to the "fault" of either party or properly be described as accidental. These are cases in which the impossibility is due to some contemplated or normal use of the subject-matter of the contract. Such impossibility will quite commonly exclude the right to terminate. But there are cases in which this would be an inappropriate solution: particularly those in which the deterioration or loss occurred in the course of a normal trial of the thing[1243] and those in which the defect only became apparent in the course of use of the thing.[1244] Two cases of this kind have been accorded special treatment.

The first arises where the party seeking to terminate the contract has disposed of the performance received by him. One possible solution, adopted in GERMANY, is to suspend the right to terminate until the aggrieved party can get the thing back.[1245] In ENGLAND a decision which ruled out such a solution was subsequently reversed by statute.[1246] An alternative possibility, which is supported by some AMERICAN and SOUTH AFRICAN cases, is to allow the aggrieved party to terminate on restoring the proceeds of the disposition.[1247] Of course it is assumed that the aggrieved party does not at the time of the disposition know of the circumstances on which his right to terminate is based.

The second special case arises where the aggrieved party alters the nature of the thing which he has received. Here GERMAN law starts with the general principle that termination is excluded (CC § 352); but this is subject to the important qualification that it does not apply in cases of sale if the defect only appears in the course of the transformation.[1248] ENGLISH law starts with the same general principle as GERMAN law, but it has been suggested that alteration of the subject-matter does not irretrievably deprive the aggrieved party of the right to terminate.[1249] The limitations (if any) on the scope of the principle are, however, obscure.

The destruction or deterioration of the subject-

1238 *Enneccerus and Lehmann* 169, 445-446; GERMAN CC § 351; *a fortiori* under FRENCH CC art. 1647 par. 2; *cf.* ULIS (*supra* s. 7) art. 79(1); cases of excused non-performance are excluded by ULIS art. 79(2).

1239 GERMAN CC § 351 sent. 2; ULIS art. 79(2)(e) is more restrictive.

1240 See *Enneccerus and Lehmann* 170.

1241 CC § 350; criticised by *Enneccerus and Lehmann* 169; *cf.* ULIS art. 79(2)(d).

1242 *Atiyah*, Sale of Goods (ed. 3 London 1966) 122; *Benjamin (-Finnemore and James)* 321.

1243 See, *e.g.*, *Treitel* 321; ULIS art. 79(2)(b).

1244 *E.g.*, GERMAN CC § 352.

1245 CC § 353; *Enneccerus and Lehmann* 170.

1246 *Hardy & Co. v. Hillerns and Fowler*, [1923] 2 K.B. 490 (C.A.), reversed by the ENGLISH Misrepresentation Act 1967 (*supra* n. 312) s. 4 (2).

1247 *Marr v. Tumulty*, 256 N.Y. 15, 175 N.E. 356 (1931); *Willie and Millin (-Coaker and Schutz)* 103, 194; *cf. Corbin* § 1114.

1248 CC § 467 sent. 1; *cf.* ULIS art. 79(2)(c).

1249 *Western Bank of Scotland v. Addie* (1867), L.R. 1 Sc. & Div. 145, 159, where ENGLISH authorites were discussed on an appeal from SCOTLAND.

matter which should have been restored may also give rise to a liability in damages. This possibility arises where the thing which the defaulting party is liable to restore has perished or deteriorated in his hands; or where the thing which the aggrieved party is liable to restore on termination perishes or deteriorates after he has exercised the right to terminate.

In GERMAN law CC § 347 imposes a severe standard of liability: there may be liability for loss or deterioration for which the party who is bound to restore is not truly at fault;[1250] and the liability may exist in respect of any loss or deterioration taking place after the moment of the receipt of the performance which is to be restored (so that there may be liability in respect of acts or omissions before termination). CC § 347 only applies in terms to a contractually reserved right to terminate, and in such cases the severe standard of liability may be justified on the ground that the parties should have taken the possibility of having to make restoration into account.[1251]

The provisions of CC § 347 only apply "correspondingly" to cases in which the right to terminate is conferred by law (CC § 327 sent. 1). Here the severe standard of liability may be justified against a person who is responsible for the circumstances giving rise to the right to terminate.[1252] But the same standard is not applied against the aggrieved party who is innocent in this respect. This party's liability under CC § 347 will only exist (if at all) in respect of acts or omissions taking place after notice of circumstances giving rise to the right to terminate.[1253] In respect of earlier acts or omissions the liability of such a party is normally limited to one to restore the extent of his enrichment.[1254]

In ENGLISH and AMERICAN law a buyer who is in possession of the goods is treated as a bailee who is bound to exercise reasonable care for their safety.[1255] In ENGLISH law this seems to be his only duty; it is expressly provided that he is not bound to return the goods to the seller.[1256] Under the AMERICAN Uniform Commercial Code a merchant buyer may be bound to return the goods to the seller on the latter's request, and also on such request to do certain other acts, such as reselling the goods (s. 2–603). As in GERMAN law, such duties do not arise out of the original contract: they spring up as consequences of termination.

iii. *Effects of Termination on Right to Damages*

183. *General introduction.* – A party who fails to receive the performance which was due to him under a contract may wish to pursue a number of remedies. For example, the buyer of a machine which fails to operate in accordance with the seller's undertakings as to its capacity[1257] may wish to claim one or more of the following: cure of the defect; termination in the sense of returning the machine and getting his money back; damages for the cost (incurred by him) of installing the machine; damages for loss of expectation; and damages for consequential loss.[1258]

It obviously does not make any practical sense for the buyer to claim both cure (a form of specific relief) and termination; and there is no dispute on the question that enforced performance (where available) cannot be combined with termination in respect of the same obligation. But there is also thought to be a difficulty about combining termination with damages. Here the difficulty is not that the combination makes no practical sense; in practical terms the aggrieved party is simply claiming a sum of money and the only question is as to the size of the award. The difficulty is thought to be a logical one, arising from the retrospective effect of termination: if the parties are to be put back into the position in which they would have been if the contract had never been made, how can damages be awarded for its breach?[1259] In the case of a continuing contract, a further argument can be put in relation to failure to perform obligations not yet due at the time of termination: ignoring the principle of retrospective operation, the contract "ceases to exist" with regard to these "future" obligations so that no further breaches occur on which a right to damages can be founded.[1260]

These arguments are in fact far from compelling. The principle of retrospective operation does not necessarily apply for all purposes; nor do such

1250 So *Larenz* I 297 ("*kein echtes Verschulden*"); contrast BGB-RGRK § 347 no. 2.

1251 *Larenz* I 296.

1252 *Enneccerus and Lehmann* 166; *Larenz* I 297.

1253 BGB-RGRK § 347 no. 6.

1254 See *supra* s. 181. CC § 327 sent. 2.

1255 UCC s. 2–602 (2)(b); *Benjamin (-Finnemore and James)* 400.

1256 Sale of Goods Act, 1893 (*supra* n. 312), s. 36.

1257 *Millar's Machinery Co., Ltd. v. David Way and Son, supra* n. 308.

1258 For the distinction between these various kinds of damages, see *supra* s. 49–53.

1259 *Klang and Gschnitzer (-Gschnitzer)* IV 1 § 921 no. I (p. 493).

1260 See *Treitel* 732 for ENGLISH cases in which this view was expressed.

statements as that a contract has "ceased to exist" carry any necessary connotations as to the extent to which damages are recoverable for its breach. They refer only to the primary obligations under the contract, so far as these have not been performed. Nevertheless such arguments have been influential in a number of systems of law to limit the extent to which termination can be combined with damages. Their effect has been greatest in GERMAN law and least felt in FRENCH law; other systems occupy intermediate positions.

184. *Particular applications.* – GERMAN law distinguishes, more sharply than other systems, between two senses of termination (*supra* s. 144): refusal to accept performance and *Rücktritt* in the sense of an act by the aggrieved party giving rise to mutual duties of restoration. Refusal to accept performance is not regarded as termination; and there is no doubt that such refusal can be combined with a claim for damages.[1261] It is, perhaps, also relevant that a buyer who is entitled to damages for breach of an express undertaking as to quality may either return the subject-matter and claim damages for breach of the whole contract, or retain it and claim damages in respect of the diminution in value due to the defect and consequential loss.[1262] Even the former course, however, is not regarded as termination in GERMAN law: it differs from this remedy in that the aggrieved party does not seek to recover back his own performance. Where a contract is terminated in the sense that one party duly declares *Rücktritt*,[1263] the Civil Code makes termination alternative to damages for non-performance,[1264] so that the two remedies cannot be combined.[1265] This rule applies not only in cases of impossibility and delay (where it is expressly laid down) but also in cases of so-called *positive Vertragsverletzung*.[1266]

SWISS and AUSTRIAN law likewise start with the principle that the aggrieved party can either claim damages for non-performance or terminate the contract.[1267] But each of these systems in fact attenuates the general rule. In SWISS law termination may be coupled if the other party cannot disprove fault with a claim for negative interest (CO art. 109 par. 2) and in case of sale for further damages.[1268]

AUSTRIAN law goes further in CC § 921, which provides that termination does not affect the aggrieved party's claim for compensation for loss caused by non-performance.[1269] This provision is reconciled with the general rule that termination and damages for non-performance are alternatives by restricting the claim under CC § 921 to a so-called "difference claim".[1270] The aggrieved party can only claim the difference in value between the promised performance and his own performance which he retains or recovers (as the case may be). This is said not to be a claim for expectation interest (*Erfüllungsanspruch*); and this is true in the sense that the party who terminates does not have the normal choice of basing his claim on either the "exchange" or on the "difference" theory (*supra* s. 73): he is restricted to the latter. Even so, the "difference claim" allowed on termination by AUSTRIAN law appears to be in effect one method of protecting expectation interest in the sense that the aggrieved party can recover the amount of money by which the value of the performance due to him exceeded the value of his own performance.

In COMMON LAW countries, the supposed logical impossibility of combining termination and damages has had some influence; but that influence has steadily declined. It was particularly strong in the UNITED STATES where at one time the notion that the aggrieved party must elect between "rescission" and "damages" enjoyed a considerable vogue.[1271] In some states this view has been expressly reversed by legislation;[1272] and in relation to sales of goods the Uniform Commercial Code contains a number of provisions which make it clear that "cancellation"[1273] can be combined with damages.[1274] Thus claims for termination have been successfully combined with claims for

1261 CC § 280 par. 2, 286 par. 2; *Enneccerus and Lehmann* 212, 222.

1262 *Enneccerus and Lehmann* 437.

1263 Under CC § 349.

1264 As distinct from damages for delay (*cf. supra* s. 75).

1265 CC § 325 par. 1 sent. 1, 326 par. 1 sent. 2.

1266 *Supra* s. 75; *Enneccerus and Lehmann* 238.

1267 SWISS CO art. 107 par. 2; AUSTRIAN CC § 918 par. 1, 920.

1268 *Supra* s. 59. CO art. 208 par. 3. If the seller can disprove fault, he is nevertheless liable for "indirect" damage under CO art. 208 par. 2 (*supra* s. 59).

1269 *Cf.* also AUSTRIAN CC § 932 par. 1 sent. 2.

1270 *Klang and Gschnitzer (-Gschnitzer)* IV (*supra* n. 1259).

1271 *Corbin* § 1217-1221.

1272 CALIFORNIAN CC § 1692; *cf.* NEW YORK Civil Practice Law and Rules – C.P.L.R. – (McKinley's Consolidated Laws of New York Book 7 B) § 3002 (e).

1273 As defined by UCC s. 2-106 (4).

1274 UCC s. 2-703, 2-711 (1), 2-721.

reliance and consequential losses;[1275] and there seems to be no reason why a claim for expectation loss should not also be available together with termination. It is true that traces of the older view (requiring election of remedies) remain;[1276] but it is to be expected that they will be increasingly discredited, under the influence of the provisions of the Uniform Commercial Code.

ENGLISH law has been almost entirely free from the supposed necessity to elect between termination and damages; and the remedies can be freely combined. In a case resembling the example given at the beginning of s. 183 above, the buyer of the defective machinery not only recovered back the price but also recovered installation expenses (reliance loss) and damages in respect of the profits which he would have made, had the machinery not been defective (expectation loss).[1277] The only slight difficulty in this connection arises out of the habit of some COMMON LAWYERS to refer to any money claim as "damages" even though it is in fact a claim for an agreed sum; and such a sum cannot be recovered if it would only have fallen due after the date of termination. If, for example, the owner of a chattel has hired it out and terminates the contract, he cannot recover any payments of hire falling due after the date of termination;[1278] but this does not preclude the possibility of his terminating and recovering damages for the hirer's repudiation of the contract.[1279] The ENGLISH rules are followed by the INDIAN Contract and Specific Relief Acts;[1280] and also in a number of CIVIL LAW jurisdictions within (or formerly within) the BRITISH COMMONWEALTH.[1281]

In FRENCH law the argument that termination and damages are "inconsistent" remedies has been largely disregarded. Under CC art. 1184 par. 2 *résolution* may be combined with damages.[1282] The damages are assessed on the normal basis:[1283] they are not limited to reliance loss or in any other way that is not equally applicable where damages are claimed by way of substitute performance. There can be no doubt that the FRENCH approach is more convenient than that which starts with the assumption that termination and damages are "logically" inconsistent and therefore alternative remedies.[1284] Such an approach leads at best to needless complexities and at worst to the risk of serious injustice in denying the most appropriate remedies.

ULIS (*supra* s. 7) similarly allows damages and termination to be combined[1285] and the damages where the contract is avoided may include expectation loss, such as loss of profit (art. 87). The main distinction under ULIS between cases in which the contract is terminated and those in which it is not relates to the time for assessment (*supra* s. 71).

In this section our only concern has been with the availability of damages *in principle* together with termination. We have not been concerned with the *measure* of recovery. The relevant part of that topic was discussed in s. 54 to 65 above, where we saw that various elements of recovery could properly be combined so long as this did not result in double recovery for the same loss. The need to guard against double recovery is of course particularly strong where a party seeks both to terminate and to recover damages. But it does not follow that damages and termination should never be combined since the combination by no means necessarily leads to double recovery.

F. RESTRICTIONS ON THE RIGHT TO TERMINATE

185. *General.* – The balancing of interests which the courts undertake in deciding whether or not termination is justified appears mainly in the rules which determine whether a right to terminate exists at all. But it exerts its influence also in a further group of rules which are based on the

[1275] *Clark v. Ohio Prefab. Homes, supra* n. 306; *Sheridan Drive-In Inc. v. State, ibidem.*

[1276] *E.g., Balon v. Hotel and Restaurant Supplies,* 6 Ariz.App. 481, 433 P.2d 661 (1967). The case was not governed by the AMERICAN Uniform Commercial Code.

[1277] *Millar's Machinery Co., Ltd. v. David Way & Son, supra* n. 308.

[1278] See *Treitel* 732.

[1279] *Ibidem; cf. Moschi v. Lep Air Services, Ltd., and others,* [1973] A.C. 331 (H.L.). The position may be different where an actual court order for "rescission" has been obtained.

[1280] INDIAN Contract Act, 1872 (*supra* n. 241) s. 75; Specific Relief Act, 1877 (*supra* n. 136) s. 38, 41 (still in force in, *e.g.,* PAKISTAN but replaced in INDIA by Specific Relief Act, 1963 (*ibidem*) s. 30, 33).

[1281] *E.g.* SRI LANKA: *Weeramantry* II § 1013; SOUTH AFRICA: *Willie and Millin (-Coaker and Schutz)* 102-103 (stating the obvious limitation that there must not be double recovery); SCOTLAND: *Walker* I 584, II 1092 (but contrast *Smith* 857 and *Gloag and Henderson* 132: these references may be to actions for an agreed sum).

[1282] *Cf.* CC art. 1630, laying down a similar rule in case of eviction.

[1283] *Mazeaud,* Leçons III no. 1016; *De Page* III no. 104.

[1284] *Zweigert and Kötz* 201.

[1285] Art. 24, 41, 55, 63.

assumption that a right to terminate does or did exist, and which proceed to restrict the exercise of that right. Some such rules have already been considered. The most important of these is the rule which requires the aggrieved party to restore the performance which he has received (*supra* s. 181, 182). Limitations on the ground of good faith or on the ground that the defaulting party may be entitled to perform out of time or that he may have a liberty to cure could also be placed under this general heading; and the same is true of rules limiting the effects of termination in cases of continuing contracts and of partial default.[1286]

A number of additional rules limiting the right to terminate will be considered in the following sections. These rules are for the most part more highly developed in COMMON LAW than in CIVIL LAW countries; and this fact is perhaps explicable on the ground that some corrective is necessary for the absense of any formal machinery of termination in the COMMON LAW (see *supra* s. 152). The general policy behind these rules is that termination is likely to cause undue prejudice to the defaulting party, where he is led to believe that this remedy will not be claimed, and the defective performance has been actually received and retained for some time by the aggrieved party. The right to terminate is therefore limited in cases of waiver and acceptance, and by the failure of the aggrieved party to assert the right promptly.

186. *Waiver and acceptance.* – In COMMON LAW countries it is well settled that the right to terminate a contract is lost by "waiver".[1287] This takes place when a party, knowing of the circumstances giving rise to a right to terminate, nevertheless continues with the performance of the contract or fails to assert his right to terminate. It may amount to a complete waiver, excluding even the right to damages, or merely to a waiver of the right to terminate, leaving the right to damages unimpaired. In the case of a stipulation as to time which is of the essence of the contract, the waiver may be temporary so that an extension of time becomes in turn of the essence of the contract.[1288]

A common situation analogous to waiver arises where a buyer has "accepted" goods delivered in performance of a contract of sale and the goods turn out to be defective. In ENGLISH law the buyer thereby loses any right which he may have had to terminate the contract for breach of condition, though he may still be entitled to terminate for misrepresentation or for a "total" or "fundamental" or frustrating breach[1289] (see *supra* s. 164, 166). The principle is distinct from waiver since "acceptance" may take place without knowledge of the breach.[1290]

In the UNITED STATES the Uniform Commercial Code distinguishes between "rejection" and "revocation of acceptance".[1291] The former is precluded by acceptance which may take place without knowledge of the non-conformity of the goods;[1292] the latter is in principle precluded only if the acceptance was made with knowledge of the non-conformity.[1293] But the Code goes on to provide that a buyer who has accepted is barred from any remedy if he does not notify the seller of the non-conformity after he has discovered it *or should have discovered it.*[1294] Thus the right to terminate may be lost in respect of goods which the buyer has accepted even though he has no actual knowledge of the non-conformity. Indeed the AMERICAN rule is more severe than the ENGLISH under which only termination is generally precluded: failure to give notice of the defect bars the buyer from *any* remedy, including damages.

GERMAN law recognises a general principle that the right to terminate a contract can be renounced either expressly or tacitly.[1295] Acceptance of late performance will often, but not invariably, be regarded as tacit renunciation.[1296] Renunciation appears to require knowledge of the defect and thus to correspond to the COMMON LAW principle of waiver rather than to that of acceptance. This requirement of knowledge is also stated in a special sale provision governing the case in which a buyer accepts the subject-matter knowing it to be physically defective. In such a case the buyer loses not only his right to terminate but also his right to a price reduction and certain rights to damages, unless the acceptance is made subject to an express reservation of his rights.[1297] The COMMON LAW does not appear to give the buyer any such right to accept defective performance subject to a reservation of his right to terminate except per-

1286 *Supra* s. 171, 174, 175, 180.

1287 *Corbin* ch. 40, esp. § 755; *Treitel* 707-708; UCC s. 2-209 (5); *Clark v. West*, 193 N.Y. 349, 86 N.E. 1 (1908).

1288 *Treitel* 723.

1289 *Idem* 710-712.

1290 This is true under the UNITED KINGDOM Sale of Goods Act, 1893 (*supra* n. 312) s. 35 even after its amendment by Misrepresentation Act 1967 (n. 312) s. 4 (2): *e.g.* where a buyer retains goods for more than a reasonable time without intimating rejection.

1291 UCC s. 2-602, 2-608.

1292 This is implicit in UCC s. 2-607 (2).

1293 *Ibidem;* and *cf.* UCC s. 2-608.

1294 UCC s. 2-607 (3) (a).

1295 BGB-RGRK § 346 no. 1.

1296 *Idem* § 360 no. 4; *Enneccerus and Lehmann* 172.

1297 CC § 464; *cf.* CC § 640 par. 2.

haps where he has accepted defective goods in the reasonable belief that the defect can be cured.[1298]

In the case of a commercial sale, the buyer is under the GERMAN Commercial Code moreover bound to examine the goods (if this is reasonably practicable) and to give immediate notice of defects; if he fails to do so he again loses not only the right to terminate but also rights to price reduction and damages.[1299] The principle here is analogous to the COMMON LAW rule in cases of acceptance as the right to terminate may be lost even without actual knowledge of the defect; it resembles the AMERICAN rather than the ENGLISH rule in that it results in loss of a number of rights and not only in loss of the right to terminate.

The FRENCH Civil Code contains no express provision regulating the loss of the right to terminate in cases of acceptance of defective subject-matter; but it is established that the right to termination may be renounced after it has arisen.[1300] This seems to be a less severe limitation than that of waiver or "acceptance"; but where the right to terminate would be extinguished in other systems on such grounds a FRENCH court could perhaps exercise its discretion to refuse termination. There appears to be no special rule in cases of sales corresponding to the principle of "acceptance" in COMMON LAW countries; but in practice similar results can be reached under the rules relating to the time during which a buyer can claim redhibition (or price reduction) on account of latent defects (*infra* s. 187).

187. *Lapse of time.* – The prejudice which termination can cause to the defaulting party obviously increases the longer the aggrieved party delays in claiming this remedy; and most systems of law contain provisions designed to ensure that the right to terminate is exercised without undue delay. To some extent these overlap with the rules as to "acceptance" discussed in s. 186 above.

In FRENCH law, a claim for redhibition on account of latent defects in the subject-matter of a sale must be brought "*dans un bref délai*" (CC art. 1648). This period is computed not from the time of the sale but from the time of delivery, that being the point at which the buyer first acquires the opportunity of discovering the defect.[1301]

The AMERICAN Uniform Commercial Code similarly provides that the right to reject non-conforming goods must be exercised within a reasonable time of delivery or tender (s. 2-602 (1)); and that the right to revoke acceptance must be exercised within a reasonable time after the buyer has discovered or should have discovered the non-conformity.[1302]

In ENGLAND delay in asserting a right of rejection for breach of "condition" has likewise been held to bar the right.[1303] Normally such delay will in any case amount to acceptance and bar the right on that ground.[1304]

Under ULIS (*supra* s. 7) a buyer to whom defective goods have been delivered may similarly lose the right to terminate by lapse of time: *i.e.* if the buyer does not exercise it promptly after giving the required notice of non-conformity (art. 43). This notice must itself be given promptly after the buyer ought to have discovered the non-conformity and in any event within two years of delivery unless the goods have been guaranteed for a longer period (art. 39(1)). Failure to give such notice deprives the buyer of *all* rights to rely on the non-conformity. This is similar to the AMERICAN rule[1305] except that it operates quite irrespective of "acceptance".

In GERMAN law lapse of time does not as such deprive the buyer of his right to terminate; but where he alleges the existence of a defect the seller may take the initiative by setting a term within which the right to terminate must be claimed; if it is not claimed within that time the right is lost (CC § 466).

All the above rules deal with a buyer's claim to terminate on account of some breach by the seller or (even where this is not a breach) on account of a defect of quality. They do not in terms deal with a seller's right to terminate for non-payment of the price, nor with other situations in which the right to terminate may be exercised on account of contractual default. Nevertheless it seems to be recognised in most systems[1306] that they represent a general contract principle. This is particularly clear in GERMAN law where the principle that the defaulting party can set a term within which the right to terminate must be exercised is stated not only in relation to particular contracts such as sale (CC § 466) but also in relation to contracts gener-

1298 See UCC s. 2-607 (2) and 2-608 (1) (a).

1299 Comm.C § 377, 378; *cf.* Comm.C § 381 par. 2; *Larenz* II 42.

1300 *Mazeaud*, Leçons III no. 1012, 1017.

1301 *Idem*, Leçons III no. 989.

1302 UCC s. 2-607 (3) (a); 2-608 (2).

1303 *Panchaud Frères S.A. v. Etablissement Général Grain Co.*, *supra* n. 1024.

1304 Under Sale of Goods Act, 1893 (*supra* n. 312) s. 11 (1)(c), 35.

1305 UCC s. 2-607 (3) (a); see *supra* s. 186.

1306 But in FRENCH law the seller's right to terminate for non-payment of the price is exercisable at any time within the period of prescription: *Mazeaud*, Leçons III no. 1017.

ally and in relation to the obligations of either party (CC § 355). Under this rule, the onus is to some extent on the party in breach, who is thus given a method for determining how long he is at risk of having the contract terminated.

In COMMON LAW countries, too, the rule that termination must be sought without undue delay is of general application; in some jurisdictions this rule is expressly stated by statute.[1307] The COMMON LAW rule puts the onus of terminating within the required time entirely on the aggrieved party. The party in breach does not have to call on the aggrieved party to declare his option; but on the other hand the defaulting party has no right to fix a time within which the option to terminate must be exercised. No doubt if the defaulting party asks the aggrieved party to declare his option, this request may, as a matter of fact, abridge the time during which the option can be exercised.

The problem whether termination is barred by mere lapse of time does not often arise in COMMON LAW countries. Where the default is known to the aggrieved party, delay in asserting the right will normally be regarded as evidence of waiver (*supra* s. 186). But where the default is not known, mere lapse of time would probably bar the right to terminate, on the analogy of the similar rule which applies in cases of misrepresentation.[1308]

Under ULIS the basic distinction is between cases in which the defaulting party has not performed at all (*e.g.* by failing to deliver or pay) and those in which he has performed defectively (*e.g.* by delivering late, or at the wrong place, or by delivering non-conforming goods). In the first situation, lapse of time does not lead to loss of the right to terminate. On the contrary, failure to require performance within a reasonable time leads (if the breach is fundamental) to "*ipso facto* avoidance".[1309] A seller who has failed to deliver at the date fixed in circumstances amounting to a fundamental breach can ask the buyer whether he intends to require performance (art. 26(2)); failure by the buyer to respond promptly again leads to "*ipso facto* avoidance". In the second situation, the right to terminate is lost if it is not exercised promptly after the defective performance has been rendered or the required notice of non-conformity been given.[1310]

The lapse of time considered in this section is a lapse of time falling short of the normal period of limitation laid down by law for a particular type of claim. Such periods of limitation are maximum fixed periods applicable to all remedies for a particular type of default; the rules discussed above refer to indeterminate periods, shorter than the fixed limitation periods, within which certain remedies must be exercised.[1311]

G. ANALOGOUS REMEDIES

188. *Variation or suspension of the contract.* – In some cases termination of the contract is felt to be too drastic a remedy while damages are insufficient or inappropriate. It may be possible for the courts to adopt a middle way by upholding the contract while varying one or more of its terms. It is true that the general tendency, both in CIVIL and in COMMON LAW countries, is somewhat hostile to this course, which is felt to infringe the sanctity of contracts.[1312] But in fact a number of rules which have already been considered do have the effect of modifying the contract: for example the rule under which an aggrieved party may be entitled to a price reduction, and that under which a defaulting party may be entitled to extra time to perform.

Variation may again be appropriate in the case of an instalment contract which provides for deliveries on credit. If the buyer fails to pay only one instalment in accordance with the contract termination may not be justified, but the court may uphold the contract on the terms that in future the seller need only make deliveries against cash.[1313] Again, on breach of a contract to render services to a person for life it was held on the latter's claim for termination that a more appropriate remedy was to grant him an annuity for life. Although the judgment was expressed to be one for damages, it has been suggested that it amounted to a variation of the contract.[1314]

Suspension of the contract is a common in-

[1307] CALIFORNIAN CC § 1691 (1); Revised Codes of MONTANA (*supra* n. 137) § 13-905 (1); NORTH DAKOTA Century Code (*supra* n. 154) § 9-09-04 (1); OKLAHOMA Statutes (*supra* n. 187) § 17-233 (1); SOUTH DAKOTA Compiled Laws (*supra* n. 154) § 53-11-4.

[1308] See *Leaf v. International Galleries*, [1950] 2 K.B. 86 (C.A.).

[1309] Art. 26 (1), 30 (1), 62 (1). *Supra* s. 178.

[1310] Art. 26 (3), 30 (3), 43.

[1311] Thus we have not been concerned with provisions such as GERMAN CC § 477 which governs proceedings not only for termination but also for price reduction.

[1312] For example, in FRENCH law such modification might be thought to conflict with CC art. 1134.

[1313] *Ex p. Chalmers* (1873), L.R. 8 Ch.App. 289; Restatement of Contracts (1932) § 287.

[1314] *Zweigert and Kötz* 199.

stance of variation. Giving the debtor extra time to perform is one kind of suspension. Another kind arises where the creditor's liability to pay is suspended while the agreed counter-performance is not being rendered: for example where a customer's liability to pay is suspended on account of a builder's delay.[1315] Suspension of this kind often arises under the express terms of the contract: for example where a time charterparty provides that a ship is to be "off hire" while she is not available for service.[1316]

In the cases mentioned so far, suspension has been of the obligations (or of some of the obligations) of one party only; it is not true suspension in the sense that it leaves open at least in theory the liability of the defaulting party in damages. Suspension in the full sense requires a postponement of obligations on both sides. This solution has, in particular, been adopted in some legal systems to deal with the situation in which services are not rendered under a contract of employment on account of a strike.[1317] Where non-performance gives rise to suspension in this sense, it is not properly speaking default at all, and therefore falls outside the scope of the present chapter.

189. *Adequate assurance of performance.* – The right to terminate a contract usually depends on some kind of default.[1318] This may take various forms. In COMMON LAW countries a mere refusal to perform may, under the doctrine of anticipatory breach, constitute sufficient default and justify termination before the time for performance has arrived. But at COMMON LAW the mere belief of one party (however reasonable) that the other will not be able to perform his obligations when they fall due is not a ground on which termination or even refusal to perform can be justified.[1319] There must be a breach, actual or anticipatory, and this is still the position in ENGLAND.

In the UNITED STATES, however, a striking departure from this principle has been made by the Uniform Commercial Code, s. 2-609 (1) of which provides: "A contract for sale imposes an obligation on each party that the other's expectation of receiving due performance will not be impaired. When reasonable grounds for insecurity arise with respect to the performance of either party the other may in writing demand adequate assurance of due performance . . ." Such a demand has two effects. First, the party making it may, until the assurance is received, suspend any performance for which he has not received the agreed return. Secondly, a failure to provide such assurance within a reasonable time not exceeding 30 days is a repudiation of the contract.[1320]

The main purpose of the section is to free the party seeking the assurance from the contract so that he does not have to render performance while the uncertainty lasts, and so that he can make alternative arrangements (*e.g.* buy or sell elsewhere) if the uncertainty is not removed within a reasonable time. The need to grant such relief may be particularly strong where the party seeking the assurance was under the contract bound to perform before the other party, and events after the contract make it uncertain whether he will receive the agreed counter-performance. Thus termination[1321] and a defence in the nature of the *exceptio non adimpleti contractus* are entirely appropriate remedies in this context. But in treating the failure to provide the assurance as a "repudiation" the Code in addition makes the remedy of damages available to the party seeking the assurance;[1322] and it is questionable as a matter of policy whether this remedy should be available against a person who is not in actual default and who has not refused to perform. Such a rule is certainly not justified by the analogies on which the section is based.[1323]

The lack of case law on the section may suggest that claims for damages under it are not often

[1315] *Cf. Corbin* § 1293.

[1316] As in *Hongkong Fir Shipping Co., Ltd. v. Kawasaki Kisen Kaisha, Ltd., supra* n. 955.

[1317] See, *e.g., Morgan v. Fry,* [1968] 2 Q.B. 710, 728 (C.A.). See generally this Encyclopedia vol. XV ch. 15.

[1318] Of course this is not invariably so: termination may be justified on account of excused non-performance (*e.g., Poussard v. Spiers, supra* n. 1063) or on account of some other factor specified by law (*e.g.* GERMAN CC § 626) or by virtue of a power to terminate conferred by the contract itself.

[1319] *Small and Sons, Ltd. v. Middlesex Real Estates, Ltd.,* [1921] W.N. 245 (K.B.); *Universal Cargo Carriers Corp. v. Citati* (*supra* n. 1025). Some variation may however be justified on the principle of *Ex p. Chalmers* (*supra* n. 1313), though in that case there had been an actual breach.

[1320] S. 2-609(1) and (4).

[1321] Called "cancellation" by the AMERICAN Uniform Commercial Code which uses "termination" in a different sense: s. 2-106(3), (4); *supra* n. 954.

[1322] This appears to follow from the treatment of repudiation in UCC s. 2-703, 2-711.

[1323] One of these (mentioned in Official Comment 2 to s. 2-609) is the right of stoppage *in transitu,* the exercise of which gave no claim to damages. The other (mentioned *ibidem*) is the doctrine of anticipatory breach, but this is based on a definite refusal to perform or on actual inability to do so.

made, for if they had been made they would surely have been contested. Doubt as to the appropriateness of the remedy of damages in this type of situation is, moreover, strengthened by a consideration of similar provisions in CIVIL LAW countries.

In GERMAN law CC § 321 provides a special defence for a party who is obliged to perform in advance. This defence is available when, after the making of the contract, there has been a substantial deterioration in the financial position of the other contracting party. If the deterioration is such as to endanger the former party's claim to the agreed counter-performance, he is entitled to refuse to render his own performance until the counter-performance is rendered, or until security for its performance is given.

This provision is in one respect broader than that of the Uniform Commercial Code, in that it is of general application and not restricted to sales. But in all other respects it is narrower. It is restricted to cases in which the party complaining of insecurity was obliged to perform in advance; and to a particular ground of insecurity, *viz.* the substantial deterioration of the other party's financial position.

Even when these conditions are satisfied, their sole effect under CC § 321 is to suspend the obligations of the party who was bound to perform in advance. The obligations of that party are not extinguished (except under a special analogous provision relating to contracts to make loans, CC § 610); nor is that party entitled to exercise the right of termination (*Rücktritt*) merely because the circumstances envisaged by CC § 321 have occurred.[1324] Thus he would not be entitled to recover back any performance that he had already rendered before the deterioration in the other party's financial situation. If the latter party refuses to comply with a request to perform concurrently or to give security, a right of *Rücktritt* may, however, arise on the ground that such refusal is contrary to the general good faith requirement stated in CC § 242.[1325] Even in such a case, however, the refusal does not give rise to a right to damages: this only arises on actual default in the performance of the obligation originally undertaken.[1326]

SWISS CO art. 83 contains a provision similar to GERMAN CC § 321.[1327] In particular it is confined to cases in which a party's financial situation has deteriorated. The SWISS provision is not in terms restricted to the case where one party is bound to perform in advance, though no doubt it will in practice most commonly operate in cases of this kind. More significantly, the SWISS provision differs from the GERMAN in that it entitles the party who seeks security to set a reasonable term for it to be given, and to terminate the contract (*zurücktreten*) if it is not given. Here again, however, the right is simply one to terminate. Even though in SWISS law the right to terminate for contractual default is normally coupled with a right to damages (see *supra* s. 184) the latter right is not available to a party who terminates in the absence of default under CO art. 83.[1328]

In FRENCH law the principle of giving security where counter-performance is imperilled is stated in CC art. 1613. This applies where a seller who has agreed to deliver on credit is in imminent danger of losing the price on account of the buyer's bankruptcy or insolvency. In such a case the seller is relieved from his obligation to deliver unless the buyer gives security for payment.[1329] The various rights of an unpaid seller and the effects of bankruptcy on contracts are considered elsewhere.[1330] CC art. 1613 is only mentioned here because of its reference (unusual in the context of unpaid sellers' rights on bankruptcy) to giving of security. It will be noted that the only right conferred by the article is one to withhold delivery.

ULIS (*supra* s. 7) similarly deals with the situation in which, after the conclusion of the contract, the economic situation of one party appears to have become "so difficult that there is good reason to fear that he will not perform his obligation" (art. 73 (1)). In such a case the other party can *suspend* the performance of his obligations: this is the sole remedy provided by the law. No provision is made for giving security or assurance of performance.

(Completed in May 1972)

[1324] BGB-RGRK § 321 no. 4.

[1325] *Ibidem; Palandt* § 326 no. 3.

[1326] BGB-RGRK § 321 no. 4; but see *Larenz* I 156, 157.

[1327] See also SWISS CO art. 316, on promises to make a loan.

[1328] *Guhl* 39.

[1329] *Cf.* also FRENCH CC art. 1188, accelerating the liability of the debtor in certain cases of deterioration of his financial circumstances. CC art. 1188 is not, however, concerned with the right to terminate.

[1330] See this Encyclopedia vol. VIII ch. 3 *sub* III A and vol. XVI ch. 14.

V. CONTRACTUAL REMEDIES IN SOCIALIST LEGAL SYSTEMS

Gyula Eörsi*

A. GENERAL PRINCIPLES

190. *Specific performance.* – While economic development may cause specific performance to lose some of its significance,[1331] this remedy nevertheless remains the most conspicuous and characteristic feature of the system of contractual remedies available in Socialist legal systems.[1332] Its importance results from the socialisation of the national economy and the planning system. In a socialised economy the immediate purpose of production is the satisfaction of social needs which are fixed by the national economic plan for a given period. This purpose almost always implies reliance on specific performance, as the present system of planning rarely permits the existence of a market where damages received may be utilized for purchase of substitutes. Monetary or other material incentives such as damages – both liquidated and unliquidated – which reduce the gains of the enterprise and consequently both the investment fund and the participation fund of the employees exert an indirect pressure but don't replace the lost performance as they can in systems based upon private ownership.

A third reason for the overwhelming importance of specific performance for the foreign trade among the members of the CMEA[1333] is the absence, at present, of a convertible currency, a fact responsible in part for the slow development of the claim to damages and of discharge in the General Conditions of Delivery 1968 (GCD).[1334] It is, however, suggested that even if a convertible currency were created, no radical change could be expected in the near future in the general policy of the GCD.[1335] Whereas the Uniform Sales Law of 1964 (ULIS)[1336] by the frequent resort to *ipso facto avoidance* tends to facilitate the termination of contracts, the GCD tend to oblige the parties to perform the contract, even in difficult circumstances.

ULIS and GCD constitute two extremes which demonstrate that the "natural" remedy in a free market model is damages whereas in a planned economy it is specific performance. Although this is a gross generalisation and simplification, yet it may safely serve as a starting point in the discussion of the system of remedies for breach.

191. *Socialist co-operation.* – Another general principle of Socialist contract law pervading as well the system of remedies is the principle of socialist co-operation[1337] which is a far-reaching negation of the principle that each party must protect its own interests, as expressed for sales law in the maxim of *caveat emptor.* To give an example, occasionally it is not sufficient that goods conform to the sample examined by the buyer at the time of the conclusion of the contract; the seller, who is generally an expert in questions of manufacturing, must satisfy the demand of the buyer with goods of good quality which are fit for the purpose which the contract is designed to achieve.[1338] A violation of this principle usually obliges the seller to pay damages.[1339]

Another manifestation of this principle is that a sales contract creates in the obligee not only a right to delivery of goods but also an obligation to perform all acts expected of him to enable or facilitate performance, irrespective of whether such acts have been expressly spelt out by the parties as duties under the contract. The violation of these obligations constitutes a distinct kind of breach known as the default of the obligee (*supra* ch. 15).

192. *Sectoral differences.* – The fundamental characteristics of the system of remedies are in general the same whether one is dealing with the sphere of the socialised economy or with trans-

* Professor at the University of Budapest (Hungary). The author is indebted to Professors *A. Faĭnshteĭn* (Moscow), *A. Gams* (Zagreb) and *L. Stepniak* (Warsaw) for valuable information received from them in respect of SOVIET, YUGOSLAVIAN, respectively POLISH law.

1331 *Bratus* 103.

1332 See *supra* ch. 6 subch. I.

1333 Council of Mutual Economic Assistance; in the West frequently called COMECON.

1334 See *Szász* 238, 250. Nevertheless there is a marked development if the 1968 version of the GCD is compared with that of 1958: the system of remedies was intensified and extended (*Kanda* 576).

1335 For the English text of the General Conditions of Delivery of Goods between organizations of the member countries of the CMEA see *infra* List of General Conditions.

1336 Convention Relating to a Uniform Law on the International Sale of Goods, of 1 July 1964, see *United Nations*, Register of Texts of Conventions and Other Instruments Concerning International Trade Law I (New York 1971) 39-63.

1337 See *supra* ch. 6 subch. I.

1338 Opinion no. 5/1973 of the Presiding Judges of the HUNGARIAN S.Ct. Economic Branch, B.H. 1973, 388.

1339 See *supra* ch. 6 subch. I.

actions between citizens. However, some quite important differences flow from the fact that the functioning of the socialised economy is subject to state direction carried out mainly through comprehensive planning.

Although the state-owned enterprises enjoy a more or less extended autonomy in their dealings, at least the framework of their activity is determined by the owner, the state, mainly through the national economic plan. This situation has given rise to the concept – among others – of "contractual discipline", by analogy to "labour discipline" within the enterprises. This concept is responsible for the most important difference between remedies for transactions within the nationalised economy and those outside it; namely where circulation of goods and services as well as capital investments are involved and both parties to the contract belong to the socialised sphere (mainly state enterprises), the law provides for mandatory *liquidated damages*. The main but not the sole purpose of such liquidated damages is to raise the level of "contractual discipline", in other words, to stimulate the parties to live up to their contractual obligations and serve thereby the national interests (for details see *infra* s. 223-232). Another consequence of the planned character of the contracts within the nationalised sphere of economy is that the requirement of specific performance is more intensive in this field than outside it.

The special features of the nationalised economy have led to the creation, in the GERMAN DEMOCRATIC REPUBLIC and in CZECHOSLOVAKIA, of a new branch of law: *economic law*. It, speaking in general terms, unites and combines elements of traditional civil law and of administrative law operating in this sphere. For instance, "economic liability" in economic law covers both liability for breach of contract and liability towards the state and its public organizations in the field of nationalised economy, in contrast with separate heads of civil law liability and administrative law liability in other sectors.

The present contribution concerns itself in the main with the law within the nationalised economy.

193. *The system of remedies*. – The system of remedies is based on the various kinds of breaches of contract: the default of the obligor, the default of the obligee, defective performance, non-performance or supervening impossibility.[1340]

In every type of breach the remedies may be grouped roughly in two categories:

(1) Remedies – known in HUNGARY as *objective* remedies, and in the GERMAN DEMOCRATIC REPUBLIC as "securing rights" (*Sicherungsrechte*) – which are independent of the conduct or fault of the party in breach. They are aimed at the removal of the cause of friction or dispute (*Störungsbeseitigung*) through specific and actual performance of the contract (including substituted performance or repair) or at the restoration of the balance of performance on both sides (*e.g.*, by reduction of the price) and, in the last resort, at the release through discharge of the parties.

(2) So-called *subjective* remedies which are appropriate in cases of fault and result in an award of damages – liquidated or unliquidated; in the GERMAN DEMOCRATIC REPUBLIC the purpose of these remedies is said to be the reparation of loss or damage consequent upon breach (*Folgeschäden*).[1341]

The difference between the two groups is more important in theory than in practice because fault is usually presumed and the courts or state arbitration will only rarely exonerate a party; thus "subjective" remedies are sometimes hardly distinguishable from the "objective" ones (*infra* s. 224).

194. *Fines under administrative law*. – "Contractual discipline" is also promoted by various kinds of fines payable to the state. Such fines are mostly imposed for the production or sale of goods lacking in quality and are in addition to damages paid to the other party. Fines are not contractual remedies and will not be treated here. However, cases where a party because of his own conduct is debarred from obtaining liquidated damages which then become due to the state, will be discussed below (s. 231 (7)).

195. *No uniform solution*. – The foregoing are very general statements. The laws of the various Socialist countries vary in many points.

This is particularly true of YUGOSLAVIAN law where the state ownership of economic units is unknown; in the system of self-management prevailing there the market plays a greater role and economic planning is also less intense than in the other Socialist countries. Consequently the remedies available in the sphere of the socialised economy in YUGOSLAVIA resemble greatly the remedies resorted to in the sphere of individual consumers in other EUROPEAN Socialist states.

1340 These matters are discussed in greater detail in the preceding ch. 15.

1341 For HUNGARY: *Eörsi*, Consequences no. 5.3, and *idem*, Problems no. 148. Similarly in POLAND, communication of *Stepniak*. For the GDR: Lehrmaterial 2, 84-85. *Kanda* 574 does not distinguish between these two groups.

The dearth of reliable material has prevented the treatment of the FAR-EASTERN legal systems. The law in CUBA seems to be in a state of swift transformation, the main trends being an approach towards the laws of the majority of EUROPEAN Socialist countries.

B. SPECIFIC PERFORMANCE

i. *Introduction*

196. *Basic rules.* – We have seen why specific performance is the main remedy for breach of contract in the Socialist laws, particularly within the sphere of the nationalised economy. It places the plaintiff – so far as possible – in the position in which he would be had the contract been performed in conformity with its terms and according to the law (see *supra* s. 49).

Specific performance is enforced by the courts (or state arbitration). If the performance consists of handing over specific goods, RSFSR CC art. 217 expressly enables the obligee to apply to the court (or state arbitration) for an order that the goods be taken away from the obligor and handed over to him. A similar procedure applies to contracts for work. But in labour contracts, specific performance as a remedy is available for the employee only. Where the obligation consists of doing something for somebody else (*mandatum*, commission agency, deposit) the obligee is entitled to have the work done at the costs of the obligor.[1342] On the other hand, nobody may be forced to any action which could affect his personality, in particular his literary or artistic creativity (for instance, to produce a novel under a contract between publisher and writer).[1343]

The distinguishing feature of specific performance in Socialist laws is the fact that at least in the sphere of the nationalised economy where specific performance is available, neither party may demand, offer or accept rescission instead.

Specific performance is available irrespective of the fault of the obligor.

197. *The limits of specific performance.* – The award of specific performance is, in general, excluded by the following factors:

(1) Impossibility of performance, including impossibility of repair or replacement;

(2) specific performance, in the circumstances, yields an economically unjustifiable result;[1344]; if, however, restricted specific performance – *e.g.* through price reduction – is possible, this will be ordered instead of total rescission;[1345]

(3) in some cases it is relevant that the obligee no longer seeks specific performance. In cases of default, this rule practically always empowers the obligee to rescind the contract The obligee can also rescind, where repair or replacement of a defective performance is likely to take so much time that the delay amounts to default and where the refusal to take delivery of goods is due to serious nonconformity with the contract and thereby places the obligor at default (*infra* s. 213). A corollary of these rules is the ability of the obligor to put an end to the contract where the obligee continues in default upon his obligation to enable and facilitate performance for a prolonged period (*infra* s. 211). These gaps in the principle of specific performance are inevitable since an unending default might lead to a deadlock;

(4) the rules as to remedies contained in the civil codes are optional, not mandatory. Therefore in contracts governed by the civil codes the parties may stipulate the right of rescission even in cases where rescission would not be otherwise permissible. On the other hand, in the sphere of the nationalised economy the rules on remedies are mandatory[1346] except in the case of internal contracts serving the purposes of foreign trade (for instance, a contract between a producer and a foreign trade enterprise of the same country);

(5) even within the sphere of the nationalised economy, the doctrine of specific performance is more flexible for contracts of delivery (of sale) than for other categories of contracts, *e.g.*, those for work or for construction;[1347]

(6) in the field of international trade other than between Socialist countries, the principle of specific performance finds application in about the same way as in WESTERN CONTINENTAL laws.[1348]

[1342] SOVIET UNION: RSFSR CC art. 218. See the comparable provision in the POLISH CC art. 580 for cases of default.

[1343] *Bratus* 101.

[1344] Lehrmaterial 2, 92.

[1345] *E.g.* POLISH CC art. 637 par. 2.

[1346] In a HUNGARIAN case a contractor sought to restrict his liability to the observance of the technical requirements because the work under the contract involved the application of new methods. This restriction was held to be void because of the mandatory character of the rules on remedies in the sphere of the nationalised economy: S.Ct. Gf. V. 23.021/1974, B.H. 1974, 374.

[1347] For the SOVIET UNION see *Bratus* 102.

[1348] See *Kanda* 575, 578.

ii. *Default of the Obligor*

198. Where the obligor is in default the main rule is that the obligee may insist on performance;[1349] rescission in such cases is subject to special requirements (*infra* s. 212). For contracts of delivery, HUNGARIAN law reinforces this rule by obliging the party in default promptly to set up new terms for his own performance. If he fails to do so or the new terms do not satisfy the obligee, the court will, at the request of the obligee, provide the new terms.[1350]

iii. *Default of the Obligee*

199. The default of the obligee in itself does not, as a rule, relieve the obligor of his obligations: he must remain able and willing to perform.[1351]

Where under the contract goods have to be physically transferred and the obligee refuses to accept the tender the goods are retained by the obligor for and on the obligee's behalf at his cost and risk; alternatively the obligor may store the goods at the cost and risk of the obligee.[1352] In both cases, title in the goods passes; the obligor is no longer owner or lessee but the "responsible custodian"[1353] (in case of sale the risk passes and the price falls due, and in case of a lease there is no further obligation to pay rent).[1354] Further the obligor is entitled to perform through deposit in court if this is feasible.

HUNGARY has introduced for its nationalised economy a radical rule. Where under a contract of delivery the buyer does not present himself at the plant of the seller to take delivery, the seller may transport or forward the goods to the address of the buyer.[1355]

These rules promote specific performance in cases of default by the obligee. Yet they seem to create the possibility of "endless situations" in which the obligor might remain bound to his obligation infinitely despite the breach by the other party. Such situations evidently need to be regulated (see *infra* s. 211). Similar rules appear in WESTERN CONTINENTAL laws but not under the heading of specific performance.

iv. *Defective Performance*

200. *In general.* – Defective performance is the common denomination in all cases of nonconformity with the contract or the law, except default, such as (1) delivery of defective goods, goods of bad quality or an *aliud;* (2) deficient performance; (3) incomplete performance; (4) defective packing, lack of labelling or marking; (5) incomplete documentation (in greater detail *supra* ch. 15).

We shall concern ourselves mainly with the first three cases. In these instances specific performance is served by the following means:

(1) rescission is permitted in specified conditions only; it is particularly rare under the GCD of the CMEA (*infra* s. 214) because the possibility of a cover purchase is minimal here;

(2) the obligee is, as a rule, entitled to repair or replacement of defective goods or services as well as to a reduction in the price (*quanti minoris, supra* s. 67).

In dealing with these problems various legal systems distinguish between specific goods and generic goods; between serious defects and not so serious defects; between *Gewährleistung* and *Garantie* and between the nationalised economy and the sphere of citizens.

201. *Specific and generic goods.* – Where specific goods are sold, replacement as a remedy is excluded. The obligee has an option between repair, reduction of price and, in certain circumstances, rescission.[1356] The problem is more difficult in contracts for work where the work performed is unfit for the purposes of the con-

[1349] SOVIET UNION: RSFSR CC art. 225; BULGARIA: Code of Obligations (CO) art. 79; HUNGARY: CC § 300; POLAND: CC art. 477; CZECHOSLOVAKIA: Economic Code (EC) § 139, International Commercial Code (ICC) § 230, 235, 237. For YUGOSLAVIA see *Goldštájn* 180. The GCD of the CMEA do not state the rule expressly but there has never been any doubt in this respect (see *Szász* 239–242). For the default of the obligor see *supra* ch. 15.

[1350] Government Decree 10/1966 Korm. of 14 Feb. on Contracts of Delivery (DecrCD) (*A szállítási szerződésekről*), M.K. no. 11/1966, § 35 (French transl.: Rev.dr.hongr. 1969 no. 1, 41) amended by Decrees 46/1967 Korm. of 5 Nov., M.K. no. 78/1967 (Engl. transl.: Hung.L.Rev. 1969 no. 1, 35), 2/1970 Korm. of 3 Feb., M.K. no. 7/1970, and 35/1973 MT of 24 Dec., M.K. no. 87/1973.

[1351] See, *e.g.*, *Ioffe* 411; *Eörsi*, Consequences no. 11.

[1352] This is expressly stated in the POLISH CC art. 552 par. 2 as well as in the HUNGARIAN DecrCD (*supra* n. 1350) § 39 par. 1. For YUGOSLAVIA see *Goldštájn* 182–183.

[1353] HUNGARIAN CC § 196; SOVIET CP 84, CG 86.

[1354] *Ioffe* 411.

[1355] DecrCD (*supra* n. 1350) § 39 par. 2. On the other hand, in YUGOSLAVIA the Supreme Economic Court has ruled that the seller cannot ask the court to compel the buyer to take delivery. See Economic Court 16 June 1958, Zb. III 2 (1958) no. 384 (English Summary in Appendix), as quoted by *Goldštájn* 162–163.

[1356] For HUNGARY see CC § 305.

tract. Replacement would amount to the obligor having to do the work anew. This creates no particular difficulty where the work consists of repairing something: bad repair work must be redone. In cases of construction, however, the demolition of the defective building and the erection of a new one involve excessive cost to the detriment of the national economy and sometimes put a serious strain on the capacity of the construction industry. Therefore, the usual solution is a combination of repair and reduction of price or rescission; only very exceptionally is the building demolished and rebuilt.[1357]

202. *Refusal to accept performance.* – A distinction between serious and not so serious defects is made in the SOVIET UNION and in the GERMAN DEMOCRATIC REPUBLIC. In cases of serious defects or incomplete performance – in the field of the nationalised economy – the obligee is entitled to reject performance.[1358] In the SOVIET UNION the obligee is obliged, and not merely entitled, to reject goods which fail to conform to the compulsory technical standards or technical conditions, and where they are incomplete. In some other cases where, *e.g.*, the quality of the goods conforms to the compulsory standards but falls below the standards set by the contract (or is of a lower quality) the obligee has an option between refusal and taking delivery.[1359] RUMANIAN law goes even further. Here any defect in performance is qualified as serious enough[1360] to oblige the buyer in a contract of delivery between socialised units to refuse delivery in each and every case.[1361]

Rejection is neither repudiation nor rescission and does not necessarily mean that the goods are sent back to the obligor. The rejection of performance has – at least in the GERMAN DEMOCRATIC REPUBLIC – no bearing on the obligation to take possession of the goods (*supra* s. 199).[1362] Thereby a situation similar to responsible custody is created If, upon the demand of the obligee, the obligor does not make any disposition, the obligee may store the goods at the expense of the obligor or – with his consent – send them back or keep them as a commission agent on behalf of the obligor.[1363]

The legal consequences of the refusal of delivery are (1) the obligor is in default; (2) consequently the payment does not fall due; (3) liquidated damages for the default will reach their maximum amount (*infra* s. 229) earlier than in cases where delivery is taken; (4) in RUMANIA the acceptance by the obligee of defective goods is regarded as contributory negligence (*infra* s. 237).

Thus the main purpose of the refusal to take delivery is to accelerate specific performance by placing the obligor under an increased financial strain.

203. *Defective and unfit goods and work.* – In the fields of contracts of delivery and for work between nationalised enterprises, HUNGARIAN law distinguishes between defective goods and work on the one hand and goods and work unfit for their purpose, the delivery of an *aliud* included, on the other hand. Different remedies are available in the two cases (*infra* s. 206, Table 4). Where the goods or work are unfit, the period of limitation is longer than in cases of defects in the goods or work. Where the goods are unfit, the obligee may withhold payment, whereas in cases of defective goods he is entitled to withhold 20 per cent of the price only.

204. *Gewährleistung and Garantie.*[1364] – Traditionally *Gewährleistung* is the quasi-absolute statutory liability for defects in onerous contracts and *Garantie* is a contractual clause to the same effect. This is the line of distinction in the economic law of the GERMAN DEMOCRATIC REPUBLIC and the basic theoretical approach in POLAND[1365] supported by CC art. 556 and 571. This delimi-

[1357] In HUNGARY, for instance, where within the sphere of the nationalised economy a construction work is unfit for its purpose, the obligee has a right to rescind the contract but the *obligor* may offer to rebuild. The obligee has no right to demand this (GCB § 31). On the other hand, in POLAND, the GCB art. 33 par. 1 no. 3 provides that the construction work must be done again.

[1358] GDR: Contract Law (Law on the Contract System in the Socialist Economy (*Gesetz über das Vertragssystem in der sozialistischen Wirtschaft – Vertragsgesetz* –) of 25 Feb. 1965, GBl. I 107) § 90 and 101; see Lehrmaterial 2, 92 and 7, 60-62 (*Abnahmeverweigerung*); SOVIET UNION: RSFSR CC art. 261; CP 61, 62, CG 62-66.

[1359] *Kleĭn and Petrov* CP 66, CG 67 no. 2.

[1360] Law no. 71/1969 on Economic Contracts (*Legea no. 71 privind contractelor economice*), B.O. no. 154 of 29 Dec. 1969, art. 14, and Law no. 2/1970 on the Assurance and Control of Goods (*Legea no. 2 privind asigurarea şi controlul calităţii produselor*), B.O. no. 28 of 28 March 1970, art. 22, 39 and 40.

[1361] *Sterescu a.o.* 38-39.

[1362] GDR: Contract Law (*supra* n. 1358) § 90 par. 3 and *Spitzner and Panzer* § 90 no. 2.2.

[1363] GDR: Contract Law (*supra* n. 1358) § 90 par. 4.

[1364] See *Harmathy and Lontai*, Discussion sur quelques questions d'importance de la réglementation relative à l'exécution défectueuse des contrats: Act. Jur.Hung. 10 (1968) 349-357; *Kemenes*, A jótállási rendszer néhány időszerü elvi kérdése: J.K. 1973 no. 2, 64-73.

[1365] For instance, *Madey* 70 ss.; *Czachórski* 448. In HUNGARY, on the other hand, it has been held by the

tation is, however, no longer accurate because a *Garantie* is now frequently imposed by legal regulations. This is particularly so where durable goods – especially machinery in the braod sense – are sold by state enterprises or co-operatives to citizens.

Another frequently alleged difference is that in contracts of sale and for work *Gewährleistung* requires that the goods or work should be free of defects at the moment of taking delivery whereas *Garantie* requires that they should remain free of defects during a given period of time. This, however, is only half the story. In both cases the defect must originate from factors present before delivery and in both cases the goods or work must be free of defects during a given period.

A third possible difference is the burden of proof. Some legal systems place it upon the obligee in cases of *Gewährleistung* and upon the obligor in cases of *Garantie*. But many writers doubt whether this difference is reasonable. Moreover, the burden of proof has only slight importance in Socialist laws where the judge or state arbitrator is obliged to take an initiative, if necessary, to ascertain facts not brought before the tribunal by the parties.[1366]

A fourth difference – at least in HUNGARIAN law – is that *Garantie* may apply to all categories of breach (CC § 248) whereas *Gewährleistung* applies only to defective performance. Nevertheless *Garantie* is hardly ever used outside the sphere of defective performance.

The real difference between the two seems to lie in the fact that the rights flowing from *Garantie* differ in many respects from those arising from *Gewährleistung*, both in respect of their variations and of their enforcement. In principle, *Garantie* should place the obligee in a better position than *Gewährleistung;* but this is not always the case. In POLAND, for instance, the law is almost invariably criticized on the grounds that sometimes *Garantie* is less favourable to the obligee than *Gewährleistung*.[1367] Very frequently *Garantie* offers in certain respects more, and in others less, favourable rights to the obligee than does *Gewährleistung*. The basic difference is that, on the one hand, *Garantie* permits a longer period of time and facilitates the enforcement of the claim and, on the other hand, it restricts the options available to the obligee under the rules on *Gewährleistung* (invariably awarding repair, but ordering replacement and rescission in special circumstances only and the reduction of price very rarely). To balance the advantages and disadvantages, HUNGARIAN law permits a choice between *Gewährleistung* and *Garantie*.[1368]

The economic law of the GERMAN DEMOCRATIC REPUBLIC has departed from the originally very "German" notions of *Gewährleistung* and *Garantie*. The former was replaced by *Garantie*, a variant of the old *Gewährleistung* and regulated by the mandatory rules of Contract Law § 41-43; and the old *Garantie* by the so-called *Zusatzgarantie* (additional guaranty), a contractual clause whereby the obligor remains liable for defects for an additional period (§ 44). During this additional period defects are no longer covered by the *Garantie* and the rights of the obligee can be restricted by the contract.[1369]

Thus *Garantie* and *Zusatzgarantie* relate to successive periods of time. *Gewährleistung* and *Garantie*, in the original sense, run at least in part concurrently; the obligee either has an option of invoking *Gewährleistung* or *Garantie* until the term of *Gewährleistung* expires, or of being content with the *Garantie* although the term of *Gewährleistung* has not yet expired.

In the SOVIET UNION there is no special regulation for the *Garantie*. Instead RSFSR CC art. 283 par. 2-3 provide that where durable goods are involved or the goods are handed over for preservation, compulsory standards or technical conditions as well as a contractual stipulation may prescribe a longer term for a demand for repair or replacement than is provided by the general rules on defective performance.

Supreme Court that a contractual clause which stipulates a longer term than provided by the law for rejecting defective goods does not create an obligation of *Garantie* but remains within the field of *Gewährleistung* (Opinion no. 50/1973 of the Conference of the Presiding Judges, S.Ct. Economic Branch, B.H. 1973, 630). GDR: see Lehrmaterial 7, 57; *Such* 350, 407.

[1366] The second and third difference can be observed in § 28 and 34 of the GCD of the CMEA (critically: *Szász* 257-258).

[1367] See, for instance, *Madey* 71-72; *Czachórski* 449, 451; *Ohanowicz and Górski* 225; *Soltysinski*, Odpowiedzialnosc producenta wobec konsument za szkody wyrzadzone wprowadzeniem do obruto rzeczy z wadami: Studia Cywilistyczne 1969 no. 15, 162 ss.; communication of *Stepniak*.

[1368] S.Ct. XXX.P.E.D., Polgári Elvi Határozatok (Budapest 1969) 110; Ministerial Decree 4/1969 BiM-KGM-KipM-KkM-NIM of 30 March on the compulsory minimum limit of *Garantie* for certain durable consumption goods (*Egyes tartós fogyasztási cikkek jótállásának legkisebb kötelező mértékéről*), M.K. no. 24/1969, §2 par. 2; in the sphere of the nationalised economy: Opinion no. 30/1973 of the Conference of the Presiding Judges, S.Ct. Economic Branch, B.H. 1973, 540.

[1369] Lehrmaterial 7, 53-57.

205. *Spheres of economy and contract types.* – The respective spheres of nationalised economy and of citizens are governed by the same principles and, to a very great extent, by the same or similar rules; except that in the first group "contractual discipline" is much more emphasised. Differences can also be found in the different types of contracts, such as contracts of sale (between citizens), contracts of delivery (sales between nationalised units), and contracts for work, of construction, or for technical and financial planning of construction projects (in both spheres of the economy).

The remedy of specific performance in cases of defective performance is weakest in the field of sales. In SOVIET law[1370] the buyer is *always* entitled to opt for rescission; the principle of specific performance does not apply. In POLAND the same rule applies both for contracts of sale and of delivery,[1371] except that the seller can avoid rescission by offering replacement or repair; specific performance depends in these cases on the seller's option. In addition, where specific goods produced by the seller are sold the seller may rescind the contract. This also applies to a contract of delivery where the buyer, having originally opted for repair has, after a *Nachfrist*, chosen to rescind.[1372] Under HUNGARIAN law (CC § 305) in all cases – including where the parties to the contract are citizens – and in SOVIET and POLISH law, in all cases other than those mentioned above, rescission depends upon further special conditions (*infra* s. 212).

The remedy of specific performance is maintained, though weakened, by the fact that in all contract types mentioned above both within and outside the sphere of the nationalised economy the obligee may also opt for a ***reduction of the price*** (*quanti minoris*). This, in essence, combines specific performance and the restoration of the balance of performance and counter-performance.

206. *Variants.* – In the following tables some variants are presented in respect of the contract-types mentioned in the preceding section.

*Table 1: Contract of **Sale** (citizen(s) involved)*

SOVIET UNION RSFSR CC art. 246	POLAND CC art. 560–561	HUNGARY, generic goods CC § 305
Replacement (generic goods) or *Reduction of price* or *Repair* by obligor or at his costs	*Replacement* or *Reduction of price* or *Repair* if unsuccessful during an additional term (*Nachfrist*): rescission; seller may refuse to repair if it involves high costs	*Replacement* or *Reduction of price* or *Repair* obligee may repair himself or have it repaired by a third person; obligor may offer replacement instead of reduction of price or repair
or *Rescission*	or *Rescission* seller may offer repair or replacement instead	*Rescission* in special circumstances only

Table 2: Contract for Work (citizen(s) involved)

SOVIET UNION RSFSR CC art. 364	POLAND CC art. 636	CZECHOSLOVAKIA CC § 273
Repair or *Costs of self-repair* if so provided by contract	*Repair* if unsuccessful during an additional term: rescission;	*Repair*
or	if not possible in due time·	if not possible within a fixed time:
Reduction of price	*Reduction of price* if defect not substantial	*Reduction of price* if defect not substantial
Rescission under special conditions only	*Rescission* under special conditions only	*Rescission* under special conditions only

For HUNGARY see Table 1 (CC § 305)

[1370] RSFSR CC art. 246.
[1371] CC art. 560, 612.
[1372] CC art. 561, GCD 52.5.

Table 3: The Sphere of the Nationalised Economy

GDR: all contracts in the field of production, trading and technical development (*Leistungsverträge*): Contract Law § 91-93	POLAND: contracts for technical and financial planning of construction projects, building contracts (contracts of delivery: as in sale between citizens)
Repair	*Repair*
if agreed upon	if no excessive costs involved (GCP 13.1, GCB 33.3)
otherwise	or – where possible –
Repair by the obligee	*Repair by the obligee* (GCB 33.4)
if economically warranted or obligor has failed to repair or replace within an additional term	or
	Cover purchase (GCD 52.1-3)
or	or
Replacement	*Remaking* if *repair* impossible
Refusal to accept performance (*supra* s. 202)	
or	or
Reduction of price	*Reduction of price* (GCP 13, GCB 33)
Rescission	*Rescission*
if any other remedy fails	under special conditions

Table 4: Nationalised Economy – HUNGARY

Contracts of delivery and for work (DecrCD § 40, DecrCW[1373] § 23-24)	Building contracts (GCB § 29-31)	Contracts for technical and financial planning of construction projects (GCP § 13)
1. *Defects:*	1. *Defects* (if substantial):	1. *Defects:*
Repair or	*Repair* if no excessive cost involved; if not possible (in time) but work not otherwise unfit:	*Repair* if defect not substantial:
Reduction of price	*Reduction of price*	*Reduction of price*
Contracts of delivery: *Repair by the obligee* if defect not substantial – or if obligor has failed to repair in time; however: the obligor may offer replacement instead of repair or reduction of price[1374]		
Contracts for work: *Repair by the obligee* if the obligor is not ready to repair (in time); however: the obligor may remake instead of repair or reduce the price, unless this would cause such a delay that the obligee would lose his interest in the contract		
2. *Unfitness:*	2. *Unfitness:*	2. *Unfitness:*
Replacement (contracts of delivery) *Remaking* (contracts for work) or		*Remaking*
Rescission under special conditions	*Rescission* but: the obligor may offer to rebuild	

[1373] Government Decree 44/1967 Korm. of 5 Nov. on Contracts for Work Between Enterprises (DecrCW) (*A vállalatok vállalkozási szerződéseiről*), M.K. no. 78/1967 (Engl.transl.: Hung.L.Rev. 1969 no. 1, 65; French transl.: Rev.dr.hongr. 1969 no. 1, 69).

[1374] The obligee may refuse this offer if replacement would prejudice his interests (Opinion no. 12, S.Ct. Economic Branch, B.H. 1973, 453).

SOVIET law is very detailed in this field. For instance, it has special rules for cases where performance does not conform to the compulsory technical standards or technical conditions,[1375] for cases where the defect can be eliminated at the place where the goods are,[1376] where the quality of the goods does not meet the requirements of the contract or of the certificate of quality,[1377] where delivery is incomplete,[1378] for defective technical constructions in the experimental stage or in cases of special, individually manufactured machinery (CP 65), where quality falls into a much lower class of specifications than required,[1379] and so on.

In YUGOSLAVIA, in the field of commercial sales the principle of specific performance – in the present YUGOSLAVIAN law – can always be defeated by rescission. The General Usages of Trade of 1954[1380] give the buyer the following rights in cases of defective performance:

(1) Rejection of the goods and rescission;

(2) rejection of the goods and specific performance (under no. 155 the buyer is not entitled to reject the goods if: he has made any disposition of the goods in his own name and for his own account, or the difference in quality of the goods does not exceed the usual tolerance limits unless the clause "without tolerance" or a similar clause appears in the contract);

(3) reduction of the price proportionate to the decrease of the value of the goods delivered;

(4) repair within a reasonable time where repair is possible.

These remedies are rather traditional and differ much from the remedies open to the obligee in the field of the nationalised economy in the other Socialist countries. The main reasons for these differences are briefly stated above (s. 195).

Table 5: GCD of the CMEA

<table>
<tr><th>Gewährleistung, § 75 par. 2–7</th><th>Garantie, § 31</th></tr>
<tr><td colspan="2">Elimination of the defect –
the buyer may choose between
Repair or Replacement</td></tr>
<tr><td>or</td><td>or</td></tr>
<tr><td>Reduction of the price</td><td>Reduction of the price</td></tr>
<tr><td></td><td>the seller may choose between:
Repair
Replacement
Reduction of the price;
if elimination of the defect is not accomplished in due time, the buyer may demand
Reduction of the price</td></tr>
<tr><td colspan="2">Rescission, provided that:
the parties are entitled to rescind by a bilateral international agreement or by the contract and, unless otherwise stipulated by the agreement or the contract, the foreign trade arbitration panel is satisfied that the seller cannot eliminate the defect by repair or replacement and the buyer – despite the reduction of price – cannot use the defective goods for the purposes of the contract (see also infra s. 214).</td></tr>
</table>

207. *Summary.* – The foregoing may be summarised (except for YUGOSLAVIA) as follows:

(1) The rules are much more detailed and differentiated for the nationalised economy than in other sectors;

(2) in the nationalised economy the obligee's options between various remedies are much more restricted than outside this sphere; for instance, in HUNGARY the nationalised units have a very restricted possibility to choose between remedies (in cases of defective goods and services they may not opt for a reduction of price); and the option of the obligee may be eliminated by the obligor in many cases,[1381] *etc.*;

(3) the principle of specific performance has a much greater impact in the nationalised economy than in other sectors.

[1375] CP 61, CG 62.
[1376] CP 62, CG 63.
[1377] CP 63, CG 64.
[1378] CP 64, CG 66.
[1379] CP 66, CG 67.
[1380] See General Usages no. 154.
[1381] GCD of the CMEA and other laws.

C. RESCISSION, TERMINATION

208. *The concepts.* – *Rescission* is a unilateral declaration[1382] whereby the contract is terminated *ab initio;* the contract is treated as if it had never been concluded. Each party in consequence is obliged to return what it has received under the rescinded contract (*restitutio in integrum*). If performance cannot be reversed – particularly in cases where the obligee is entitled to possess the property of a third party (for instance lease) or where the obligor is under a legal obligation independent of the contract to do something for a third party (for instance agency), rescission is not available.

In such cases rescission is replaced by unilateral *termination by notice.* Termination by notice puts an end to the contract *ex nunc,* at the moment when the notice becomes effective; however, the balance of performance and counter-performance must be restored, if necessary. In the following discussion, rescission includes termination by notice.

Rescission as a remedy is, in general, an *ultima ratio:* it operates where the principle of specific performance is inappropriate (*supra* B).

i. *Default of the Obligor*

209. *Cases of rescission.* – Where the obligor is in default, there are, in the various Socialist laws, four situations in which the obligee may rescind the contract. In addition the GCD of the CMEA permit rescission in one further instance.

(1) The parties have stipulated a "fixed term" in their contract – *i.e.,* they expressly state that the obligee is not to be bound to take delivery after the time of performance has expired[1383] (the words used are immaterial). The "fixed term" does not, however, oblige the obligee to rescind the contract: it only empowers him to do so; he may nevertheless demand performance after the expiration of the "fixed term";[1384]

(2) it is evident that the time of performance is of the essence of the contract[1385] (*e.g.,* where a bus is hired for a Sunday excursion);

(3) the obligee can prove that due to the default performance is no longer meaningful;[1386]

(4) in any other case after the expiration of an additional term (*Nachfrist*) for performance fixed by the obligee.[1387] The expiration of the extended period terminates the contract; the obligee may nevertheless continue to demand performance;

(5) the GCD of the CMEA for the reasons briefly stated above (s. 190) are, in general, hostile to rescission. Nevertheless they grant rescission in addition to cases within no. (1), where default becomes prolonged. Either party may rescind the contract

(a) where an unavoidable circumstance (*vis major*) impedes performance and this lasts for five or eight months according to whether performance is due within twelve months after the conclusion of the contract or thereafter;

(b) in other cases where default continues for more than four or six months.[1388]

210. *Cover.* – A cover purchase necessarily involves rescission. As a cover purchase usually requires a free market, it is not typical for Socialist countries, except YUGOSLAVIA, where it has substantial importance. In countries other than YUGOSLAVIA there are, however, certain goods in which there is such a market; particularly since the economic reforms cover purchases occasionally occur. The POLISH CC art. 153 expressly provides for cover purchase as a remedy where the obligor fails to deliver generic goods.[1389]

This shift in the attitude of Socialist countries, however, should not be overemphasised. Firstly, cover purchases have not at all become an everyday occurrence. Secondly, the fact that nothing fundamental has changed in this field can be seen in the grounds given by the HUNGARIAN Supreme Court in admitting cover purchases for contracts of delivery. The court stated that the main obligation of state enterprises is to meet the social demands. It is therefore not proper that an enterprise should acquiesce in the fact that the obligor

[1382] In RUMANIA due to the FRENCH influence in the past, rescission may only be granted by a court (CC art. 1021).

[1383] HUNGARY: CC § 300 par. 2; GDR: Contract Law (*supra* n. 1358) § 45 par. 3; CZECHOSLOVAKIA: CC § 86; POLAND: CC art. 492 (for reciprocal contracts); YUGOSLAVIA: *Goldštájn* 185; CMEA GCD § 77, 86.

[1384] CZECHOSLOVAK CC § 140; CMEA GCD § 86 par. 2.

[1385] HUNGARY: CC § 300 par. 2.

[1386] BULGARIA: CO art. 79; CZECHOSLOVAKIA: CC § 86, ICC § 235-238; HUNGARY: CC § 300 par. 1; POLAND: CC art. 477 par. 2; SOVIET UNION: RSFSR CC art. 225 (in the field of the nationalised economy if permitted by the law or stipulated by the contract). With slightly different wording: GDR: Contract Law (*supra* n. 1358) § 98 par. 1.

[1387] CZECHOSLOVAKIA: CC § 85 par. 1, EC § 139 (except goods for export or defense); HUNGARY: CC § 300 par. 2; POLAND CC art. 491 par. 1 for reciprocal contracts; YUGOSLAVIA: *Goldštájn* 180.

[1388] CMEA GCD § 70 and 85 par. 1.

[1389] In the nationalised sphere of the economy an additional term is required before a cover purchase (GCD 52). In YUGOSLAVIA notification suffices (*Goldštájn* 181).

is in breach of performance since this would frustrate the aim of the contract. One must therefore expect the enterprise to ensure that the social demand is met, if possible and economically warranted,[1390] through another seller (see also *infra* s. 235).

ii. *Default of the Obligee*

211. *The main rules.* – By virtue of the principle of specific performance the obligor remains obliged to perform the contract until the obligee declares himself ready to take delivery (*supra* s. 199). This situation, however, cannot last forever. The law, therefore, not only puts pressure on the obligee to perform, but also opens the way for the obligor to terminate the contract.

On the one hand, the obligee is induced to accept the obligor's tender of performance since otherwise he will have to pay interest upon a sum of money due by him; and, in the sphere of the nationalised economy, he will also become liable to pay liquidated damages.

On the other hand, the contract can be terminated by the obligor in the following circumstances:

(1) the obligor who has become a "responsible custodian" (*supra* s. 199) may sell or consume the goods where, after demand, the obligee fails to remove them within a reasonable time or where disproportionate difficulties arise in caring for the goods or meeting incidental expenses;[1391]

(2) the obligor may rescind a bilateral contract after expiration of an additional term for performance;[1392]

(3) in POLAND the obligor is entitled to sell the goods after expiration of an additional term; the same is true in the SOVIET UNION for contracts for work where the customer fails to collect the goods for six months and after two notices (*e.g.*, where things are left at the dry-cleaner, in the shoe-repair shop, *etc.*).[1393] In other countries, including HUNGARY, general conditions and standard contract forms under government control serve to take care of such situations.

iii. *Defective (Deficient, Incomplete) Performance*

212. *Rescission as a last resort.* – Rescission is the *ultima ratio* coming into play where it has become impossible to achieve an economically warranted solution by any other means, especially by specific performance. To modify a WESTERN expression: a "very fundamental" breach is needed in such cases, although the wording of some pertinent rules seems to indicate that a "fundamental" breach suffices. The commentary on the Contract Law in the GERMAN DEMOCRATIC REPUBLIC emphasises that rescission in cases of defective performance amounts to a breakdown of the principle of specific performance. It can be resorted to only when the purpose of performance is defeated and only in so far as this purpose can no longer be pursued. Since the products lose their value, economic interests have to be kept in mind in deciding upon rescission. An example from the practice of the Contract Court of the GERMAN DEMOCRATIC REPUBLIC is defects rendering impossible the satisfaction of the needs of the population.[1394]

The conditions for the granting of rescission are expressed variously in the relevant legal rules, *e.g.*,

(1) substantial defect and impossibility of repair or replacement (permanently or at the material time);[1395]

(2) impossibility of repair or replacement (permanently or at the material time) performance being no longer useful even with a price reduction; if part only of the performance is thus affected, rescission is granted in part only;[1396]

(3) substantial, repeated or numerous defects;[1397]

(4) unfitness for the proper purpose, the obligee not being interested in replacement or remaking.[1398]

In POLAND, a contract for technical and financial planning of a construction project or building within the nationalised economy may be rescinded by the obligee on the ground of defects only where economically justifiable reasons exist.[1399]

[1390] Opinion no. 64/1973 of the Presiding Judges, S.Ct. Economic Branch, B.H. 1973, 700.

[1391] HUNGARY: CC § 197 par. 1; the rule does not apply to goods in social property and in the hands of a Socialist organization. POLAND: CC art. 551 par. 2 without this restriction.

[1392] POLISH CC art. 491, stated also in art. 640 (contracts for work).

[1393] POLAND: CC art. 551 par. 1; SOVIET UNION: RSFSR CC art. 366.

[1394] *Spitzner and Panzer* no. 1 and 2.1 § 93; Central Contract Court 14 March 1959, VS 1959, 285; District Contract Court Leipzig 16 Feb. 1961, VS 1962, 31.

[1395] POLAND: CC art. 636.

[1396] GDR: Contract Law (*supra* n. 1358) § 93 par. 1.

[1397] CZECHOSLOVAKIA: CC § 273 in cases where citizens buy from socialised units of trade.

[1398] HUNGARY: DecrCD (*supra* n. 1350) § 40 par. 4-5, DecrCW (*supra* n. 1373) § 24.

[1399] GCP 23.1 GCB 51.1.

This rule is stated as follows: the plan is not fit for erecting a building (GCP 13.1) or a defect of the building cannot be repaired and renders it useless for its purpose (GCB 35.1.2).

213. *Reduction to default.* – In the previous section we have briefly touched upon the fact that repair or replacement should be effected within the proper time. A fusion of the idea of default with that of defective performance may be helpful at this point: default in repairing or replacing a defective performance may lead to rescission.

Defective performance may give rise to default in cases where the obligor is under an obligation to repair the defects or replace the defective goods. This may take a considerable time after the expiration of the term of performance, during which time the obligor is in default; and it is not too difficult to avoid a contract where the obligor is in default (*supra* s. 211). After all, from the economic point of view it is immaterial whether default is caused by defective performance or by some other circumstance.

Consequently where the time taken for eliminating a defect becomes a ground for rescission or termination through default, the contract can be rescinded (this is called "reduction to default"). Sometimes the provisions as to rescission for defective performance contain such a rule.[1400]

In other cases of reduction to default the obligee may rescind the contract if the defect is not eliminated within the period of time for repair or replacement set by the obligee.[1401] Here we are faced with a special kind of additional term during which the obligor is bound to repair or replace the goods instead of effecting a simple delivery as in other cases of an additional term.

Reduction to default may be brought about in cases of refusal to accept performance (*Abnahmeverweigerung*) (*supra* s. 202); if, after the goods have been rejected, the obligor does not perform within the time agreed upon by the parties he is in default.[1402]

A reduction to default is not, however, always possible. Where the obligor is obliged by the compulsory rules of the national economic plan to deliver, a reduction to default is not permissible. In such cases rescission remains possible only in genuine cases of serious defects (*supra* s. 212); the contract may be terminated for supervening impossibility (*infra* s. 216) and the obligor is compensated by liquidated damages which may here have an additional punitive character (*infra* s. 231).

214. *The CMEA General Conditions of Delivery.* – In cases of defective performance, rescission serves as an *ultima ratio* where the performance is backed by a *Garantie.*[1403] In other cases, rescission is expressly permitted by the GCD of the CMEA where a provision to this effect is contained in a bilateral international agreement or the contract between the parties (*supra* s. 206 Table 5). Provision for rescission is enough; its conditions will be established by the arbitration tribunal.[1404]

Does this mean that the parties may not rescind the contract on account of defective performance in the absence of such an agreement or contract? An argument *e contrario* would support such a contention. On the other hand, it might be argued that the GCD are silent on this question and, therefore, the door is open for an analogy or for the application of the seller's law under § 110 (see *infra* (2)).

(1) It has already been mentioned that a default of four or six, or five or eight months, as the case may be, creates the possibility of rescission (*supra* s. 209 *sub* (5)). This rule might be applied by way of analogy where the elimination of defects takes that long (reduction to default, *supra* s. 213). This suggestion is supported by the fact that in both cases liquidated damages become due according to § 83 dealing with liquidated damages for default. On the other hand, *Szász* (p. 248) points out that the periods of time mentioned above start to run at different times for the two categories in question – in cases of default, from the time of performance, in cases of defective performance, from the time when notice is given in respect of the defect. On this ground he denies the possibility of an analogy. Nevertheless, it is possible to argue that a partial analogy may be

1400 For instance, rescission instead of replacement or repair is granted also when a substantial defect cannot be eliminated "in time" (HUNGARY: CC § 305 par. 1 *lit.*d, DecrCW (*supra* n. 1373) § 24; POLAND: CC art. 367 par. 2, contracts for work). The GCD of the CMEA in § 75 par. 4 provide that in cases of repair and replacement the obligor is bound to pay the same liquidated damages as in cases of default (*Szász* 248 doubts that this is a case of reduction to default, – see also next section).

1401 For instance, see POLAND: CC art. 636, 637 par. 1 (contracts for work), GCD 52.5. CZECHOSLOVAKIA: ICC § 305 (contracts of delivery).

1402 GDR: Contract Law (*supra* n. 1358) § 90 par. 2.

1403 CMEA GCD § 31 par. 8; *Kanda* 578.

1404 According to *Kanda* 578 this is a case where the contract is rescinded by the arbitration tribunal and not by the parties. The writer is inclined to disagree with this view.

admitted where some only of the facts in the two categories coincide, while others may be different.

(2) GCD § 110 provides that, in the event of gaps in the GCD, the law of the seller applies. If the GCD are silent on rescission in cases of defective performance, the contract can, under certain circumstances, be rescinded where the seller is a BULGARIAN, HUNGARIAN, POLISH or SOVIET enterprise; and the arbitration tribunal may rescind the contract where the seller is from RUMANIA. The question, therefore, is whether the GCD are silent on the subject of rescission. The GCD provide that rescission may be stipulated by an international agreement or by a contract between the parties but they do not state that these are the only ways of creating the possibility for rescission. If the provision is understood as excluding other possibilities of rescission then there is no gap in the GCD in this respect and § 110 cannot apply. If, however, this is not so, § 110 will apply and new ways are open for rescission. This is an open point; arbitration tribunals in different Socialist countries hold different views.[1405]

215. *Expenses.* – The expenses intimately connected with the exercise of the rights flowing from *Gewährleistung* or *Garantie* (*e.g.* loading or unloading of goods, transport to and from the place where repair takes place, storage, *etc.*) must be borne by the obligor irrespective of fault[1406] although in cases of fault expenses are usually treated as elements of damages.

iv. *Supervening Impossibility*

216. *Definitive impossibility.* – Definitive supervening impossibility puts an end to the contract.[1407] The contract may also be terminated in those rare cases where, for reasons of supervening unforeseeable events, performance would cause an extraordinary hardship (economic impossibility[1408] or impossibility in connection with the interests of a party).[1409] In such cases, performance, although not physically or legally impossible, cannot reasonably be insisted upon, having regard to the new situation, to the interest of the parties, to the national economy as a whole, and to the possible consequences of the performance in the given situation. By the termination of the contract, the parties share the consequences of supervening, burdensome circumstances and the obligor is relieved from bearing exclusively all unforeseeable, extraordinary and heavy risks.

There is one contract-type where this kind of impossibility is fairly frequently encountered but does not always lead to the termination of the contract. In contracts of maintenance, where, owing to the conduct or the circumstances of one (or both) parties, personal maintenance in the household of the obligor has become impossible, the court may convert the contract into a life-annuity contract instead of terminating it.[1410]

In other cases of impossibility, the court will not modify the terms of the contract; termination seems to be the only reaction to impossibility. This solution permits the more drastic and bars the less drastic measures, particularly in legal systems which are keen on specific performance. This result is usually justified by the consideration that it would go beyond the functions of the courts to alter the terms agreed upon by the parties. This principle does not apply in the field of plan-contracts or economic contracts (*supra* ch. 6 subch. I) between socialised units of the economy as in this field the national economic plan furnishes the foundation for the agreement between the parties. Therefore, state arbitration may modify the terms of a plan-contract to secure the fulfilment of the plan; modification is also permitted where performance has become impossible. Further, the principle is weakened in HUNGARY by the provision that the court may modify a contract where it violates some substantial lawful interest of one of the parties in consequence of any circumstance which has occurred and which affects the permanent relationship between the parties subsequent to their making the contract (CC § 241). Although this rule is not connected either with impossibility or with a breach of contract, the situation described in this rule comes very close to "economic impossibility" and could also be – but is not for the time being – applied in such cases.

217. *Temporary impossibility.* – Where performance becomes impossible due to a temporary circumstance only, the contract remains in force

[1405] *Szász* 248-249; *Engelmann, Kemper a.o.* 182-183, who state that a majority of arbitration tribunals do not permit rescission.

[1406] GDR: Contract Law (*supra* n. 1358) § 94 par. 1 (incidental claims); CZECHOSLOVAKIA: CC § 402 (necessary costs and expenses); HUNGARY: in cases of *Garantie* under Decree 4/1969 (*supra* n. 1368) § 2 par. 1.

[1407] HUNGARY: CC § 312; POLAND: CC art. 475 par. 2.

[1408] SOVIET UNION, communication of *Faĭnshteĭn*; POLAND: *Ohanowicz and Górski* 195; *Czachórski* 197 ss.

[1409] HUNGARY: *Eörsi*, Consequences no. 23.3.

[1410] HUNGARY: CC § 589 par. 2; POLAND: CC art. 913.

but the parties are temporarily relieved from the duty to perform. This situation may also undergo a "reduction to default" (*supra* s. 213); if, due to the duration of the impeding factor, a party ceases to be interested in the performance, he may then terminate or modify the contract.[1411]

218. *Salvage and subrogation.* – It may happen that as a result of supervening impossibility, a remainder (*residuum*) is left (the hide of an animal, the ruins of the burnt down house). It is also possible that the obligor receives compensation for the destruction of the object of performance (*surrogatum*), such as insurance benefits or compensation from a tortfeasor. In such cases the obligee may claim the surrender of the remainder or other benefits, but remains liable for the proportionate part of his counterperformance.[1412]

219. *Repudiation.* – Repudiation by the obligor is treated in the same way as impossibility. In HUNGARY, however, the obligee may choose between the remedies for default and those for supervening impossibility (CC § 337). This means that he is free either to claim performance (the right granted in cases of default), or to rescind the contract without proving that his interest has ceased (the right resulting from impossibility).

v. *Restitutio in integrum*

220. *Restitution is possible.* – Rescission cancels the contract *ab initio:* it is treated as if it had never been concluded. Where, however, the parties have performed the contract, in part or *in toto*, the delivered goods must be returned *in specie*[1413] and if this is no longer possible, then in value.[1414] This obligation is not dependent on fault. Some laws provide that such restitution is governed by the rules on unjust enrichment.[1415] This, however, is not true for HUNGARY where different rules apply to restitution of an unjust enrichment and to cases of rescission.[1416]

221. *Restitution is impossible.* – HUNGARIAN law takes into account cases where performance is impossible *ab initio.* This happens frequently where a party is seemingly entitled under an alleged contract of lease to the use of property of the other party and pays rent for such use, or where a party is legally obliged to act on behalf of the other party (agency) but receives benefits for such act. Since restitution of what has already been done is impossible, in such cases rescission is replaced by the termination of the contract *ex nunc.* Consequently, restitution *in integrum* does not take place, but the balances of performance and counter-performance, if any, are returned.[1417]

222. *Expenses.* – The parties may have incurred expenses connected with the conclusion of the rescinded contract or with later developments (*e.g.* freight charges for delivery, storage, the taking of delivery, expenses of restitution, *etc.*). Such expenses are not reimbursed by the other party, at least not in the absence of fault.

POLISH law, however, provides a apecial rule for sales. Where the buyer on the ground of defective performance rescinds the contract or demands reduction of the price, he may demand his expenses (negative interest, *supra* s. 50) even in the absence of fault;[1418] if the seller is at fault, the buyer may even demand full damages (positive interest).

D. REMEDIES STIMULATING PERFORMANCE

i. *In General*

223. *Functions.* – The remedies treated above serve the purposes of (1) specific performance, (2) the restoration of the balance between performance and counter-performance (through reduction of the price) or (3) the termination of the contractual relations. We now turn to remedies whose main function is to induce the parties to performance but which serve, as well, to effect reparation in cases where one party has suffered loss and to facilitate government control over contractual discipline in the sphere of the nationalised economy (function of signalisation).[1419]

Remedies which perform this function are: liquidated damages, damages, and price-sanctions. All are designed to serve each of the three functions which are, in this context, inseparable. For instance, if damages are paid, the party in breach is deterred from committing further breaches; the

[1411] SOVIET UNION, communication of *Faĭnshteĭn.*

[1412] HUNGARY: CC § 312.

[1413] GDR: Contract Law (*supra* n. 1358) § 93 par. 2; *Spitzner and Panzer* no. 2.2. § 93 states that in the sphere of the nationalised economy CC § 346 ss. find no application, not even in a complementary way.

[1414] *Ioffe* 466–467.

[1415] POLAND: CC art. 495 par. 1.

[1416] CC § 361 par. 2.

[1417] CC § 237 par. 2.

[1418] CC art. 566 par. 1.

[1419] See, *e.g.*, *Antimonov* 21–22; *Mamutov, Ovsienko and Iudin* 35: "Liability serves as an instrument for localisation of defects and information relating thereto." Signalisation must indicate the causation of damage and not only cases where damage has been caused through fault (*idem* 44–48; *contra: Malein* 42–43); see also *Kanda* 576.

other party receives reparation; and, in the sphere of the nationalised economy, the money goes compulsorily through the state-owned bank – which enjoys a monopoly in this respect – so that the controlling government organs, by looking into the bank account of the enterprises, can see how frequently and seriously contractual discipline is violated.

224. *The requirement of fault.* – Fault is, as a rule, essential for the application of most remedies in this group.

From the theoretical point of view, the fault principle is of the utmost importance. According to present Socialist legal thinking liability has – in concert with many other factors – an educative effect on society; however, liability can elicit the desired educative effect only if it depends upon fault. The most extreme view expressed is that there is no liability without fault and that therefore cases of strict liability should be excluded from the field of liability altogether.[1420] Others support the view that only liability for fault is genuine liability, the cases of strict liability constituting rare exceptions which may, in future, become more numerous.[1421] Particularly where state enterprises are involved, much hope is placed in the educative effect of liability. Here both fault and liability are in a way "collective". The acts and omissions of every member of the collective working in such an enterprise are deemed to be the acts and omissions of the enterprise itself[1422] and the shortcomings of individual members are mirrored in the fault manifesting itself in the shortcomings of organization, direction, discipline, equipment, training, and so on. This is why *Pflicke* advocates a liability system which would, above all, stimulate the workers' collective and would concentrate on the exploitation of all possibilities open to the collective.[1423] The fault concept as here utilized has not much in common with the *mens rea* of an individual and is based on the social expectations and failure to live up to those expectations.

The damages paid out by the enterprises are part of the financial liabilities of the enterprise and, as such, diminish its investment fund as well as the employees' participation fund, thereby creating a collective interest in eliminating the sources of damage.[1424]

Although an imposing majority hold these views, they are not shared by all.

For instance, *Posch* is very sceptical of the educative effect of liability of state enterprises for fault: he advocates strict liability of enterprises and fault liability for torts of citizens.[1425] On the other hand, *Such* (p. 334) is of the opinion that the fault principle must be used both where enterprises and individuals are involved; only the standards must be different in the two cases. In the SOVIET UNION, *Mamutov, Ovsienko and I͡udin* distinguish between liquidated damages and damages. Damages, in their view, are the correction of the impaired balance of the assets of the parties, which should therefore not depend on fault.[1426] Arguing with *Malein*, they maintain that the payment of damages stimulates production even in the absence of fault. On the other hand, liquidated damages should be regarded as having a punitive character and therefore should depend on the degree of fault.[1427]

Their views do not enjoy large support. Legal writers in the GERMAN DEMOCRATIC REPUBLIC maintain that the trend is to increase the objective character of liability. If this is so, it becomes increasingly difficult to extend the notion of fault and yet distinguish it from liability without fault. Probably one should renounce the notion of fault in economic law altogether.[1428]

In practice the problem is much less acute. Fault is presumed[1429] and exoneration difficult because, as we have seen, fault does not require a genuinely reproachable conduct: it is measured, by and large, against the social expectation in the given situation. This is clearly expressed in the HUNGARIAN Civil Code. There the article defining tort liability, which also applies to contractual liability, does not even mention the word "fault". This article provides that the obligor is relieved from liability if he can prove that he has been acting in such a way as might, in general, be

1420 *Malein* ch. 1 no. 2 entitled "Fault – Necessary Basis for Liability".

1421 *Matveev*, Osnovanii͡a grazhdanskopravovoĭ otvetstvennosti (Moscow 1970) 86, quoting also other authors.

1422 See this Encyclopedia vol. XI ch. 4 s. 323.

1423 *Pflicke* 1558–1559.

1424 Described in some detail by *Eörsi*, Quelques problèmes no. 3.

1425 *Posch* 1116–1122.

1426 *Mamutov, Ovsienko and I͡udin* 38–42.

1427 *Idem* 43–44.

1428 *Spitzner and Panzer*, Preliminary Remarks to Part IV where other authors are referred to.

1429 BULGARIA: CO art. 45; CZECHOSLOVAKIA: ICC § 249; HUNGARY: CC § 339 par. 1; RUMANIA: CC art. 1082, 1156; SOVIET UNION: RSFSR CC art. 222, see *Malein* 75–76; POLAND: CC art. 471 is not quite clear on this question. *Czachórski* 242 is of the opinion that fault is presumed, but see *contra: Warkałło*, Wykonywanie zobowiazan i skutki ich niewykonania według kodeksu cywilnego: PiP 1965 II 204–222 (English, French and Russian summary in Appendix).

expected in the given situation.[1430] Certain standards are applied when deciding whether fault has played a role in the breach.

These standards differ for the various branches of the law. For example, a lower standard applies in respect of citizens, a higher in respect of state enterprises;[1431] the standard is lower in the case of unqualified persons and higher in the case of professionals. In this way the domain of fortuitous events – *casus minor* – has lost its more or less clear-cut borderlines; these borderlines vary according to different categories. The highest standards are those applicable to state enterprises.

HUNGARIAN law, for instance, develops the above rule in the following manner: The party in breach "is relieved from liability if it can prove that it has been acting in performing the contract in such a way, as might, in general, be expected from a Socialist organization in the given situation. When forming a judgment as to the conduct of the party in breach, the possibilities generally available to Socialist organizations and the requirements which can be imposed on them having regard to these facts, shall serve as a starting-point".[1432] The law stresses a "general" – that is, a social – expectation in respect of "a" Socialist organization and not of "the" Socialist organization which has in fact committed the breach.

In other countries, the exoneration clause similarly centers around a social expectation that all possible means be mobilised to perform duly the contract.[1433] These standards are applied in such a way that exoneration becomes extremely difficult. In practice only an external and unavoidable circumstance is strong enough to achieve exoneration;[1434] this formula is identical with that for circumscribing liability without fault in FRENCH contract law. Thus *casus minor* tends to disappear from the sphere of the nationalised economy and liability for and liability without fault are hardly distinguishable any more.[1435] There are, however, some further cases of strict liability in various Socialist countries, particularly in the field of forwarding contracts and hotelkeepers' contracts. In these cases, exoneration is based by and large upon proof of *vis major* or contributory negligence of the other party.

225. *Instances of liability for fault.* – Reverting to liability for fault, we shall discuss some typical situations which demonstrate the full impact of this liability.[1436]

(1) Internal factors such as a breakdown of machinery or lack of man-power, materials or equipment do not constitute good defenses, unless they are the direct consequence of unavoidable

[1430] CC § 339 par. 1, made applicable by § 318 for contractual relations.

[1431] POLAND: Directive no. 2/1958 of 17 April 1958 on the Liability for Non- or Undue Performance of an Obligation (published with comments by *Buczkowski*, Glosa do uchwały nr. 2/58 Kolegium arbitrażu GKA: PiP 1958 II 225).

[1432] DecrCD (*supra* n. 1350) § 48 par. 1-2; DecrCW (*supra* n. 1373) § 21 par. 1-2.

[1433] In the GDR exoneration becomes possible according to Contract Law (*supra* n. 1358) § 82 par. 1 only where the circumstances leading to a breach could not have been avoided despite the exploitation of all possibilities created by the Socialist relations of production. The SOVIET state arbitration has ruled that the starting-point in deciding the question of fault is that in the interest of the national economy the state enterprise is bound to take all measures to assure the unconditional performance of its contractual obligations and to exploit entirely its possibilities within the planned system of the economy (Letter of Instruction of the State Arbitration of the Government of the USSR of 28 Dec. 1967 no. I-1-59: Sbornik instruktivnykh ukazanii Gosudarstvennogo Arbitrazha pri Sovete Ministrov SSSR (Moscow 1968) no. 27 p. 61).

[1434] Although contractual liability is considered to be liability for fault in POLAND, Directive no. 2/1958 (*supra* n. 1431) provides that an external fortuitous event is needed for exoneration; the party must prove unforeseeability plus that it could not prevent the breach despite the utmost care. Consequently an internal fortuitous event never exonerates.

[1435] See for POLAND: *Szwaja* 97; *Buczkowski and Nowakowski* 182. HUNGARY: *Eörsi*, Quelques problèmes no. 5; SOVIET UNION: *Gribanov*, Voprosy sovetskogo grazhdanskogo prava v praktike sud i arbitrazha (Moscow 1960) 374; *contra*: *Malein* 76. In the GDR *Spitzner and Panzer* also find it extremely difficult to discern fault liability under Contract Law (*supra* n. 1358) § 82 (liability giving rise to liquidated damages and damages) from liability without fault under Contract Law § 83 ("liability" in other cases, described *supra* B and C); their solution is that in the first case the impediment of performance must be of such a nature that it becomes impossible for the particular enterprise in question to eliminate it, whereas in the second case it must be extraordinary to such an extent that its elimination should be impossible not only for the party involved but for *any* state enterprise (§ 83 no. 2.2). In other countries, however, liability for fault includes cases where it is not proved that it was impossible for *any* state enterprise in the same situation as the party in breach to eliminate such impediments (*supra* in this section). Under such circumstances *casus minor* can only survive in a marginal sense.

[1436] As to liability for third persons see *supra* ch. 15.

external events.[1437] A better management or organization might have eliminated their adverse effect on the performance of the contract. For instance, neither an epidemic nor the call of workers to military service can the defendant exonerate himself on the ground that it was impossible to recruit a sufficient number of employees.[1438] In a very wide range of cases, these circumstances, and others of a similar character, are not accepted as excuses since they reveal a defect in the organization, even if the specific kind of defect or the organizational level at which it occurred is not known.[1439] A COMMON LAWYER would express this as *res ipsa loquitur*.

(2) In a planned economy the parties to the contract may receive instructions from superior state agencies such as ministries. Such instructions may affect contracts already concluded. The superior organ, for some economico-political reason, may on occasion even prohibit the performance of a contract or of a group of contracts in order to secure, for instance, the satisfaction of the needs of the population; thus contracts between manufacturers and export-import enterprises may be cancelled. If such instructions emanate from an organ which is the superior organ of both contracting parties – for instance, the government – this is an act of God (or: state) or a supervening legal impossibility, and no liability arises. If, however, the instruction is issued or other measure taken – for instance modification of the allocation of raw materials – by an organ superior to the obligor only, the obligor is not relieved from performing the contract. If he fails to perform, the instruction or measure of the superior organ will not be a good defence[1440] even where the enterprise is bound to obey the instructions and could not avoid the breach of contract. This may seem surprising as the enterprise is a legal person separate from the state organs of economic management and, therefore arguably not liable for damage caused by a distinct body of economic management acting in the exercise of public power. In fact, however, unless otherwise provided, this rule applies exclusively within national boundaries where the entire economy constitutes a closed system and all participants manage the property of one person, *viz.* the state. In these circumstances, the rule serves the purpose of allocating the loss consequent upon a breach to that branch of the state-owned economic system in which the cause of the breach arises, rather than permitting it to affect other branches. Thus the enterprise in breach must pay liquidated damages and any additional damages; the enterprise frequently obtains indemnity from the organ which has caused the breach through its instruction or action.[1441] In this way the superior organ is restrained from needlessly interfering with contracts already concluded. It must be added, however, that these rules apply only where the instructions or measures affect specific and already concluded contracts rather than the economic activity of the enterprise as a whole. The rules do not apply, for instance, where the superior organ refuses to accept the export plan of the enterprise.[1442]

226. *Council for Mutual Economic Assistance.* – The GCD of the CMEA open with a very stringent provision – "only" *vis major* exonerates.[1443] The obligor must promptly inform the other party about the circumstances and possible consequences of the event and these circumstances must be certified by the Chamber of Commerce in the obligor's country (§ 69). No sanctions are attached to the violation of these obligations although the practice of the arbitration tribunals is not uniform in this respect. In HUNGARY and RUMANIA the arbitration tribunals hold that *vis major* does not exonerate a party which violates these obligations, whereas the POLISH, CZECHOSLOVAKIAN, and BULGARIAN tribunals exonerate a party on the grounds of *vis major* but award damages to the obligee if he has thereby suffered damage.[1444]

Vis major may not be, however, the only ground for exoneration. CMEA GCD § 68 par. 3 provides that "The parties shall also be relieved of

[1437] For POLAND see the Directive no. 2/1958 (*supra* n. 1431).

[1438] GDR: State Contract Court 5 July 1957, VS 1957, 21; Central Contract Court 4 June 1959, *ibidem* 1959, 219; State Contract Court 1 July 1958, *ibidem* 1958, 226; see *Spitzner and Panzer* § 82 no. 2.3.

[1439] POLAND: Directive no. 2/1958 (*supra* n. 1431); GDR: *Spitzner and Panzer* § 83 no. 2.8.

[1440] HUNGARY: DecrCD (*supra* n. 1350) § 48 par. 3; POLAND: Directive no. 2/1958 (*supra* n. 1431); SOVIET UNION: *Kleĭn and Petrov* CP 59, CG 60 no. 20; *idem* CP 61, CG 62 no. 13. CZECHOSLOVAKIA: EC § 145 par. 2; GDR: Contract Law (*supra* n. 1358) § 82 par. 2 no. 2.

[1441] GDR: *Spitzner and Panzer* § 82 no. 2.21-25.

[1442] GDR: Government Contract Court 30 Dec. 1958, VS 1959, 59; *Spitzner and Panzer* § 82 no. 2.21.

[1443] § 68 par. 1; *vis major* is defined in par. 2 as "circumstances which arise after conclusion of the contract as a result of events of an extraordinary character, unforeseen and unavoidable by the party".

[1444] See *Katona*, The International Sale of Goods Among the Member States of the Council for Mutual Economic Assistance: 9 Colum.J.Transnat.L. 226-282, 270 (1970).

liability for partial or complete non-performance of obligations under the contract, if such relief is provided for by the bilateral agreement, or by the contract, or by the substantive law of the seller's country applied to the given contract." The latter, however, does not necessarily mean that the same strict standards are applied as those mentioned in the previous section, although even there exoneration is not easy. For instance, the RUMANIAN arbitration tribunal has not accepted bad harvests as a ground for exoneration at least when the weather at the time of the conclusion of the contract was already unfavourable and the bad harvest was, consequently, foreseeable.[1445]

ii. *Liquidated Damages*

227. *General rules.* – Liquidated damages are necessary accessories to plan-contracts or economic contracts through which the exchange of goods and services within the nationalised economy takes place. In each country, other than YUGOSLAVIA, the law (1) imposes liquidated damages for most kinds of breach of contract, *i.e.* default of the obligee, defective performance,[1446] and impossibility (repudiation, definitive non-performance) and (2) fixes the amount of liquidated damages.

These rules provide for a mandatory minimum. They become part of the contract even in the absence of a stipulation by the parties and they prevail over any stipulation undercutting the prescribed minimum. On the other hand, the parties are free to stipulate liquidated damages for additional kinds of breaches and are free to agree upon a higher amount of liquidated damages than that fixed by the law.[1447]

228. *Council for Mutual Economic Assistance.* – The GCD of the CMEA contain no rules on liquidated damages in the case of default of the obligee or non-performance or impossibility of performance. In other instances they reduce all kinds of breach to the default of the obligor.

The GCD expressly provide for the payment of liquidated damages where the obligor is in default (§ 83).

This provision also applies in cases of defective and deficient performance until the goods are repaired;[1448] the obligor is in default until he delivers goods conforming to the contract.

It follows from this concept that where the obligee has opted for a reduction of price, no liquidated damages are due. Nevertheless, even in such cases the obligor has the right to repair or replace the goods instead of reducing the price. If he does this, he is bound to pay liquidated damages for default.

Non-performance and impossibility constitute protracted default on the obligor's part giving rise to the maximum amount of liquidated damages for default of the obligor. Foreign trade arbitrations in HUNGARY and the GERMAN DEMOCRATIC REPUBLIC apply the same rule to an obligor who refuses to perform. SOVIET foreign trade arbitration holds that these cases are not covered by the GCD, making the seller's law applicable under § 110 – that is, the buyer may demand performance and/or damages as appropriate.[1449]

No liquidated damages are payable in the case of the obligee's default; in the absence of a rule in the GCD, the seller's law, which does not provide for mandatory liquidated damages, applies (*supra* n. 1449).

The GCD contain no rules dealing with the reduction of liquidated damages. Here again silence is construed in two different ways. Some argue that the solution is left to the seller's law under § 110,[1450] in which case reduction becomes possible; others believe that silence implies negation, so that the GCD do not allow reduction.[1451]

229. *Some details.* – As a rule, liquidated dam-

[1445] No. AZ-449/67 of 5 June 1967, see *Katona* (*supra* n. 1444) 268.

[1446] In RUMANIA there are no special rules on liquidated damages for defective performance because taking delivery of defective goods is prohibited (*supra* s. 202) and administrative, labour law or – in more serious cases – penal sanctions attach in such cases (Law no. 2/1970 (*supra* n. 1360) art. 39-40). Nevertheless liquidated damages for default will be due where repair is successful; and liquidated damages for non-performance will be due where repair is impossible or unsuccessful (*Sterescu a.o.* 38-39 with further references who states that this is a moot point). Thus the prohibition against taking delivery of defective goods results in all cases in a "reduction to default" (or non-performance) (*supra* s. 213).

[1447] GDR: Contract Law (*supra* n. 1358) § 52.

[1448] § 31, 75; *supra* s. 214.

[1449] See *Szász* 239-266; *Engelmann, Kemper a.o.* 155. It is noteworthy that according to CMEA GCD § 110 par. 2, the "seller's law" is always the general civil law of the seller and never the special rules applicable in the field of the nationalised economy. These general civil law rules never provide for compulsory liquidated damages, but damages may be due.

[1450] HUNGARIAN Arbitration no. 1013, 1015 and 69036 – unreported, see *Katona* (*supra* n. 1444) 274. BULGARIAN Arbitration no. 9/61 – unreported, see *Szász* 241.

[1451] BULGARIAN Arbitration no. 11/5, 17/60, 4/61 – unreported, see *Katona* (*supra* n. 1444) 274.

ages are a fixed percentage of the value of the goods or services due under the contract. This applies also to incomplete performance where the basis for the calculation of liquidated damages is the total value of the contractual obligation and not the value of what remains to be delivered. In cases of default, a certain percentage is fixed for each day or decade of delay up to a maximum percentage: once the liquidated damages reach this ceiling, they do not increase any further. The liquidated damages for a defective performance are a certain fixed percentage, very frequently the same as the maximum percentage for cases of default. These percentages vary widely in different countries, sometimes according to fixed categories.

In the course of development, the percentages have been decreasing in the various countries. Paradoxically enough, liquidated damages tend to decrease in direct proportion to the increase of the material prosperity of the enterprises. The increase in the importance of material stimulation enhances the sensitivity of the enterprise to economic *stimuli*. The increasing sensitivity leads to the result that the enterprise begins to suffer from smaller liquidated damages much more than from larger amounts in previous epochs of total absence of material interest, when even liquidated damages as high as 20-50 per cent did not substantially affect an enterprise. To illustrate the present situation it may be noted that liquidated damages for defective, deficient and incomplete performance amount to 5 per cent in the SOVIET UNION and in HUNGARY, to 8 per cent within the Council for Mutual Economic Assistance, and to 10-15 per cent in the GERMAN DEMOCRATIC REPUBLIC and POLAND; special punitive liquidated damages in the SOVIET UNION (*infra* s. 231(5)) are fixed at the rate of 20 per cent;[1452] these rates frequently also constitute the maximum for liquidated damages.

230. *Cumulation and absorption.* – It may happen that the obligor commits more than one breach within the framework of a single contract. This raises the problem whether the liquidated damages due for each breach can be cumulated.

(1) If the breaches are separate and independent from one another – *e.g.*, late performance and also defective performance – cumulation takes place.[1453] If, however, one breach becomes irrelevant because of the succeeding one, liquidated damages are due only for the second breach. When, for instance, a default leads to rescission, no liquidated damages are due because of the lack of a certificate of quality.[1454]

(2) If the breaches are interconnected, either absorption or cumulation takes place. Where a default results in non-performance (rescission), it is only the maximum amount of liquidated damages which is usually due.[1455] Where, on the other hand, default is due to defective performance (*e.g.* repair or replacement takes some time after the time for performance has expired), cumulation is frequently the rule.[1456]

231. *Punitive character.* – Liquidated damages which always have a reparative function, may also have a punitive character. This punitive aspect extends beyond the common view that a party who is obliged to make good the damage it has caused is thereby "punished" except where the

[1452] SOVIET UNION: CP 59, CG 60; CP 60, CG 61. HUNGARY: DecrCD (*supra* n. 1350) § 49 par. 2 *lit.* c, DecrCW (*supra* n. 1373) § 30 par. 2 *lit.*c. CMEA GCD § 74 par. 4, § 83. GDR: First Implementing Regulation to the Contract Law (*Erste Durchführungsverordnung zum Vertragsgesetz*) of 25 Feb. 1965, GBl. II 249; POLAND, communication of *Stepniak*.

[1453] GDR: *Spitzner and Panzer* § 104 no. 2.5; SOVIET UNION: *Klein and Petrov* CP 59, CG 60 no. 3.

[1454] RUMANIA: see *Sanivelici and Macovei* 68.

[1455] GDR: Lehrmaterial 7, 68; *Spitzner and Panzer* § 104 no. 2.8. CMEA (*supra* s. 228). On the other hand, in RUMANIA where during a default the goods perish because of a *vis major*, the obligor is bound to pay liquidated damages both for default and impossibility (*Sterescu a.o.* 41, *Sanivelici and Macovei* 67-68), except in the case of building contracts. See also: Instruction no. 8 of the President of the State Arbitration, Collection of the Presidential Instructions of the State Arbitration (Bucarest 1966) 236; decisions of the President of the State Arbitration P.A.S. 2908 of 30 Nov. 1964, Arbitrajul de Stat 1965 no. 1, 82 and P.A.S. 2057 of 14 Aug. 1967, Arbitrajul de Stat 1967, no. 5, 86. *Sanivelici* 68 explains this rule by the punitive character of liquidated damages.

[1456] GDR: Lehrmaterial 7, 68; *Spitzner and Panzer* § 104 no. 2.8 up to a maximum amount. HUNGARY: Opinion no. 100/1973 of the Presiding Judges, S.Ct. Economic Branch, B.H. 1973, 850 (contracts of delivery; in the field of contracts for work liquidated damages for default will merge with those for defective performance: DecrCW (*supra* n. 1373) § 30 par. 2 *lit.*c). RUMANIA: In the case of hidden defects earlier decisions of the state arbitration (for instance, P.A.S. 2908 of 30 Nov. 1964 (*supra* n. 1455)) rule that liquidated damages for defective performance and default must be cumulated. Under the new legislation, however, which prohibits acceptance of defective goods, the problem becomes irrelevant because if the buyer shall not accept defective goods such goods are not *delivered* and therefore there is no place in the system for liquidated damages for defective performance (*Sterescu a.o.* 38-39). Consequently only the reduction to default — and the other measures mentioned (*supra* n. 1446) are possible.

value of an unjust enrichment only is required to be repaid. The punitive character of liquidated damages is particularly clear-cut within the sphere of the nationalised economy.

(1) Liquidated damages can be viewed as furnishing average compensation where the obligee's right to damages arises irrespective of the actual extent of damage suffered and additional, actual damages cannot be recovered. In the sphere of the nationalised economy, however, a party may sue for damage not compensated by an award of liquidated damages; in this case the latter are not average but minimum damages (*infra* s. 238).

(2) Liquidated damages are frequently cumulated and may then have an expressedly punitive character (see *supra* s. 230).

(3) Liquidated damages are due irrespective of whether the obligor has repaired or replaced the defective goods or whether the price has been reduced. They are also due where the obligee has chosen rescission; the rule is not "rescission or damages" but rescission *and* liquidated damages plus excess damages. Although a replacement of goods or reduction of price may satisfy the interests of the obligee, he is nevertheless entitled to liquidated damages. They are independent of specific performance.

(4) In some countries the amount of liquidated damages may depend on the degree of fault. The SOVIET state arbitration may, for instance, *ex officio* increase the amount of liquidated damages by 50 per cent if the conduct of the obligor has been reproachable to a high degree (such as, *e.g.*, repeated breaches, long lasting default, substantial damage caused, intentional breach, *etc.*).[1457] It may also reduce damages in an appropriate case. This latter rule applies also to damages in other countries.[1458]

(5) The amount of liquidated damages may also depend on the economic significance of the breach – which is something different from the damage actually suffered by the obligee. For instance, in the SOVIET UNION, liquidated damages, which usually amount to 3-5 per cent of the value of the contractual obligation, may amount to 20 per cent where the goods fail to conform to the compulsory standards and technical terms or, again in the case of incomplete performance where the obligor has failed to repair within a fixed period.[1459] Liquidated damages may also reach 20 per cent if the goods delivered are inferior in quality to those specified in the contract.[1460]

(6) In the SOVIET UNION, in the case of defective and incomplete performance, liquidated damages are payable in addition to *full* damages;[1461] here liquidated damages are in the nature of a contractual penalty payable to the other party.

(7) Finally in some countries state arbitration may partly or wholly deprive a party – otherwise entitled thereto – of liquidated damages and may order their payment to the state. This may happen in the SOVIET UNION where the plaintiff himself has violated the law, and this violation does not affect the defendant's liability.[1462] In the GERMAN DEMOCRATIC REPUBLIC, liquidated damages are

[1457] This 50 per cent goes to the state budget and does not enrich the obligee. See the Government Decree no. 988 of 27 Oct. 1967 on the economic liability of enterprises and organizations for not performing their tasks and obligations art. 31 (see *Kleĭn and Petrov* 279). *Idem* CP 85, CG 87 no. 6 quoting the Letter of Instruction of the State Arbitration of the Government of the USSR of 28 Dec. 1967 no. I-1-59 (*supra* n. 1433).

[1458] GDR: Contract Law (*supra* n. 1358) § 107: reduction because of contributory negligence or because of the disproportion between the liquidated damages and the damage actually suffered. HUNGARY: Opinion no. 17 of the S.Ct. Economic Branch, B.H. 1973, 623, based on CC § 247 par. 1 (the same principle as in the GDR). In POLAND the situation is about the same on the grounds of CC art. 484 par. 2 (*Szwaja* 135 ss.; *Dawidowicz*, Miarkowanie kar umownych w obrocie uspolecznionym: Przegląd Ustawodawstwa Gospodarczego 1971 no. 4, 117-121; *Kziezopolski*, Uwagi o miarkowanie kar w obracie uspolecznionzm: PiP 1970 I 518-528 at 519-521, 523-526). SOVIET UNION: CP 85.5, CG 87.5: a reduction is possible in exceptional cases only, where regard is had to the interests of the parties, the degree of fault, *etc.*; liquidated damages cannot be lower than the damage actually suffered and may only be reduced, not remitted (see *Kleĭn and Petrov* CP 85, CG 87 no. 5 quoting the Letter of Instruction of the State Arbitration of the Government of the RSFSR of 19 Jan. 1968 no. I-2/2). CZECHOSLOVAKIA: reduction very exceptional (EC § 144). On the other hand, no reduction is granted under RUMANIAN law (see *Sterescu a.o.* 37-38 on the basis of Law no. 71/1969 (*supra* n. 1360) art. 20).

[1459] CP 61, CG 62; CP 64, CG 66, CP 62, CG 63, These liquidated damages are called *shtrafnaı͡a neustoika*, that is "punitive liquidated damages"; see *Malein* 119.

[1460] CP 66, CG 67.

[1461] Fundamentals of the Civil Legislation of the USSR and the Union Republics of 8 Dec. 1961 (VVS SSSR 1961 no. 50 pos. 525) art. 50 par. 3 (see *Kleĭn and Petrov* 282-283). *Idem* CP 88, CG 90 no. 1.

[1462] Government Decree no. 648 of 30 June 1962 (*Kleĭn and Petrov* 227) art. 13, Letter of Instruction of the State Arbitration of the Government of the USSR of 27 Nov. 1962 no. I-1-37: Instrukt͡sionnye ukazanii͡a Gosudarstvennogo Arbitrazha pri Sovete Ministrov SSSR – Sistematizirovannyĭ Sbornik (Moscow 1964) 87-90.

payable to the state where a party is in breach of his obligation to enforce his claim to liquidated damages[1463] (*infra* s. 245).

232. *Other cases.* – Outside the field just discussed, liquidated damages are widespread in the field of transport contracts. In the case of default, the carrier is liable for liquidated damages which are calculated as a percentage of the freight. The figure must not exceed the amount of the freight and damages are, as a rule, average, not minimum compensation (*supra* s. 231(1)). Damages in excess of liquidated damages are only due where the carrier, with knowledge of the importance of timely performance, has undertaken in writing to comply with the term of performance, and is unable to show that the delay was due to *vis major*.[1464] Liquidated damages frequently figure in contracts for the delivery of agricultural products concluded mainly between agricultural producing cooperatives and state trading enterprises. Liquidated damages in this field are governed by special rules similar in many ways to those appearing in the sphere of the nationalised economy, in contracts of delivery, and in contracts for services.

In other cases, liquidated damages are somewhat rare, although they are not unknown to the general civil law legislation. In the case of defective performance, the obligee is entitled both to specific performance (repair, replacement, *etc.*), and to liquidated damages; in the case of non-performance he may, except in POLAND[1465] and in HUNGARY (where the option of performance is not open),[1466] choose between performance and liquidated damages. The courts have power to order reduction of excessive liquidated damages;[1467] in BULGARIA and POLAND this power may be exercised where the obligor has partly performed the contract.[1468] The relevant rules may assume importance in contractual relations within the CMEA where, in the absence of a direct regulation, these rules determine on the basis of § 110 whether damages other than liquidated damages are payable (*infra* s. 238).

iii. *Damages*

233. *Full compensation.* – The Socialist laws follow the GERMAN principle originating in the nineteenth century: the party in breach must pay full compensation consisting of *damnum emergens* and *lucrum cessans* (positive interest) (*supra* s. 49).[1469] The rules of tort law which in most countries permit reduction of damages in exceptional cases do not apply to contractual liability.[1470]

234. *The calculation of damages.* – As far as the calculation of *damnum emergens* is concerned, one has to bear in mind that the damaged or destroyed goods do not belong to the state *enterprise*; they belong to the *state*, whether the damage has occurred at the level of the manufacturer, or of the wholesale or retail trader, provided that all these are state enterprises. What is the value of such goods? What is the loss to the national economy? Should this be decided depending on the link in the chain at which the damage has occurred; and what is the appropriate solution where different owners are involved at the various levels of the chain? In some countries this question is answered in the negative; the loss is considered to correspond to the retail price regardless of the level at which the damage occurred.[1471] It is evident that this calculation, in addition to *damnum emergens*, contains an element of *lucrum cessans* from the viewpoint of the entire national economy as well as some additional enrichment except where the damage is in fact caused in the last link of the chain. The manufacturer may sue for the entire retail-price, thereby obtaining the profits of the wholesale as well as the retail trader without incurring the expenses of these enterprises.

[1463] Decree on the Tasks and Methods of Activities of the State Contract Court (*Verordnung über die Aufgaben und die Arbeitsweise des Staatlichen Vertragsgerichts*) of 18 April 1963 (GBl. II 293) as amended on 9 Sept. 1965 (GBl. II 711) § 48.

[1464] The latter rule is a HUNGARIAN one; see CC § 500 par. 1.

[1465] See *Czachórski* 361; *Ohanowicz and Górski* 207; *Szwaja* 114 ss.

[1466] CC § 246 par. 3.

[1467] BULGARIA: CO art. 97 par. 3; HUNGARY: CC § 247 par. 1; POLAND: CC art. 484 par. 2; SOVIET UNION: RSFSR CC art. 190; YUGOSLAVIA: General Usages no. 252.

[1468] BULGARIA: CO art. 97 par. 3; POLAND: CC art. 484 par. 2.

[1469] For instance, GDR: Contract Law (*supra* n. 1358) § 106 par. 1 and HUNGARY: CC § 358 par. 1 mentioning expenses as a third group of damage which, however, has an independent role in tort much more than in contract; SOVIET UNION: RSFSR CC art. 219 and POLAND: CC art. 361 par. 2 without mentioning expenses.

[1470] HUNGARY: CC § 318; POLAND: CC art. 440; SOVIET UNION: *Kleĭn and Petrov* CP 85, CG 87 no. 5. On the other hand, GDR Contract Law (*supra* n. 1358) § 107 permits an extraordinary reduction of damages having regard to the efforts of the obligor to prevent or mitigate the consequences of damage and to the proportion between liquidated damages and the damage.

[1471] SOVIET UNION: *Kleĭn and Petrov* CP 87, CG 89 no. 1-3; HUNGARY: see *Eörsi*, Manual no. 366.

Expenditure is calculated separately from loss of profit in the GERMAN DEMOCRATIC REPUBLIC and in HUNGARY. In the GERMAN DEMOCRATIC REPUBLIC, for instance, such expenses include wages paid to workers who, as a result of the breach, have had to stop working.[1472]

Loss of profit is always more or less hypothetical. Some countries try to eliminate uncertainty by requiring the obligor to repay the profits envisaged by the economic plan.[1473] Such gains are, of course, also hypothetical but at least they are known in advance and can, therefore, be calculated without the necessity of adducing evidence in this respect. Loss of profit is also compensated where, due to defects in the goods, the price has had to be reduced in conformity with the price regulations.[1474] In other countries, distributive justice seems to be more important in this respect than the certainty inherent in the method just mentioned: the quantum of the loss of profit must be proved.[1475]

Where the court or the state arbitration is satisfied that the plantiff has suffered damage but its exact extent cannot be established, the defendant in some countries will be ordered to pay an estimated sum (the so-called "general damages" in HUNGARY).[1476]

235. *Damages and cover purchases.* – Considering that cover purchase is at present a somewhat rare occurrence in most Socialist countries (*supra* s. 210), the question whether the calculation of damages should be based on the abstract or on the concrete principle (*supra* s. 69) is rather theoretical. In the present conditions the abstract principle can only rarely be used. A cover purchase must usually actually take place and the damages are calculated on the basis of the actual price paid. In HUNGARY, Opinion no. 64/1973 (*supra* n. 1390) states that a higher price than that stipulated in the original contract can be taken into account only in so far as this is inevitable in the given circumstances.

In YUGOSLAVIA, where cover purchases are more frequent, the applicable law is in consequence more developed. A notice to the seller is needed in order to entitle the buyer to the price-difference and the expenses incurred in connection with the cover purchase.[1477] According to the Supreme Economic Court, the buyer has an option between the abstract and concrete methods of calculating the price-difference. The concrete calculation may be applied irrespective of whether the cover purchase in fact takes place unless it is a purely fictitious arrangement.[1478] Where the buyer is in default, the seller may demand the difference between the contract price and the average price at the place of delivery on the first working day after the termination of the contract. Alternatively he may either demand the loss actually suffered or sell the goods to a third person and apply the concrete test in calculating his damages, claiming in addition his expenses.[1479]

236. *Full compensation?* – It would be impracticable to compensate all kinds of possible damage including extravagant and inconsequential items. The difference in fact between legal systems which limit contractual liability and those which permit so-called full compensation is that the latter systems must find special techniques to keep compensation within reasonable bounds. Among Socialist countries, POLISH law thus limits liability when it restricts liability in contract to the compensation of "normal" damage.[1480] Other Socialist laws come close to this position without such an explicit rule. This is accomplished mainly by resorting to doctrines of causation in law, such as "basic", "necessary", "essential", and "decisive" causes. Causes which convert the mere possibility of damage into reality are used in SOVIET law as a test; "adequate cause" in POLAND determines what is "normal"; and in HUNGARY the legally relevant cause serves this function.[1481] Sometimes "direct" and "indirect" consequences are distinguished, where a "direct" consequence is the first link in the chain of consequences.

There are also types of cases where the law puts a limit to compensation. Thus in contracts of affreightment, loss of profit is not compensated;

1472 *Spitzner and Panzer* § 106 no. 2.3; District Contract Court Neubrandenburg -32-N-48/67-, VS 1968, 533; see also *supra* n. 1469.

1473 GDR: *Spitzner and Panzer* § 106 no. 2.2; SOVIET UNION: *Klein and Petrov* CP 88, CG 90 no. 2 (as one possible way to calculate loss of profits).

1474 GDR: *supra* n. 1473.

1475 RUMANIA: Law no. 71/1969 (*supra* n. 1360) art. 20 par. 2; *Sterescu a.o.* 45-46. In HUNGARY this is the only possible way to calculate loss of profits because here the state enterprises do not receive compulsory plan-figures from the state.

1476 HUNGARY: CC § 358 par. 1; POLAND: CCProc. of 1964 art. 322; GDR: Contract Law (*supra* n. 1358) § 106 par. 3.

1477 General Usages no. 211.

1478 Economic Court (*privrednog suda*) 29 Feb. 1956, Zb. I 1 (1956) no. 249, 11 May 1956, Zb. I 2 (1956) no. 575, as quoted by *Goldštájn* 183-184.

1479 General Usages no. 212-213; *Goldštájn* 184.

1480 CC art. 361 par. 1.

1481 See the review of SOVIET doctrines in *Matveev* (*supra* n. 1421) 100 ss.; POLAND: see *Czachórski* 131; *contra: Ochanowicz and Górski* (adherents of the "necessary cause" doctrine). HUNGARY: see *Eörsi*, Manual no. 263 ss.

in the field of hotel-keepers' strict liability the same rule applies and, in addition, a maximum amount is prescribed which may only be exceeded where the fault of the hotel-keeper is proved.

237. *A special case of contributory negligence.* – We have seen earlier (s. 202) that RUMANIAN enterprises may not take delivery of defective goods. If they do so inspite of an overt defect, it amounts to contributory negligence. The damage occasioned by the defective performance must then be borne by the obligee to the extent of his contribution to the loss considering the weight to be attached to his fault in accepting the defective goods.[1482]

238. *Liquidated damages and full damages.* – As mentioned above (*supra* s. 231), liquidated damages are minimum damages; if a party can prove that his loss is not adequately compensated for by the liquidated damages, he may recover for the excess damage. This is the position in the majority of Socialist countries.[1483]

The GCD of the CMEA are silent on this question. As to the consequences of this silence, opinions differ. Some hold that silence means the exclusion of such damages and others that silence opens the road to the seller's law.[1484] The majority seems to regard silence as a gap to be filled by the seller's law unless there are bilateral complementary protocols to the GCD between member states which provide otherwise. In fact, such protocols frequently exclude damages in excess of liquidated damages; where, however, this is not the case, the seller's law applies.[1485] In fact, a much debated question is whether development of the GCD should expressly open the way to such damages or whether the level of liquidated damages should be raised instead.[1486]

iv. *Price Sanctions*

239. *In general.* – Price sanctions in the narrow sense of the word are a special remedy in the economic law of the GERMAN DEMOCRATIC REPUBLIC.[1487] A fixed sum is added to or deducted from the price, as the case may be, in the case of violation of a contractual obligation, if so prescribed by the law or stipulated by the contract. Price sanctions may replace, or be due in addition to, liquidated damages. Where price sanctions are stipulated, the contract may exclude damages. The obligor cannot be exonerated from the payment of price sanctions.

Price sanctions have nothing in common with the reduction of price within the framework of *Gewährleistung;* the price is "reduced" by a fixed sum and the reduction has no relation to the gravity of a possible defect. Price sanctions resemble contractual penalties; in fact they are regarded as a special kind of liquidated damages, and are another variation of the doctrine of contractual liability.[1488] They supply further evidence of the confluence of fault liability and liability without fault (*supra* s. 224). The advantage of price sanctions lies in the rapidity of the economic effect: they are automatically and invariably added to or deducted from the price. They find application particularly where contractual duties of relatively minor importance are frequently violated.[1489]

240. *Other cases.* – Price sanctions may serve as a remedy in other fields where performance and counterperformance are interdependent because payment is not due before delivery so that the remedy can operate more or less automatically. An example is furnished by a case where perfor-

[1482] Law no. 71/1969 (supra n. 1360) art. 14 par. 5. *Sanivelici and Macovei* 62-63, referring to cases prior to the enactment of this law but not overruled by it: Decision of the President of the Central Arbitration P.A.S. 1575 of 7 May 1959, Arbitrajul de Stat 1960 no. 4, 49; P.A.S. 2545 of 19 Oct. 1964, Arbitrajul de Stat 1964 no. 6, 74; Arbitration of the Ministry of Machine Industry Hot. no. 2377/1958 Arb.C.M., cited by *Manolescu and Apostol,* Rolul contractului tip de proiectare şi al contractului de antepriza pentru construcţii capitale in lupta pentru ridicarea calităţii şi reducereaa preţului de cost al construcţiilor: Arbitrajul de Stat 1958 no. 5, 3-23, 19. The obligee may, for instance, be liable for the further deterioration of defective goods taken over by him.

[1483] BULGARIA: CO art. 92 par. 1; GDR: CC § 340 par. 2; HUNGARY: CC § 246 par. 2; SOVIET UNION: RSFSR CC art. 189 awards damages in excess to liquidated damages. *Contra:* CZECHOSLOVAKIAN ICC § 1193; POLAND: CC art. 484 par. 1; HUNGARY: Introductory Law to CC (Law-Decree 11/1960 of 12 April (*A Polgári Törvénykönyv hatálybalépéséről és végrehajtásáról*), M.K. no. 28/1960) § 46A for foreign trade contracts in which the GCD of the CMEA are not applicable.

[1484] GCD § 110. See the different views in *Engelmann, Kemper a.o.* 243-244. *Kanda* 577 suggests that it is a fundamental principle of the GCD that the possibility of claiming damages is excluded.

[1485] *Engelmann, Kemper a.o.* 244-245.

[1486] See *Szász* 253-257 who proposes that damages not covered by liquidated damages should be awarded but within limits only.

[1487] Contract Law (*supra* n. 1358) § 53.

[1488] *Spitzner and Panzer* § 53 no. 1.1.

[1489] *Ibidem.*

mance is not accepted because of defects in the goods.[1490] Where the obligee refuses to accept a tender or fails to take the necessary measures towards performance price sanctions, in the form of an addition to the price, can be used but do not operate automatically.

In some cases, price sanctions do not operate automatically. For instance, in HUNGARY, where defective goods are delivered under a contract of delivery, the obligee may retain not more than 20 per cent of the price; and where the goods are unfit, he can retain the total price.[1491] This has a stimulative effect and serves at the same time as a kind of security supplying a financial basis for a possible repair or reduction of price.

E. ALLOCATION OF RISK

241. *General remarks.* – Risk allocation is here considered only in so far as it is connected with a breach of contract. A breach of contract may cause the passing of the risk (*infra* s. 242), prevent the passing of the risk (*infra* s. 243) or increase the risk already borne by a party (*infra* s. 244). Risk allocation in these cases can be considered as a remedy.

242. *Default of the obligee.* – The default of the obligee in accepting a due tender or in taking other steps necessary to enable the obligor to perform operates to pass the risk from the obligor to the obligee even though the goods remain in the former's possession.[1492] In the GERMAN DEMOCRATIC REPUBLIC an example of such default is furnished by the buyer who fails to give instructions for the dispatch of the goods under the contract of delivery so that the person delivering is obliged to store the goods.[1493]

In the GERMAN DEMOCRATIC REPUBLIC, HUNGARY, and POLAND fault on the obligee's part is not required, whereas in the SOVIET UNION the risk passes only where fault on the part of the obligee is proved.[1494] In POLAND, risk passes generally only where the obligee deposits the goods in court (where a sale is involved, the seller needs only store the goods); the risk also passes to the buyer under a contract of delivery who is obliged to collect the goods and has failed to do so in due time.[1495]

243. *Defective performance.* – Where the obligee accepts delivery, but refuses to treat the same as performance on the obligor's part[1496] because of defective or deficient performance, the risk does not pass to the obligee.[1497] In other cases, as well, of defective performance the obligee is not entitled to return the defective goods but must await the obligor's instructions. In such cases, he holds them in "responsible custody" (*supra* s. 199) and the risk remains with the obligor.

The same rule applies where the obligee demands replacement but provisionally retains the defective goods in "responsible custody". Finally if, after the risk has passed to the obligee, the goods are sent back to the obligor for repair the risk shifts to the obligor while the goods remain in his possession.[1498] In all these cases fault is irrelevant.

244. *Increase of liability.* – The obligor carries the risk incidental to his performance, independently of any default on his part. His risk, however, may increase where he is in default. If specific goods which have been sold perish before the time of performance, the obligor bears the loss and the contract is terminated because of supervening impossibility. If, however, he is already in default when the specific goods perish or deteriorate, he may incur liability to pay damages to the other party apart from the loss he suffers; and this will happen irrespective of whether the damage is caused by an act of *vis major* or through his own fault, provided that the default can be traced to his fault (and not to an inherent defect in the goods)[1499] (*casus mixtus*).

There are other cases where the obligor who has committed a breach of contract may have to bear the consequences of increased liability. The following examples may be mentioned:

(1) Where a party entitled to the use or possession of another's property under a contract parts therewith contrary to the contractual terms and

[1490] *Abnahmeverweigerung, etc.; supra* s. 202.

[1491] DecrCD (*supra* n. 1350) § 42. If under contracts for work goods are defective the obligee may retain or claim back a proportionate part of the price (DecrCW (*supra* n. 1373) § 23 par. 5).

[1492] GDR: Contract Law (*supra* n. 1358) § 48 par. 3; HUNGARY: CC § 303 par. 2 *lit.*b; POLAND: CC art. 486 par. 1, 551 par. 1; SOVIET UNION: RSFSR CC art. 138 par. 2, 227 par. 3; *Fleĭshits* § 227 no. 2; YUGOSLAVIA: *Goldštájn* 182.

[1493] *Spitzner and Panzer* § 59 no. 2.3.

[1494] GDR: Contract Law (*supra* n. 1358) § 48 par. 3; HUNGARY: CC § 303 par. 2 *lit.*b; POLAND: CC art. 486, GCD 65.2. SOVIET UNION: RSFSR CC art. 227.

[1495] GCD 65.2, see *Buczkowski and Nowakowski* 210.

[1496] *Abnahmeverweigerung, etc.; supra* s. 202.

[1497] GDR: Contract Law (*supra* n. 1358) § 90 par. 3.

[1498] POLAND: CC art. 580 par. 3.

[1499] HUNGARY: CC § 303 par. 2 *lit.*b; POLAND: CC art. 472; SOVIET UNION: RSFSR CC art. 138 par. 2, 225 par. 1; *Fleĭshits* § 225 no. 2; YUGOSLAVIA: *Goldštájn* 181.

the property, while in the possession of the third party, perishes or deteriorates due to a fortuitous event or act of nature.[1500]

(2) Where a party, entitled under a contract to the use of another's property, uses the same contrary to the contractual conditions, he is liable for all consequences of such use regardless whether his fault caused the damaging event or circumstance.[1501]

(3) Where a party contractually bound to act on behalf of another, partly or wholly delegates his duties to a third person in breach of the contract, he will be liable for all adverse consequences regardless whether these flow from the third person's fault.[1502]

In some of these cases, the defaulting party's risk may not be increased if the damage would have occurred independently of any breach of the contract.

F. ENFORCEMENT OF OBLIGATIONS

245. *Enforcement – an obligation.* – Perhaps the most outstanding feature of remedies in the present Socialist laws is that the obligation to stipulate liquidated damages frequently goes hand in hand with the obligation to enforce them. Where liquidated damages are compulsory, this obligation frequently extends to claims for additional damages.

This rule took shape before the economic reforms. It was thought – and in part the view still prevails – that since the director of a state enterprise is merely the agent of the state within the enterprise, he is not entitled to renounce liquidated damages or damages in addition thereto which are due, not to him, but to his master and owner of the enterprise, namely the state; contractual discipline requires not only the exact performance of contractual obligations but also the enforcement of claims. Directors of enterprises ought not, in this view, to be able to accord waivers to each other. This rule resulted in increased and protracted litigation between state enterprises. In order to live in peace with their superior organs, the enterprises sued each other even where there was no hope of success. With the advent of the economic reforms – one of whose main purposes was to increase the autonomy of the enterprises – the rule lost much of its vigour in many countries. The idea gained ground that if the director of an enterprise is entitled to make decisions on highly important business and management issues, why should he not be free to decide whether to enforce a claim to liquidated damages? At the same time the reforms have increased the material interestedness of the enterprises, resulting in greater inclination than in the past to enforce claims.

Breach of the duty to enforce claims may give rise to consequences under labour law or administrative law – principally disciplinary measures. It may also result in the liquidated damages not sued for being payable to the state. The state arbitration is in fact empowered (*ex officio*) to award liquidated damages or additional damages in cases where the obligee has failed to enforce a claim.

RUMANIA has a fully effective rule to this effect: no state enterprise may waive a claim to specific performance, liquidated damages or damages. Even the State Insurance Company is obliged to enforce its subrogation rights unless relieved by a commission at the Ministry of Finances.[1503] Violation may lead to a fine under administrative law as well as activate the financial liability of managers in labour law for failure to enforce the enterprises' claims.[1504]

In the GERMAN DEMOCRATIC REPUBLIC, an express obligation to enforce claims no longer exists. Nevertheless, the omission to enforce claims for liquidated damages may amount to a violation of contractual discipline and may then give rise to disciplinary penalties (*Ordnungsstrafen*); the Contract Court may, in addition, order the liquidated damages to be paid to the state.[1505]

In POLAND, the general conditions for contracts for technical and financial planning of construc-

[1500] HUNGARY: CC § 426 par. 2 (sublease), 584 par. 2 (loan for use); POLAND: CC art. 714 (loan for use).

[1501] POLAND: CC art. 714 (loan for use), art. 841 (deposit, where the obligor uses the deposited thing or guards it at a place or in a way which violates the contract).

[1502] HUNGARY: CC § 388 par. 3 (contract for work), 475 par. 3 (agency). POLAND: CC art. 739 (agency).

[1503] See *Eörsi*, General Report. Socialist Laws: AIDA Le Congrès Mondial 1974 no. 18; this obligation exists in certain insurance cases also in POLAND and in the GDR: *ibidem* no. 16.

[1504] *Sterescu a.o.* 46-47; see Law no. 68/1970 on sanctions against contraventions of the laws concerning financial discipline, taxes, duties, and contributions to compulsory insurance (*Hotărîre pentru stabilirea și sancționarea contravențiilor la normele legale privind disciplina financiară, impozitele, taxele și primele de asigurare prin efectul legii*), B.O. no. 6 of 13 Feb. 1970, art. 6; Law no. 306/1970 on some measures to implement the Law on Economic Contracts (*Unele măsuri pentru aplicarea legii contractelor economice*), B.O. no. 35 of 15 April 1970, art. 3 par. 2.

[1505] Decree on the State Contract Court (*supra* n. 1463) § 48; *Spitzner and Panzer* § 104 no. 2.12; Lehrmaterial 2, 96.

tion projects or buildings between socialised units impose an obligation to claim liquidated damages and additional damages.[1506]

In the SOVIET UNION there are certain situations where a party is bound to sue for liquidated damages. One example is a buyer who has wrongfully refused to pay the purchase price.[1507]

In HUNGARY, the duty to sue is confined to the very rare case where a contract of delivery or for work between nationalised units is financed directly from the state budget and not from the funds of the enterprise or by way of bank-credits. Even in such cases the duty is discharged where a party, for good reasons, believes that the other party will not be held liable or where the breach of contract is not substantial.[1508]

246. *Jurisdiction.* – In cases of breach of contract the parties may resort either to the ordinary courts or to state arbitration (in HUNGARY to the economic division of the court and in YUGOSLAVIA to the economic courts). In the GERMAN DEMOCRATIC REPUBLIC, the Contract Courts with an organization, jurisdiction, and procedure similar to that of the state arbitrations in the other countries are the proper tribunals. The jurisdiction and procedure of the state arbitration and economic court are discussed by *Knapp.*[1509]

247. *Defective performance.* – The rights attached to *Gewährleistung* or *Garantie* (see *supra* s. 204) must be enforced within a relatively short period. The main variants in this field are:

(1) The time available to the obligee may either operate as a period of limitation or as a time for forfeiture. In the first case, the claim is barred and hence enforcement by the courts or state arbitration also, but the right as such continues to exist. But in exceptional cases, enforcement may be permitted even after the period of limitation has run.

(2) Time commences to run either from the taking of delivery or the conclusion of the examination of the goods (but see *infra* (4)).

(3) For each category of cases a single period of time is prescribed for suing the other party. More frequently, there is one period prescribed for giving notice of defect to the obligor and a second, subsequent period for instituting proceedings.

(4) In most cases a distinction is made between patent and latent defects. Patent defects are those which may be discovered on a proper examination of the goods; whether a defect is patent or latent will frequently depend on the method of examination prescribed by the law. In the case of latent defects, the obligee must give notice thereof within a short prescribed time of its discovery (subjective term) and not later than a longer prescribed period after the taking of delivery (objective term).

These periods of time vary from country to country and also according to the goods involved.[1510]

In the case of *Garantie*, the obligee must always give notice to the obligor within the life of the guarantee and must present the document of *Garantie*. Here the distinction between patent and latent defects has no relevance.

248. *Rescission.* – A contract is rescinded by the unilateral declaration of the party entitled to rescind. In RUMANIA, however, only the court may declare a contract rescinded (*supra* n. 1382).

249. *Prescription.* – Socialist laws contain special rules on prescription in the sphere of the nationalised economy. The period is three years in the SOVIET UNION, five in HUNGARY, and ten in POLAND. However, for claims between state enterprises, *inter se*, at any rate money claims, including damages, a uniform period of one year is prescribed, except for claims to liquidated damages where the period is six months.[1511]

[1506] GCP 18, GCB 30.

[1507] *Kleĭn and Petrov* CP 81, CG 83 no. 1; no. 35 of the Letter of Instructions of the State Arbitration of the Government of the USSR of 29 July 1963 no. I-1-36 (*supra* n. 1462) 177.

[1508] DecrCD (*supra* n. 1350) § 58, DecrCW (*supra* n. 1373) § 32.

[1509] This Encyclopedia vol. XVI ch. 13 s. 23-25.

[1510] Thus in POLAND notification of defect must be given, in the case of dealings within the nationalised sphere promptly upon discovery (CC art. 565 par. 2), and in other cases within one month of the sale (CC art. 563 par. 1). In HUNGARY notification must be given within eight days of examination of goods or discovery of defect, and proceedings commenced within six months thereafter (CC § 306) except that in the nationalised sphere proceedings must be commenced within six months after the taking of delivery (DecrCD (*supra* n. 1350) § 41, DecrCW (*supra* n. 1373) § 25); in the latter case the period is three years where the goods are unfit for the purpose for which they were acquired. The general limitation in the SOVIET UNION is six months except in the case of building contracts where it is one year. These are only examples which may, in specific cases, be controlled by more detailed regulations. In particular, care should be taken to distinguish limitations for notification of defects from those for instituting proceedings. Not every Socialist system has this dual limitation aspect.

[1511] GDR: Contract Law (*supra* n. 1358) § 109; POLAND: CC art. 118, GCD 72; SOVIET UNION: RSFSR CC art. 78-79; HUNGARY: CC § 324 par. 1, 408 par. 1, but § 55 of the Introductory Law to the CC (*supra* n. 1483) provides that money-claims of an agri-

250. *Security.* – Where, under a contract, one party has the use or possession of property belonging to the other, – as *e.g.* in certain types of agency – or the goods or property of a party are kept on the premises of the other – as in the case of a lease of land or house – a charge arises by operation of law in favour of the obligee – *i.e.*, the agent in the one case and the owner in the other. This charge secures the agent's claim to commission and expenses or the owner's claim to rent; the security does not cover any possible claims for damages.

G. COMPARATIVE REMARKS

251. *Similarities.* – Contractual remedies in WESTERN systems and in SOCIALIST laws manifest important similarities. The inventory of remedies is essentially the same: it consists of specific enforcement, termination of the contract, damages, liquidated damages and penalties. This similarity arises from the fact that in both societies contracts form the normal instrument between legally distinct units of the economy for the exchange for money of goods, other property or services. If the contractual promise is not kept, the aggrieved party generally has the choice between insisting upon its enforcement and seeking its termination. In either case he may, in addition or by way of substitution, ask for damages.

252. *Differences.* – Yet, within this general framework are also discernible differences of equal importance between the solutions of the two groups of countries – differences which may be traced back to the divergencies in their social-economic structures.

(1) In WESTERN societies, the main purpose of the parties to most commercial contracts is to make profits. In such cases the interests of the aggrieved party are almost always satisfied if he receives damages. Even where the motive of the aggrieved party is not to make profits (*e.g.*, where he is a private consumer who buys for personal use) his interests are normally considered to be satisfied by an award of damages making it possible for him to acquire a substitute. In the SOCIALIST system, on the other hand, the main goal is to satisfy social needs even if the profit motive is also incidentally present. The social needs are not satisfied if one state-owned enterprise pays damages to another. This is so even where the possibility of a cover purchase exists for, although the obligee will have acquired the goods or services it needs through the cover purchase, these will ordinarily not be produced and, accordingly, will not be available to the economy.

(2) The WESTERN economy is essentially a market economy, whereas the SOCIALIST economy is a state planned economy, although, of course, traces of state planning are to be found in the WEST just as traces of a market in SOCIALIST countries. A market economy presupposes the availability of a relative abundance of goods and services; in planned economies – at any rate at the present time – demand in most cases exceeds supply. This makes cover purchases – and even cover sales – relatively easy in a very wide range of cases in the WEST. In the SOCIALIST countries cover purchases would be a rare occurence; cover sales, on the other hand, are possible as there is typically a ready market for goods.

These basic considerations favour damages in the WEST and specific performance in SOCIALIST countries.

(3) One of the important consequences of a state planned economy is what is termed "contractual discipline" within the sphere of the socialised economy. Contractual discipline reflects the fact that state-owned enterprises and co-operatives conclude contracts in order to fulfill the national plan. The main manifestations of contractual discipline in the field of remedies are the frequent administrative penalties and labour disciplinary measures – not discussed in the present chapter – as well as the system of compulsory liquidated damages. Of course in WESTERN systems as well administrative and criminal remedies are occasionally found in a contractual context, but their use is regarded as exceptional.

Thus the principle of *pacta sunt servanda* which prevails in both systems of law is stricter in SOCIALIST countries than in WESTERN law, firstly, because it entails the obligation of specific enforcement, and, secondly, because it is supported by administrative and labour law sanctions as well.

253. *Party freedom to select the remedy: The "system" of remedies.* – Where the purpose of contractual remedies is the protection of the interests of the injured party, this may be achieved either by specific enforcement or by damages. From this point of view, the object of the two types of remedies is, in WESTERN countries, similar, and there is no need for what in SOCIALIST countries is known as the "system" of remedies. Where, as in the latter group of countries, the main goal of the

cultural producing cooperative against another co-operative or a state enterprise become barred after two years.

law of contract is the satisfaction of social needs, the difference between specific performance and damages becomes very substantial. Although damages may here also have a compensatory effect for the aggrieved party, the interests of the national economy are not satisfied. Thus legal writers and laws in some countries – in particular in the GERMAN DEMOCRATIC REPUBLIC and HUNGARY – make a sharp distinction between remedies having a direct effect on the satisfaction of needs and those having a stimulative effect on the satisfaction of needs. To the first group belong specific enforcement (including repair and replacement), reduction of price and termination, and to the second, liquidated damages and damages (*supra* s. 193). In contrast, the stimulative effect is not, in general, an accepted feature in WESTERN systems, being inconsistent with the compensatory function of damages (*supra* s. 45), even if there may be minor exceptions to this.

254. *The main remedies.* – In market economies damages constitute the main remedy. The remedy is always available in COMMON LAW jurisdictions and in the EUROPEAN CONTINENTAL laws, "the limits to its scope are of more theoretical than practical importance".[1512] On the other hand, in state planned economies oriented towards the satisfaction of needs, the most adequate remedy is specific enforcement which, as a rule, extends to barring both parties from demanding, offering or accepting termination of the contract and damages in place of specific enforcement, particularly where demand exceeds supply (*supra* s. 196). Specific enforcement is the main contractual remedy except where it becomes impossible or economically too onerous.

The reasons that explain the predominance of the damage remedy in WESTERN law relate essentially to the importance and availability of markets. Accordingly, WESTERN law has no objection of principle to the remedy of specific performance, at least where the damage remedy would be inadequate. With the increasing availability of goods and services in SOCIALIST countries the principle of specific performance is losing ground. It may therefore be argued that the difference between the two groups of countries lies not so much in the law as in the fact that in one group there is an abundance and in the other a scarcity of goods. Indeed, the availability of a commodity is not without significance in WESTERN systems; the fact that the goods contracted for are in short supply is precisely the ground on which COMMON LAW courts will sometimes order specific performance of a contract for the sale even of purely generic goods.[1513] The approach can thus be seen as essentially the same: specific performance is granted where this is warranted by the circumstances and is replaced by damages in other cases; it is only the scarcity of goods and services which assigns a very broad role to specific performance. Yet the argument contains only a half-truth: a state planned economy's objection to the damage remedy is one of principle that yields only to rather compelling considerations. Accordingly, such societies will probably always lay a heavier stress on specific performance than does a market economy. Nor should the importance of tradition be overlooked in this connection. In the atmosphere of SOCIALIST laws and court practice the predominant importance of specific performance is an important aspect of legal culture, whereas in the WEST it is more usual to regard damages as the normal remedy.

255. *Termination.* – This consideration must also be kept in mind in comparing the possibility of terminating the contract for breach. Here there is seemingly no difference between the two law groups as termination is, in both groups, justified only if the breach is a serious one. Yet two points should be added to this general statement. The first is that in SOCIALIST countries a breach, for the purposes of termination, is a serious one only if performance has become impossible or economically extremely burdensome, whereas in WESTERN legal systems the requirements that must be met in order to qualify a breach as a serious one for this purpose are somewhat less strict. The second point is that in most WESTERN legal systems the injured party is, in the normal case, entitled to damages and to put an end to the contract, whereas in the SOCIALIST legal systems the latter remedy is more severely restricted.

256. *Liquidated damages and penalty clauses.* – The most prominent feature of the remedies available in the socialised sphere of economy in SOCIALIST countries has no counterpart in WESTERN legal systems. This consists of a mandatory system of liquidated damages for breach, coupled frequently with an obligation to seek the enforcement of the claim. These rules rest on the concept of "contractual discipline" and frequently have a punitive character since the amount recovered occasionally goes beyond compensating the damage caused by the breach. The main purpose of the rules respecting liquidated damages is to

1512 *Supra* s. 226.

1513 See *Sky Petroleum Ltd. v. V.I.P. Petroleum Ltd.*, [1974] 1 All E.R. 954 (Ch.) where, during the 1973 oil shortage, an oil company was restrained from cutting off supplies to one of its customers, in breach of contract.

stimulate the parties to live up to their contractual obligations as well as to ensure fulfilment of contractual obligations by the other party (*supra* s. 227-231). On the other hand, in COMMON LAW systems – though not in most CIVIL LAW systems – penalty clauses may be invalid precisely if their object is the stimulation of performance by the stipulation of a sum that has a punitive character, going beyond compensation.

(Completed in April 1975)

LIST OF GENERAL CONDITIONS

(cited in subch. V)

COUNCIL OF MUTUAL ECONOMIC ASSISTANCE

CMEA GCD – General Conditions of Delivery of 1968. Russian text: *Tokareva* (ed.), Mnogostoronnee ekonomicheskoe sotrudnichestvo sofsialisticheskikh gosudarstv (ed. 2 Moscow 1972) 530-562; English transl.: *United Nations*, Register of Texts of Conventions and Other Instruments Concerning International Trade Law I (New York 1971) 72-102; English, French and German transl.: *Zweigert and Kropholler* (ed.), Sources of International Uniform Law / Sources du droit uniforme international / Quellen des Internationalen Einheitsrechts I (Leyden 1971) E 155, F 155, G 155.

HUNGARY

GCB – General Conditions of Building Contracts (*Az építési szerződések alapfeltételei*), Annex to the Ministerial Decree EVM 5/1968 of 6 April, M.K. no. 29/1968;

GCP – General Conditions of Projecting Contracts (*A tervezési szerződések alapfeltételei*), Annex to the Ministerial Decree EVM-KGM-NIM 10/1968 of 10 Oct., M.K. no. 80/1968.

POLAND

GCB – General Conditions of Contracts of Realisation of Building Investments and Execution of Repairs (*Ogólne warunki umów o realizacje inwestycji budowlanych oraz o wykonywanie remontów budowlanych i instalacyjnych*), Annex to the Implementing Order of the Minister of Construction and Construction Material Industry of 8 April 1974, Mon.Polski no. 14 poz. 94.

GCD – General Conditions of Contracts of Sale and Contracts of Delivery Between Units of the Socialised Economic Sector (*Ogólne warunki umów sprzedaży i umów dostawy między jednostkami gospodarki uspołecznionej*), Annex to Resolution no. 192 of the Council of Ministers of 3 Aug. 1973, Mon. Polski no. 36 poz. 218.

GCP – General Conditions of Contracts of Work on Construction Projects (*Ogólne warunki umów o prace projektowe w budownictwie*), Annex to the Implementing Order of the Minister of Construction and Construction Material Industry of 8 April 1974, Mon.Polski no. 14 poz. 94.

UNION OF SOVIET SOCIALIST REPUBLICS

CG – Rules on the Delivery of Goods for National Consumption (*Polozhenie o postavkakh tovarov narodnogo potrebleniia*), ratified by the Decree of the Council of Ministers of the SSSR on 9 April 1969, Sobr.post. SSSR 1969 no. 11 pos. 64;

CP – Rules on the Delivery of Products for Industrial-Technical Purposes (*Polozhenie o postavkakh produktsii proizvodstvenno-tekhnicheskogo naznacheniia*), ratified by the Decree of the Council of Ministers of the SSSR on 9 April 1969, *ibidem*.

YUGOSLAVIA

General Usages – General Usages of Trade of 1954 (*Opšte uzanse za promet robom*), Sl.l.Y. no. 15/1954; English transl.: *Blagojević* (ed.), The General Usages of Trade (Collection of Yugoslav Laws no. 9) (Beograd 1964); French transl.: *idem*, Usages commerciaux au trafic de marchandise (Receuil des lois de la RSF de Yougoslavie no. 9) (Beograd 1964).

LIST OF PRINCIPAL WORKS

(1)

1. COMPARATIVE LAW: *Eörsi*, Fundamental Problems of Socialist Civil Law (Budapest 1970), cited Problems; *idem*, Quelques problèmes de la responsabilité civile délictuelle selon le droit soviétique et le droit hongrois: Rev.trim.dr.civ. 1971, 735-749, cited Quelques problèmes; *von Mehren*, The Civil Law System (Englewood Cliffs, N.J. 1957); *Rabel*, Das Recht des Warenkaufs I (Berlin and Leipzig 1936); *Zweigert and Kötz*, Einführung in die Rechtsvergleichung auf dem Gebiete des Privatrechts II (Tübingen 1969).

2. COUNCIL OF MUTUAL ECONOMIC ASSISTANCE: *Engelmann, Kemper a.o.*, Liefervertrag, Montagevertrag, Kundendienstvertrag im Aussenhandel der RGW-Staaten ([East] Berlin 1967); *Kanda*, K problematice odpovědnosti hospodářských organizací ve vzájemných vztazích členských států RVHP za nesplněni źavazků ze smluv o dodávce zboží: Práv. 1971 no. 7, 574-592; *Szász*, A KGST Általános Szállitási Feltételei (Budapest 1974).

3. AUSTRALIA: *Cheshire and Fifoot (-Starke and Higgins)*, The Law of Contract (Australian ed. 4 Sydney 1974); *Spry*, Equitable Remedies (Melbourne 1971).

4. AUSTRIA: *Klang and Gschnitzer* (ed.), Kommentar zum Allgemeinen bürgerlichen Gesetzbuch IV 1, V (ed. 2 Vienna 1968, 1954), *Klang* (ed.) VI (ed. 2 Vienna 1951).

5. BELGIUM: *Dekkers*, Précis de droit civil belge (Brussels 1955); *De Page*, Traité élémentaire de droit civil belge II, III (ed. 3 Brussels 1964, 1967).

6. CANADA: *Baudouin*, Le droit civil de la Province de Québec (Montreal 1953).

7. FRANCE: *Carbonnier*, Droit civil IV (ed. 6 Paris 1969); *Marty and Raynaud*, Droit civil II (Paris 1962); *Mazeaud, H., L. and J.*, Leçons de droit civil II, III (ed. 2 Paris 1962, 1963), cited Leçons; *idem*, Traité théorique et pratique de la responsabilité civile délictuelle et contractuelle II (ed. 6 Paris 1970), cited Traité; *Mazeaud, H. and L., and Tunc*, Traité théorique et pratique de la responsabilité civile délictuelle et contractuelle (3 vol.) (ed. 5 Paris 1957-1960), I (ed. 6 Paris 1965), cited Traité; *Planiol and Ripert*, Traité pratique de droit civil français VII, X (ed. 2 Paris 1954, 1956).

8. GERMANY (DEMOCRATIC REPUBLIC): *Pflicke*, Die subjektive Voraussetzung der materiellen Verantwortlichkeit für die Verletzung der Wirtschaftsverträge und das System ökonomischer Hebel: StuR 1964, 1520-1559; *Posch*, Die materielle Verantwortlichkeit des Bürgers und der Betriebe im Zivilrecht: StuR 1970, 1111-1128; *Spitzner and Panzer*, Kommentar zum Kooperationsrecht (Berlin 1970); *Such*, Der Liefervertrag (Berlin 1967); *idem and Schüsseler* (ed.), Lehr- und Studienmaterial zum Wirtschaftsrecht II, VII (Berlin 1972, 1973), cited Lehrmaterial.

9. GERMANY (FEDERAL REPUBLIC): *Enneccerus and Lehmann*, Recht der Schuldverhältnisse (ed. 15 Tübingen 1958); *Esser*, Schuldrecht (2 vol.) (ed. 4 Karlsruhe 1970-1971); *Larenz*, Lehrbuch des Schuldrechts (2 vol.) (ed. 10 Munich 1970-1972); *Lindacher*, Phänomenologie der "Vertragsstrafe" (Frankfurt 1972); *Palandt*, Bürgerliches Gesetzbuch (ed. 29 Munich 1970); *Reichsgerichtsräte*, Kommentar zum Bürgerlichen Gesetzbuch (ed. 11 Berlin 1960), cited BGB-RGRK.

10. HUNGARY: *Eörsi*, The Legal Consequences of the Breach of Contract and the Anticipatory Breach: *Péteri* (ed.), Essays in Comparative Law (Budapest 1966) 173-194, cited Consequences; *idem*, A polgári jogi kártérítési fellelősség kézikönyve (Budapest 1966), cited Manual; *Harmathy and Lontai*, Discussion sur quelques questions d'importance de la règlementation relative à l'exécution défectueuse des contrats: Act. Jur.Hung. 10 (1968) 349-357.

11. INDIA: *Dutt*, Indian Contract Act (ed. 4 Calcutta 1969); *Pollock and Mullah (-Kapur)*, The Indian Contract and Specific Relief Acts (ed. 9 Bombay 1972).

12. NEW ZEALAND: *Cheshire and Fifoot (-Northey)*, The Law of Contract (New Zealand ed. 2 Wellington 1974).

13. PAKISTAN: *Mahmood*, The Contract Act (Lahore 1969).

14. POLAND: *Buczkowski and Nowakowski*, Prawo obrotu uspolecznionego (Warsaw 1971); *Czachórski*, Prawo zobowiązań w zarysie (Warsaw 1958); *Madey*, Rekojma przy dostawach w obrocie uspolecznionzm w PRL (Warsaw 1965); *Ohanowicz and Górski*, Zarys prawa zoboviazan (Warsaw 1970); *Szwaja*, Kara umowna wedlug kodeksu cywilnego (Warsaw 1967).

15. RUMANIA: *Sanivelici and Macovei*, Raspunderea contractuala protrivit legii contractelor economice: Rev.rom.de drept 1971 no. 11, 60-68; *Sterescu, Georgescu-Vilcea and Gheran*, Raspunderea contractuala in raporturile dintre organizatii socialiste: Rev.rom.de drept 1971 no. 7, 34-48.

16. SOUTH AFRICA: *Kerr*, Principles of the Law of Contract (Durban 1967); *Lee and Honoré*, The South African Law of Obligations (Durban 1950); *Maasdorp and Hall*, Maasdorp's Institutes of South African Law III (ed. 8 Cape Town 1970); *Wessels (-Roberts)*, Wessels' Law of Contract in South Africa (2 vol.) (ed. 2 Durban 1951); *Willie and Millin (-Coaker and Schutz)*, Mercantile Law of South Africa (ed. 16 Johannesburg 1967).

17. SRI LANKA (CEYLON): *Weeramantry*, Law of Contracts (2 vol.) (Colombo 1967).

18. SWITZERLAND: *Gmür and Becker*, Berner Kommentar zum schweizerischen Zivilgesetzbuch VI 1 (ed. 2 Berne 1941-1946); *Guhl*, Das schweizerische Obligationenrecht (ed. 5 Zürich 1956); *Oser and Schönenberger*, Kommentar zum Schweizerischen Zivilgesetzbuch V 1 (ed. 2 Zürich 1929).

19. UNION OF SOVIET SOCIALIST REPUBLICS: *Antimonov*, Osnovadiâ dogovornoĭ otvetstvennosti sotsialisticheskikh organizatsiĭ (Moscow 1962); *Bratus*, Predmet i sistema sovetskogo grazhdanskogo prava (Moscow 1963); *Fleĭshiŝ*, Nauchno-prakticheskiĭ

kommentariĭ k GK RSFSR (Moscow 1966); *Ioffe*, Sovetskoe grazhdanskoe pravo I (Moscow 1971); *Kleĭn and Petrov*, Nauchno-prakticheskiĭ kommentariĭ k polozheniiam o postavkakh produktsiĭ proizvodstvenno-tekhnicheskogo naznacheniia i tovarov narodnogo potrebleniia (Moscow 1971); *Malein*, Imushchestvennaiia otvetstvennost v khoziaĭstvennykh otnosheniiakh (Moscow 1967); *Mamutov, Ovsienko and Iudin*, Predpriiatie i materialnaia otvetstvennost (Kiev 1971).

20. UNITED KINGDOM: *Anson (-Guest)*, Anson's Law of Contract (2 vol.) (ed. 23 London 1969); *Benjamin (-Finnemore and James)*, A Treatise on the Law of Sale of Personal Property (ed. 8 London 1950); *Cheshire and Fifoot (-Furmston)*, The Law of Contract (ed. 8 London 1972); *Chitty (-Guest a.o.)*, Chitty on Contracts (2 vol.) (ed. 23 London 1968); *Gloag*, The Law of Contract – A Treatise on the Principles of Contract in the Law of Scotland (ed. 2 Edinburgh 1929); *idem and Henderson*, Introduction to the Law of Scotland (ed. 7 Edinburgh 1968); *Lawson*, Remedies of English Law (London 1972); *McGregor*, On Damages (ed. 13 London 1972); *Smith, T. B.*, A Short Commentary on the Law of Scotland (Edinburgh 1962); *Treitel*, The Law of Contract (ed. 3 London 1970); *Walker*, Principles of Scottish Private Law (2 vol.) (Oxford 1970).

21. UNITED STATES OF AMERICA: *Corbin*, Contracts (St. Paul, Minn. 1963); *Farnsworth*, Legal Remedies for Breach of Contract: 70 Colum.L.R. 1145-1216 (1970); *Fuller and Perdue, Jr.*, The Reliance Interest in Contract Damages: 46 Yale L.J. 52-96, 373-420 (1936/37); Restatement of Contracts (1932); *Williston*, On Contracts (15 vol.) (ed. 3 Rochester 1957-1972).

22. YUGOSLAVIA: *Goldštájn*, The Law of Sales in Yugoslavia: Law in Eastern Europe no. 14) Leyden 1967) 125-196.

(2)

DETAILED TABLE OF CONTENTS

Volume VII

CONTRACTS IN GENERAL

Arthur von Mehren · Chief Editor

PROVISIONAL TABLE OF CONTENTS

FSC
www.fsc.org
MIX
Papier | Fördert gute Waldnutzung
FSC® C083411

Kolibri 360 GmbH
Ferdinand-Jühlke-Straße 7
99095 Erfurt, Deutschland
produktsicherheit@kolibri360.de